Listening to Salsa

MUSIC / CULTURE

A series from Wesleyan University Press

Edited by George Lipsitz, Susan McClary, and Robert Walser

Published titles

FRANCES R. APARICIO

✠

Listening to Salsa

GENDER, LATIN POPULAR
MUSIC, AND PUERTO RICAN
CULTURES

✠

WESLEYAN UNIVERSITY PRESS

Published by University Press of New England

Hanover and London

WESLEYAN UNIVERSITY PRESS
Published by University Press of New England, Hanover, NH 03755
© 1998 by Frances R. Aparicio
Printed in the United States of America 5 4 3 2 1
CIP data appear at the end of the book

ACKNOWLEDGMENTS

Every effort has been made to obtain permission from the copyright holders to reproduce the photograph on page 144.

A partial and earlier version of chapters 11 and 12 appeared in "'Así Son': Salsa Music, Female Narratives, and Gender (De)Construction in Puerto Rico," *Poetics Today*, Winter 1994.

Lyrics from "Ligia Elena" and "Ella se esconde" reprinted with permission of Rubén Blades Publications.

"Llegó de Roma" by Manuel Jiménez Canario, also known as "El Obispo." Copyright © 1959 by Peer International Corporation. Copyright Renewed. International Copyright Secured. Used by Permission.

"Tintorera del Mar" by Manuel Jiménez Canario. Copyright © 1978 by Peer International Corporation. International Copyright Secured. Used by Permission.

"Cuando las Mujeres Quieren a los Hombres" by Manuel Jiménez Canario. Copyright © 1930 by Peer International Corporation. Copyright Renewed. International Copyright Secured. Used by Permission.

"Somos Diferentes" by Pablo Beltrán Ruiz. Copyright © 1945 by Editorial Mexicana de Música Internacional S.A. Administered by Peer International Corporation. Copyright Renewed. International Copyright Secured. Used by Permission.

"Obsession" by Pedro Flores. Copyright © 1947 by Peer International Corporation. Copyright Renewed. International Copyright Secured. Used by Permission.

"Mujer" by Agustín Lara. Copyright © 1931 by Peer International Corporation. Copyright Renewed. International Copyright Secured. Used by Permission.

"Arráncame la Vida" by Agustín Lara. Copyright © 1934 by Promotora Hispano Americana de Música S.A. Administered by Peer International Corporation. Copyright Renewed. International Copyright Secured. Used by Permission.

Continued on page 279

Dedicated to the puertorriqueñas in my life,
to Mamita, my hermanas Diana and Vivian,
to my hijas chicana-riqueñas
Gabriela and Camila,
and to all my Latina compañeras in culture.

Contents

✠

Illustrations

✠

Preface

✠

This book originally emerged out of my desire to give personal and cultural meaning to academic work, that is, out of a profound need to reclaim the knowledge about Puerto Rican culture that had been denied to me through a colonial education. But to limit the impact of this interdisciplinary study to the ways in which it has allowed for my personal decolonization would not do justice to the larger issues it has provoked. By now it has become commonplace for prologues to become personal confessions, a site, as poststructuralists would say, for "locating the writing subject." As much as this project has enhanced my own life, here I neither claim the role of organic intellectual (my upper-class upbringing limited my identification with salsa music), nor do I feel compelled to "tell my story." Rather, a more productive framework for these preliminary words would include tracing the process of the research project; reviewing the dilemmas, goals, and tensions experienced by those of us who juggle popular culture in and out of the prudish and disembodied spaces of academic production; and reflecting on the tenuous location that popular culture still holds in academe despite its commodification as cutting-edge scholarship.

This interdisciplinary incursion is, first of all, an act of love toward the Latina/o culture and people. I have seen, among those Latinas and Latinos whom I have known and loved, the destruction and pain that cultural displacement, exclusion, and internalized colonialism can create. At the same time, I have also witnessed firsthand the strength that we hold in our power of affiliation, cultural resistance, and reaffirmation. My efforts at analyzing our social contributions to popular music sincerely reflect the respect, admiration, and responsibility that I feel toward these collective expressions, a cultural legacy that was denied to me by my class upbringing and that this research project attempts to recover for myself, my daughters, and for future students of Latino and Latina cultures.

Simultaneously, this project is a declaration of war. As a puertorriqueña who still resists being labeled a "feminist" scholar, I cannot but critique, from within, the traditional masculine discourse that continues to imbue our everyday lives as Latinas/os with blatant objectifications and insidious mutings of women. Thus, I must address those social contradictions posited by salsa and the larger Afro-Caribbean musical tradition from which it emerges. Certainly, salsa—by the very racial and class positionings of its composers and interpreters—has historically represented, because of its marginality, a delimited freedom with which to carve a space for social change and for cultural resistance. However, as a musical industry dominated by men, salsa music continues to disseminate lyrics laden with problematic, misogynist, and patriarchal representations of women. Thus, like other sites of popular music, it too articulates the heterogeneous values and cultural negotiations of gender that Latinos and Latinas experience. While Afro-Caribbean women, such as La Lupe, India, Celia Cruz, Deddie Romero, Olga Tañón, Albita, and other emerging feminist singers have sung with or against these discursive traditions, the politics of distribution and marketing, coupled with masculinist historiography, have systematically rendered mute their voices, relegating them to the margins of mainstream attention.

A revealing example of this marginalization is the September 1994 issue of *Latin Beat,* dedicated to salseras and, more generally, to Latina musicians. "The Women's Issue," as it is titled, textually embodies the problematic location of women within the industry and their ensuing contradictory representations. While many of the articles, authored by men, attempt to contest women's invisibility and document the musical contributions of Latinas such as La India, Gloria Estefan, Selena, Deddie Romero and of female groups like La Noreste and Wild Mango,[1] the "special" nature of this issue reveals the systematic invisibility of women in *Latin Beat*'s regular issues—and in the music industry in general—while emphasizing their extraordinary, marked presence as women within the male-dominated world of popular music.[2] In an otherwise honest and productive attempt to render Latinas visible, "The Women's Issue" nonetheless frames women's professional success as derivative. That is, it emphasizes the woman's genetic predispositions to music making (as in the case of Deddie Romero, who comes from a family of musicians); it explains the woman's success as a result of her male mentoring and management, as the brief discussion of La India suggests.

Eroticizing associations, analogous to the objectifying discourse of merengue and salsa songs, continue to inform descriptions of female groups such as the Bay Area's Wild Mango.[3] In Cali, Colombia, where eleven female salsa bands have emerged since 1990, Olga Lucía Rivas attests to the ways in which the male producers and managers exert their power in choosing the names of the groups. In addition, they also determine the provocative clothing that many of the women felt personally uncomfortable wearing onstage.[4] Briefly put, while Latina musicians and singers are gradually becoming more visible, their representation within the music industry is systematically mediated by male gaze and authority.

Here I share with Tricia Rose her very tenuous position as a woman of color working on a musical tradition that has been culturally oppositional yet deemed as egregiously misogynist. Like Rose, who was asked why she defended rap and why she would consider Salt and Pepa as feminists when they wore high heels and lipstick, I have also found myself having to explain the ambiguities of women's participation in salsa as both subjects and objects. Taking salseras seriously means grappling with the ideological complexities behind feminist Latina singers who wear high heels and bright red lipstick and perform seminaked, a tension that emerges, in part, from imposing Anglo feminist values on a particular Latina aesthetics of the body.

Intercultural tensions such as the above became particularly striking when I presented my work in progress to various cultural audiences. When lecturing on gender and salsa music to a predominantly Anglo audience, I was always wary, and rightly so, that my feminist analysis of the lyrics would reaffirm the all-powerful images of macho Latinos that circulate in this country.[5] Simultaneously, when sharing my work with Latina/o audiences, I found that many Latino men would try to undermine the impact of salsa's sexism by reminding me that contemporary salsa male singers in the 1990s (e.g., Gilberto Santa Rosa) were representing women in much more sensitive ways and that machismo in salsa was really a thing of the past. While I recognize that in the 1970s salsa songs articulated much more blatant forms of violence against women, I am still convinced that neither salsa, the merengue, nor the bolero has yet transcended any of the masculinist tendencies that I identify here. Even now, when the participation of women salsa performers has increased, the authorial control over composition is still very much in the hands and pens of male composers and producers. Strong, radically feminist voices such as La Lupe's have been relegated to the margins; women's central role in the early stages of salsa's development has been dismissed by music historians.

With emerging figures such as La India and Albita Rodríguez, along with the posthumous renaissance of La Lupe's works, I hope that my present gender critique will be deemed outdated. In fact, the fast rhythm of change in popular culture today makes this type of study vulnerable to quickly losing its timeliness. Yet the question is not whether salsa is *still* machista. Rather, how does this music continue to inscribe gender, how is it gendered itself, and what is the impact of gender politics on its listeners? As Tricia Rose has eloquently explained, we need to confront the contradictions in popular expressions and "incorporate them into an analysis which explores how and why they retain currency—not simply dismiss them because they do not measure up to an imaginary standard of politically consistent expression."[6]

While some Latino men have felt a strong ambivalence and even disavowal toward my work, it is in the act of "speaking the unpleasant," to borrow a phrase by Adalberto Aguirre Jr., and at the risk of being labeled a "vendida" (as Sonia Saldívar-Hull reminds Latina feminists) that I have found it possible to unite individual conscience and a desire for social change.[7] Some years ago, when I first taught a graduate course on popular music and contemporary Puerto Rican literature at the University of Michigan, a Latina student came to my office to inform me that she was going to drop the class because the feminist perspectives and critiques of salsa music that we discussed in the classroom were beginning to cause too many conflicts in her relationship with her fiancé. He was angry at her deconstructions of his favorite songs, lyrics that he identified as part of his national culture and that reminded him of his childhood in the Caribbean. Salsa was for him a tool for cultural reaffirmation. His anger at her feminist "betrayal" was channeled at the professor, accusing me of invading and destroying his own popular culture and musical legacy with those feminist ideas. He asserted that I did not have the right, as an intellectual (and as a woman?), to invade this cultural space nor to trespass on his personal life.

After a long conversation with my student, I persuaded her to finish the semester but not without having to reflect on my role as a Latina scholar working on popular culture. Leaving my office that late afternoon, I was reminded of the immeasurable power that we hold as teachers of popular culture and of issues of everyday life, a power that had affected the personal life and intimate relationship of one of my students. Although this power was intimidating, I also felt the greatest satisfaction and joy ever in my years of teaching, for then I realized that this course was transforming students' values, attitudes, and ways of being.

This incident underscored the fact that teaching popular culture is beginning to radicalize traditional notions of how and by whom knowledge is produced. Thus, the issue for me is not whether students have read the most fashionable and required theory or literary texts or literary criticism as a quantifiable measure of their erudition but rather whether the course and the readings promote the potential for personal and social transformations in my students, myself, and our communities through the sharing of interdisciplinary approaches to culture.

The case detailed above also introduced me to the difficulties of attempting to bridge academic values and popular practices, what I call mixing deconstruction with dancing. When I go dancing to Latin music with my Latino and Latina friends, they often complain that my analysis spoils their fun. Perhaps that is the curse shared by cultural studies scholars, for we furnish evidence that there is no such thing as "pure" or unmediated cultural pleasure. However, the greatest danger here lies in assuming that cultural critique is the exclusive product of academic training. As Part Four of this book demonstrates, the most profound and serious theorizing about the meanings of salsa came from working-class Latinas who articulated the ways in which they negotiate salsa music and culture to reimagine themselves and their relationships with men.

Although popular culture is not yet fully institutionalized and rather tenuously accepted and acceptable, many cultural critics, including myself, have accrued true material benefits and professional privileges from our incursions into popular culture. While these contradictory circumstances have allowed for the publication of studies that might otherwise have been deemed irrelevant, the danger lies in accepting such privileges without questioning them, without assuming a degree of accountability to the "masses"—musicians and artists on whom we depend. To assume this accountability implies pushing academe into accepting the public role of intellectuals, rather than letting cultural analysis become another item in the assembly line of intellectual activity, extracted from the everyday lives in which popular culture emerges. This means advocating, through our work, for the value of publishing outside exclusively academic journals and convincing our colleagues that learning should not be quantifiably measured by how many European and Anglo intellectuals one can quote but by the social and cultural impact of our ideas and actions. In short, it means taking risks to transform the dangerously comfortable spaces that we inhabit as intellectuals.

This book addresses the relations between gender and Latin popular music in ways that escape a particular disciplinary approach, weaving the voices of Puerto Rican literary texts and Latin popular music to unify its different parts. (Unless otherwise noted, all translations are my own.) What began in 1987 as a research project that examined the presence of popular music in contemporary Puerto Rican narratives grew into a larger and more complex interdisciplinary enterprise that deploys both musical and literary texts as equally significant cultural voices in exploring larger questions about the power of discourse, gender relations, intercultural desire, race, ethnicity, and class. What seemed, at first, a book project on music and literature in the manner of comparative literature, began to define itself gradually as a book on culture and gender (not without the wonderful insistence of my former colleague, Eliana Rivero). Since 1990, when the University of Michigan "discovered" me as a potentially interesting cultural studies and Latina scholar, my research questions began to change through stimulating intellectual exchanges in the Program in American Culture, where our own brand of cultural studies, informed by theories of race and ethnicity, was beginning to emerge. This community has offered me larger "culturescapes" in which to locate my own intellectual preoccupations. In the route from the deserts of Arizona to the bookish culture of Ann Arbor, this book began to take on a life of its own.

Rather than a history of women salseras, or interpreters, which is sorely needed, this book offers readers cultural studies interventions into gender, culture, and music. It deals with the gendering of music and with the ways that music negotiates gender roles. It focuses mostly on Puerto Rican music, but it necessarily connects these with Cuban and other Latina/o musical forms. The central musical references that I use emerged mostly from their presence in the *nueva narrativa* of Puerto Rico. For instance, Rosario Ferré's short stories, demonstrating her fascination with the cultural history of Ponce, highlighted the danza and the plena. Luis Rafael Sánchez's rewritings of boleros and Ana Lydia Vega's feminist narratives on salsa, urban life, and sexual politics in San Juan all directed me to the particular songs used in this book. In their literary works, these authors intuited how larger discursive structures and cultural texts mediate gender, race, class, and ethnic identities.

The first part, "The Danza and the Plena: Racializing Women, Feminizing Music," is a detailed genealogy of the patriarchal discursive tradition in Puerto Rico that has juxtaposed the danza and the plena, two central forms of Puerto Rican Creole music, as either white or black. Here I also identify the patriarchal strategy of feminizing music evident in canonized and foundational Puerto Rican essays since the end of the nineteenth century, a nationalist discourse that still informs the works of contemporary male writers such as Edgardo Rodríguez Juliá and Antonio Benítez Rojo, otherwise lauded for their postmodern and hybrid approaches to Caribbean culture. This first part, then, discusses the historical gendering of music and the resistance of the dominant sector against the Africanization or creollization of European dance forms, the concomitant racialization of women in Puerto Rican society, and issues of interracial desire explored in the short stories of Puerto Rico's major feminist writer, Rosario Ferré, whose work I read as oppositional rewritings of this patriarchal discursive tradition.

"The Plural Sites of Salsa" (Part Two) constitutes a postmodern analysis that attempts to escape the futile efforts of defining salsa as ideologically homogeneous. By offering a critical collage of diverse and conflicting definitions of salsa music proposed by musicians, musicologists, and intellectuals and by unmasking the nationalist underpinnings of various texts about salsa, this section strives to illuminate the heterogeneous social and political locations in which salsa has been inserted. Despite its pan-Caribbean genealogy, salsa has been deployed as a marker of national identity by Cubans and Puerto Ricans alike, and it has also been a marker of racial and class conflict in Puerto Rico during the 1980s. Within the postcolonial conditions of the diaspora, U.S. Latino/a communities engage this music as a space for cultural reaffirmation. To complicate matters further, salsa music also is being constructed by Anglo audiences, who, in many ways, continue to give it meaning in eroticizing and depoliticizing modes, thus engaging in a process of feminization analogous to what I discuss in Part One. Here, however, issues of crossover, appropriation, and cultural (mis)translation are salient, given the cross-cultural and colonial underpinnings of this context.

The third section, "Dissonant Melodies: Singing Gender, Desire, and Conflict," is perhaps the most expectedly traditional approach from a scholar "disciplined" in literary criticism. While I originally wanted to avoid a monodisciplinary reading of songs as literary texts, the dearth of studies in gender and Latin(o) popular music creates the need to situate some overarching representations and images of women within particular musical forms such as the bolero, salsa, merengue, and rap. Here I argue that the motif of the "absent woman" in the boleros coincides with modernization, urbanization, and women's systematic entrance into the labor force since the 1930s, that is, with women's departure from an exclusively domestic realm. Together, as Afro-Caribbean musical forms, salsa, merengue, and rap share figurations of black women and mulattas as food to be consumed and continue to articulate ambivalent feelings of both desire for and disavowal of the mulatta through the synecdoche of her rhythmic butt. This patriarchal image, in turn, is appropriated—"rebutted"—by female musicians, such as Lisa M, who deploy it to reaffirm their own power over men.

Equally urgent is the need to insert less well-known women's voices into the discussion of male-inflected lyrics, thus offering the reader/listener a dialogic medley of gender, desire, and conflict as they are articulated in song. Of particular significance is the shift in lyrics about gender relations between men and women, mostly during the 1970s. Analogous to the conflictive dynamics between men and women that Deborah Pacini Hernández identifies in *Bachata: A Social History of a Dominican Popular Music*, salsa music of the 1970s is also characterized by male anger and hostility toward women, thus articulating "the growing social and economic as well as emotional tensions between men and women" that ensued from urban migration and economic transformations in the household.[8] The medley in Part Three also examines the bolero, traditionally deemed heterosexual, romantic music in Latin America, through contemporary homoerotic rewritings by Luis Rafael Sánchez and Iris Zavala.

The final part of this study, "Así Somos, Así Son: Rewriting Salsa," is the most innovative in light of the dearth of audience research on salsa music in the Latina/o community, with the exception of Edgardo Díaz Díaz's ground-breaking study of a Latin club in Austin, Texas. After listening to salsa songs for years, I realized that neither textual nor discourse analysis would offer an adequate venue for understanding issues of audience reception and what Henry Giroux has called the moment of "the productive." Most Latin American cultural analysts prefer their own individual readings and analysis of verbal, visual, or even musical lyrics over what the "masses" may have to say. Very little cultural analysis integrates theorizing with the voices and ideas of those outside academe. Even the highly praised works about the masses and popular sectors by Néstor García Canclini, Beatriz Sarlo, Jesús Martín Barbero, and Ariel Dorfman fail to incorporate these perspectives.[9] Notwithstanding the primary role of these works in establishing the terrain of popular culture since the 1970s and 1980s as a serious field of inquiry, this domain remains a scholarly territory inhabited and articulated by a chosen few of the intelligentsia. Some Latin Americanists have even expressed an elite-ridden anxiety over the perceived mainstreaming of mass culture and the concomitant demise of the written word.[10] In this light, little has been advanced in terms of democratizing the production of knowledge about popular culture. This final section, then, constitutes what I call the critical praxis of "listening to the listeners," allowing their voices and their experiences as producers of meaning(s), to complement my own feminist readings in Part Three.

The materials for this audience research emerged out of lengthy interviews with eight working-class Latinas from Detroit and Ann Arbor, Michigan, ten Latina students at University of Michigan, and eight Latinos from Ann Arbor. Interviews began with a series of questions regarding age, class, national origin, migration, and musical tastes and practices and continued with open-ended questions about two songs, "Así son" by El Gran Combo and Willie Colón's "Cuando fuiste mujer," which were played during the interview. These two songs were selected among innumerable other possibilities, first, because Ana Lydia Vega and Carmen Lugo Filippi had chosen "Así son" as an epigraph to their own story and thus, as a recognizable cultural text among Puerto Ricans. Willie Colón's song was chosen because it represents a sample of *salsa romántica* so in vogue now. Although I do not engage in ethnographic work per se (i.e., as participant observer), these interviews constitute, I hope, a small but important contribution to much-needed audience research on salsa.

Given the tools of ethnography, it is no longer sufficient to speak about popular culture without including the voices and knowledge of others. Too many of us think of ourselves as democratic, socialist, or even radical scholars, yet we speak only from written interventions that privilege our own voices and those of other "experts" to the exclusion of nonacademic perspectives. Moreover, how radical can this scholarship be when theorizing is still protected as the exclusive power of those formally "educated"? Or when this scholarship is not accessible to those nonacademic or "popular" sectors who indeed finance those very same cultural products? While I am fully aware that this book, as it is now written for an academic audience, may not necessarily be accessible to those outside our well-guarded territory, we must continue to strive toward expanding the dialogue beyond academic settings, thus reaching via radio, journals, television, and newspapers the very communities that constitute popular culture. If we continue to speak to each other implosively, like a concentric force that rejects any "outside" element, then our work will fail to truly radicalize the production of knowledge that has kept popular culture outside the canon.

Over more than six years this book was made, unmade, and remade by many others besides the designated author. First, I want to acknowledge the financial support that I received from The Ford Foundation/National Research Council for the postdoctoral fellowship in 1987–88 that allowed me to initiate this project. In addition, the University of Michigan generously granted me two semester-long leaves of absence and a small research grant, the latter funded by the Office of the Vice-Provost for Research. I especially want to thank Dr. Lester Monts, Vice-Provost for Academic and Multicultural Affairs, for allowing me the uninterrupted time to complete the first draft of the book during the fall of 1994.

I also want to thank my previous colleagues and wonderful *compañeras*, Eliana Rivero and Elizabeth B. Davis, with whom I shared very difficult years in the *canículas* of Arizona and who also had the pleasure of being *co-colas* displaced in the southwestern regions of the country. Thanks also to those friends and scholars at University of California, Berkeley, who made the 1987–88 fellowship year a most special time in my life: Marisol Berríos-Miranda, Shannon Dudley, Pablo Furman, Quique Cruz, Lichi Fuentes. Together they provided me with important knowledge about Latin American music and with long fiestas and real music making, *en fin*, with a *co-munidad* musical.

Words of appreciation are merited by those colleagues and scholars whose work and commitment to popular music have enhanced my perspectives here, including Deborah Pacini Hernández, Juan Flores, Jorge Pérez Rolón, Peter Manuel, George Lipsitz, Robin Kelley, Steve Loza, Manuel Peña, Jorge Duany, Angel Quintero Rivera, and Edgardo Díaz Díaz. My warmest gratitude to Don Pedro Malavet Vega, who graciously shared with me his books about popular music in Puerto Rico in the very early stages of the project, and to Raúl Fernández, whose erudition as a *cocolo* has been extremely helpful. I owe particular gratitude to those friends, colleagues, and students who have read, commented on, and edited parts of the manuscript at different stages: Francine Masiello, Doris Sommer, Laura Pérez, Susana Chávez-Silverman, and Cándida Jáquez. Lisa Quiroga and Wilson Valentín worked as my research assistants in the stages of interviewing. I also want to thank Margarita de la Vega Hurtado, who bought books for me on salsa and *cancioneros* during her frequent trips to Colombia; Lise Waxer, who has been in touch from Illinois and Cali, Colombia, sharing ideas and materials; and Bridget Morgan, for her generosity in sharing resources and materials with me. To Christina José-Kampfner a thank you from *el corazón* for her solidarity. To Renee Moreno and especially to Alexandra Marchevsky and Brenda Cárdenas who worked as my research assistants, an immense thanks for their attention to detail and style and for their lucid suggestions. I also want to thank Eileen McWilliam, Suzanna Tamminen, and the staff at University Press of New England for their support and professional attention.

I want to thank personally El Gran Combo and Derek Cartagena, Rubén Blades, and Willie Colón for their generosity in sharing their lyrics and photos for this book. Also, my gratitude to Ms. Claire Johnston from Peer International for being practical and realistic in her licensing agreement. Mercedes Pérez Glass from Ansonia Records helped me track down some record companies. Sonia Alvarez from ASCAP and Jessie Lema at BMI spent many hours identifying music publishers for numerous songs; Jason Baluyut, from the Department of Romance Languages and Literatures at the University of Michigan, spent an inordinate amount of time sending and receiving faxes.

Unfortunately, I was not able to quote directly many of the songs performed by women, nor was I able to publish some photos that would have enhanced my discussion on women in music. While some producers did not cooperate, others were difficult to locate and still others charged too high a fee. However, these were the exception. Most of the individuals that I worked with showed a genuine interest and enthusiasm for this book and were very generous in allowing me to share these materials with my readers. *¡Muchas gracias a todos!*

I feel deep gratitude to my parents, Jorge and Vicky, who initially expressed reservations about this work but who came through, as parents always do, by becoming my Puerto Rico–based research assistants. My immense love and debt go to Julio, from whom I have learned about *activismo*, dedication, and integrity; and to my daughters, Gabriela and Camila, who have had to sacrifice the pleasures of having a mother available twenty-four hours a day but who, in the process, have learned to recognize practices of gender exclusion as well as the clave beat. Without their unconditional love and their unexpected patience, this book would not have been written. Last but not least, I want to recognize the contribution of all the Latinas and Latinos who were interviewed for this project. Coming from settings as diverse as Detroit and Ann Arbor, these voices, in my opinion, made this book a truly interdisciplinary and collective project, offering insights that I could have never articulated on my own. *¡Gracias!*

PART ONE

✠

THE DANZA AND THE PLENA: RACIALIZING WOMEN, FEMINIZING MUSIC

✠

A Literary Prelude

✟

Music is a Woman.
—Richard Wagner

The logic of binary oppositions appears to have become an obsessive fatal attraction.
—Henry Giroux, *Border Crossings*

Whether or not we can in fact escape from the structuring imposed by language
is one of the major questions facing feminist and non-feminist thinkers today.
—Elaine Marks and Isabelle de Courtivron, *New French Feminisms*

In 1975, when Rosario Ferré first published "When Women Love Men" in the journal *Zona de carga y descarga*, the story "caused a terrible scandal" because it honored the memory of Isabel "La Negra" Luberza, a famous or infamous black prostitute from Ponce, also Ferré's hometown, who had been shot to death in a drug-related homicide. The black-and-white format of the journal highlighted the racial binary examined in the story as well as mourning for this controversial Afro–Puerto Rican woman. Because Ferré's story contained "every obscene word in existence," the Ramayo brothers, who had been partially financing the publication of *Zona*, decided to withdraw their support, a decision that ultimately led to the demise of this radical and historically significant journal.[1]

Prophetically, this scandal prefigured the continuing and profound impact that this short story has had on Puerto Rican letters and on Latin American feminism. Like "The Youngest Doll" and "Sleeping Beauty," "When Women Love Men" has been one of Rosario Ferré's most widely read and analyzed short stories.[2] The author's personal and revealing essays examining the genesis of this story—in Spanish titled "¿Por qué quiere Isabel a los hombres?" and in English, "Why I Wrote 'When Women Love Men'"—evince its canonized status as one of the most representative texts of Puerto Rican feminist writing.[3] "When Women Love Men" portrays the contradictions and desires of two socially opposed female characters: Isabel

Luberza, a white aristocratic lady and wife to Ambrosio, and Isabel La Negra, a black prostitute. Both love Ambrosio, and after his death they have an encounter that is simultaneously competitive and mutually desirous. The ending, which has led critics to categorize the story as "fantastic," suggests a fusion of both women into one indivisible entity.

In this light, most critics have read the story as an articulation of the common oppression of all women, regardless of their race or class status.[4] This particular reading, informed by Elaine Showalter's concept of a "woman's culture," erases the power differentials among women in diverse race and class locations and fails to show these gender(ed) identities as problematic constructs in Puerto Rican patriarchal discourse. It is now compelling to situate this story, as well as two other less-read stories from *Papeles de Pandora* (The youngest doll), within a tradition—and against the grain—of a white, Eurocentric patriarchal discourse in Puerto Rico that has historically constructed women within a racial binary: white ladies, black prostitutes. In this first part of this book I analyze how these sexual and racial iconographies have been imposed on the discourse of musicology and, more generally, on discussions of national and cultural identity within the Puerto Rican essay tradition.

In her article "Papeles de Pandora: Devastación y ruptura," Ivette López Jiménez alludes to the "paradigmatic" level of Rosario Ferré's stories. This term, coined by Juri Lotman, refers to the presence of allusions, references, and borrowed discourse (intertexts) from cultural areas outside literature per se. Thus, the meaning of the text is structured around other systems of signs or cultural expressions, such as music, art, journalism, and the like.[5] Like other stories in *The Youngest Doll*, "When Women Love Men" is indeed constituted by musical intertexts and subtexts (source texts) that refer the reader to the terrain of Puerto Rican popular culture, particularly to the Afro–Puerto Rican musical forms of plenas and bombas and to the European-derived danza. The integration of popular codes within the literary text, evidence of a postmodern poetics, possesses significant political, cultural, and literary repercussions. As Juan G. Gelpí and other critics have observed, the use of extraliterary references and allusions, particularly those regarding popular music and mass culture, has become since the early 1970s a countercanonical strategy that democratizes literature and destabilizes the patriarchal and elite ideologies that had characterized Puerto Rican literature since the end of the nineteenth century. This earlier patriarchal literary discourse is clearly represented in the writings of Salvador Brau, for example, and reaches its apex with the rhetoric of "cultural nationalism" in the works of the generation of the 1930s: Antonio Pedreira, Tomás Blanco, and René Marqués.[6]

Musical subtexts and intertexts suggest, first of all, a new definition and location of the literary text that questions and displaces the privileged site of literature as an art for and by the elite. The postmodern politics of integrating popular music—neither classical nor art music—within fiction destabilizes the modern(ist) notion of art as a space exempt from the "vulgar" reality of the masses: it questions the idea of literature as a new reality that can substitute for and transcend the social spaces of the masses. As Henry Giroux explains,

In treating cultural forms as texts, postmodernism multiplies both the possibilities of constructing meaning as well as the status of meaning itself. In this sense, postmodernism redraws and retheorizes the objects and experiences of politics by extending the reach of power and meaning to spheres of the everyday that are often excluded from the realm of political analysis and pedagogical legitimation. In this case, the field of political contestation is not restricted to the state or the workplace, but also includes the family, mass and popular culture, the sphere of sexuality, and the terrain of the refused and forgotten.[7]

In Puerto Rico, this postmodernism that blurs the boundaries between the elite and the popular has been engaged in by writers who reexamine, contest, and ultimately deconstruct the hegemonic articulations of Puerto Rican culture.[8] Among these dominant paradigms one central social construct remains: the unified, homogeneous, and harmonic society devoid of racial and social conflict, emblematized by the image of the *gran familia puertorriqueña*, a central political, cultural, and social rhetoric on the island since the early part of the century.

This image originated in the writings and political discourse of the *hacendados* (landowners), in their dealings with the Spanish colonialist government during the latter half of the nineteenth century. It was later activated as a strategic response to the economic and social displacement suffered by them after 1898, precisely as U.S. absentee capitalism began to buy and mechanize the sugar production process previously controlled by this sector. According to Arcadio Díaz Quiñones, by the 1930s the Puerto Rican economy was virtually monopolized by U.S. corporations and by a Puerto Rican bourgeoisie that was both "allied and subordinated" to the interests of the metropolises. Another sector of the bourgeoisie, however, had remained displaced by these transformations, and thus its members and heirs attempted to create alliances with the workers' movement in order to confront the colonial power.

There emerged, then, two bourgeois sectors in conflict: the displaced, anticolonialist group and the new bourgeoisie that benefited from the U.S. presence in the Puerto Rican sugar-based economy.[9] To garner the support of the workers for an anti-U.S. stance, the political party of the displaced landowners summoned up the image of the patriarchal dynamics that structured the haciendas in the past, within the semifeudal relations under which workers and patrons (*padrinos*) lived together (*convivencia*) on the same terrain and social unit, the latter protecting and even acting as family (*padrinos*) to the former (the workers), who provided the labor force necessary for profit making. A homogenizing discourse of unity, harmony, and most important, *convivencia* was produced by the heirs of this displaced social sector.

This discourse, however, was exclusionary and hegemonic by its very subject location. It has resurfaced throughout the twentieth century, particularly during the 1930s, when writers like Antonio Pedreira, Tomás Blanco, and later René Marqués, as descendants of the displaced *hacendado* families, yearn for a nostalgic recuperation of this preindustrial and premodern past. As Arcadio Díaz Quiñones has observed, the patriarchal icon of the *gran familia puertorriqueña* has emerged historically during times of crisis against the colonial presence of the United States. Puerto Rican bourgeois writers have invoked an ideal past that never truly materialized, by locating social harmony and *convivencia* within a specific historical time and space (Ponce, the haciendas, and pre-1898). Thus, they were able to displace the gaze of their readers from a present moment of strife, social conflict, racial emergence of the black proletariat, women's participation in labor, migration to the cities, and a more visibly heterogeneous society to the tenets of a historical period very much desired strategically. To contest the presence of the United States in Puerto Rico, writers like Antonio Pedreira and Tomás Blanco constructed a bipolar tension between Anglo values imposed by the colonizing and imperialist power and the old, traditional and safe values held by the white, European-bred Puerto Rican aristocracy.

The ensuing hispanophilia, a result of this discourse of resistance against Anglo domination, underlies Puerto Rican cultural discourse even today. For instance, the conflicting views currently voiced concerning Puerto Rican literature in the United States written in English and about the diasporic community that produces it are excellent examples of how this hispanophilia informs controversies around Puerto Rican identity. The discourse of resistance against U.S. colonialism that has emerged on the island has led, ironically, to a static, fixed, and preterite construct of puertoricanness that excludes and silences those "other" Puerto Ricans of the diaspora. This attitude, however, should not be dismissed as arbitrarily reactionary, but it must be understood in terms of its historical genesis, that is, as an initial expression of resistance.

Music, gender, and race necessarily converge in tracing this genealogy of patriarchal and phallocentric power that men have held, both sexually and discursively, over Puerto Rican women of all racial configurations. Moreover, art music as well as particular forms of popular music have been consistently mediated by images of women, that is, feminized in a pejorative and problematic way. In the terrain of musicology, as Susan McLary notes, this feminization assumes diverse values and meanings, contingent on its historical moment and on the writer's own ideology.[10] Nevertheless, it is clear that the gendered icons of music in Puerto Rican patriarchal discourse subsume race and class factors.

In this larger, interdisciplinary framework, Rosario Ferré's short story, which suggests an integration of Afro–Puerto Rican plenas with the European aristocratic danzas, white ladies with black whores, and desire with erotic pleasure can be better understood not only as a feminist text by a Puerto Rican woman writer but as a feminist text that also speaks to and from a Puerto Rican history of racial and discursive constructs. Located within this broader historical and discursive frame, "When Women Love Men" is not reduced to a text that speaks to the homogenized oppression of all women but instead emerges as a polemical fictional rendering of the cultural dualities and oppositions that mark westernized, masculine writing.[11] By opposing plena versus danza, black versus white, and pleasure versus desire, Rosario Ferré contests the bourgeois literary tradition that has authored, and authorized, patriarchal definitions of women, of music, and of culture. She proposes new modes of writing and reading a national Puerto Rican cultural identity in more complex and, hopefully, democratic ways. Invoking Judith Butler, I have chosen to read Ferré's story as "a genealogical critique" that "refuses to search for the origins of gender" and instead "investigates the political stakes in designating as an origin and cause those identity categories that are in fact the effects of institutions, practices, discourses with multiple and diffuse points of origin."[12] In other words, Isabel Luberza and Isabel La Negra are significant as culminations of and, simultaneously, as deconstructive icons of this patriarchal discursive tradition.

CHAPTER ONE

A White Lady Called the Danza

✝

The Puerto Rican danza is a particular dance form that evolved from the English and European country dance (contradanza) and became transculturated in the Caribbean. While the term *danza* in Spanish usually refers to dance in general, in the Caribbean the danza is closely associated with the Cuban *habanera* or *danzón*, to which it is related. Most scholarship on the danza focuses on its much-debated origins, locating its genesis as far back as the *cantigas* of Alfonso X the Wise, as Samuel R. Quiñones does, or in the Spanish country dance, which entered Puerto Rico through Colombian immigration in 1813, as Cesáreo Rosa Nieves suggests.[1] Historically, the danza became the national music of the island, representing in fact the hegemonic interests of the dominant class sector at the turn of the century and throughout its first half. At present the Puerto Rican danza is regarded more as an art form than as popular music or dance, thus following the dominant ideology that has constructed it as the dance that evokes the yesteryears of the haciendas, as many rum and cigarette advertisements produced in Puerto Rico continue to do.

However, the danza has also evolved into new songs, with political content and social protest, and it has recently been revitalized by popular singers in Puerto Rico. The political value of this musical form as a vehicle for resistance against imperialism, against tyranny, and against hegemony has been systematically silenced throughout Puerto Rican history. The African heritage that forms part of its structure and musical texture also has been subjected to erasure through systematic efforts to whitewash African-derived cultural elements from Puerto Rico's social imaginary. A closer genealogical look at the danza as textualized in essays and literary texts since the late nineteenth century will reveal in more complex detail the patriarchal and hegemonic motivations underlying racial and gender- and class-based inscriptions.

In 1849, Manuel A. Alonso published *El Gíbaro* in Spain, where he had lived for seven years.[2] The fifth chapter of this first exemplar of Puerto Rican literature is dedicated to the "bailes de Puerto Rico" [dances of Puerto Rico], which he categorizes as three: (1) dances of society, which are no more than the echo or repetition of those of Europe (he includes the country dance and the waltz as examples); (2) the properly Puerto Rican–Creole hybrid dance forms, which Alonso names "*bailes de garabato*"; and (3) the "bailes de bomba," the "least important" for the author, those of African origin that have not been "generalized ever." Alonso, in fact, does not describe or mention examples of the last because, as he explains, black dances "do not merit inclusion under the title of this chapter, for even though they are seen in Puerto Rico, they have not been generalized" [no merecen incluirse bajo el titulo de esta escena, pues aunque se ven en Puerto Rico, nunca se han generalizado].

Thus, in 1849, writing from Spain, Alonso deems invisible and unimportant the cultural presence and production of the African population in Puerto Rico. Given their still unemancipated status as slaves, the "politics of inclusion" of African popular forms was surely not a consideration for his elite reading public. Historically, indeed, the plena, the popular Afro–Puerto Rican dance and song form, does not truly emerge as a singular, delineated musical form until the beginnings of the twentieth century, precisely when the African population migrates into the cities to constitute an emerging urban proletariat. At the time of Alonso's writing, however, the bomba was performed as a primary musical expression for the slaves in the plantation societies. Alonso's utter dismissal of this song and dance form ensues from the marginalized status of African cultural expressions, from their social construction as primitive, and from their invisibility in the national paradigm.

Alonso engages centrally in the feminization of music as he describes the country dance being performed in Puerto Rico:

Sus pasos adquieren mayor encanto con la gracia de las hijas del Trópico; es imposible seguir con la vista los movimientos de una de aquellas morenitas de mirar lánguido, cintura delgada y pie pequeño, sin que el corazón se delate queriendo salir del pecho. . . .
Oh hijas de mi patria! nadie os iguala en el baile, nadie derrama como vosotras ese raudal de fuego puro como vuestras frentes, ni esa voluptuosidad encantadora que solo nace en nuestro clima.

[These steps acquire greater charm with the graciousness of the daughters of the Tropics; it is impossible to follow with one's eyes the movements of one of those dark-skinned young women with languid gaze, slender waistline and small feet, without having one's heart reveal itself wanting to come out of one's chest. . . .

[Oh daughters of my fatherland! no one surpasses you in dancing, nobody spills over like you that fire, pure like your foreheads, nor that charming voluptuosity that is only born in our climate.]

In Alonso's eyes, the European country dance is enhanced by the tropical-izing effect, indeed the transcultural elements, of the Caribbean culture, here discursively equated with the Caribbean climate and its biological product, the Creole female, the daughters of the Tropics [hijas del Trópico]. From exile, Alonso's desire for the Puerto Rican woman and her beauty finds a language that channels that absence into nostalgia for the land, the music, and the women. Puerto Rico (the fatherland, the *patria*), the music, and women converge as a master metaphor for the distance im-posed by his student years in exile away from his native island. The central epithets employed to describe Caribbean women—the languid look, gra-ciousness, and charming voluptuosity, the "raudal de fuego puro," the fire and heat that emanate from the women's bodies while they dance—prevail in Puerto Rican cultural discourse.

In a similar vein, Amaury Veray, a composer, musicologist, and radical nationalist thinker explained, in an essay published in 1956, the change from the rigid rhythms of the country dance to the flexibility and arpeggio-type structure of the Puerto Rican danza as the expression of an overarch-ing tropics: "Se dijero [*sic*] que venía a satisfacer este ademán de facilidad mediante el cual los trópicos expresan sus manifestaciones artísticas" [It may be said that (the changes) satisfied this gesture of facility by which the tropics expresses its artistic manifestations].[3]

Across the Atlantic, Alonso's male gaze imagines and discursively con-structs a Puerto Rican woman—Creole or mulatta—who possesses both a European-associated languor and an African-derived sensuality, a voluptu-osity that Sander Gilman has identified in its medical and aesthetic reper-cussions throughout Europe.[4] This languor will continue to be associated with the Puerto Rican danza and its concomitant aristocratic lady, the dama, while the African-derived sensuality, dangerous promiscuity, and voluptuosity will characterize the discourse about the plena, about Afro–Puerto Rican music in general, and analogously, about the mulatta and black woman.[5]

Salvador Brau's essay "La danza puertorriqueña," first published in 1885 in the *Almanaque de damas* [Almanac for ladies] corrects Manuel Alonso's romantic description of the tropicalized country dance, the contradanza.[6] A master figure of positivism and heir to the values of the Enlightenment, Brau denounces the juvenile enthusiasm and the nostalgic tone underlying

Alonso's romanticized evocation of the country dance. Brau follows his critique with an explanation of the differences between the European country dance, a figure dance, and the Puerto Rican danza, whose main part, called the merengue (named for its sweet tone and nature), was at the time performed by individual couples, a transformation that signaled an ideological shift from a premodern collectivity to an ascending individualism marked by Western capitalism.[7]

Brau traces the transculturation of the European country dance in Puerto Rico to around 1842 or 1843, when a new dance from Havana, Cuba, known as upa or merengue, began to displace the traditional country dance. While this thesis has been the most widely accepted among musicologists, others, such as Braulio Dueño Colón, propose that the country dance was initially transformed by the Venezuelan immigration to Puerto Rico around 1835–1840, an influx of upper-class *venezolanos* that brought with it two central changes in the dance: from figure dancing to couple dancing and the dismissal of the *bastonero* (the guide or leader who led the dance with his cane). These two changes signaled the danza as a more democratic practice (by dismissing the strongly rooted authority of the *bastonero*), which in turn also led to more intimacy between the man and the woman, who could now whisper to each other while dancing, a practice totally unacceptable according to the traditional mores of the European country dance.[8]

The so-called *upa*, a term that was subsequently forgotten, was generally replaced by the more popular term, *merengue*. This Cuban dance form, itself a transcultural product of the European country dance in Cuba, consisted of a 4/4 beat, like its predecessor. It had two parts, the first of which was eventually called the *paseo* (promenade), made up of eight fixed measures repeated in a slow tempo. The second part also consisted of eight measures and also was repeated, but it was characterized by more agitated, playful rhythms, the danceable part per se. Edgardo Díaz Díaz reminds us that whereas the paseo was danced by interdependent couples or as figure dancing, the merengue was performed by independent couples who embraced as they danced throughout the salon. Thus, in its own internal structure the danza allegorizes the social tensions mentioned above.[9] While Brau names this second part the merengue, Amaury Veray later makes clear that the merengue is only the final part of the dance, not the whole second part.[10] Significantly, the merengue penetrated the ballrooms of the Philharmonic Society by 1846, and by 1854 the original 8 measures had extended to 34 and later to 130! Thus, Salvador Brau appropriately describes the merengue as an "invading or invasive march," a "revolution."[11]

Many individuals from the older generation, as well as traditionalists, opposed the performance of merengues in social dances. Veray confirms this:

El llamado merengue pronto se hizo popular entre los jóvenes de la época y debido a su desenfrenada interpretación fue motivo de escándalo para los decorosos contertulios que asistían a los bailes a ver bailar la juventud. Fueron muchos los ciudadanos peninsulares que se escandalizaron con tan deleznable atrevimiento.[12]

[The so-called merengue soon became very popular among the youth, and because of its unbridled performances, it caused a scandal among the decorous people who attended the dances to see the young people dance. There were many Spaniards who were scandalized by this daring, unacceptable behavior.]

Significantly, Veray identifies the resistance to this dance not only as a generational or moral issue but also as an articulation of the tensions between *gachupines* (Spaniards) and Creoles. Despite the fact that the General Don Juan de la Pezuela officially prohibited the dance in 1846, by 1850 the merengue had totally replaced the Spanish country dance.[13]

This musical revolution, this transculturation, also produced changes in instrumentation. Brau documents that in 1853 the güiro joined the orchestras "with its Indian reminiscences."[14] Echoing the colonialist persecution and censorship of drumming among the slaves, the presence of this non-European instrument led to the arrest and imprisonment of the güireros or güiro players. Yet the gradual creolization of the dance orchestras continued to increase with the addition of the timbal, or redoblante, the percussion box that Brau correctly traces to the African bomba, but his observations about it reveal the anti-African stance that also informed Manuel Alonso's dismissal of this Puerto Rican dance form:

[El timbal] recuerda los sacudimientos peculiares de la bomba africana, acentuando la cadencia de baile de un modo obsceno, adaptable a las contorsiones grotescas y lascivas de esos abigarrados botargas que recorren las calles en la época de nuestro extraordinario carnaval.[15]

[(The timbal) reminds us of the peculiar rumblings of the African bomba, accentuating the cadence of the dance in an obscene manner, adaptable to the grotesque and lascivious contortions of those who traverse the streets during the season of our extraordinary carnival.]

For the positivist author the presence of the güiro is acceptable because of its nostalgic or folkloric value, but that of the timbales announces the overt Africanization of the orchestra. This becomes the pivotal point around which the danza degenerates, for Brau, into obscenity, primitivism, and mere physicality. Yet Brau's language in this quotation reveals an interesting degree of ambiguity regarding his own subject position. In these lines he rejects the timbal because of its association with the negative and primitivized gestures of the Puerto Rican carnival, yet he simultaneously considers the carnival part and parcel of his collective culture (nuestro extra-ordinario carnaval). The use of the possessive, also deployed by Braulio Dueño Colón in the quotations below, suggests an ambivalent self-location on his part as a member of the patriarchal bourgeoisie. The insistence on the possessive marks, discursively, a struggle for the ownership and control of cultural practices. The ambivalence rests, then, on this sense of owner-ship of and identification with Creole cultural productions and on a simul-taneous distancing from the racial presence of African elements that these cultural practices were making visible and audible.

Braulio Dueño Colón's observations in 1913 about the danza's African elements reaffirm this steady Africanophobia: "no negaremos que hubo un tiempo en que nuestra danza degeneró de modo lamentable debido al mal gusto artístico de ciertos compositores y directores de orquesta que uti-lizaron la bomba africana, imprimiendo a la danza un ritmo grotesco y, por ende, antiestético"[16] [we will not deny that there was a time when our danza lamentably degenerated due to the bad artistic taste of certain com-posers and orchestra directors, who employed the African bomba, pressing upon the danza a grotesque and thus antiesthetic rhythm]. Read together, the colonialist and racist reactions of both Brau and Dueño Colón stress the primacy of European musical structures in the musical canon as well as defining what is beautiful and "aesthetic." The non-European, African structures and rhythms, described as "antiesthetic," "grotesque," and primitive, prove to be too subordinate to claim inclusion within a national paradigm of culture.

Revising and deconstructing this Eurocentric resistance to *lo africano* in essays about the danza, Angel Quintero Rivera has recently examined the presence and the role of the bombardino instrument in twentieth-century danza orchestras. The bombardino is a wind instrument that produces a sound similar to that of the clarinet but resembles a type of French horn. It became one of the principal instruments in Puerto Rican danza orchestras; in fact, black musicians like Cocolía built their fame on their bombardino interpretive skills. Angel Quintero Rivera suggests that the tone and tex-ture of the bombardino were used, in fact, to camouflage the sounds of the African drums that were prohibited from entering the elite hacienda ball-rooms.[17]

The invasion of non-European instruments into the space of the upper-class landowning families also resulted in rhythmic innovations and trans-formations. The use of the dot and the sixteenth note [el puntillo y la semi-corchea] was, according to Amaury Veray, the beginning of what later was to be called the *tresillo elástico* (flexible triplet)—a term coined by Don Fer-nando Callejo; its incorporation into the danza has been attributed to

Manuel G. Tavárez. The *tresillo elástico* refers to the use of three notes against two within the same beat, thus creating a syncopation in the rhythmic and melodic structure of the danza. Angel Quintero Rivera has analyzed this *tresillo elástico* as also African-derived because it creates a rhythmic tension, a pull and push between the offbeat notes and their resolution toward the principal beat.

The prohibitions against the merengue, the pejorative arguments against the faster rhythms, the incarceration of the güireros, and the resistance to the new intimacy and the corporeal movements of the dancing couple, are clearly founded in the Africanophobia of a repressive colonial system, an ideology consistently articulated by the local patriarchal bourgeoisie and justified through sexual and racial constructs, inscriptions, and associations that linked "Africanness" and the black population to exoticism, eroticism, unbridled sexuality, and indolence. The forces of civilization were obliged to contain these sites of unlimited passion, for the "domino theory" of passions assumes that "sexual passions have no self-regulating mechanisms, no internal limits."[18] Salvador Brau's ambivalence toward the new, transcultural danza is expressed precisely in the context of this Africanizing process. For him, tradition (i.e., European elements and structures) remains the desired state for Puerto Rican music, while innovation and cultural syncretism are mostly equated with degeneration and with the concomitant profanation of its European subtexts. However, as Angel Quintero Rivera also notes, Brau analyzes the danza as an instance of the "stratified integration" by which the Puerto Rican bourgeoisie attempted to construct this image of the *gran familia puertorriqueña*. A racial and cultural allegory underlies Brau's view on how the sounds of the Indian güiro and the "trepidations" of the savage timbal are fused and harmonized (to be read as contained) by the strings, the European instrumental legacy.[19] Nevertheless, "both the Afro-Caribbean syncopation and the transition to couple dancing were explicitly identified . . . with creole aesthetics and naturalism," as Peter Manuel observes about both Cuba and Puerto Rico.[20]

The racializing and racist power of Brau's argument is further revealed when he deems this syncretism positive only in the context of borrowings or contacts with European or U.S. composers. He first comments on the valuable influence of the danza rhythms—ironically, those same rhythms that he describes as grotesque and lascivious—on the work of Louis M. Gottschalk, who was "inebriated by the voluptuosity of this hybrid music."[21] Brau also mentions the work of Don Félix Astol, the Cataluña-born composer of "La Borinqueña," a danza that remains Puerto Rico's national hymn. Astol also was seduced by the eroticized rhythms of the danza. While Brau boasts about the international influence and the impact of Puerto Rican danza rhythms on other musical forms, a vision parallel to what we call "world beat" music today, he fails to recognize that the power of the danza to attract the attention of foreign musicians and composers had actually rested also on the eroticization of the habanera rhythm, a tropicalized otherness that Gottschalk himself desired, capitalized on, and integrated into his own compositions.

What Brau could not assess, then, is the central role of the New Orleans–born pianist and composer in the development of the Puerto Rican danza. According to Federico A. Cordero, Gottschalk's visit to Puerto Rico in 1859 marked the earliest composition of a danza that contained the basic structure that Juan Morel Campos would later standardize. Gottschalk's *Danza Opus 33* is, to this date, the oldest danza to be found. In other words, the genesis of the Puerto Rican danza as such is located in the intercultural circulation of the habanera rhythms as erotiziced by Gottschalk.[22]

Salvador Brau's ambivalence toward the danza is also informed by the duality and binary oppositions—emotion versus reason, the body versus the mind—characteristic of the discourse of the Enlightenment. Despite the fact that the hybrid nature of the danza supposedly degrades the purity of its European sources, Brau still confesses his "love" for this music, a passion that developed during his youth and to which his memories of the past are inextricably linked.[23] At the end of his essay, however, Brau insists that the Puerto Rican danza should not be experienced in the ballroom, where sensuality and psychological perturbation may abound, but instead should be analyzed alone in the study, where, through reason, one can discover the cultural syncretism and the diverse musical elements that the danza incorporates.

This very duality between reason and the affective also surfaces when Brau seeks to establish his own credibility and authority as an objective writer. While his love for the danza stems from his youth—and from its characteristic emotional upheavals—his essay is the product of a rational, scientific approach typical of maturity and, moreover, of his identity as a man of letters who can translate into verbal discourse the dangerous pleasures that the music can trigger in him, a translation between the arts that reeks of containment. This self-ascribed authority leads him to conclude that "this danza, such as it exists among us, must disappear."[24] The death of the danza in its Africanized and transcultural state, as summoned by Salvador Brau, is necessarily followed by a positivist message articulated through icons of music and dance—images mediated by Brau through which the African, non-European aspects of the music and the feminine are displaced and replaced by the "ronda sagrada del Trabajo y del Progreso, a compás de las armonías solemnes de la Ciencia, de la Justicia y de la Fraternidad universal"[25] [sacred circle of Work and Progress, to the beat of the solemn harmonies of Science, Justice and of universal Brotherhood].

For Brau, the ascribed non-European (i.e., the erotic and emotional) aspects of the danza, synthesized as its feminine traits—"danza femenina de la molicie" [feminine dance of softness]—must be eradicated and supplanted by the values of work and justice, by the masculinity of science and reason. The westernized discourse of Salvador Brau functions here to counteract the transcultural processes that symbolize a threat to positivism and to the Enlightenment. Brau mourns the loss of the cultural purity that the European country dance embodied and all that it represented, and he denounces the antirational values of indolence, melancholy, and eroticism that he locates in his constructed others: women and Afro–Puerto Ricans. By equating femininity with an essentialized African lasciviousness and obscenity in this "objective" and "scientific" study of the danza, Brau succeeds in constructing a hegemonic discourse about Afro-Caribbean music and culture that still informs current attitudes about popular culture in Puerto Rico and elsewhere. The feminization and simultaneous tropicalization (read Africanization and erotization) of the European creolized contradanza, as devalued by Salvador Brau, continues to privilege a patriarchal, Eurocentric ideology over other cultural sectors that constitute Puerto Rico and Puertoricanness, thus preparing the terrain for the contemporary struggles over cultural discourse that Juan Flores summarizes.[26]

Brau's essay also may be read as a phobic, defensive reaction to the period of postemancipation and to the possible cultural and racial displacements that the freeing of slaves entailed after 1873. In this context, Quintero Rivera also reads a substantial degree of fear in Brau's essay about the danza, although mostly political and class-marked rather than racial. This fear underlies the ideological shift of the Puerto Rican *hacendados* from a liberal stance to a much more rigid conservative position:

. . . desconfianza de las iniciativas populares rayando en temor ante la explosión de actos de masa durante las transformaciones políticas del cambio de siglo (las partidas sediciosas, las turbas republicanas, la organización propia del proletariado en la Federación Libre de Trabajadores y su prédica socialista), aunque no los mencione Brau por su nombre [27]

[. . . a mistrust over popular initiatives that borders on fear over the explosion of mass events during the political transformations of the turn of the century (insurrectionary forces, republican forces, the organizing of the proletariat through the Free Federation of Workers and their socialist preachings), although Brau does not mention them].

Brau's feminization of the danza also dovetails with the still-strong literary tradition of romanticism in the Caribbean colonies at the time, a movement that also explains the gendering of the Puerto Rican danza. As romantic music, the danza is usually based on a biographical sentimental experience, and as programmatic music its titles and lyrics refer us systematically to the female loved one, the *amada*. Songs such as "Margarita," "Violeta," and "Laura y Georgina" are but three of the best-known danzas in Puerto Rico, and they all sing to women.[28]

During the nineteenth century, a time of exile for many Latin American liberal writers, the desire for the idealized woman extended also to the fatherland, to one's birthplace. (Notice the linguistic irony of the term in Spanish, *patria*, with its patriarchal root; yet the cultural tradition includes both, as in the phrase "la Madre Patria" [The Mother Fatherland]). This extended metaphor suggests the conflation of three central signifiers: woman, country, and nature. José Gautier Benítez, Puerto Rico's most illustrious romantic poet, evinces this phenomenon in his poem titled "Ausencia" [Absence]. He addresses Puerto Rico, his beloved island:

Tú das vida a la doncella	[You give birth to the lady
Que inspira mi frenesí	Who inspires passion in me;
A ella la quiero por ti,	I love her because of you,
A ti te quiero por ella.[29]	And I love you because of her.]

In this romantic tradition, already seen in the work of Manuel Alonso, the absence of the loved one translates into the absence of the country (the national and political allegory), which itself increases the male subject's desire for both. In this light, the romantic danzas in Puerto Rico have been valued as much for their sentimental lyrics as for their articulation of a patriotic and national desire.

Also indebted to the positivist legacy, Antonio S. Pedreira, in his seminal essay on Puerto Rican culture and identity, *Insularismo,* employs the feminizing strategy to describe the landscape of the island and, metaphorically, the supposedly docile and "insular" character of the Puerto Rican people.[30] According to Pedreira, in contrast to the epic and grandiose geographic dimensions of other Latin American countries like Chile, Argentina, or Mexico, Puerto Rico consists of "a tender, soft, bland, crystalline landscape," thus constituting a geography "of a minor tone," like that of "our danza which tends towards languor and intimacy." This danza, "predominantly lyrical" in its tone, "adopts a soft air, . . . lovely, and profoundly feminine." Pedreira concludes these remarks by equating music, gender, and geography: "The danza, like our landscape, is of a feminine condition, soft and romantic."[31] Pedreira's descriptions are meaningful in the context of his colonizing thesis about the Puerto Rican, whom he defines as docile, "aplatanado" [self-defeating] and passive toward history.

The danza "Laura y Georgina," composed by Juan Morel Campos, was originally dedicated to the Capó sisters, whose first names inspired the title. Piano music published in 1958 by the Instituto de Cultura Puertorriqueña. Courtesy of the Instituto de Cultura Puertorriqueña.

This contested vision of Puerto Rican identity[32] links the Puerto Rican to his/her geography: in a syllogistic argument, Pedreira equates the poorly epic island landscape of "a minor tone" with the purported intellectual and cultural inferiority of the Puerto Rican. Moreover, the slow and languid rhythm of the danza represents for Pedreira an additional symptom of our supposed docility as a nation, a rhythm that stands in contrast to the fast rhythm of the North American fox trot. Here Pedreira essentializes historically developed musical forms as static, ahistorical symbols of a particular culture, explicitly gendering the respective national characters of Puerto Rico and the United States. He defines the feminine as Puerto Rico's assumed weakness, while the masculine is associated with the epic, the grandiose, the North American culture, a discursive gendering that emulates the colonizing gesture of first world countries toward those of the third world.[33]

Despite Salvador Brau's anti-Africanizing sentiments, the danza became the national music for Puerto Ricans precisely because its African elements were mediated and whitened. In 1942, Antonio Pedreira reread the danza as a metaphor for the colonizability of Puerto Ricans evident in the slow rhythm of production of Puerto Rican life. This is a rather ironic stance given his own position as a world aristocrat—in the tradition of Rodó and Ortega y Gasset—against the commercial, mass society of the United States. Yet if "[b]y the 1930's . . . most Puerto Ricans were coming to view the danza as archaic and quaint," as Peter Manuel documents, then Pedreira's privileging of North American rhythms over the "soft, romantic" texture of danzas is perhaps his way of negotiating his own fledgling entrance into modernity.[34]

Yet the traits that he essentializes as a sign of the docile and self-defeating Puerto Rican character have very little to do with the value of the danza as a national music. He proposes a circular argument that results at best in a redundancy. In a totalizing way, he reduces the danza to "a minor tone," a structural element that signals its supposed "blandness," but the fact is that, musically speaking, not all danzas are written in a minor tone. And even if a substantial number of danzas were composed in this modality, this particular trait has nothing to do with the maleness or femaleness of the culture from which they emerge but rather with the predominant modalities of romantic music that characterize them. Yet if it is true, as Susan McClary posits in *Feminine Endings*, that even the most traditionally neutral musical structures have been subjected to gendered constructs and valued as such, the feminization and consequent devaluation of specific musical structures or features—like the cadences that McClary analyzes in her book or the minor tonality that Pedreira feminizes—are integral to the dissemination of patriarchal ideology.

Pedreira is hardly alone in his attempt to ascribe cultural, gendered and social meanings to the minor tonal system, a system whose characteristics are based on intervals and relational tones.[35] This feminization, then, cannot be explained by any inherent gender value in the minor tonality but rather by a larger project of constructing an image of Puerto Rican society that would reaffirm the masculinist and patriarchal values of a Puerto Rican bourgeoisie that no longer controlled the land and thus clung to control over language and cultural discourse. Pedreira himself explains neither his gendering of Puerto Rican culture nor that of the danza, as he takes for granted the fixed meanings associated with femininity. By not questioning gender in his discourse, Pedreira simply confirms the central role of the gendered constructs in the discourse of nationality. Pedreira succeeds in reaffirming the stereotypes and negative values ascribed to the nonwhite, nonmale, non-European elements of Puerto Rican culture as deviations from the norm, images that have survived under the myopic lens of historical amnesia.

This feminized image of the danza, still current in contemporary musicology,[36] can be easily contested with one historical example, unsurprisingly omitted by Brau, by Pedreira, and by most musical histories in Puerto Rico. "La Borinqueña," the national anthem of Puerto Rico, is a danza in its musical features. Yet its own genealogy illustrates the significant silences and omissions in official history that undermine the very myths and gendered constructs on which Eurocentric patriarchy stands. The current lyrics of "La Borinqueña" were composed in 1901 by Don Manuel Fernández Juncos (1844–1928), a Spanish-born Puerto Rican statesman, writer, and composer, whose lyrics for "La Borinqueña" even Pedreira criticizes as "una danza bailable con tema ramplonamente bucólico" [a danceable danza with an exaggeratedly bucolic theme]. Pedreira's judgments about Juncos were intended to prove his point about the "blandness" of the Puerto Rican national character. The original melody of "La Borinqueña," composed by Paco Ramírez, became the official anthem of the island in 1952, when the current governmental status of the Commonwealth of Puerto Rico was established. And in 1977, the lyrics by Manuel Fernández Juncos officially became the new text. Pedreira was accurate in his assessment of this text, a highly patriotic song that was also politically safe in its pastoral description of the island's landscape:

La tierra de Borinquen	[The land of Borinquen
Donde he nacido yo.	Where I was born
Es un jardín florido	Is a florid garden
De mágico primor.	Of magical beauty.
Un cielo siempre nítido	An ever-clear sky
Le sirve de dosel	Covers it as a canopy
Y dan arrullos plácidos	And the waves at its feet
Las olas a sus pies.	Are its placid lullabies.
Cuando a sus playas	When Columbus arrived

Vino Colón.	At its shore
Exclamó lleno de admiración:	He exclaimed full of admiration:
Oh! Oh! Oh!	Oh! Oh! Oh!
Esta es la linda tierra	This is the beautiful land
Que busco yo;	That I have searched for;
Es Borinquen la hija	This is Borinquen the daughter,
La hija del mar y el sol	The daughter of the sea and the sun
Del mar y el sol	Of the sea and the sun
Del mar y el sol.	Of the sea and the sun.]

Juncos's lyrics reaffirm Pedreira's constructs regarding the melancholy, docility, and passive nature of the Puerto Rican danza. Nevertheless, Pedreira's feminization of the danza and of Puerto Rican culture is also heir to the romantic discourse to which Manuel Alonso and Manuel Fernández Juncos are also indebted. Fernández Juncos's text, like Gautier Benítez's poetry, conflates woman and island, thus creating a double, allegorical discourse of love and politics, of romantic desire and national beauty, which has been lucidly examined in nineteenth-century Latin American literature by Doris Sommer.[37]

The palatability and political neutrality of Juncos's version of "La Borinqueña," uncontested in the 1952 call for new lyrics to the national anthem,[38] stand in sharp ideological contrast to a previous version written by Lola Rodríguez de Tió, a Puerto Rican woman poet who struggled for Puerto Rico's independence from Spain and who died in Cuba after years of exile.[39] Lola Rodríguez de Tió capitalized on "La Borinqueña"'s already popular melody (the one composed by Paco Ramírez) and wrote a revolutionary version that was supposedly used during the insurrection of El Grito de Lares in 1868. It thus became known as "El himno de Lares."[40] This text is a call to violence and to nationalist patriotism, a summons to the defense of the masses. It contains the image of the machete that later inspired nationalist radicals (the macheteros) and became a symbol of the nationalist revolutionary struggles of recent years. It also reveals "a Caribbean consciousness that becomes a thematic concern for the women writers in the contemporary period"[41] and for Nueva Trova singers like Pablo Milanés, who interpreted some of Tió's poetry, particularly the verses "Cuba y Puerto Rico son / de un pájaro las dos alas."

> ¡Despierta Borinqueño
> que han dado la señal!
> ¡Despierta de ese sueño
> que es hora de luchar!
>
> ¿A ese llamar patriótico,
> no arde tu corazón?
> ¡Ven! nos será simpático

el ruido del cañón.

¡Mira! Ya el cubano libre será;
le dará el machete la libertad.

Ya el tambor guerrero dice en su son
que es la manigua el sitio de reunión.
¡Bellísima Borinquen a Cuba hay que seguir!
¡Tú tienes bravos hijos que quieren combatir!

¡Ya más tiempo impávidos no podemos estar!
¡No queremos, tímidos, dejarnos subyugar!
Nosotros queremos ser libres ya:
Y nuestro machete bien afilado está.

¿Por qué hemos de estar dormidos
y sordos a esta señal?

No hay que temer, Riqueños, al ruido del cañón,
pues salvar la patria es deber del corazón.
No queremos más déspotas. Caiga el tirano ya.
Las mujeres indómitas, también sabrán luchar.

¡Queremos la libertad! ¡Nuestro machete nos la dará![42]

[Wake up, borinqueño,
the signal has been given!
Wake up from your sleep
It is time to fight!

Does not your heart burn
to this patriotic call?
Come! for we will be pleased
to hear the noise of the cannons.

Look! The Cubans will already be free;
the machete will reward them with freedom.

The war drums speak with their sounds
that the grassland is the meeting place.
Most beautiful Borinquen, let's follow Cuba
You have courageous sons who want to fight.

We cannot remain impassive any longer!
We do not want to be shy, to be subordinated!
We want to be free now;
and our machetes are already sharpened.

Why should we be asleep
and deaf to this signal?

We should not fear, Riqueños, the noises of the cannon,
for saving our country is the duty of our hearts.
We want no more tyrants. May the tyrant fall!
Women, unconquerable, will also know how to fight!

We want liberty! Our machetes will assure it for us!

Lola Rodríguez de Tió's hymn, a summons to both men and women to take up arms and fight against the Spanish troops, challenges the images of Puerto Ricans as docile, passive and melancholic. These lyrics, a far cry from the innocuous pastoral discourse of Fernández Juncos, were popularized and learned by all Puerto Ricans, thus becoming the counterofficial patriotic hymn during these times of struggle. Rivera Montalvo has indicated that this text marks precisely the historical instance when "La Borinqueña leaves the aristocratic salons and becomes the hymn of all Puerto Ricans." But as history has shown before, this version was censored by the Spanish government, who correctly considered it a "song of rebellion" against the Spanish regime.[43] That Pedreira strategically ignored and did not even allude to Lola Rodríguez de Tió's "Borinqueña," a text that belies his characterizations of the danza as feminine and passive (in its lyrics as much as in its authorship), is not surprising given the radical oppositionality that Tió's text embodies. That the most aggressive, "masculine," politically dangerous, and collectively powerful version of "La Borinqueña" was written by a woman undermines Pedreira's arguments regarding the "feminine" aspects of Puerto Rican culture and about women themselves. This historical example demonstrates, moreover, the imperative of restoring the historical memory that patriarchal strategies attempt to suppress.

As time has proved, when Salvador Brau called for the disappearance of the Africanized danza at the end of the century, his exhortation was useless and antiprophetic at best. Indeed, the Puerto Rican danza, in its most creolized (read Africanized) form, acquired the status of national music, representative of the island and of the culture at the turn of the century. Its most lauded representatives were the composers Juan Morel Campos and Manuel G. Tavárez, both of whom were mulatto sons of artisan families in the Ponce area. What is relevant is not so much the origin of these composers but, as Angel Quintero Rivera has indicated, "the musical analysis of the danza is very revealing as music produced by artisans precisely in the midst of the process of their struggles for the recognition of their civil rights."[44] Indeed, the manifestations of the artistic and cultural presence of the mulatto, camouflaged within the discursive and aesthetic frames of the European-born and aristocratic dances of the upper-classes, reveal, in their historical development, the struggles of the working class—in this case artisans and mulattoes—to achieve a certain degree of hegemony. The previously discussed examples of the timbal, the bombardino, and the syncopated rhythms in the *tresillo elástico*, indicate the mediated forms by which the African-derived elements could be integrated into European forms, that is, accepted by the dominant class and acceptable as a national symbol.

It is not a coincidence, either, that the social, historical, and political locus in which the danza developed was the southern city of Ponce during the second half of the nineteenth century. Ponce was also the historical and social site in which the Puerto Rican Autonomist Party was born. This political party promoted the image of the *gran familia puertorriqueña* in its confrontations with the Peninsular government. Within the context of national politics, the *hacendados* took on the role of *padres de agrego (appointed parents)*, toward the artisans, *los honestos hijos de la labor* (the honest sons of labor). The presence and the contributions of the mulatto sector to the musical culture of mainstream society at the time, albeit in camouflaged nature, was facilitated by the paternalistic ideology of the dominant landowning sector. It is no coincidence, then, that Ponce, "la ciudad más puertorriqueña de Puerto Rico" [the most Puerto Rican city in Puerto Rico], according to Luis Muñoz Marín, was the geocultural hub of the landowners, of the *gran familia puertorriqueña* ideology, of the plena, of Isabel La Negra, and of Rosario Ferré's life and works.

More recently, after some decades of silence and oblivion, the danza has resurfaced in Puerto Rican musical culture in truly different contexts from the aristocratic ballrooms in which it was performed. From dancing music of the aristocracy and from national music at the turn of the century, the danza has survived mostly as a musical form interpreted and performed by pianists and orchestras. Since the 1980s, however, the danza has undergone a process of *metalepsis*,[45] a cultural transvaloration of meaning by which a musical form assumes a cultural and social meaning different from that of its origins. In other words, the danza has been popularized and decontextualized, no longer bound to the upper-class landowner society that sanctioned it as Puerto Rico's national music. It is no longer art music only, nor the music of nostalgia for the patriarchal order that many Puerto Ricans still may want to evoke. Amaury Veray, for instance, points to the danza's social value in his arguments against its "death" or disappearance. Yet he recognizes that the danza's prestige and life have been limited to its performance and interpretation as art music. It is no longer danceable, thus its value as an expression of social cohesion and collectivity has been diminished, if not totally annulled.

In 1981, however, Danny Rivera, a Puerto Rican popular singer of ballads and of autochtonous music (plenas, música jíbara, and political nueva canción) recorded a two-record album titled *Danzas para mi pueblo* [Danzas for my People].[46] Included were some of the best known romantic pieces by Juan Morel Campos, Manuel G. Tavárez ("Margarita"), and Angel Mislán ("Tú y yo"), side by side with Lolita Rodríguez de Tió's revolutionary and historically silenced "La Borinqueña" and a more recent composition by Vitín Calderón titled "Lolita." The last was dedicated to

Lolita Lebrón, the nationalist political figure who was released from jail by Jimmy Carter in 1979, along with the other political prisoners who had been convicted of attempting to assassinate President Truman and of attacking Congress in 1954 and jailed for twenty-five years. The danza, then, in 1980, was employed as a musical form that vindicates the contributions of two radical and revolutionary women in Puerto Rican history, both of whom are named Lolita. Vitín Calderón's danza in honor of Lolita Lebrón evokes the same revolutionary call to arms that Lolita Rodríguez de Tió had penned more than a hundred years ago.

Danny Rivera's inclusion of both "La Borinqueña" and of Calderón's "Lolita" is significant, as it represents a newly embedded ideological feminization of the danza; that is, it continues the tradition of the gendering of this musical form, yet the very figures that speak or that are spoken about in these pieces are the embodiment of radical action and revolutionary struggle in Puerto Rico, an oppositional and liberating icon given the "colonial dilemma" of the island.[47] This ideological shift in the ways that women are associated with the danza, congruent with the solidification of the feminist movement in Puerto Rico during the 1970s, overturns the negatively valenced gender constructs of the danza, of women, and of Puerto Ricans, inscriptions that both Brau's and Pedreira's patriarchal writings helped to constitute.

In Mapeyé's album *Criollo y más*, two danzas, "La sensitiva" by Manuel G. Tavárez and "Marisel" by Modesto Nieves, are performed as jíbaro music, with its rhythms, instrumentation, and arrangements.[48] Yet this synthesis of the European white lady called the danza with the autochthonous music of the Puerto Rican mountains is not new. Antonio Cabán Vale's ("El Topo") famous song, "Verde luz," also a danza, has already become the unofficial Puerto Rican anthem among the youth, the politically active, and the Left. Mapeyé's criollo renderings of danzas as instrumental music reposition them away from the classical musical canon and the traditional danza orchestra, integrating them within the popular canon of jíbaro music. The cuatros, guitarras, and güiros, the same that were prohibited from participating in orchestras and dances earlier in the century, are now the instruments that give voice to the danza.

These examples show how musical forms are rescued from oblivion and transformed in the process of recovery. The democratizing and popularizing trend of the Puerto Rican danza is not surprising given the powerful movement of the Nueva Canción that has characterized Puerto Rican popular music since the 1960s. This movement has revitalized all Puerto Rico's musical culture and integrated the danza into the musical context of a larger audience, the mulatto sector, returning it, transformed, to the social and racial groups that historically contributed to its development. This recent metalepsis has challenged the discursive dualities and oppositions established by the Eurocentric patriarchy in Puerto Rico in the struggles for discourse and power that motivate these social constructs. The binary correspondences between the danza, the aristocratic white lady, and the plena, the black prostitute and national site of pleasure, have been deconstructed by Puerto Rican musicians since the 1960s. The danza, democratized, now emerges as another vehicle for popular expression and for the reaffirmation of a radical ideology, an oppositional stance against the colonial status of the island. In this sense, the danza now converges with her antagonist in discourse, the African-derived plena.

CHAPTER TWO

A Sensual Mulatta Called the Plena

✝

If the feminized and racialized danza was the national music of Puerto Rico by the turn of the century, the Afro–Puerto Rican plena, along with the bomba, was historically and discursively marginalized, erased, and dismissed as *música de negros* (music of Blacks). This opposition, which negates the racial hybridity of the Puerto Rican people as well as the basic processes from which its transcultural manifestations emerge, continues to inform musicology. Moreover, it builds the historical framework for current manifestations of racial binaries in the young, urban musical culture of Puerto Rico, as the rockero-cocolo paradigm during the 1980s illustrates (cf. Part Two, "The Plural Sites of Salsa"). Like the danza, the plena is, after all, a hybrid musical form that integrates both European and African elements in its form and lyrics. Their respective differentialized genesis, racially and class-located, have led music historians and essayists to present the danza in opposition to the plena, systematically denoting the former as "our national music" while relegating the latter to the fringes of culture as "folklore." Like the danza, the plena also becomes an object of feminization in Tomás Blanco's essay, "Elogio de la plena,"[1] which I pose here as a central subtext to Rosario Ferré's "When Women Love Men."

The origins of the plena, a form of song and dance practiced by the black and mulatto proletariat, have been located by most musicologists in the coastal towns and areas of southern and southeastern Puerto Rico, that is, in the sugar-growing plantation areas where the African population resided.[2] While its chronological origins are still undefined, most scholars date its emergence from around the turn of the century. Among some hypotheses, it has been proposed that the term *plena* came from the tradition of singing and dancing outside during the evenings, particularly in nights of full moon (*luna llena* or *luna plena*). Thus, the adjective for *luna plena* became synonymous with the dance and the music.[3] Many scholars have also indicated the English-derived partial origins of the plena, as they recount the presence of a couple, immigrants from St. Kitts, who used to play the guitar and tambourine on the streets of Ponce to make a living. The husband used to tell the wife, "Play, Anna!" or "Play now!" which was heard and rewritten into Spanish as *Ple-na*.[4] As Juan Flores has observed, the English source of the Puerto Rican plena has not always been documented by music historians, yet it reveals the "multiple intersections and blending of cultures as working people scatter and relocate," as well as the "regional Caribbean context for the emergence of twentieth century song forms in all nations of the area: son, calypso, merengue, and many other examples of the 'national popular' music of their respective countries were all inspired by the presence of musical elements introduced from other islands."[5]

Juan Flores contributes to the growing scholarship on the origins of the plena by calling attention to the legacy of the semilegendary Joselino "Bumbún" Oppenheimer (1884–1929), from the area of La Joya del Castillo, a proletarian barrio in Ponce, where Flores locates the historical beginnings of this music. He recounts the "humble beginnings" of this music in the work of Bumbún, whose job plowing the land was accompanied by singing and improvising plenas. The call-and-response structure characteristic of this musical form was practiced and developed by Bumbún, who sang the solo while his *cuarteros* (plowboys) responded with the refrains. Joselino Oppenheimer, also known as "King of la Plena," left his trade as plowman and began the first plena band, dedicating himself to the music full-time. According to Flores, he was also a popular *panderetero* (tambourine player), famous for his virtuosity in improvising as well as for his body performance with the pandereta: "In the midst of a vibrant improvisation he would rest it suddenly on his shoulder, bounce it off his head, or roll it along the floor, all the while twisting and jerking his body in a wild frenzy."[6]

The historical recovery of a figure such as Joselino Bumbún Oppenheimer and the identification of the English couple in Ponce—John Clark and Catherine George, the latter known as Doña Catín—are significant contributions to the historical reconstruction of the plena per se; Flores's documentation is valuable mostly in the context of an overarching silence that has veiled the authorial contributions of specific individuals of the working class to the development of a national culture or music. By minimizing the individual authorship of plenas under the rubric of anonymous oral tradition, musicology has virtually erased the presence of working-class artists such as Joselino Oppenheimer from scholarship and official histories. Authorship for white, European, and upper-class males has consistently been recognized and glorified under the Western tradition of individualism and the romantic tenet of the "genius," yet the authority and creativity of black working-class individuals is systematically diluted under the rubric of folklore and collectivity.[7] This issue is doubly poignant in the case of women's authorship in popular music traditions.

Other theories suggest that the plena was born in 1916, during World War I as a result of U.S. influence on musical taste, but this theory is quite unconvincing because of its lack of documentation. What is clear is that by the 1930s this Afro–Puerto Rican musical form had been embraced as the "authentic" and "representative" music of the Puerto Rican people.[8] Puerto Rican writer Edgardo Rodríguez Juliá suggests, in fact, that the plena, "our first proletarian music," displaced the European-derived music in Puerto Rico, the danza, the contradanza, the minuet, and the rigodon.[9] As I have shown, the class struggles embodied in this musical displacement are evident in this case, for it was the popularity of the plena that filled the void of a dwindling danza from the second decade of the century. This displacement reflects the class and economic transitions created by the presence of U.S. absentee capitalism, a new economic structure that replaced the dominant power of landowners with a capitalist wage labor, both in agriculture and later in the industrialization of the urban areas. As Juan Flores states, "the emergence of the plena coincided with the consolidation of the Puerto Rican working class":

The first two decades of the century, when plena was evolving from its earliest traces and disparate components into a distinct, coherent form, saw the gravitation of all sectors of the Puerto Rican working population—former slaves, peasants and artisans—towards conditions of wage labor, primarily in large-scale agricultural production set up along capitalist lines. More and more workers, formerly inhabiting worlds separated by place and occupation, came into direct association, both at the workplace and in their neighborhoods; their life experience and social interests were converging, and assumed organized articulation with the founding of unions, labor federations and political parties.[10]

The power of the plena to document and express the struggles of the working-class sector surfaces in many of its lyrics. Structurally and aesthetically, the Puerto Rican plena has been compared to the German moritaten, the Mexican corrido, and the Spanish romance, for like them, it narrates historical events from the point of view of the masses, of *el pueblo*. Taking a satirical, parodic tone and perspective, the plena summarizes the events and the subsequent subjective reaction of the people in stanzas structured according to the Hispanic oral tradition, featuring eight-syllable lines with assonant rhyme. Unlike its above-mentioned counterparts, the plena is much more concise. Its lyrics are characterized by a call-and-response structure between the soloist and the chorus, which sings the refrain, an element clearly derived from the African musical heritage and that is part of the tradition of salsa music. The Africanness of the instrumentation—panderetas, guitar, cuatro, güiro, maracas, bongos, and a conga—and its percussive predominance, along with the assumed "simplicity" and "repetitious" character of its lyrics and rhythm, have been deemed primitive and unsophisticated by Eurocentric standards, an attitude that surfaced in the controversy around the Bellas Artes Center.[11] Yet the felicitous dissemination of the plena throughout Puerto Rico, across the Atlantic, and into New York had to do precisely with what those lyrics and African musical elements symbolized in a historical period of economic and social change. As Ruth Glasser observes, "[T]he development of an important plena scene in New York City had everything to do with the United States' relationship to Puerto Rico. The very processes that sent musicians and their working-class compatriots into economic 'exile' in New York were also responsible for the city's highly developed record industry."[12]

Two of the most poignant examples of the marginality of the singing subject and of its ensuing decolonizing stance are "Mamita llegó el obispo" ("Mother, the Bishop Arrived") and "Tintorera del mar" ("The Female Shark").

In "Mamita llegó el Obispo," first recorded by Manuel Canario Jiménez in 1927, the singer describes the arrival of a foreign bishop in the city of Ponce.[13] The characterization of the foreign figure and of religious authority defies the appropriate respect expected by the church toward its officials:

Mamita llegó el Obispo llegó el Obispo de Roma; mamita, si tú lo vieras ¡qué cosa linda, qué cosa mona!	[Mother, the Bishop arrived the Bishop of Rome arrived; Darling, if you could see him he's so handsome, he's so cute!
Tiene los ojos azules la cara muy coquetona ¡ay, mami, si tú lo vieras! ¡qué cosa linda, qué cosa mona!	He has blue eyes and a flirtatious face Darling, if you could see him he's so handsome, he's so cute!
El Obispo no confiesa Nada más que a las fregonas con esa boquita dulce ¡qué cosa linda, qué cosa mona!	The Bishop offers confession Only to kitchen maids with that sweet mouth he's so handsome, he's so cute!
Y dicen las hermanitas del Sagrado Corazón: "Muchachas, tengan cuidado, porque el Obispo es un gran león.	And the nuns of the Order Of the Sacred Heart say: "Girls, be careful because the Bishop is a great lion."
El Obispo no come piña que lo que come es toronja, ¡ay, mami, si tú lo vieras! ¡qué cosa linda, qué cosa mona!	The bishop doesn't eat pineapple instead he eats grapefruit, Oh Darling, if you could see him he's so handsome, he's so cute!

El Obispo no toma ron	The Bishop doesn't drink rum
que le gusta la cañita	instead he likes "moonshine"
Mamita, si tú lo vieras,	Darling, if you could see him
¡qué cosa linda cuando se pica!	he's so cute when he gets drunk!
Los hombres están rabiosos	The men are very angry
al ver cómo están las cosas,	at the way things are going
pues, dicen que las mujeres	for they say that the women
ahora se han vuelto todas devotas.	have all become devout.
Dicen que el Obispo es jockey	They say that the Bishop is a jockey
y monta la yegua Nora,	and he rides Nora, the mare,
Mamita, si tú lo vieras,	Darling, if you could see him
¡qué cosa linda cuando la monta!	he looks very good when he rides her!
La plaza de las Delicias	The Square of the Delights
se llena cuando él se asoma;	is crowded when he comes out;
y hay una que le ha pedido	and one woman has asked him
un paseito en carro con gomas.	for a ride in his car with rubber tires.
Mamita, un obispo solo	Darling, one lone bishop
no da para ser de todas.	is not enough for all of us.
Mamita, yo lo que quiero	Darling, I wish to have him
es que me lo dejen para mí sola.	all for myself.]

The refrain, "Darling, if you could see him, he's so handsome, he's so cute," replaces the social respect that should be accorded a bishop with sexual desire. The song develops this motif throughout; the eighth stanza reveals that the men are angry because all the women have suddenly become religious devotees. The view of the foreign bishop as a human being, fraught with vices and indulging in pleasures—he is sexually appealing, he rides a mare (a pun for sexual activity), he likes to drink the local moonshine—is ironically encapsulated in the reference to the "Plaza de las Delicias" (Square of Delights). The final stanza strongly suggests that this song may have been authored by a woman, for the last word *sola* reveals the female subjectivity behind the poetic voice. This female perspective is not surprising, given the constant reference to the foreign white male as an object of desire; it stands as an inversion of the phallocentric discourse about women of color that permeates popular music.

Rosario Ferré herself offers a personal version of the political deployment of this plena. According to her, in 1952, the bishop of Ponce, who was Irish, James MacManus, publicly opposed Luis Muñoz Marín for reelection, even threatening to excommunicate parishioners who voted for the latter given his relationship to a woman outside of marriage. The Popular Democratic Party, headed by Muñoz Marín himself, revised the traditional plena about the foreign bishop and played it on radio stations all over the island. This is when Ferré first heard it. As a result, Ferré observes, Muñoz Marín won the election by 400,000 votes, "half of the population was excommunicated from the Catholic Church, and some time later Bishop MacManus was ordered to return to New York."[14] Thus, the oppositionality of this plena is double-edged: it speaks against religion and its institutional representatives, and also inverts the discourse of sexual desire usually directed toward women.

This oppositionality has been deployed by Edgardo Rodríguez Juliá to frame an essay about the historical visit of the pope to San Juan, Puerto Rico. In "Llegó el Obispo de Roma"[15] the author-chronicler capitalizes on this subject position of the plena to indulge in a satirical, social critique of class divisions and racial inequities in Puerto Rican society through a journalistic narrative of this historical event. Rodríguez Juliá analyzes and documents the humor that still prevails among the male Puerto Rican proletariat, a humor that distances itself from social institutions through parody and linguistic puns.

"Tintorera del mar" [The female shark] narrates the tragedy of a U.S. lawyer who visited Puerto Rico to represent the interests of an American company during a strike. The song narrates the incident, which has become legend, of the lawyer being attacked and bitten by a *tintorera* while swimming in the beautiful tropical waters of the island. The song addresses not the lawyer, but rather the *tintorera*, reminding listeners through anaphoric repetition of her power:

Tintorera del mar,	[Female shark,
tintorera del mar,	female shark,
tintorera del mar,	female shark,
que te comiste a un americano.	you ate an American.]

This emphasis on the power of local fauna to destroy the foreign element, the lawyer, a figure who represents not only the authority of the law but U.S. capitalist interests at their best, can be read as a political allegory against capitalist intervention on the island. Again, the powerful nature of the female shark, who triumphs over the masculine hegemony of the United States, offers an inflection different from those gendered dualities that Pedreira employed in 1942. In the popular imagination the female shark is seen as an agent of power, an allegory for a culture of resistance in the colony against imperialist intervention represented throughout various cultural texts as male, a textualization that culminates in Rubén Blades's popular hit "Tiburón" (Shark).

The plena, like the danza, did not escape changes in its class-based social meanings. After the turn of the century, the interests of the U.S. recording industry in "race" music found in Puerto Rico's folklore a new source of revenue. Thus, Manuel "Canario" Jiménez, the most important singer and interpreter of plenas, was responsible for their first recordings in New York since 1926 and subsequent dissemination internationally.[16] Mediated by the new technology of the LP and the radio (introduced in Puerto Rico in 1922), the plena was inserted into different contexts of reception, creating new listening practices and reaching a larger, more diverse audience, beyond the working-class sector from which it emerged. Commercialization of the plena led to its international dispersion, yet as Jorge Pérez-Rolón has accurately shown, it also led to the trivialization of its content.[17] In New York, plenas appeared as part of the dancing repertoire in social clubs and dance halls as large as the Palladium, a new environment that ultimately led to the plena's transformation in terms of lyrics and ideology.

The second chapter of the history of the plena, 1925 to 1950,[18] is marked by the performances of Manuel "Canario" Jiménez, who because of the nature of recording technology, sang shorter plenas, omitting many narrative details and emphasizing the repetition of its refrains. The first signs of commercialization arise in Manuel Canario's instrumentation, which promotes the melodic instruments over the traditional rhythmic section,[19] a shift that corresponds to the systematic muting of the African elements and polyrythmia in the hands of the dominant sector. The oppositionality of traditional plenas, still alive in Canario's recordings, was drastically displaced by an emphasis on entertainment characteristic of César Concepción and his orchestra and Joe Valle, his singer. This major metalepsis was motivated by the popularity of the big band sound and the mambo in New York among the middle-class Puerto Rican, Latino, and Anglo audiences. Changes in instrumentation to include winds, trumpets, and saxophones accompanied this change in function, and César Concepción's orchestra embodied the shift from a plena conjunto to a dance orchestra with the big band sound. The invention of the electric microphone[20] allowed for larger dance halls and larger orchestras. The mambo style, popular at the time, was synthesized with plenas, thus creating the plena-mambos that César Concepción and Joe Valle made famous.

Nestor García Canclini has called these changes the resemantization of popular culture under the influence of capitalism,[21] which again illustrates the struggles for power between the dominant sectors and the subordinate classes. By appropriating the oppositional plena for entertainment purposes, the upper classes and the U.S. music industry cripple its radical ideology and the marginal subjectivity in the lyrics as well as in the rhythms. From collective, communal music, improvised and oppositional, the plena turns into an individualized expression, much briefer and more contained. Indeed, a musical historian has termed this period "the decline of the plena," arguing that a myriad of factors led to its demise.[22] Nevertheless, the renewed popularity with an international audience, as well as the revitalization represented in its musical syncretism with the Cuban mambo and the experimental innovations and effects made possible with new technology, have been considered positive aspects of the plena's commercial status.[23]

This appropriation, however, did not last long. During the plena's third historical stage, the 1950s and 1960s, black musicians Mon Rivera, Rafael Cortijo, and Ismael Rivera vindicated the plena, doing away with what they saw as trivial entertainment, and returned it to the black Puerto Rican proletariat from which it originally emerged by making "full use of recording technology" and creating "ingenious innovations to style."[24] In this sense, Rafael Cortijo, like African-American rappers today, reappropriated the tools of the master—technology—to reaffirm the musical and cultural presence of the marginalized. Indeed, to speak about technology and about media only as hegemony, as Leonardo Acosta does in *Música y descolonización*, is to miss the strategic appropriations of that media by marginalized sectors, a process that historically has led to innovation and experimentation and to new traditions, as Peter Manuel has proposed in the context of India and Tricia Rose has explored lucidly in African-American rap.[25]

Edgardo Rodríguez Juliá, in *El funeral de Cortijo*, pays homage to Cortijo's music and historical presence in Puerto Rican culture.[26] Juliá employs intertexts and subtexts from plenas to metaphorize the problems of Eurocentric discourse and the contemporary displacement of the sources of power in Puerto Rican society. The narrative form of the chronicle employed by Juliá is "appropriate to [the] relational method of cultural analysis" that Juan Flores proposes as an alternative to the essentialist methods and "still prestigious metaphors of organic growth"[27] prevalent in Puerto Rican cultural discourse. This "relational" approach, a contemporary response to both "Eurocentric, elitist privileging and to the relativism of the syncretic model," aims to "identify not some originary identity but the contacts and crossings experienced by the culture as social practice." In other words, the relational approach does not focus on either an exclusively Afrocentric view of Puerto Rican culture nor a Eurocentric one but rather analyzes the "interplay with the non-African, elite and folkloric components."[28]

In this light, Rodríguez Juliá's chronicle of Rafael Cortijo's funeral documents and reaffirms, with a self-ironic twist, the social and racial conflicts that inform Puerto Rican urban society today. His acute analysis of social changes that Puerto Ricans have witnessed since the 1940s as a result of the island's industrialization and Operation Bootstrap, what Juliá calls the "desarrollismo muñocista" [Muñoz-led development] of the times, is embodied in the concept of *desclasamiento* (declassing). The author proposes this concept to refer to the dismantling of the hegemony of the once dominant landowning sector, and to the ensuing mobility of many families from the rural areas to the city, a migratory flux that created hybrid living conditions within the "metropolitan area" of San Juan. This *desclasamiento* led to the emergence of a mass culture and, as José Luis González has indicated, to the full-fledged development of a popular culture in Puerto Rico.[29]

The popularity of Rafael Cortijo y su Combo around the 1950s becomes the representative icon of the "revolution of the Puerto Rican Black" in the cultural terrain, a central part of the so-called *trastocamiento interno de valores culturales* (inner shift or inversion of cultural values) that José Luis González observes not only in popular culture but in the new narrative of the 1970s, of which Rosario Ferré, Ana Lydia Vega, and Luis Rafael Sánchez are some of the most important representatives. Rafael Cortijo's historical significance lies in the *visual* presence of blacks on television (in his show *La Taberna India*) and in their musical prominence in radio; in other words, they "occupied" the social space of media and entertainment that threatened and contested the "whiteness" [*blanquitismo*] of social clubs and dance halls. Moreover, Rafael Cortijo relocates the plena away from the orchestra and within the combo, a conjunto-type group that, unlike the orchestra, articulates a plurality of rhythms, a true polyphony of voices and instrumental performances that are not subsumed under an orchestral score.

Cortijo's revolution in the world of Puerto Rican popular music also implies a decentering of the signifier within the musical and verbal text, that is, a shift from a representational and denotative language to a more centrifugal, connotative language coded in the colloquialisms of the proletariat. This new role of language is reflected in the Puerto Rican *nueva narrativa*, which Rosario Ferré deploys in her short story "Maquinolandera." Edgardo Rodríguez Juliá traces this shift:

La Elena proletaria de Canario, aquel paradigma de la plena antigua cuya concreción siempre parte de una anécdota y algunos detalles felices, aquí se ha convertido el soneo vago, quizás más sugerente, definitivamente más irónico: la plena abandona el contorno proletario y se acerca a los límites imprecisos de un lenguaje en clave, para iniciados, jerga del exclusivismo lumpen del arrabal y el caserío. Toda la música de Cortijo es así, rica en connotaciones malevas y pobre en denotaciones realistas.

[The proletarian Elena of Canario, paradigm of the old plena whose concreteness comes from an anecdote and some happy details, here (in Cortijo's music) has become a vague *soneo*, perhaps more suggestive, definitely more ironic: the plena abandons the proletarian terrain and aproaches the imprecise boundaries of a coded language, for initiates, the exclusive dialect (*jerga*) of the lumpen of the ghetto and the housing project. All of Cortijo's music is such, rich in delinquent connotations and poor in realist denotations.][30]

SALP 1476

STEREO

Ansonia
RECORDS

Rafael Cortijo playing the timbales on the album cover for *Noche de temporal*, Ansonia Records, SALP 1476. Licensed by Ansonia Records.

Cortijo's art of signifying, through linguistic puns and centrifugal discourse—in "El yo yo," "El bombón de Elena," and "Maquinolandera," among others—was associated with the Afro–Puerto Rican bomba. It paved the way for the development of salsa music in the early 1960s in New York (where Cortijo also performed with Ismael Rivera). Juliá's observation of the "exclusivist" nature of this coded language of the lumpen suggests that the black marginalized sector was no longer content with a mediated presence in cultural production, with a "Juan Morel Campos . . . negro vestido con el frac del arte blanco"[31] ["Juan Morel Campos . . . a black dressed with the tuxedo of white art], as the cultural negotiations of the danza exemplified in history. In the 1950s, Rafael Cortijo and Ismael Rivera occupied the public space of radio and television, articulating the needs and interests of a long-forgotten social sector that was, however, assuming a larger role in the economics of the island as well as in the economy of the mainland. Salsa music in the 1960s represented the apex, the heightened presence of the working-class Puerto Rican, not only on the island but on the mainland United States. (The fact that El Gran Combo de PR was a continuation of Rafael Cortijo y su Combo reveals this historical continuity.)

Rodríguez Juliá thus proposes a new way of reading Puerto Rican society and culture through the relational approach that Juan Flores identified. This polyphonic and decentered perspective is informed precisely by Cortijo's new plenas with their centrifugal language: the voices of the black urban proletariat, the residents of Barrio Obrero (Worker's Neighborhood) where Cortijo and Ismael Rivera lived, and the so-called punks (*títeres*) of Luis Llorens Torres public housing projects assume a dialogic role with and against the homogenizing discourse of the dominant white sector.

Given the displaced powers of official sources of authority in a colonial Puerto Rico, illustrated by the authority of the U.S. Secret Service over the local police during the pope's visit in "Llegó el Obispo de Roma" (Juliá's literary text), both the church and the U.S. consumer economy impose their own strategies of warfare on power.[32] These institutions constantly confront the masses, placing them within divided spaces and class boundaries, as exemplified in the mise-en-scène of the pope in the parking area of Plaza las Americas, the largest shopping mall in the Caribbean, or via the stratification of language. This division of space clearly illustrates a "strategy" as Michel de Certeau defines it, in opposition to the ways in which the powers-that-be manage, distribute, and control the place, the tactics, and "the space of the other"; they "make use of the cracks that particular conjunctions open in the surveillance of the proprietary powers."[33]

In Rodríguez Juliá's text, these tactics are articulated in the voices of the proletariat, the poor and the marginalized, which are heard through the fissures of the master narratives also imbedded in the chronicle. The jokes about the pope through which the "ancestral anti-clerical sentiment" is filtered,[34] the sexual discourse *a lo mamichulin* directed toward women, the satiric perspective that pokes fun at authority mediated by the traditional plenas (as in "Mamita llegó el Obispo"), counteract in a dialogic mode the traditional and mystifying music of the church ("Holy, holy, holy shall be God" [Bendito, bendito, bendito sea Dios]). This popular discourse, rooted in the musical dialogism and the satiric perspectives of the plena, informs the new narrative of the 1970s, thus establishing the power and primacy of this musical form as a vehicle of a Puerto Rican collective consciousness that has been able to articulate the social, class, and racial struggles for hegemony that have characterized Puerto Rican cultural history.[35]

In this light, Tomás Blanco's influential essay of 1935, "Elogio de la plena" (In praise of the plena), has been hailed as a "landmark essay" that fostered the "wide recognition" of the bomba and the plena "as the most distinctively Puerto Rican musical tradition."[36] But although Tomás Blanco, a medical doctor, historian, journalist, and defender of civil rights in Puerto Rico (1896–1975), wrote to praise and exalt Afro–Puerto Rican music, his own subject location as a white male and member of the generation of the 1930s places him alongside Antonio Pedreira and René Marqués, among other patriarchal figures. Tomás Blanco's "Elogio de la plena" should not be read in isolation but in the context of his own class and racial subject position and especially in relation to his other contributions to racial definitions and to the racial debate in Puerto Rico, namely, *El prejuicio racial en Puerto Rico* (1937). That controversial, problematic, and ambivalent piece was written only two years after the publication of "Elogio de la plena."[37]

To acclaim "Elogio" as antiracist discourse is to ignore the racial and gender constructs underlying Puerto Rican cultural thought that permeate his writings. Not as virulently anti-African as was Antonio Pedreira, Tomás Blanco assumes a conciliatory stance toward racial conflict in Puerto Rico, a perspective plausible only through the silencing of social and racial conflicts on the island. An overarchingly homogenizing discourse, *El prejuicio racial en Puerto Rico* minimizes the intensity and dangers of racial attitudes in Puerto Rico by positing an antinomy between its expression on the island, which Blanco characterizes as "juego de niños" [children's game], and the violent racism (lynching) and segregation (Jim Crow laws) exercised in the South of the United States, which Blanco terms "authentic" racial prejudice. He compares racist terms in English and in Spanish and concludes that English terms are "pejorative," while those in Spanish are "healthy euphemisms."[38] He analyzes the economic, religious, and social factors that motivate racism in the United States and contrasts them to Puerto Rico, where he minimizes the economic centrality of the sugar plantation; where Catholicism, unlike Protestantism, allows for racial tolerance;[39] and where social integration permits all individuals equal rights and living conditions.

Dismissing all the historical and analytical flaws of these arguments—which Arcadio Díaz Quiñones lucidly addresses in his introduction to the 1985 edition—Blanco concludes that the little racial prejudice in Puerto Rico is indeed "mimetic" and "imported" from the United States. This projection of blame is also extended to the Puerto Rican woman, who, he concludes, is "the carrier of Puerto Rican prejudice" [la portadora del prejuicio puertorriqueño].[40] Blanco's strategic displacement toward his others, in this case the United States and women, appears systematically in the writings of Pedreira and of René Marqués, and it is not surprising to find this strategy in Blanco, who, after all, shares with them the same class and gender subject position.

Tomás Blanco's ambivalence toward race and mestizaje in Puerto Rico is also articulated in "Elogio de la plena," which displays language and discourse as racially informed social sites.[41] The ideological discrepancy between what Tomás Blanco says explicitly in "Elogio" and what his choice of metaphors and imagery subtly reveal, the semantic ambiguities and interstices that surface throughout his writing reaffirm the centrality of language in defining race and gender constructs. Blanco introduces his essay on the plena as an apology, a defense of this Afro–Puerto Rican form in view of the attacks it has been subjected to as "savage music of Blacks." Like Salvador Brau before him, Blanco maintains the binary between the danza and the plena, the central axis on which the author formulates and builds his argument. He sees the plena as the musical form that will survive the danza, for the latter, limited to a particular social class and "transplanted" from Europe, will not endure as a dance form. In contrast, the plena, born "in the soul of the people," is vigorous enough to withstand the test of time.

This "organic" metaphor—summarized in the image of the danza as a "greenhouse plant" and of the plena as a "wild flower"—subsumes the danza under the rubric of foreign, alien, a European cultural product "transplanted" to the tropics.[42] While Blanco is correct in his allusion to the European origins of the danza and to its transculturation, he actually inverts the historical tradition of the danza as Puerto Rico's "national music" and the Afro–Puerto Rican forms as the music of the primitive Other. Blanco's apparently progressive openness toward acknowledging the black racial element in Puerto Rican culture, emblematized in this initial metaphor, is further developed in his observations regarding the true "mulatto" constitution of the Puerto Rican:

En general, debe parecer evidente a todo el que tenga ojos y haya considerado el asunto con alguna objetividad, que Puerto Rico es la más blanca de todas las Antillas; que casi no tenemos negros puros; y que el número de blancos puros—computados a grosso modo pero con mayor fidelidad que en el censo oficial—no alcanza a la mitad de la población. Por lo tanto, la mayoría de las gentes del país es de sangre mezclada; mestizos, morenos, mulatos, grifos, o blancos con dosis más o menos homeopática de pigmento negroide (40).

[In general, it must be evident to those who can see and who have considered this issue with some objectivity, that Puerto Rico is the whitest of all the Antilles; that here we don't have pure blacks; and that the number of pure whites—grossly calculated but with greater fidelity than in the official census—does not reach even half of the population. Thus, the majority of the people in this country are of mixed blood; mestizos, morenos, mulatos, grifos, or whites with a more or less homeopathic dose of negroid pigmentation.]

This reaffirmation of racial mestizaje, also articulated in *El prejuicio racial en Puerto Rico,* unfolds, nevertheless, from an ambivalent ideological stance. The hybrid racial constitution of Puerto Ricans may be read as an argument for the recognition of the black sector in Puerto Rico. Simultaneously, within a dominant discourse such as that of the generation of the 1930s, mestizaje is also the sign for whiteness, the rationale for the denial of pure blackness. This ambivalence, or rather duplicitous logic, is encapsulated in another observation by Blanco: "Tenemos abundante sangre negra, de la que no hay por qué avergonzarse; empero, haciendo honor a la verdad, no se nos puede clasificar como pueblo negro" [We have abundant black blood, for which there should be no shame; however, honoring the truth, we cannot be classified as a black people]. Mestizaje, then, becomes the necessary tool to prove the absence of racial prejudice in Puerto Rico. The mulatto figure "incarnates . . . reconciliation and convivencia. It is a paradigm of social and racial harmony"[43] in the works of Tomás Blanco, "a reconciliatory paradigm that erases the sexual domination and violence exercised on the bodies of the female slave."[44]

Moreover, Blanco's definition of mestizaje is limited to racial miscegenation, excluding and denying any form of cultural hybridity in Puerto Rico and reinforcing the superiority of white European culture over the transcultural forms. This position, articulated two years after "Elogio," seems to contradict Blanco's apologetic discourse on the plena and his reaffirmation of the mulatto character of Puerto Ricans. Yet his Eurocentric and even racist ideology, albeit subtly disguised, is already inscribed in his essay "Elogio de la plena."

Tomás Blanco's veiled racist discourse can only be mediated by gender constructs. He establishes the duality of the danza and the plena in a language that duplicates the rhetorical and aesthetic traditions of each musical form yet is still entrenched within the patriarchal recourse of feminization. The danza, according to Tomás Blanco, leads us to the European romantic iconography of the woman à la Rubens:

A tal hembra convenía la sensualidad pamplona que se regodea en los compases de las danzas. Lacrimeo suplicante y metáforas regordetas prestigiaban de romanticismo el falso ambiente en que se acuñaba la galantería aristocrática de la época. Y entre floripondio y floripondio de cumplidos banales, eran los merengues de la danza la florinata pura de aquella galante aristocracia de papel de estaño.

[The languid sensuality that revels within the measures of the danzas is agreeable to this female. Pleading tears and plump metaphors gave a romantic prestige to the false ambiance in which the aristocratic gallantry of the times found itself at home. And between the flowery words of banal flattery, the merengues of the danza were the pure essence of the gallant tinfoil aristocracy.][45]

In contrast to this parodic reconstruction of the romantic style, the plena is described as "la morena tendinosa, musculosa, espigada o redonda, tiernecita o madura; pero con jarretes y axilas en vez de pie y de aire" [the dark-skinned, tendinous woman, muscular, slender or round, tender or mature; but with hocks and underarms instead of feet and of air]. She is

"mulatica de tez dorada como ron añejo; de pelo lacio y ojos pícaros que pueden pasar por andaluces; de parla castellana, un poco arcaica; y, de ágil paso sensitivo, como de bestezuela selvática. Sinuosa y llena de vigor, tiene olores de tierra y sabor de marisco"

[a charming mulatta of golden complexion like aged rum; with straight hair and roguish eyes that can pass for Andalusian; she speaks Castilian, a bit archaic; and, with an agile sensitive step, like that of a small jungle animal. Sinuous and full of vigor, she smells like the earth and tastes of seafood].[46]

The subtexts to these opposing portraits comprise a contrastive aesthetics of the danza and the plena that contain the respective structures and elements indicated by musicologists; in other words, Blanco's verbal iconographies are translations of the respective musical styles. While the danza is "cursi" (affected), the product of an epoch of "banal flattery" and "gallantries," allusions that hyperbolize the very rhetorical artifice of nineteenth century taste and romantic discourse, the plena is "burlona, traviesa y arisca" (mocking, mischievous, and surly).[47] The plena speaks in simple, direct statements. It tries not to "empalagar cuando acaricia" [overwhelm with its caress] and occasionally is "chocarrera" (coarse). [48] Blanco's stylistic antinomy seems to privilege the more direct, ironic, and humorous perspective of the plena over the artificial and inflated rhetoric of the danza, an indication in fact of the changing styles and tastes to which the dated danza no longer responded.

Blanco's portrayal of the danza as a white aristocratic lady from a nineteenth-century salon and his sexually charged images of the plena as a roguish mulatta are not original. The iconic, visual nature of Blanco's danza and plena is not arbitrary, given the "function of visual conventions as the primary means by which we perceive and transmit our understanding of the world about us."[49] In other words, the mythification of race, class, and gender identities assumes even more powerful ideological impact through visually expressed artistic representations. Even though Blanco's descriptions are not directly visual but verbal translations of musical forms into images, a sort of literary portrait, they still evoke in the reader/viewer associations between the individual image and the "general qualities ascribed to a class,"[50] in this case, to black, white, and mulatta women. In this context, Tomás Blanco's female icons of the danza and the plena are an integral part of the conventional European iconography of white and black women throughout the nineteenth century. In particular, the plena articulates the values associated with the African woman, represented throughout Europe in the figure of the Hottentot Venus. Sander Gilman's influential work on the ways in which the European gaze constructs the African woman as site of "concupiscence,"[51] as an "icon for deviant sexuality," and ultimately, for disease, conforms to the overarching historical and patriarchal discursive framework within which Tomás Blanco's voice and gaze fall.[52]

The collective fetishizing of the black woman also has been linked to the hegemony of Victorian ideals for the white European female, thus projecting male desire onto the female Other in order to guarantee the virginity and purity imposed on the white female. In fact, Gilman's research shows that the anatomical characteristics of the Hottentot Venus associated with deviant sexuality, primitivism, and disease were eventually also imposed on the white prostitute and representations of her. This gender construct and its racially informed historical consequences—sexual aggression and violence on black women and mulattas—easily extended to the New World, where the imperialist politics of the Conquest facilitated and justified systematic sexual violence against indigenous and African women.

It is revealing that Blanco's discursive danza is not figured iconically as woman but rather as rhetoric, language, and gesture, whereas the plena— the sensuous, roguish mulatta—is figured by a prominent corporeality that exposes Blanco's own patriarchal and Eurocentric biases: the emphasis on her skin color, her underarms, her feet, her muscles, and most significantly, her musky odor, unveils a male desire for the mulatta, always already primitivized through her corporeality. Thus the danza–plena antinomy reflects the decorporalizing of the white woman, desexualizing and effacing of her physicality, and the concomitant, inverse hypersexualizing and corporalizing of the black and mulatta. As José Blanco suggests, the "less body" of the white upper class may be explained "because they fulfill their personality above all in the material or symbolic extensions of property, capital, state, commerce, "religion."[53] Yet a distinction is in order between white male bodies and those of white women whose constructed sexuality has been informed and muted by Victorian ideals since the nineteenth century. In addition, the discursive constructs of bodies of color as hyperbodies, as mere physicality, responded to various colonizing and hegemonic projects, especially the ways in which the economics of labor dictated social constructs that would justify the exploitation of subjugated peoples.

Frantz Fanon's analysis of interracial desire in the 1950s as a symptom of internalized colonialism on the part of the black male, as a strategy for de-racializing the subject (i.e., for self-whitening), illuminates the hidden asymmetries of power that Tomás Blanco refuses to engage in this essay.[54] By concentrating on a modern, urban context where mestizaje is blessed by the church through marriage, Blanco dismisses the historical evidence of sexual violence and rape against indigenous women and African female slaves, the real beginnings of mestizaje throughout Latin America. More-over, he locates the mulatta as an erotic axis for mestizaje, around which both the white male and the mestizo man hover. Yet his choice of relational words (*casarse* vs. *mezclarse*) to refer to the location of men and white women, on the one hand, and men and mulatta women, on the other, maintains the racial boundaries required by a racist society, that obligatory *marginality* of the relations between the white man and the mulatta woman:

La mezcla de razas se efectúa hoy mayormente a través de la mujer mulata. Entre las clases mezcladas, la tendencia del hombre es casarse con mujeres más claras; pero al mismo tiempo, por lo regular, es con ese mismo tipo de mujer mulata con la que se mezcla el hombre blanco. El color melado claro de la piel parece tener valor estético o de selección erótica.[55]

[The racial mixture takes place today mostly through the mulatta. Among the racially mixed classes, the tendency of the man is to marry women with lighter skin; at the same time, however, normally the white man mingles precisely with that same type of mulatta. It seems that the light color of her skin has aesthetic value or is of erotic choice.]

The white male's desire for the female racial Other—the black or mu-latta—is not seen as a problem by Blanco; it is legitimized as another exam-ple of Puerto Rico's civilized *convivencia* between whites and blacks that ul-timately erases the concept of whitening underlying the use of *mestizaje*. Indeed, the historical context of sexual interaction between white males (the *señoritos*) and the mulatta women in Cuba in the nineteenth century was precisely in the *bailes populares* to which the *señoritos* went to escape from the decorum and Victorian repression of sexual behavior, a social practice that also displays the symbolic erotic value that Afro-Cuban music held for the upper classes.[56] The marginal relations between white males and mulattas, usually never made official, have indeed been the structural principle that maintained the growth of mestizaje in the Caribbean islands.

However, despite the demographic impact of interracial relations, the fact remains that this particular racial and gender configuration has not transformed the disempowered and subordinated status of the mulatta. Literary characters such as Luis Rafael Sánchez's La China Hereje in *La guaracha del Macho Camacho*, Rosario Ferré's Isabel la Negra, and countless mulattas in Latin American soap operas attest to the pervading sublocation of such women within the social strata and the hierarchies of power. Tomás Blanco, then, only succeeds in replicating the already rooted social asymmetry between the sexes and between the races that has not necessarily improved, as the prevalence of this figure in literature, popular media, and music attests.

To conclude, I want to underscore the historical continuity of a white male writing subject within this genealogy of patriarchal discourse in Puerto Rico, beginning with Manuel Alonso's earlier descriptions of the gracious and desirable beauty of the "daughters of the Tropics," who articulates his own veiled desire for the mulatta or black woman through the language of music. The universal metaphor of music as woman is a discursive consequence of male hegemony in music as an institution, as composers, musicologists, and critics within the larger cultural arena have illustrated. In Puerto Rico this specific discursive construct is doubly informed by processes of racialization. In the case of Manuel Alonso, the Creole woman becomes an object of desire that supplants and symbolizes the desire to return to his Madre Patria. Salvador Brau does not articulate any desire for the mulatta or Creole woman but only because he displaces that desire onto a past, to his youth and the emotional upheavals that characterized it. He thus associates the erotic with the racial otherness of Afro-Caribbean music, situating it in opposition to reason, work, and progress. His misogyny and racism are justified and thus legitimized in his positivist argument for de-Africanizing the danza.

Tomás Blanco's ambivalence toward the African presence in Puerto Rican culture is expressed in the contradictory and uneven arguments of *El prejuicio racial en Puerto Rico.* Yet while his "Elogio de la plena" may vindicate him as one of the most progressive or antiracist writers of his generation, it is *in* and *through* gender constructs that his racism surfaces. While Blanco attempts to undermine the value of the danza as an outdated form in 1935, recognizing the predominance of the plena as Puerto Rico's authentic music, he can achieve this only by perpetuating the very racism that he so forcefully tries to fight at the beginning of his essay. This laudatory stance toward the plena could be framed only within a discourse of primitive otherness and racialized eroticism. By locating the plena in the still functional otherness that Brau successfully articulated at the end of the past century, Tomás Blanco's apology for this Afro–Puerto Rican music can be more readily accepted by his elite audience. To construe the plena as a mulatta and the mulatta as plena, as music, was a way of asserting dominance over a racially subordinate female as well as sublimating desire for a racial Other, a desire that proves itself unfailingly persistent throughout history.

CHAPTER THREE

Desiring the Racial Other
Rosario Ferré's Feminist Reconstructions
of Danza and Plena

✛

Nosotras, tu querida y tu mujer, siempre hemos sabido que debajo
de cada dama de sociedad se oculta una prostituta . . . siempre hemos
sabido que cada prostituta es una dama en potencia.
—Rosario Ferré, "Cuando las mujeres quieren a los hombres"

We, your lover and your wife, have always known that every
lady hides a prostitute under her skin. . . . A prostitute, on the
other hand, will go to similar extremes to hide the lady under her skin.
—Rosario Ferré, "When Women Love Men"
(translated by Rosario Ferré and Cindy Ventura)

As a woman writing from the same class location as that of Manuel Alonso, Salvador Brau, Antonio Pedreira, and Tomás Blanco, Rosario Ferré appropriates the discursive tradition on music, race, and gender analyzed above, rewriting and subverting it from her own multiply inflected subject position. This is achieved in her controversial short story, "When Women Love Men."

"When Women Love Men" is not so much a short story as a portrayal, a dialogic text constituted by two female voices that have been socially antagonistic and opposed. Isabel Luberza is the literary embodiment of the lady, the dama or señora, Ambrosio's widow and is a white aristocrat who lives confined within the boundaries of her white mansion and submits herself wholeheartedly to the social tenets of the perfect wife. As this chapter proposes, Isabel is also, implicitly, a literary embodiment of the Puerto Rican danza. Isabel la Negra (Isabel the Black), Ambrosio's *mujer* and *corteja* (lover), a fictional rendering of the well-known prostitute in Ponce, is associated in the text with eroticism, sex, and concupiscence. Isabel La Negra embodies the Puerto Rican plena, as the epithets used to describe her are evidently generated in the untranslatable puns, sounds, and rhythms of an Afro-Antillean language mediated by the works of Luis Palés Matos: "la Rumba Macumba Candombé Bámbula: Isabel La Tembandumba de la Quimbamba, contoneando su carne de Guingambó por la encendida calle antillana"[1] [the Rumba, Macumba, Candombé, Bámbula, Isabel the Tembandumba de la Quimbamba, swaying her okra hips through the sun-swilled Antillean streets].

Isabel the wife and Isabel the lover exemplify a split of the female subjectivity, according to Hispanic marianista tradition, into virgin (wife) and whore. These two literary characters bring to the fore the patriarchal gender dynamics at play in Puerto Rican urban society (although not exclusively there, as patriarchal traditions of "casa chica" in Mexico and other Latin countries continue to attest) by which men extract sexuality and pleasure from the marital relationship and displace it onto the affair. In "Respeten, que hay damas" [Be respectful around the ladies], Edgardo Rodríguez Juliá probes this gender construct through verbal recreations of photography:

En el reverso de la señora, la mujer, aquella es mujer de su casa, a veces adorno del santuario puertorriqueño burgués; ésta es mujer de la calle, amenaza del sacro hogar. El hombre puertorriqueño apenas se decide: la señora es algo así como un testaferro sexual de la madre, la mujer es la negación de tanta pureza, laberinto de variantes que en su último extremo conduce al Club Riviera.
Cuando la señora es más obligación que sensualidad, se busca la mujer, me echo la corteja, le pongo casa a una querida, ya me oíste.
En esta madeja de inclinaciones y gustos amamantados desde la más tierna infancia, se debate la sexualidad del hombre puertorriqueño, casi siempre herida, casi siempre confusa hasta el límite de la infidelidad o el ridículo. Hay una fisura fundamental en este inquieto y envanecido varón: una vez edificada la pureza de la esposa como garantía de fidelidad (los cuernos son el bochorno máximo para ese honor hispánico que confunde la honra con la obstetricia) desfallecen los ardores del sexo, el amor se amansa en hábito, conveniencia doméstica sazonada con la responsabilidad de educar a los hijos.[2]

[On the inside of the wife is the woman, the former is the woman of her home, sometimes adorning the burgeois Puerto Rican sanctuary; the latter is the woman of the street, a threat to the sacred home. The Puerto Rican man hardly makes up his mind: the wife is something like the sexual container for motherhood, the woman is the negation of such purity, a labyrinth of variants that in its most extreme form leads to the Club Riviera (the brothel).
[When the wife becomes more of an obligation than sensuality, one looks for the woman, I take on a mistress, I buy her a home, you heard me.
[Within this web of inclinations and tastes that have been breast-fed since the earliest infancy, the Puerto Rican male sexuality is being debated, almost always wounded, almost always confused up to the limits of infidelity or ridicule. There is a fundamental fissure in this agitated and proud male: once the wife's purity has been built as a warranty of fidelity (to be cheated on is the worst shame for that Hispanic honor that confuses social honor with obstetrics), sexual passion is di-

minished, love is domesticated by habit, a domestic convenience seasoned by the responsibility of educating the children.]

Rodríguez Juliá's social analysis of the wife/whore dichotomy as it is manifested in everyday sexual relations in Puerto Rico is followed by a verbal translation of two portraits, one of a lady whose pose and elegant background serve to efface and cover her body; the other, her inverse image, the woman on the street. Proposing a textual and ideological continuity with Tomás Blanco's race and gender icons, the elegant lady reveals a visage that lays bare her class-based objectification: "El rostro perfectamente ovalado refleja una vaga tristeza, quizás esa inocencia melancólica de la mujer excesivamente protegida. Todo es suavidad en el porte de esa mujer más concebida como adorno que como amante."[3] [The perfectly oval-shaped face reflects a vague sadness, perhaps that melancholy innocence of a woman who has been excessively sheltered. All is softness in this woman's bearing, a woman who has been conceived more as adornment than as lover.]

The antithesis to the señora, whose oppression is directly proportional to the elegance of her surroundings, is the woman on the street. Significantly, she is posing outside, on the street, not inside within the domestic sphere accorded to the señora. Her setting is not an artificial, stiffly elegant arrangement but rather houses that expose their lower-middle-class background. Her physical description reveals the icons of gesture and dress that accord dignity to her social location as the female Other:

Esa falda pegada a las carnes acentúa su hembrismo. Los zapatos de trabilla, esas uñas pintadas de rojo que ardientemente asoman entre las tiras de cuero, insinúan una sensualidad encendida, condición de hembra leal a sus encantos. Sostiene en sus brazos a un bebé, ese fruto de algún amor prohibido o frustrado.[4]

[Her skin-tight skirt accentuates her femaleness. Her shoes with straps, those red-painted nails that ardently peek out between the leather straps, insinuate a fiery sensuality, the condition of a woman faithful to her charms. She holds a baby in her arms, the fruit of some forbidden or frustrated love.]

This woman, either lover or divorcée, is othered precisely because of the unconcealable evidence of her past sexual experience: her child. No longer admissible for the role of sacred mother (mythified only by marriage) and pure wife, the divorced woman or the single, unmarried mother has to be content with her marginal role as lover, as *la mujer*. Juliá's emphasis on this woman's markers of sexuality—her bright red nail polish, her strappy shoes, her clinging skirt, and ultimately, her child—characterizes her as analogous to Isabel la Negra, emphasizing the central role of the male gaze in representations of female sexuality.

The socially visible "respect to the ladies" that Latino men consciously exhibit and articulate serves as a mask for the underlying, profound resentment that the (Puerto Rican) male holds toward women. The Freudian-based "fundamental fissure" that Edgardo Rodríguez Juliá identifies in the Puerto Rican male, or *varón*, refers to a lack that converts his wife into an empty vessel of pleasure, a "warranty of fidelity" with which he himself cannot abide. As such, the wife ends up representing "the patient character custody of the mother's unconditional love," a projection that justifies his sexual exploits with other women; that is, by identifying his wife with his mother, the *varón* minimizes his sense of guilt or infidelity.[5] Elizabeth Grosz summarizes the Freudian-based relations between this unmediated duality and the contradictory requirements of "symbolic functioning":

on the one hand, the boy's sexuality is virile, active, predatory; yet, on the other hand, it must be controlled, repressed, sublimated, and redirected. This split attitude may effect [*sic*] the man's choice of love-object. For example, Freud suggests that men may feel split between feelings of tenderness, respect, affection, and sexual "purity"; and feelings of a highly sexual yet debasing kind. Affection and sexual desire seem to inhabit different spheres, often being resolved only by splitting his relations between two kinds of women—one noble, honourable, and pure (the virgin figure), the other a sexual profligate (the prostitute figure). He treats the first with asexual admiration, while he is sexually attracted to, yet morally or socially contemptuous of, the second. Here the male lover attempts to preserve the contradictory role of the mother (as pure and as seducer), while removing its contradictions by embodying its elements in separate "types" of women, either virgin or whore, subject or object, asexual or only sexual, with no possible mediation.[6]

At best, Juliá attempts to delve into the sexual psychology of the Puerto Rican male. At worst, he does not problematize the asymmetrical relations of power between men and women, as he also fails to integrate race as a factor in these relations. Thus, his verbal translations of gender roles, as metaphorized through photography, continue to inscribe the dualities of the *eterno femenino*—virgin/whore—onto the consciousness of the reader. By leaving this patriarchal discourse untouched, by not questioning its role, and by suggesting a unilateral view of the victimized male as a result, "Respeten que hay damas" becomes yet another repetition, in the 1990s, of the phallocentric discourse that continues to locate the *mujer*, the lover, and the whore as an overdetermined site of eroticism, pleasure, and sexuality. The wife, or señora, continues to be emptied of her own desires and sexual agency, naturalized into a useless appendage only functional at social events, a role that the author accepts, in his own words, as *comme il faut*.[7]

Rosario Ferré, instead, appropriates these patriarchal constructs that are still in active circulation, discursive reaffirmations of prevailing social relations of power between men and women, and polemicizes them by imbuing both women, Isabel Luberza and Isabel la Negra, with a mimetic desire for each other, a desire that resolves itself in the final fusion or merging of both figures. While this "fantastic" ending has been interpreted from a feminist approach, my discussion of this story integrates the roles of race, class, and otherness—articulated through musical intertexts—in the social formulation of gender roles. The plena lyrics and Afro-Antillean voices systematically construct Isabel la Negra, and the European Judeo-Christian tenets and values articulated through Bible quotations and social traditions comprise the ideology beneath Isabel Luberza's behavior and repressed desires.

While Isabel la Negra's main subtext, the plena, is suggested explicitly in the first epigraph of the story, Isabel Luberza's metaphoric embodiment of the danza is only suggested by default, implicit as an antinomy to the plena. It can be identified only by reading its historical subtexts, particularily Tomás Blanco's "Elogio de la plena." The plena is already present in the story's first epigraph:

la *puta* que yo conozco	[the whore whom I know
no es de la china ni del japón	is not from China nor from Japan
la puta viene de ponce	The whore is from Ponce
viene del barrio de san antón.[8]	from the San Antón neighborhood.]

Here Rosario Ferré rewrites the original, traditional anonymous plena, "la *plena* que yo conozco" (cf. the earlier epigraph), which speaks to the music's origins, by substituting *plena* for *puta*, a strategy that emphasizes the underlying feminization and erotization of the musical form that we have traced throughout Puerto Rican cultural discourse. In addition, the title of the short story, "When Women Love Men," is an appropriation of the first line of another traditional plena that narrates the tricks and strategies used by women in their efforts to control love relations, rituals based on folkloric beliefs of African origin:

CUANDO LAS MUJERES QUIEREN A LOS HOMBRES

(Plena from the oral tradition, interpreted by Manuel Canario Jiménez and his group.)

Cuando las mujeres	[When women
quieren a los hombres	love (want) men
prenden cuatro velas	they light four candles
y se las ponen por los rincones.	and place them in the corners.
Coro	
Compran esos libros	They buy those books
que se llaman de colecciones	which are called collections
van a la cocina	they go to the kitchen
y les hacen sus oraciones.	and they do [to them] their prayers.
Coro	
Rompen las camisas	They rip their shirts
los calzoncillos, los pantalones	their underpants, their pants

Pobres de los hombres	Poor men
ni las comidas se las componen.	They don't even prepare their food.
Coro	
Les echan huesos de muerto	They throw on them bones from the dead
agua florida también les ponen	flower water they also place on them
ay madre querida	Oh dear mother
ten cuidado con esos hombres.	be careful with those men.
Coro	
Si son de Guayama	If they are from Guayama
hechizos ellas les ponen	they put spells on men
en un vaso de agua	in a glass of water
todo el cuerpo le descomponen.	they can make their bodies decay.][9]

These lyrics acquire meaning in the first paragraph of the story, when one of the women addresses Ambrosio and sketches out the story for the reader: Ambrosio has died and left each Isabel half of his inheritance, a decision that forces both women to meet and negotiate between them the use of the mansion, which also was divided between the two. The female speaker then adds that "anyone would say that you did what you did on purpose, just for the pleasure of seeing us light a candle in each corner of the room, to see which one of us had won."[10] Women fighting against each other for the love or property of a man signals a patriarchal strategy that glorifies the masculine ego while it subjugates women by keeping them disjointed, divided. Yet what follows in the text suggests that the final fusion or merging of both Isabels is indeed the actualization of what Ambrosio staged through his will and inheritance, an intention "to melt" them, "to make [them] fade into each other like an old picture lovingly placed under its negative, so that [their] own true face would finally come to the surface."[11]

René Girard's model of triangular desire[12] is effective in deciphering Ambrosio's role as a mediator between the desires of both women. By coming face to face with each other—that is, by dismantling the allegorical binaries that each represents—"their own true face" would finally come *to the surface*. What surface metaphorically and textually, I propose, are the racial, class, and gender constructs penned by the patriarchal writers such as Brau, Pedreira, and Blanco. That "own true face" will be, I hope, not only the "desire for acknowledgement and for knowledge," for the "truth" that has been traditionally associated with eroticism,[13] but the underlying presence of blacks and of women in paradigms of Puerto Rican culture and identity, silenced throughout official discourse as speaking and acting subjects in their own right.

The musical and cultural intertexts (the plena and its lyrics) also inform the pretextual antagonism already established between the two protagonists. The plena song "Cuando las mujeres quieren a los hombres" outlines the alternative ways that women exert power over men, but it does so by portraying women as witches, *brujas*. The gender ambivalence that permeates the song—"poor men, / be careful with those men"—is even clearer in the short story, where Ferré demonstrates the negative and positive effects of such positionings. Indeed, the strategies used by women to control the love of their men more clearly reverberate in the allusion to Isabel Luberza's "ancient wisdom I had inherited from my mother, and my mother from her mother before her,"[14] a wisdom that nevertheless proved futile in keeping Ambrosio's undivided love for herself. Thus, the "wisdom" of the white European female tradition is rendered impotent, in contrast to the power and strategies used by the African woman, a differential form of power that will be discussed later. Contrary to what some critics have observed,[15] the first paragraph of the story begins to deconstruct the antinomy of women by foreshadowing the final fusion of the white lady and the black whore.

The text unfolds into two alternating narrative voices: the voices of Isabel Luberza and Isabel la Negra. In the final paragraph, the fusion of Self and Other has reached its apex, and the reader can no longer discern who speaks. In addition to Ambrosio, an obvious point of convergence for both women, a number of motifs anticipate and prefigure the final fusion, a structure that characterizes the neofantastic story and its detective story–like plot. Most prominently, the motif that serves as a psychological and structural nexus is the bright red nail polish, "Cherries Jubilee," they both use. The color, alluded to by Rodríguez Juliá in his description of the woman on the street, is equated with lower-class, black aesthetics; it is appropriated by Isabel Luberza in her desire to become her Other, thus challenging and renouncing the muted and self-effacing colors of her upper-class repressed sexuality. While the Cherries Jubilee has been explained as an instance of American capitalism on the island,[16] it has also been read by Debra Castillo as an "objective correlative" that suggests the resistance of both women, "at the textual level," to pleasing men. This is what makeup purportedly does but for emancipatory purposes,[17] thus achieving the "shifting of surfaces and classes and races over one another through the polishing of nails."

The large white home of Isabel Luberza and her late husband Ambrosio also becomes a space symbolic of the identification between both women. Ambrosio's will dictates that each woman will own half of the house, thus satisfying Isabel la Negra's class-based desire that she felt growing up in deprivation:

... her yearning to live in the house, her dream of sitting out on the balcony behind the silver balustrade, beneath the baskets of fruit and garlands of flowers, ... She suffered from a nostalgia that had become incandescent over the years, burning in her heart like a childhood vision. In this vision, which flashed back to her whenever she walked past Isabel Luberza's house, she'd see herself again as a young girl, barefoot and dressed in rags, looking up at a tall, handsome man dressed in white linen and Panama hat, who stood leaning out on the balcony next to a beautiful blond woman, elegantly dressed in a silver lamé gown.[18]

Isabel Luberza initially mourns the transformation that the house will inevitably suffer, from decent family home to brothel, from white-painted wall of purity and decorum to "those gaudy shades that persuade men to relax." Its "shocking pink" balcony, its "snow-white, garlanded facades" will turn "chartreuse green fused into chrysanthemum orange,"[19]— changes in color that Luberza can no longer resist, as they symbolize the metamorphosis of her own upper-class aesthetics into those bright colors that exude a tropicalized sensuality and sin. This shift signals the metaphoric encroachment of the culture of the lower class into the spaces of the aristocracy, a displacement that Puerto Ricans experienced as a result of the economic changes brought forth by the United States and later by Operation Bootstrap and the industrialization program, which motivated the flux of workers from the rural areas into the city. This phenomenon has been described by José Luis Gonzáles as the "plebeyismo" of Puerto Rican culture, which Juan G. Gelpí has identified as a thematic continuity in Ferré's narratives.[20]

By the end of the story it is Isabel Luberza who most desires to become her racial Other, Isabel la Negra. She takes off her attire, exposing her fair skin to the sun, self-flagellating herself in order to purify the Other. She desires the unbridled sexuality of Isabel la Negra and mimics the freedom never alloted her as a "wife," for "the male is always the one who has to take the initiative." If desire marks a fundamental absence, the void underlying the white lady's desire for the Other is what propels her to give up her female role as a passive, dependent wife, as adornment, in order to gain the power that she finds in the black prostitute. This desire, as Elizabeth Grosz puts it, is "concerned only with its own processes, pleasures and internal logic, a logic of the signifier":[21]

but today I've begun to see clearly for the first time. Today I'll confront the perfect beauty of her face to my absolute sorrow in order to understand. Now that I've drawn nearer to her I can see her as she really is, her hair no longer a cloud of smoke raging above her head but draped like a soft, golden chain about her neck, her soft skin no longer dark, but spilled over her shoulders like dawn's milk, a skin of the purest pedigree, without the merest suspicion of a kinky backlash, now swaying back and forth defiantly before her and feeling the blood flow out of me like a tide, my treacherous turncoat blood that has even now begun to stain my heels with that glorious, shocking shade I've always loved so, the shade of Cherries Jubilee.[22]

While Isabel la Negra's skin is whitened at the moment of fusion, the "I" that speaks and that utters the fusion is that of Isabel Luberza, a singular pronoun that by the end of the story has become doubled. Lost in the English translation, a key utterance in the original Spanish text marks that psychic and symbolic fusion: "tongoneándome yo ahora para atrás" (now I am swaying back and forth). The "I" here, already marked by doubleness, is accompanied by a noticeably African-derived verb, *tongonear* (synonymous with *contonear*, swaying), a linguistic instance of what gender politics would deem an ambivalent Afro-Antillean and erotic discourse that constitutes the majority of Isabel la Negra's descriptions.[23] Similarly, the bright red "Cherries Jubilee" becomes the red of blood, the hidden African blood that was flowing "out of [her] like a tide," a gush that can only reveal the repressed, contained conditions of her hidden racial identity.

This fusion of the two women proposes multilayered interpretive possibilities that move beyond the Anglo-centered idea of Elaine Showalter's common woman's culture.[24] First, in the social context of racial conflict and myths, this fantastic ending is not a metaphor for a facile, reconciliatory paradigm of racial mestizaje, similar to the one textualized earlier by Tomás Blanco. Instead, it proposes a vision of cultural dialogism by which the central role of African-based culture in Puerto Rico would be recognized as equally as that of the European-based one. This vision is opposed by many *blanquitos* in Puerto Rico. The history of musical syncretism and of transculturation portrayed in the development of both the danza and the plena suggest this type of reading. Again, the musical intertexts are key here, for they open up Ferré's story to larger cultural contexts than those previously articulated by feminist approaches. The racial myths prevalent in upper-class Puerto Rican society are alluded to in the text: "al que tiene raja siempre le sale al final" [black blood always surfaces at the end], "dicen que eso requinta" [they say that African blood always comes out], myths that articulate the phobia of racial mixture among the upper class.[25] Perhaps Ferré's fusion cannot be read as participation in cultural dialogism without a recognition and acceptance of racial mixture among and within this class. Tomás Blanco himself reminded his readers, in "Elogio de la plena," that we can no longer deny this racial reality among Puerto Ricans: "no podemos tapar el cielo con las manos" (we cannot cover the sky with our hands).[26]

In other words, the cultural exchange between the European and the African-based sectors cannot be proposed before the systematic whitewashing and discursive erasure of blackness is recognized and stopped. Read within the discursive domains established by Eurocentric partriarchal writers who created a historical tradition for the gestures of racial erasure, for whitewashing the "dark" aspects of their family histories and of the cultural productions of the islands, the equitable fusion of Isabel Luberza and Isabel la Negra is not a simplistic call for a glorified mestizaje that continues to elide racial conflict but instead a radical, positive valuation of the centrality of African-derived elements in Puerto Rican society and culture. Instead of unilaterally "improving the race" (*mejorar la raza*) by whitewashing Puerto Rican society, as interracial marriage and paradigms of mestizaje have been interpreted, Ferré proposes to "mulattize" (my own expression) upper-class Puerto Rican society in a transcultural gesture that will symbolically darken and re-Africanize it, as it is embodied in the white lady called Isabel Luberza and her desire for the Other. Given the masculinist genesis of mestizaje that Vera Kutzinski identifies in Caribbean literary history,[27] Ferré's story can also be valued as an attempt to place women within that particular discursive tradition. She fictionalized, in 1976, what revisionist scholars such as Angel Quintero Rivera and Juan Flores are currently achieving in their recovery of the African presence within the history of a Caribbean island that prided itself on being whiter than its Antillean neighbors.

In addition to Ferré's rewriting of racializing processes in Puerto Rico, to conflate metaphorically the white dama/danza and the black puta/plena is a critique of class conflicts in Puerto Rico, divisions marked by clear racial boundaries and with profound implications for women's roles. Financially dependent on her husband, Isabel Luberza desired the relative financial independence that her Other, "a self-made woman," enjoyed. In Puerto Rico the real Isabel "La Negra" Luberza was powerful enough to contribute to charity and to the church, developing, as a result, a sort of social status and visibility rarely or never alloted to prostitutes. Yet it is also a fact that the church did not accept many of Isabel's donations because of her past and because of the illicit nature of her profession. As Vera Kutzinski has analyzed in the context of nineteenth-century Cuba, visual representations of the mulatta were consistently associated with prostitution and concubinage, and the use of "money obtained from illegal commerce of all sorts" became a "substitute for pedigree and concurrent social privilege," a phenomenon that marked "major socioeconomic changes in nineteenth-century Cuba."[28] Thus, the image of women of color and their overdetermined sexuality have been very much accompanied by a concomitant criminalization that revealed, in more profound ways, the threat of socioeconomic permeability and privilege that emerged from modernization and urbanization. In the case of Isabel La Negra, however, financial gains did not necessarily translate into social power or entry into the old lineage of the aristocracy. Ironically, in Ferré's story it is this financial and economic privilege that Isabel Luberza desires since, in her case, it has been systematically sabotaged by her own social position as "wife" of the bourgeoisie.

By her ironic treatment of this class boundary, which La Negra proves permeable, Ferré calls into question the social binaries that subordinate women, both black and white, proletarian and upper-class, into rigid delineations of their sexual roles. This ensuing process of (de)erotizing women, according to race and class locations, is a cross-cultural class phenomenon that in the Caribbean is clearly rooted in the economic institution of slavery.[29] Isabel Luberza, sexually repressed by the patriarchal dictates of her upper-class upbringing, desires to mimic the free sexuality and unbridled eroticism that define her Other. As a dama and as a wife, she must remain passive in her sexuality since it is the role of the man to "take the initiative." Yet the sexual knowledge that allows men to lead in sexual interaction is transmitted precisely by Isabel la Negra. She not only possesses experience and offers total sexual freedom to men: "porque en los brazos de Isabel la Negra todo está permitido, mijito, no hay nada prohibido" (because in Isabel la Negra's arms everything is allowed, son, nothing is forbidden"). More significantly, because her racial identity as a black woman is rendered negligible—"yo no soy más que Isabel la Negra" (I'm just Isabel la Negra)—and thus an ensuing inferior status is accorded to her, a social invisibility, men can open up to her without risk. They can be vulnerable; they can present themselves as inexperienced, naïve, as virgins.

In other words, because of her lack of social power, both recognizable and recognized, Isabel la Negra acquires a kind of power that other socially visible women are not privy to: she is allowed entry to men's most profound realities—their emotions, their fears, their weaknesses—aspects of their identities that are systematically masked from society and from their own wives. Recalling the traditional plena that informs the short story's title, the power of women in Afro-Caribbean societies to "possess" men comes not only from the effects of rituals but, in a modern, Ferrerian rereading of that plena, from a black woman's contradictory social and sexual positionings.[30] Isabel Luberza, the dama of privileged social status and economic comfort and luxury, received only "la sabiduría antiquísima de su madre"[31] [the antiquated wisdom of her mother], a legacy that proved useless in the erotic/sexual interactions with her husband.

As Mariana Valverde suggests, "where there is strong eroticism there is power."[32] Ferré's construction of Isabel la Negra's sexuality may then be problematic as another instance of eroticizing blacks. Ferré's own vicarious curiosity about Isabel "La Negra" Luberza and her own sense of victimization by sexual codes, articulated in the story through Isabel Luberza's voice, are revealed in more detail in her essay "¿Por qué quiere Isabel a los hombres?":

Mi descubrimiento de las sensaciones eróticas en aquel tiempo me llevó a sentirme en más de una ocasión cómplice de Isabel en mi fantasía. Recuerdo haber pensado que si lo único que ella hacía era iniciar a los amigos que me acompañaban a los bailes en esos misterios de la sexualidad que tan celosamente nos ocultaban a las alumnas del colegio no era ni la mitad de lo mala de como la pintaban las monjas. El hecho de que, algunos años más tarde, Isabel llegase a convertirse en un personaje importante del mundo de los negocios dejó también en mí una impresión indeleble.[33]

[My own discovery of erotic sensations at the time sometimes made me feel more a wishful accomplice than a disapproving judge of Isabel's activities. I remember thinking that if all Isabel did was initiate the boys I used to dance with, under the severe eyes of the chaperones, to those sexual mysteries that were strictly forbidden to us girls, she wasn't half as bad as the nuns who ranted against her in school would have had us believe. The fact that Isabel became, a few years later, a woman of means . . . made an even further impression on me.]

Debra Castillo has already observed the privileged position of Ferré and other Latin American women writers that allows them to express that "romance with the racial Other" and that "longing for a reverse mestizaje" from the subject position of a white, upper-class female writer.[34] Ferré's own vicarious desire for the sexual positioning of a black prostitute could be deemed as discursive racism if it fails to take into account the racially informed historical oppression that underlies La Negra's social role as prostitute. It may be another idealized vision of the racial Other, an image that does not truly differ much from the modes of representation that blacks have been subjected to historically throughout Puerto Rican literature. Indeed, Ferré's fictional construction of Isabel la Negra is an excellent illustration of the role of black characters as utopian loci that signal the dismantling of the bourgeois social order, a value that Rafael Falcón has identified in neo-Negrista literature in the Caribbean and Latin America.[35] In literary texts authored by whites, blacks are positioned to serve the interests of whites as they mediate the latters' liberatory articulations of social change. Despite the ideological dissidence with social institutions in which many of these authors locate themselves, their deployment of black characters can function only in relation to a liberal project separate from black agency, authority, and authorship. In other words, it is through the presence of Isabel la Negra that Isabel Luberza finally encounters her own truth and her own self.

In another of Ferré's less-discussed short stories, "Amalia,"[36] a young, white, upper-class girl, literally imprisoned within her own home by a fatal condition that prohibits her from being out in the sun, finds pleasure and happiness in the figure of the black chauffeur, Gabriel. His angelic and divine name signals the role of savior that Gabriel plays in the story. Yet this is not a classical, divine savior, but an angelic *cocolo* of sorts, reminiscent of

Madonna's black saint in "Like a Prayer," a man who is constantly associated with Afro-Caribbean music—the conga in particular—and rhythms and who introduces the young girl to erotic pleasure. An inversion of the colonialist paradigm of rape—the white man who possesses the black female slave—this coupling is subversive to the bourgeois values that permeate Ponce's upper-class society. Indeed, any sort of sexual intercourse between a "proper" young lady and a man outside her class sector and racially darker is still taboo, for it supposedly disrupts the social order and the *limpieza de sangre* boundaries necessary to secure class stability. Also, Gabriel is older than the young protagonist, insinuating a sort of sexual interaction that borders on pedophilia but is, in fact, explicitly disassociated from any form of oppression. Ferré consistently distinguishes Gabriel from the young girl's uncle who tries to molest her and who, it is implied, was the source of the girl's illness, a result of the incestuous relationship that her mother and her uncle had had over the years. Thus, Ferré raises the interracial sexual encounters between Gabriel and the young girl beyond any reproach or any indication of oppressive relations. The interracial desire is articulated as the only utopian space for the young protagonist, the only instance in which "Amalia ríe por vez primera con sus dientes de guayo chiquiquichiqui" [Amalia smiles for the first time with her grating teeth *chiquiquichiqui*].

By locating erotic pleasure only or mostly in black figures and by structuring these discoveries of erotic pleasure by victimized, upper-class white women, Ferré corroborates the class-based constructs imposed on the masses and the populace (in the Caribbean this is the black and the mulatto sectors) as the locus of pleasure and hedonism, while the realm of desire continues to be contained within the upper class.[37] This pleasure has been located historically within the social space inhabited by the others, by the marginalized and the powerless, thus establishing a discursive fissure between desire and erotic pleasure. Here Ferré is definitely articulating a class critique of upper-class mores and its impact on women. She is not "speaking for" black women or mulattas as much as she is deploying their figures to point out, through a differentiating discourse, the multiple forms of oppression of those women who are usually regarded as privileged. While the impact of erotic discourse in *Papeles de Pandora* has been acknowledged as a central feminist literary strategy, even by the author herself,[38] the question remains as to the double-edged ambivalence that this discourse implies when contained within the racial boundaries already traced by patriarchy and imperialism. As a white female narrator writing about a black prostitute, Ferré may have found herself "between identification and disavowal."[39]

The autobiographical subtexts to *Papeles de Pandora*, yet to be explored, suggest another perspective about this problem of privilege and of race, of authors and of characters. In an essay titled "Una conciencia musical"[40] [A musical consciousness], Ferré recounts the meaningful experience she had during her youth in her friendship with Gilda Ventura, a black nanny who initiated her into the popular music and culture of Puerto Rico and Latin America, an access to these differential knowledges that was very much denied by the Eurocentric cultural values of her family. Everything Ferré has written, she states, "has been an attempt to narrate the story of those years in which [she] acquired, thanks to Gilda, a musical awareness of [her] country."[41] Indeed, the dualities in "When Women Love Men"—the plenas and the danzas, the white versus the black, the socioeconomic divisions—were viscerally experienced by Ferré during her upbringing in Ponce, where La Alhambra, her elite neighborhood, came "face to face" with the Barrio de San Antón, the very poor barrio where Gilda lived and where the plena was born.

This detail is revealing of the ways in which social binaries and dualities, while undoubtedly social constructs, are not limited to discursive phenomena but also should be analyzed in terms of the concrete experiences that individuals have shared regarding class segregation, racial conflict, and the silencing of popular culture. The geophysical proximity and the disturbing social distance between these two worlds were, in many ways, mediated by Gilda, the "transgressor" who initiated the young Rosario Ferré into the pleasures of Mexican films and Afro-Caribbean music, plenas and salsa. This was, to be sure, Ferré's escape from the "silence" imposed by the Eurocentric values upheld by her family. In this sense, the black characters that Ferré portrays in such an idealistic way are an "homage" to Gilda Ventura, as she candidly explains in "La conciencia musical." Gilda was the agent for Ferré's transculturation and, perhaps more important, for her decolonization as an upper-class Puerto Rican woman. Thus, a reading of "When Women Love Men," as well as of "Amalia," should certainly take into account the personal experiences that motivate these representations. It also has implications for reconsidering erotic pleasure in a larger cultural framework. The "pleasure" of decolonization, of discovering and reconstructing aspects of one's own cultural identity that have been erased through what Ngugi wa Thiong'o has deemed "colonial alienation,"[42] is a plausible political and productive framework for reading these two short stories by Ferré.

Locating pleasure in a racial Other also implies a process of eroticizing language—the word and the text. In "Maquinolandera," the final short story in *Papeles de Pandora*,[43] Ferré experiments with the pleasure of a text imbued with Afro-Caribbean rhythms and language. Virtually ignored by critics and practically untranslatable into English, "Maquinolandera" consists of an experimental, highly poetic rendering of musical intertexts, subtexts, and allusions to Afro–Puerto Rican bombas and salsa music. It renders, simultaneously, a denouncement of the marginalized status of black and mulatto musicians and singers, both male and female, in Puerto Rico. If Ferré's stories have been characterized by countercanonical textures and ambiguous language as antipatriarchal discourse, "Maquinolandera" represents her most experimental writing in this context.

More than a narrative, this is a metaliterary text, lacking a conventional plot yet entering the world of the Puerto Rican musical farándula. The text proposes, for me at least, three levels of reading. The first consists of the description and canonical vindication of great salsa figures: Willie Colón, Eddie Palmieri, Roberto Rohena, and among the women, Iris Chacón, Ruth Fernández, and Lucecita Benítez. The second level is a pilgrimage of sorts, a traveling movement that seems to end in a concert stage, and at times is transformed into a religious procession. At the third discursive level one listens to the voice of Ismael Rivera, the *sonero mayor*, who is imprisoned. His voice embodies the metatextual search for the perfect word and the ideal sound or note. Thus, the artistic search for language and for music are doubled throughout the text, as Ferré examines the creative process not only her own as a writer but also that of Ismael Rivera as a *sonero* (a singer-improviser) and ultimately as a model for Ferré's *nueva narrativa*.

The fusion of music and literature (verbal language) is apparent from the beginning of the text, even in the very title, which refers to a bomba of the same name authored by Doña Margot Rivera, Ismael's mother, and first interpreted by Rafael Cortijo y su Combo. Afro–Puerto Rican bombas such as "Maquinolandera" are characterized by a strong presence of rhythm (instead of a melodic line) and as a result a verbal language whose meaning rests more on its phonetic values (sound and rhythm) than in its denoted meanings. Thus, one finds a predominance of *jitanjáforas* and portmanteau words such as the title itself. *Maquinolandera* a neologism that eludes a particular meaning but reproduces, in the context of modernization, the changing rhythms of urban life (*maquino/máquina*). I suggest, then, that the text is *eroticized* through the musicalization of the word and through *repetition*:[44] "Chumalacatera, maquinolandera, chumalacatera, maquinolandera . . ." The rhythms of the plena and the bomba, the African-based accentuation of words on the last syllable[45] (*Chorizá*, *maquiná*), the *jitanjáforas* popularized by Nicolás Guillén and Luis Palés Matos, the syncopation felt in the push and pull of phrases, and the anaphoric structures of the text, among other elements, help construct a musical, sensorial, and even "semiotic" texture. If "significance," as Roland Barthes defines it, is "meaning, insofar as it is sensually produced,"[46] "Maquinolandera" resists being read traditionally as a story; instead it proposes itself as a performance, an act of utterance and listening, a process of signifying more than a denotative text. This text, consciously incoherent, fragmented, and syncopated in its multiple levels of discourse, is truly revolutionary in the value of its poetics.[47]

The eroticized, musical syntax and rhythmical structures of the text transgress the boundaries of official discourse, that is, those institutionalized languages such as literature, philosophy, history, and politics that exert power constituting and legitimating social meaning for others. By subverting the literary norms imposed by a patriarchal order and by a European-based, scientifically informed realist and naturalist discourse, Ferré's *nueva narrativa* introduces the discourse and the voices of Afro-Caribbean popular music—those that Edgardo Rodríguez Juliá marked as centrifugal—into the mainstream of Puerto Rican high culture and literature, into the canon.

"Maquinolandera" also proposes a revision of the social constructs of the erotic as located in the popular sectors, which in Puerto Rico, despite claims to the contrary, remain synonymous with blacks and mulattoes. In this case, pleasure is located in the language of popular music, but is not necessarily or automatically transposed to the figure of the musicians and singers. On the contrary, Ferré's text constantly moves and shifts between the marginalized and socially persecuted vision of Ismael, Iris, and Lucecita and their representations as cultural heroes, albeit touching on the mythical and divine at times. The politics of the text, its denunciatiom of the racist cultural boundaries deployed by an elite sector in order to exclude popular Afro-Caribbean music from its proper place as a central marker of Puerto Rican culture and identity anticipates, once more and in fictionalized forms, the historical shift of popular music as an expression of *plebeyismo* to the center of Puerto Rican urban culture and postmodernity. Juan Flores has creatively termed this "Cortijo's Revenge" in the struggles for discourse and representation that have characterized Puerto Rican cultural history.

The recent shift of Afro–Puerto Rican music toward the center and into the cultural mainstream in Puerto Rico was facilitated in part by the intertextual inscriptions of popular music within the radicalizing, polyphonic texts of the *nueva narrativa*. Andreas Huyssen reminds us that "it is primarily the visible and public presence of women artists in high art, as well as the emergence of new kinds of women performers and producers in mass culture, which make the old gendering device obsolete. The universalizing ascription of femininity to mass culture always depended on the very real exclusion of women from high culture and its institutions. Such exclusions are, for the time being, a thing of the past. Thus, the old rhetoric has lost its persuasive power because the realities have changed."[48]

Although there are historical reasons to rejoice with Huyssen, salsa music, nonetheless, is still subject to feminizing constructs. Its centrality in Puerto Rican society and its simultaneous feminized marginality in the United States, as cultural Other, suggests the need for a postmodern approach to understanding current forms of Afro-Caribbean music, that is, an analysis that considers salsa in its ideological plurality: as national discourse, international mass culture, and a continuing double-edged value as a culturally appropriated musical form in the United States.

PART TWO

✛

THE PLURAL SITES OF SALSA

✛

A Postmodern Preface

✠

Porque la Salsa no existe [there is no such thing as Salsa]
—Dámaso Pérez Prado

Yo sólo conozco una Salsa que venden en botella, llamada catsup.
Yo toco música cubana [I only know a Salsa sold in a bottle
called ketchup. What I play is Cuban music.]
—Tito Puente

Soy cubana, tú lo sabes.
Aquí la Salsa . . . Soy yo!
[I am Cuban, as you know.
I am Salsa music!]
—Olga Navarro, "Nuestra música cubana"

Puerto Rico es Salsa [Puerto Rico is Salsa].
—Concierto Expo 92, Seville, Spain

Salsa es una suma armónica de toda la cultura latina reunida en Nueva York
[Salsa is the harmonic sum of all Latin culture that meets in New York].
—Willie Colón

"La música Salsa es un folclor urbano a nivel internacional
[Salsa music is urban folklore at the international level].
—Rubén Blades

"Puerto Rico es Salsa," an evening concert at Expo 92 in Seville, Spain, was the culmination of a day of festivities honoring the National Day of Puerto Rico on June 23, 1992. Yet behind the curtains of a successful stage performance by Alex de Castro, Tony Vega, Andy Montañez, and El Gran Combo de Puerto Rico, the national affirmation of salsa as Puerto Rico's music had become a controversy well before the show began. Issues of national identity, popular culture, race, and class were subtexts to this public debate that began once the government revealed that a salsa concert would represent Puerto Rico in Spain's Expo 92. For many upper-class Puerto Ricans, salsa was not an appropriate and lofty enough symbol of the island's musical traditions. Either the Puerto Rican Symphony Orchestra or a lyrical trio would have been much more acceptable. Other sectors contested that salsa was not Puerto Rican but Cuban music. Still others felt that jíbaro music had been denied its opportunity as a traditional symbol of Puerto Rico's autochthonous folklore.

Altogether and albeit their conflicting views, these opinions reveal the contested nature of salsa and the difficulties of defining a music that is syncretic and interethnically Caribbean. They also dramatize the central role of popular music as a site for the formation and definition of national identity, a process that assumes serious consequences for the Puerto Rican people because of the island's complex, lagging colonial conditions within an assumed postcolonial world. This complex and contradictory political location is informed by Puerto Rico's "uneven insertion . . . into the modern industrial configuration," what Juan Flores and María Milagros López have termed "the post-colonial colony."[1] Yet the symbolic values of popular music as a locus of national identity are not exclusively expressed by Puerto Ricans; they are also shared by Cubans, from whose African musical tradition salsa emerged, and other urban Caribbean audiences, such as Venezuelans and Colombians, who have embraced salsa as an artistic articulation of urban life and a reaffirmation of class conflict and racial identity in Latin America.

Within the continental United States, salsa music adds to this complexity as a Pan-Latino expression of cultural hybridity and resistance. Thus, because of its semantic polyvalence contingent on the cultural context in which it is listened to, produced, and performed, this particular music, fluid in its social values and cultural meanings, eludes a fixed definition. It shifts meanings among individual receptors, and it also becomes a metaphor for race, class, and gender conflicts within the diverse Puerto Rican communities (the island and the diasporas), as well as across Latin America, the United States, and the international scene. While salsa has been identified as the music of the urban, working-class black and mulatto sectors in Puerto Rico and historically rejected as such by the upper classes on the island, in the United States it has functioned as a cohesive force among Latinos in general, syncretizing, in fact, an array of Latin American musical styles into its repertoire, a "harmonic sum" as Willie Colón describes it.

Simultaneously, the history of salsa music in the United States has revealed the mechanisms by which the Anglo mainstream appropriates and co-opts the cultural productions of less dominant groups. This mainstreaming reproduces, at a larger social level, strategies of appropriation analogous to those deployed by white writers around the role of the black figure as a locus of liberation. Salsa music has been received as an oppositional, liberatory music by progressive Anglo performers like David Byrne, among others, and by Anglo audiences, particularly in major cities with Latina/o populations. This cross-cultural phenomenon readily lends itself to a continued analysis of intercultural desire as discussed in the works of Rosario Ferré.

Rather than delimiting salsa to a specific musical form or to a synthesis of structures, I prefer to interpret it as a sociomusical practice, one claimed by very heterogeneous communities for radically diverse purposes. As Willie Colón observes, more than a rhythm or a form, salsa music "es una idea, un concepto, una manera de asumir la música desde una perspectiva latinoamericana" [is an idea, a concept, a way of doing music from a Latin American perspective].[2] Its polyvalent popularity ranges from Orquesta de la Luz's performances in Japan and at Madison Square Garden to its use by the Reverend Frank Pretto in Santa Fe, New Mexico, who plays salsa with his band, Parranda, as a means of collecting funds for the poor and as a strategy, sanctioned by his bishop, to attract new members to his parish.[3] Salsa is performed in Spain and Germany, among other European countries. It is danced to in large public dance halls called *salsódromos* throughout Lima, Perú; it blares through radio stations in Tucson, Arizona, on Sunday night programs once hosted by a young Anglo miner who is a *salsamigo*, a salsa fan and expert. This music has been performed in concert halls throughout Latin American and U.S. cities, on college campuses, on the streets of the Bronx and of East L.A., and in clubs in Toronto;[4] it plays in the small living room of a Puerto Rican single woman in southwest Detroit and in the elegant living rooms of upper-class Venezuelans; meanwhile, it subtly serves as background music for a wide array of television commercials in the United States, from Duracell batteries to NBC-affiliate stations in Detroit.

Thus, to situate salsa ideologically has meant avoiding the restriction of this very heterogeneous musical expression to one ideological camp. Rather, a postmodern approach that considers the multiple meanings and social values ascribed to it by particular social and ethnic sectors is needed. In this part I will profile, first, salsa music as a marker of class and race divisions in Puerto Rico by analyzing the social dichotomy established between salsa and rock music during the 1980s. Second, I will analyze its contested national origins and its syncretism as Pan-Latina/o music and more recently as international mass culture, which has brought this Afro-Caribbean music into the foreground as global "urban folklore." It is true that the commercial label of "salsa" has been detrimental, for it homogenizes the complex history of musical forms, genres, and practices encompassed in Afro-Caribbean music. Yet contrary to Mambo King Dámaso Pérez Prado's assertion and those of many other Cuban musicians who deny the specificity of this music, salsa does exist, characterized by a specific use of rhythms, instrumentation, themes, and lyrics and by a particular historical development that is informed by Afro-Cuban music but nonetheless diverges from it.

This chapter may be read as a postmodern rendering constituted by diverse and conflicting views about salsa. It is not music history, for I do not attempt to include a complete narrative of the development of Latin(o) popular music, nor do I incorporate all of its major musicians and interpreters. Rather, I select specific case studies that illustrate the ways in which salsa music constitutes a symbolic site for negotiating issues of national identity, class, and race. I discuss this music simultaneously as mass culture, as marker of national identity, and as tropicalized ethnic expression.

To avoid the most relativist (nihilist) forms of a postmodernist analysis, this chapter refuses to deny salsa's value as a historically oppositional expression within the larger tradition of Afro-Caribbean music. Moreover, the tensions that arise from the divergent social constructions ascribed to salsa are articulated. While postmodernist theories have contributed substantially to our understanding of popular music beyond fixed, static definitions bound by nation, I agree with other critics that "this approach often seems to depoliticize such studies by emphasizing only the fluidity of boundaries rather than the actual positions they represent and the actors who constitute them."[5] As an engaged Latina scholar, I am interested in identifying and denouncing the colonialist constructions of salsa music by Anglo mainstream discourse and its concomitant othering, a political position that possibly will prove unpopular among those readers who equate crossing cultural borders with celebrating an assumed equality.

My stance, however, does not aim to defend an already anachronic or inherent concept of "authenticity" but rather to unmask the material, economic motivations and the power differentials that undergird the discursive strategies by which intercultural desire is articulated. Most important, I hope to illuminate theories and approaches to popular culture currently in circulation and to rewrite them as they are newly informed by the sociocultural practices and the perspectives of the colonized, displaced, and dispossessed cultural community of U.S. Latino/as, a perspective that remains minimally acknowledged by mainstream scholarship on popular music.

The multiple epigraphs that open this chapter illustrate the highly conflictive definitions that salsa evokes among Latino musicians and singers. Salsa music does not exist for some; for others it is only an imitation of Cuban music; and still for others, like Willie Colón and Rubén Blades, salsa is a syncretic cultural expression central to Latina/o urban communities in the United States and across Latin America, simultaneously traveling beyond borders. This plurality of ideological sites and discursive locations will illustrate the value of this music as metaphor for national identity, difference, hybridity, and oppositionality.

CHAPTER FOUR

Situating Salsa

✟

Music, Race, and Class Conflict in Puerto Rico

In Puerto Rico and other Caribbean countries, such as Venezuela,[1] salsa music has emerged as a marker of race and class differences. The cocolo-rockero dichotomy based on musical taste permeated youth culture in Puerto Rico during the 1980s. *Cocolos*, an African-derived term,[2] refers to young black men who attend salsa concerts and who drive old Toyotas with the driver's seat lowered and the loudspeakers playing salsa. The aesthetics of the car and the music, partly analogous to the Chicano lowrider tradition in the Southwest, associates salsa with this social sector. The *rockero*, or rock and roller, is the white middle-and-upper class young Puerto Rican who prefers to listen to Santana, Jimi Hendrix, Queen, and U.S. rock. While there is no particular car model that characterizes rockeros—perhaps the yuppified BMW—this audience prevails at city beaches and attends rock concerts by U.S. groups.

An event emblematic of this social duality occurred on June 12, 1987, when two concerts—one by Ratt and Poison, a couple of commercial heavy metal groups from the United States, and the other a concert in memory of salsa singer Ismael Rivera, the "sonero mayor" who had passed away recently—were planned for the same evening. They took place, respectively, in the Hiram Bithorn Stadium and in the Roberto Clemente Coliseum, two adjacent structures that share a common parking lot yet whose very names embody the racial and cultural dualities of Puerto Rican colonial society (Hiram Bithorn was a white Puerto Rican baseball player, and Clemente was black). There were fears that conflict and violence between the two groups would emerge before the events, and police were assigned to patrol the area. A few conflicts arose, yet considering that fifteen thousand fans attended the salsa concert (although the rock fans were not as numerous as expected), the evening went quite smoothly. The cocolo concert was attended by a racially diverse audience, by old and young people, by families, elders, and politicians; the rock concert was filled with youngsters dressed in the black leather, hard rock style, with long hair, many of them smoking dope.

I mention this demographic example to comment on the age-marked basis of rock audiences in Latin America and on the more diverse generational audience of salsa music in Puerto Rico. The fact that even the governor of Puerto Rico attended the concert in honor of Ismael, the same governor who organized the salsa concert in Seville, Spain, attests to the collective representativity of this music. The *San Juan Star* published a double article on the two concerts, with side-by-side pictures of two singers and two columns of text, one reviewing each event. The gap was reaffirmed in the headlines that read: "Some Like It Loud, Others Like It Lively," and the layout played with the opposition and the simultaneity of both kinds of music in relation to each other.[3] While the audience at the salsa concert booed and hissed at the mention of the next-door event, some rock fans were quoted as expressing interest in having attended the salsa event, suggesting that perhaps salsa music possesses much more acceptance and popularity in Puerto Rico than the dichotomy literally suggests.

Like all dichotomies, the cocolo-rockero one articulates a socioeconomic and racial division, yet it is also a social construct.[4] In other words, while it is true that many young men in Puerto Rico would not even dream of listening to or buying each other's music, there are those who enjoy both salsa and rock, who listen to both, who dance to both, and who even consume both. As a Puerto Rican teenager growing up in San Juan in the late 1960s and early 1970s, I attended high school dances that were almost always articulations of a double consciousness in their musical representation. Somehow we managed always to hire two bands, one that would play U.S. rock and roll and soft popular ballads (the Beatles, the Beach Boys, etc.) and the indispensable Latin music band that would perform salsa, merengue, and bolero classics. The bands would alternate shifts so that in the best of a colonized society we enjoyed nonstop live music. Quite significant, however, were the differing meanings and values of each culturally delineated musical repertoire. While U.S. rock and roll allowed us to differentiate ourselves generationally from our parents—I recall the many vigilant mothers who would sit at the front row tables as *chaperonas*—the Latin music constantly invited all in the audience to partake in the pleasures of familiar rhythms, melodies, and intimate romantic ballads to which our parents and grandparents had also sung and danced during their youth.

Like linguistic hybridity, these cultural practices cannot be explained exclusively as binary oppositions. Rather, it is essential to remember that

Some like it loud, others like it lively

Salseros jam until morning

By CARLOS GALARZA
Of The STAR Staff

If "El Sonero Mayor" Ismael Rivera had been around for his salsa music tribute at the Roberto Clemente Coliseum, he'd probably have just two words to describe it all — "Huepa Huey!"

"Huepa Huey" was Rivera's ecstatic musical war cry, and it must have been ringing in the ears of *salseros* of all ages who jammed into the coliseum Friday night to hear non-stop music into the wee hours of the morning. They danced in the aisles, drank, sang and made enough noise to drown out the roar of
See SALSA, Page 30

STAR photo by David Acevedo
Yolanda Ortiz of the Ruby Haddock salsa group belts out a number at the Clemente Coliseum.

STAR photo by Farah Rivera
Top Ratt Stephen Pearcy raises the volume at the heavy metal show at Hiram Bithorn Stadium.

Rockers give fans an earful

By JAIME PIERAS
Of The STAR Staff

The music at Hiram Bithorn Stadium was loud to the point of making you cringe.

But aside from a few fights, a few arrests and some tipsy youngsters, there was little sign of trouble among the some 5,000 fans who put down $10 to $25 apiece to see Ratt and Poison, a couple of "commercial" heavy metal groups, Friday night.

There was some disagreement over whether the groups fit the heavy metal mold, but the increasingly loud sound seemed to please the 16- to 20-year-old concert.
See METAL, Page 31

The *San Juan Star* published a double article on the salsa concert in honor of Ismael Rivera and the rock concert featuring Ratt and Poison, two heavy metal groups. Both concerts took place on Friday, June 12, 1987. Courtesy of the *San Juan Star*.

throughout an individual's lifetime, these musical choices are not fixed or stagnant. For instance, a very well known salsa interpreter in Puerto Rico, Tony Vega, was born in Philadelphia and grew up in a Jewish neighborhood. When he moved back to Puerto Rico, his favorite groups were Chicago and Santana. His first band performed "American" (U.S.) music, and as journalists interestingly commented, he is white, with green eyes and straight dark hair.[5] He has received Golden and Silver Record awards for his recordings, he performed at the Sevilla concert, and he is considered one of the most popular salseros in Puerto Rico today. However, one of Tony Vega's recent numbers, "Busca el ritmo,"[6] deploys this rockero-co-colo dichotomy to reaffirm the connection between Afro-Caribbean rhythms and the "competence" and "authenticity" of musicians and of the music in a song that reaffirms the African legacy of our cultural identity.

The song begins with a denunciation of many musicians' ignorance of the Afro-Caribbean repertoire, a lack of knowledge that, as it is implied, results from spending too much time listening to "ritmos extranjeros" [foreign rhythms], thus affecting the quality of salsa performances. The song's refrain posits an imperative both to musicians and their audience. Like an old Cuban song titled "Cambia el paso," Tony Vega exhorts his listeners and fans to give up rock and roll and to "find the rhythm" of Latino music. A tongue-in-cheek mimicry of the penetration of Anglo musical values—as in disco music—is evident in the parodically mispronounced English and code switching at the end of the song. However, the fact that English constitutes part of the surface structure of the text also implies complicity and an ambiguous self-location on the part of the singing subject. To reject rock and roll as an icon of Anglo culture and of foreign intervention and to strategically essentialize Afro-Caribbean rhythms and protect their purity seems a naïve stance on the part of the composer or at best an outdated expression of nationalism.

It also elides the multilayered musical and structural influences, including that of rock, on the development of salsa, let alone the multicultural trajectories of its own interpreters, such as Tony Vega himself. Thus, the ideological values of the song cannot be located necessarily in the individual, personal subject locations, as the case of Tony Vega and his song demonstrate, but rather are interpreted as collective, symbolic cultural spaces in which tensions between the national (in this case, the colonized) and the foreign are articulated as the fear of losing locally produced musical traditions in favor of musical imports. The contradictory facts that Tony Vega, as a musician, was very much nurtured and influenced by U.S. and British rock groups and that, moreover, salsa music as a whole has integrated rock musical structures into its diverse repertoire attest to the symbolic and strategic value of this musical positioning. A strictly musical reading of "Busca el ritmo" would not convincingly explain this value, for it resides within the larger social framework of Puerto Rican urban youth culture as well as within the longer colonial history of Puerto Rico's contradictory resistance against anything Anglo.

There are, nevertheless, already molded expectations regarding who plays or listens to salsa and who doesn't, attitudes formed partly because of the historical origins of salsa in New York's barrios as well as because of the racial and class myths created around the "bohemian" world of Latin popular music. A *Claridad* article on Tony Vega begins by asking the reader to put aside expectations of who is a salsero, for in Vega the myth of the black, drug-addict, working-class musician is dismantled.[7] Indeed, younger performers like Tony Vega, Alex D'Castro, and Gilberto Santa Rosa exemplify the recent professionalizing trend of salsa musicians. In contrast to the generation of Ismael Rivera and Cheo Feliciano, historically significant Puerto Rican black musicians and cultural heroes yet well known for their lifetime struggles with drug abuse, this younger generation of salseros exemplifies a group that has studied music in professional settings (e.g., la Escuela Libre de Música) and that rejects the myth and image of the bohemian, drug-using musician. As Andy Montañez has stated, "That vision has changed. Musicians are now interested in studying. In salsa orchestras now even the percussionists know how to read music, and this has improved the quality, thus the field has broadened, and that is why we are being invited to perform not only in Puerto Rico, but in Seville."[8] This example points out how fluidly these social dualities are negotiated within daily cultural practices and for the individual musician as well as across generations.

More important, however, these contradictory instances illustrate the shifting value of salsa as a marker of class and race in Puerto Rico. What are the implications of this shift from salsa as a cultural vehicle of oral tradition to its performance based on written notations? Will it lead to a higher level of standardization, to a diminution of its complex polyrhythmic structures, to more fixed arrangements and performances? The selection of salsa music as representative of Puerto Rico in Spain signaled the growing acceptance of this style among the island's dominant and official sector, an attitude that may have been nurtured by this racial and class-based shift in its new interpreters. Today's salsa scene is iconized by, among others, Luis Miguel, "El Príncipe de la Salsa" [The Prince of Salsa], and Gilberto Santa Rosa, "El Caballero de la Salsa" [The Gentleman of Salsa]. These singers and their bourgeois epithets encapsulate a more recent salsa sound that is not as strident as the original New York style and whose arrangements, instrumentation, and lyrics lend it a texture of soft, romantic music; thus, it is informally known as salsa romántica. While salsa musicians are becoming professionalized (read "whitened"), the musical repertoire shifts toward the individual, romantic relationship, thus diminishing the impact of its collective and political value. It is no coincidence, then, that official institutions are allowing it to be inscribed within the space of Puerto Rican official culture.

A simultaneous phenomenon, termed "validation through visibility,"[9] also helps to explain salsa's mainstreaming in Puerto Rico. Given the "globalization" of salsa music, its popularity and presence mostly mediated by the jazz tradition in Germany, Spain, Africa, and particularly Japan, it is much more acceptable now for the Puerto Rican dominant sector to validate this musical style as representative of the national culture.[10] In other words, once it acquires visibility—audibility, we may say—among European audiences, then it can be safely embraced locally. This reception, a posteriori, signals a colonialist structure of cultural circulation: the music is produced locally yet remains in the margins; then it is exported and mainstreamed by foreign audiences, to return with the endorsement of others. Like the transatlantic circulation of the tango and the analogous development of jazz, salsa music has been mainstreamed in Puerto Rico because of its newly found international and westernized legitimacy, a sort of de-Africanization ascribed to by the gaze/ear of the dominant Other.

Some of that international visibility has been due to the popularity of salsa in Japan, a truly multicultural phenomenon represented by Orquesta de la Luz and its performances. Orquesta de la Luz, composed of Japanese musicians who do not speak Spanish but sing in Spanish and who discovered salsa through the music of Tito Puente and of another Japanese salsa band, has turned out to be a wonderful exponent of this musical tradition, of its singing styles and its performance rhythms. While their 1989 performance at the Madison Square Garden Salsa Festival guaranteed them a warm acceptance on the part of the New York Latina/o community, their most recent recording, "La aventura," has not met with as favorable a sales record as their first. Initially, many Puerto Ricans on the island and on the mainland did not react favorably to what was, to them, a Japanese appropriation of their musical tradition. To be sure, I still know many Puerto Ricans who boycott their CDs for nationalist reasons, notwithstanding the fact that musically Orquesta de la Luz has rendered a most impressive collection of salsa songs and repertoire. Its large size reproduces the big band sound of 1940s Latin music, and its main female singer and male instrumentalists elicit as much energy and rhythmic coordination as any Caribbean would be expected to, singing in a clearly enunciated Spanish that belies the visual markers of their Japanese identities. This is a group that, by its very presence, has destabilized the value of salsa music as nationalist marker and as product of cultural essentialism. The experience of watching Orquesta de la Luz perform, particularly in its concert appearance at the Madison Square Garden, was truly new for most Caribbeans, including myself. Their onstage performance obliges us to recognize our assumptions about expected submissive Asian gestures, manners, and behavior. That Orquesta de la Luz thrives on this double-edged destabilizing of national/cultural constructs, on the self-tropicalizing of Japanese musicians, is most salient in some of their arrangements and lyrics.

"Somos diferentes," from their album of the same title, constitutes a rewriting of a traditional Mexican bolero authored by Pablo Beltrán Ruiz.[11] The original lyrics, in which the voice addresses the irreconcilable differences that two individuals cannot bridge despite their love, are repeated by Orquesta de la Luz and indeed sung like a bolero, respecting the original text:

> Ya me convencí que seguir los dos es imposible.
> Qué le voy a hacer
> si al buscar tu amor me equivoqué.
> Debes de saber que ni tú ni yo nos comprendemos

Orquesta de la Luz's group photo included in the album cover for *Somos diferentes* (We are different), released by BMG Victor, Japan, in 1992. Photo by Yukio Yanagi of Drago Artistic Designs, Inc. Reproduced with permission of BMG Victor, Japan.

y este es el error que ahora con dolor
pagamos los dos.
Tenemos que olvidarnos de este amor
porque un amor así no puede ser.
Somos diferentes ya lo ves
esta verdad destroza el corazón.
Hoy te digo adiós
me alejo de ti serenamente.
Todo es por demás
no lo quiso Dios
somos diferentes.

[I am now convinced
it is impossible for you and me to continue.
What can I do
if I was mistaken to search for your love.

You must know that you and I did not understand
each other
and that was the mistake that we both
pay for with pain.
We must forget this love
because such a love cannot be.
We are different, as you can see,
this truth destroys the heart.
Today I say good-bye
I walk away from you serenely.
All is useless
it is not God's will,
we are different.]

Significantly, this lyrical, romantic song of despair, fatalism, and loss becomes, in the arrangements of Orquesta de la Luz, a pretext anticipating a broader definition of "difference" that allows for a double, allegorical reading: the cultural, racial, and national differences represented by the group itself. After the initial bolero section, the group adds a montuno rhythmical section; in other words, the bolero is transformed into a salsa song that articulates an analogous "difference" deployed to highlight issues of cultural difference and musical authenticity. This second part of the song, in which difference is marked musically by the change from slow to faster rhythms, replays difference as a social construct. The lyrics invoke a Latina/o audience that, despite rejection and criticism by others, still follows and embraces the Asian others' performance and musical production: "Aunque nos critiquen, somos diferentes, cantamos con amor / al público que nos quiere" [Despite criticism, we are different, we sing with love to those who love us].

By placing their own difference in the foreground, explicitly calling Latinas/os to question their own centrality as sole producers of Latin music, Orquesta de la Luz contributes to the (de)construction of popular music as a site for negotiating national identity. Their constant articulations of a potential cultural hybridity between the East and the West but most poignantly between Japan and the Caribbean allow listeners, mostly Caribbean-based, to begin to create new modes of conceptualizing popular music. These two key ideologemes or culturally charged phrases, "Arroz con Salsa" [Rice with Salsa] and "Son del Este" [Cuban Son from the East/they are from the East], suggest doubled multicultural readings on the convergence of East and West in cultural practices. If the mention of rice signals the East, it also simultaneously plays off the local Caribbean staple; "del Este" tries to orientalize the Cuban *son*, it doubly remits us to the geographical origins of the *son*, Santiago, the "Oriente" of Cuba, the eastern part of the island.[12]

For each musical genre (salsa, boleros, merengues, rancheras, etc.) there exists a constellation of undergirding myths; social, racial, and class values; and associations that have been historically produced by dominant sectors and social institutions. As an integral part of a long tradition of Afro-Caribbean rhythms and music, born in the Latino barrios of New York during the 1960s, salsa music has been simultaneously rejected and embraced by diverse social sectors in the United States and in Latin America.

Although salsa in the 1990s has become palatable and acceptable to the Latin American bourgeoisie, it was rejected as vulgar, too sensual, and trivial because of its black working-class origins, just like the plena in the past. The Left at times has pointed out the hegemonic and repressive aspects of many of its lyrics particularly in the context of gender and in the perpetuation of violence as a social message.[13] Salsa historian César Miguel Rondón has defined it as "a music whose values are disperse, irregular and contradictory, like its characters, like the reality that produces and nurtures it,"[14] thus explicating salsa's diverse values as the unidirectional effect of realism-based art. As popular culture, John Fiske would add, salsa is contradictory, positioned between hegemonic interests and expressions of resistance.[15]

Yet to listen to Ismael Rivera's song "Mi música" (My music) is to recognize the musicians' attempts to trascend partisan politics in order to express the human reality common to the marginalized black urban sectors. When Ismael sings these words by Tite Curet Alonso, one of Puerto Rico's most renowned salsa composers, and asks that his music not be identified as either right or left, but that it stands at the center of "a very lawful drum," we know we have to resist ideological categorizations. Here I want to propose approaching salsa music also as plural ideological sites. Given the sociohistorical development of this music, its antecedents in folklore and in black counterplantation culture, and its strong contestatory stance on classism and racism, its ideological value of resistance and oppositionality continues from its origins to the present. Even when Ismael Rivera refuses to pigeonhole his music as that of the political Right or Left, a whole history of oppositionality and resistance on the part of the black sector in the Caribbean surfaces through the ironic image of the "very *lawful* drum." Even when I recognize salsa as a conglomerate of ideologies, a result of the diverse individual subject positions assumed by composers, producers, and performers, its historical continuity as the sociocultural practice and production of a marginalized community consistently illustrates this oppositional positioning.

Precisely because of the politics of its liminality, salsa music has become a target for articulation and co-optation on the part of the industry and of dominant sectors. I have just discussed the whitening of salsa in Puerto Rico, a clear case of "articulation" as Richard Middleton defines it.[16] The predominance of an individualizing salsa romántica in the 1990s accords new meanings to Felipe Luciano's words in the 1980s: "There's always a danger. Music is a double-edged sword. It is escapist, it is trendy, it is faddish . . . but it is also revolutionary, dynamic and progressive."[17] Our role as cultural critics, then, is to identify and trace the shifting ideological values of popular music. Assuming blanket statements about the contradictory nature of popular music, mostly because it is situated within the music industry and mass media, leads us to neutralize each music's sociocultural complexities and specificity, leaving no space for the importance of both musicians' and listeners' agency. The overdetermined use of "contradiction" in cultural studies has saturated how we read popular music or other texts in popular culture. As a result, a static binary has been created: hegemony equals mass media, and resistance can be located only in the subaltern musicians. While this power dynamic continues to be central to salsa music and other postcolonial contexts, particularly in the 1990s with the increasing monopoly of transnational corporations, it seems that cultural criticism has turned this binary into a fixed assumption.

By examining salsa music simultaneously as a site for negotiating national identity among Cubans and Puerto Ricans, where hegemony and resistance are dialectical forces, and where social practices like dancing allow individuals to produce relevant meanings to their own cultural displacement, I hope to go beyond the facile paradigm of "contradiction" in salsa. Ultimately, salsa's ideological plurality (not pluralism) and multiple meanings can be located in the multiple texts and discourses that the music itself produces and provokes and in its circulation as cultural text. Contradiction, then, is not inherent to the music itself but rather is located in the experience of listening, in audience response, and in the shifting values of its circulation. Like other forms of popular music, salsa has developed historically and has been subjected to social, class, race, and gender value transformations, particularly in the past ten years. Its ideological plurality needs to be examined in relation to its sociohistorical development and in terms of its geocultural location, for salsa's reception practices and, ultimately, its multiple meanings shift according to the individual musicians, its audience, its modes of production and dissemination, and its performative context.

Salsa as a Marker of National Identity

The Cuban musicologist Leonardo Acosta argues that to insist on identifying the genesis of salsa music is to erase this music as historical process. Given this caveat, I have chosen not to engage in a traditional genealogy of salsa, mainly because it tends to reify or essentialize it.[18] Through the discussions and voices of critics, writers, and musicians, salsa's contested genesis reveals itself as a site for deploying music as a marker of national identity. This systematic discursive strategy among Cubans and Puerto Ricans in particular has to be understood as another instance of the struggle for discourse and cultural authority that underlines the marginality of colonized subjects. Without attempting to do musical history or to reconstruct the chronological development of salsa in all of its diverse elements,[19] I will discuss here some of the most salient elements that particularize salsa as a sociomusical practice. Because of its multilocality (in the Caribbean, Latin America, the United States, and internationally) and because of both the heterogeneous and homogeneous uses for which the term salsa has been deployed, it is imperative to summarize what has already been presented on the development of this music.

Indirectly, salsa music is one of those unacknowledged results of the Cuban revolution. As a specific historical-cultural expression, salsa was first produced during the 1960s in the Latina/o (mostly Puerto Rican) barrios of New York City. Puerto Rican working-class musicians had been avid listeners and students of the Latin popular music mostly performed by Cuban and Puerto Rican musicians during the 1950s at the Club Palladium: among others, Arsenio Rodríguez's mambo, Machito's Cubop, Mario Bauzá's wrongly labeled Latin jazz, the Puerto Rican Tito Puente's timbales, and the voice of the other Tito, Tito Rodríguez. While Latin music in New York during that decade had been heavily Cuban, after 1959, with the success of the Cuban revolution and with Fidel Castro's taking of Havana, Latin music in New York "would never be the same."[20] The embargo on Cuba and the censorship of Cuban music in the United States led to some years of void and confusion among Latin musicians in New York, creating the need to mix musical forms. It is this syncretic tendency in Latin popular music that characterizes salsa's historical genesis.[21]

It is this clearly identified Cuban influence or pretext for the emergence of salsa music that has led most Cuban musicians and artists—and Puerto Ricans like Tito Puente—to deny the existence of salsa as a music independent of Cuban rhythms and genres. Mario Bauzá, Guillermo Cabrera Infante, Pérez Prado, Jarrín, Tata Güines, and Olga Navarro, among others, define salsa as *only* an imitation of old Cuban music.[22] Moreover, Cuban musicologist Mayra Martínez denounces salsa music's commercialization as a capitalist strategy that benefits the U.S. musical industry given the isolation and commercial blockade imposed on Cuban musical products. In other words, salsa was the strategic international marketing of Cuban rhythms by an industry whose government purposefully obstructed the marketing of Cuban music internationally.[23]

Respectful of the Cuban perspective and sensitive to the harmful economic repercussions of U.S. embargos on the island, it is important, however, to indicate that these observations by Cubans about salsa tend to conflate this music exclusively with its original Cuban rhythms. By defining salsa as a marker of Cuban national identity and cultural production, these voices erase the participation of other Latin American national groups in the historical development of the music. In fact, if salsa music was born in New York in the early 1960s, then we must also credit a group of second-generation U.S. Puerto Rican musicians (Willie Colón, Héctor Lavoe, Ray Barretto, the Palmieri brothers) with some innovations and changes to the Cuban legacy as well as Venezuelan (Oscar De León), Colombian (Grupo Niche), Dominican (Johnny Pacheco), and Panamanian (Rubén Blades) musicians who have had a central impact on its development. According to Félix Padilla, the Puerto Rican musicians from the New York barrios not only continued and developed the legacy left by the Cuban musicians, they also renovated the old forms to express more adequately the reality of barrio life.[24] In fact, there was a recontextualization of Latin popular music from spectacle (that of the big band orchestras at the Palladium) to a music produced on the street corners of New York City's Latino barrios. The musicians as artistic subjects changed, as did the location of this music and its originally intended and ideal audience.

Salsa has been defined as syncretic music, "an amalgamation of Afro-Caribbean musical traditions centered around the Cuban son."[25] The *son*, described by Cuban writer Guillermo Cabrera Infante as the "phantom that traverses America," has constituted the musical style with most impact on U.S. Latin(o) music. The *son* has been traced to a secular musical dance form that originated in the rural areas of eastern Cuba (Oriente); it is characterized by a vocal melody independent from the percussive rhythm, and it was usually performed by a tres, a botija, and a marímbula. Cabrera Infante attributes the first *son* to a 1560 song by an African woman slave named Ma Teodora, whom he deems "the first female composer in America," although this original assumption by Alejo Carpentier has been refuted by musicologists.[26] Comparable to the African American blues, the *son* has served as the basic structure for future developments in Afro-Caribbean music and salsa. For Cabrera Infante, salsa orginated in the Cuban *son;* he traces the term *salsa* to "Echale salsita," an early *son* by Ignacio Piñeiro,[27] thus modifying Rondón's thesis of salsa's origins in New York to that of a "renaissance."[28] However, Cabrera Infante's reduction of salsa music to the Cuban *son* is corrected by Willie Colón, who asserts that "while the son has a specific structure, salsa is all freedom" [mientras el son tiene una estructura específica la salsa es todo libertad],[29] an observation that is more symbolic than descriptive of the particular structures of the *son* and of salsa music.

Cabrera Infante's disputable proposal in his article "Salsa for a Salad" defines salsa exclusively as the structural presence of the *son*, rendering invisible a myriad of other genres that constitute it: other traditional Afro-Cuban dance rhythms (the guaracha and the rumba), the African musical folklore of Puerto Rico (the bomba and the plena), and the harmonies, the improvised solos, and the metal instruments borrowed from African American jazz and blues. In contrast, Rondón has indicated the specific transformations that salsa musicians achieved vis-à-vis the music of the 1950s, which can be explained by the addition of the trombones to the salsa band, a change (already in place in Mon Rivera's music) systematized by Eddie Palmieri in his album *La Perfecta*. That particular salsa sound, a bitter, aggressive and hoarse texture changed Latin music from being "ostentatious to being war-like, aguerrida, there was no more pomp but violence; the thing, was definitely different."[30] In addition, Peter Manuel enumerates other stylistic distinctions, such as the use of the timbales, the "higher pitch range" of salsa vocal lines, the style of playing congas, and the elasticity of the clave rhythm.[31]

Unlike earlier Cuban music, the lyrics of salsa have documented the *visión de mundo* of the Latina/o (mostly Puerto Rican) working-class sector in New York City in the 1970s.[32] In the Caribbean, as César Miguel Rondón has documented, salsa also has functioned as the music of the urban poor, from Cuba to Puerto Rico to Cali and Cartagena, Colombia. That salsa originated in New York City is evidence that it was a social result of the gradual industrialization and migratory movements from rural areas to urban centers that have characterized many Latin American countries throughout the second half of the twentieth century.[33] In fact, the upsurge and boom of Latin music in the United States during the 1940s and 1950s would not have been possible without the configuration of a larger Latina/o audience and market made possible by the largest migratory wave among Puerto Ricans during World War II. The movement was organized by the U.S. and Puerto Rican governments to mitigate the economic stagnation of the island at the time and provide cheap labor for U.S. industries and factories.

Historically, then, salsa is the music of the immigrant and the urban working class. It is also the music produced mostly by black and mulatto musicians, and this racial definition ties it to the functions of the bomba and the plena in Puerto Rico as much as to the Afro-Cuban forms from which it also derives. As Rubén Blades has commented, "Salsa is urban folklore," for it constitutes itself as the oral tradition of life in the cities. Its lyrics continue the traditional role of the Puerto Rican plena, the Cuban *son*, the Colombian *vallenato*, and the Mexican *corrido*—the role of narrating historical events, local situations, and stories from the point of view of the marginalized. Salsa songs of the 1970s and 1980s documented the social infrahistory of Latinas/os in the United States and of the poor urban sectors in the Caribbean and throughout Latin America. It is not surprising, then, to find a wide array of themes and issues in salsa, a diversity that helps ensure its vitality. While much commercialized salsa repertoire has been influenced by the romantic ballad since the 1980s, and as such it appeals to individual relationships, the most important salseros—El Gran Combo de Puerto Rico, Willie Colón, Rubén Blades, Celia Cruz, Ismael Rivera, Ismael Miranda, Cheo Feliciano, Ray Barretto, Héctor Lavoe—have consistently responded to historical events and social issues that affect Latina/o communities. Despite the ideological differences between, for example, Rubén Blades and Celia Cruz, both interpreters speak to the collective realities of Latinas/os in the United States and in Latin America. Their songs either address race, gender, and class conflicts or reaffirm cultural practices usually marginalized, such as santería and other African-based traditions (since religion and music converged as counterhegemonic expressions during the colonial past).[34]

In conjunction, the prevalent democratizing cultural role of salsa musicians regarding the marginalized and the urban poor continues the liberatory practices of the maroon societies during colonial slavery periods in the Caribbean. Thus, salsa's alternative values are reaffirmed as a music tied to the history of the counterplantation cultures, analogous to Jamaican reggae and African American jazz and from which the Puerto Rican bomba emerged. Salsa songs such as Eddie Palmieri's "La libertad: Lógico" (Liberty: Of course) in his album significantly entitled *Vámonos pa'l monte* (Let's go to the hinterland), Rubén Blades's and Willie Colón's "Cimarrón" (Maroon), and others reaffirm this historical continuity lucidly proposed by Angel Quintero Rivera.[35]

CHAPTER FIVE

Ideological Negotiations
Between Hegemony and Resistance

✛

Opposition in Form

Puerto Rican historian Angel Quintero Rivera has identified several structural elements of salsa music as symbolic sites of liberatory values and of freedom. First, the "free and significant combination of forms"[1] that salsa represents, as illustrated in Ruben Bladés's hit "Tiburón." This song is characterized by smooth transitions from a rumba form to harmonic elements of the seis, a Puerto Rican traditional country music form associated with a strong sense of community and friendship. Quintero Rivera believes that the diversity of the song's musical forms and the usage of the seis as a subtext for communal values are the elements that allow a strongly antiimperialist song such as this to have been a popular hit for so long in Puerto Rico. Second, the *descargas* (jamming sessions) typical in salsa performances, according to Quintero Rivera, may be constructed as an instance of freedom. Exemplified in the percussion "bursts" of "Tiburón," the *descarga* is followed by the trombone or brass section and the cuatro, also embracing the other instruments in this manifestation of virtuosity and creativity.[2] In literature, Víctor Hernández Cruz's poem "Descarga en cueros" articulates the transformative and liberating potential of a jamming session through the hyperbolic imagery of dancing: "at the bar people's drinks flew out they hands the vibrations knocked people to the floor / & the lights began to bust / & the floor to crack . . . the floor began to rock people fell off the balcony / t.p. was smiling / his face ready to rip / o.k. you win / hands in the air ready to fly / heads outside beyond the buildings."[3]

Cruz's poem plays with the blurred boundaries between dancing, jamming, and social disturbance or violence. The perceptions that many cultural outsiders have of this type of music—that it is primitive, loud, chaotic, and subversive—constitute historical repetitions of the same vestigial fears expressed by the Spanish colonial government about the performance on drums by African slaves in Cuba, also evidenced in the banning of the merengue in Puerto Rico in the first half of the twentieth century. Thus, jamming sessions in urban centers around the Americas concretized spaces of opposition and counterculture, simultaneously connecting contemporary Latinas/os and African Americans to the liberatory practices of their slave antecedents and to the cimarrones's state of mind, a maroon conscience about their own contradictory freedom and bondage found in marginality.

The soneo, the long section of improvisation in any salsa song, also exemplifies "liberty and spontaneity."[4] The soneo is characterized by a call-and-response structure between singer and chorus (the instrumentalists), and as such it is a trait that represents continuity with older forms of Afro-Caribbean musical folklore and with West African music. It allows salsa music to articulate a collective voice in its chorus section and to establish a dialogic texture in its montuno section. When the singer improvises on the main theme of the song (the art of the soneo) he or she creates new utterances and also rearticulates and culls phrases from other songs of various traditions. The singer opens up a sonorous space of freedom, improvisation, and innovation, clinging simultaneously to musical tradition and reaffirming collective memory. This structure, perhaps the most creative aspect of salsa music, also allows the lead singer, or sonero, to intersperse political commentary or social criticism in a less blatant mode.

Contesting Theodor Adorno's earlier dismissal of the liberatory value of improvisation (accusing jazz improvisation of being normalized),[5] Roberta Singer's analysis of the role of improvisation in Latin popular music vindicates this practice. Improvisation for Latina/o musicians is a complex process, although not necessarily innovative, since it lies at the roots of Afro-Caribbean musical traditions. According to the Latin musicians interviewed by Singer, improvisation implies "an incorporation of all that one knows musically" and thus the quality of improvising is a function of the musician's repertoire. The more one knows, the more freedom he or she enjoys in choosing musical selections in their potential for combination. Improvisation also implies a sensitivity to nuances, for "if you know the nuances then even repetition is not repetitive."[6] As in other forms of popular music, improvisation in salsa contests the institutionalizing processes of musical education in the Western mind and world. Music educators have generally fostered and trained students to read music, insisting that such training is the only valid method for becoming a musician, but improvisation skills also require training and practice. This "differential" expertise, rarely valued and in fact repressed in conservatories and music programs, requires a different kind of training based on practice, ear, pitch, acuity in rhythm, and most important, a true sense of dialogue with other members of the group. A collective sound emerges from the dialectic balance of improvisatory freedom and formulaic entrenchment.

Ana Lydia Vega's feminist short story, "Letra para salsa y tres soneos por encargo" (Lyrics for a salsa song and three soneos by demand)[7] deploys the soneo as a liberatory literary structure that allows readers to "improvise" the ending of the story to best fit their own needs. The story is prefaced by "La vida te da sorpresas," the refrain of a Rubén Blades song, "Pedro Navaja," a refrain that signals a commitment on the part of musicians and writers alike to deconstruct social conventions reified by class, race, and gender boundaries.[8] "La vida te da sorpresas, sorpresas te da la vida" (Life is full of surprises, surprises make up life) is not merely humorous, as the performance of the song partly suggests, but stands as an articulation of Blades's commitment to raise the consciousness of his audience (both theatrical and musical) about the need to break away from social molds. In the dramatic production of "Pedro Navaja" (a cocolo version of *The Threepenny Opera*) that broke a record as the longest-running musical comedy in Puerto Rico, the actor/narrator walks down the aisle in a Brechtian mode singing the refrain.[9] Suddenly, he points at any individual in the audience and comments: "Your wife took off with the gardener" or "Your son turned out to be gay," examples of life circumstances that oblige individuals to reflect on and perhaps destabilize fixed gender identities, class divisions, and racial boundaries. They particularize the shock value of life.

"La vida te da sorpresas" prepares the reader for an analogous feminist deconstructive strategy by Ana Lydia Vega. In her short story, a Tipa [Gal] picks up a Tipo [Guy] in one of the best-known cruising areas in Santurce, Puerto Rico. After arriving at a motel room, he freaks out in the bathroom and is thus "indisposed," unable to perform or, in musical terms, *salsear*. Given the historical sexualization of Afro-Caribbean music, Vega's own strategic use of *salsear* as a musical metaphor for sexual relations points up the masculinist centrality of salsa as a marker of gender relations in Puerto Rican urban popular culture, while it simultaneously critiques and attempts to dismantle this privileged discursive gender positioning.

In this open-ended text, Vega offers the reader three alternative endings to the narrative situation, which she labels in the title as soneos. As in its musical development, in this literary appropriation and feminist rewriting of the soneo, the structural choice emphasizes the dialogic nature of the open text as well as the need for the free, improvisational, and active role of the reader in the resolution of the story. This implies, of course, that the discursive gendering underlying the characters' sexual expectations can only begin to be dismantled through linguistic acts themselves. Indeed, the first two soneos suggest a narrative closure through two parodic articulations of institutionalized rhetoric: the first, a Marxist discursive framework; the second, a feminist discourse through which "el acto queda equitativamente consumado"[10] (the act was consumed with equity). The third soneo, however, suggests an open and demythifying, deconstructive ending. In it the couple gets dressed and the Tipa drives the Tipo back to the streets, a masculine space yet also an open locus for negotiating modern urban identities.[11] Back on the street, the Tipo resumes his ritual of *piropos* (catcalls), the same phallocentric discourse that the Tipo used to pick up the Tipa at the beginning of the story (apparently, since it was she who took the initiative).

This last alternative ending, which proposes a circular structure, is key to Vega's feminist poetics of parody and irony. In contrast to the first two soneos, with their utopian view and highly rhetoricized language, the last soneo proposes a sort of liberation from discourse itself and from narrative closure. This freedom, however, rests on the reader's awareness of the Tipo's discursive and physiological impotence, now a deconstructed one that was previously masked and falsified by his male codes, his *piropos*. The Tipo now returns to his routine, yet this circular structure allows for the new awareness that female readers now possess: a consciousness of the ironic discrepancy between the Tipo's preliminary discourse, his pretext, and his actual incapacity to perform. The call-and-response structures of the soneo have afforded feminist literature a dialogic tool by which authors like Ana Lydia Vega can democratize, culturally speaking, the literary canon while simultaneously critiquing the rigid sexual roles articulated through salsa music itself.

Yet another oppositional element in salsa's texture—both musical and textual—is its dialogism, which extends itself beyond the innovation–tradition axis. As Bakhtin has defined it, dialogism occurs when one voice, a signifier, evokes its alien, opposite term, thus suggesting a multilayered reading of reality and of opposing meanings within one text. The heteroglossia that complements dialogism, the socially stratified multiple voices that constitute any society, are very much present in salsa music.[12] A wide array of social issues—race, poverty, drugs, sexual roles, class differences, religion, politics, and most recently, AIDS—are among some of the most common themes in contemporary salsa. Yet these issues are not limited to a singular perspective. For example, Rubén Blades's "Ligia Elena," an incisive social commentary on class and race prejudice in Latin America, as clearly oppositional as it is, allows the voices of the establishment to be expressed although in parodic tone:

Solo: Ligia Elena, la cándida niña de la sociedad,
se ha fugado con un trompetista de la vecindad,
El padre la busca afanosamente,
lo está comentando toda la gente
y la madre pregunta angustiada en dónde estará.

De nada sirvieron regaños, ni viajes ni monjas,
Ni las promesas de amor que le hicieran los niños de bien.
Fue tan buena la nota que dio aquella humilde trompeta
Que entre acordes de cariño eterno se fue ella con él.

Coro: Se han mudado a un cuarto chiquito con muy pocos muebles
y allí viven contentos y llenos de felicidad.
Mientras tristes los padres preguntan en dónde fallamos
Ligia Elena con su trompetista amándose están.

Solo: Dulcemente se escurren los días en aquel cuartito,
mientras que en las mansiones lujosas de la sociedad,
otras niñas que saben del cuento al dormir se preguntan
Ay, Señor, ¿y mi trompetista cuándo llegará?

Coro: Ligia Elena está contenta y su familia está asfixiá.

Solo: Se escapó con un trompeta de la vecindad (*coro*)
Se llevaron la niña del ojo del papá (*coro*)
En dónde fallamos pregunta mamá (*coro*)
Se colaron niches en la blanca sociedad (*coro*)
Pudo más el amor que el dinero, señor (*coro*)
Qué buena la nota que dio aquel [la] trompeta (*coro*)
Eso de racismo, brother, no está en na' (*coro*)
Deja que la agarre, nos jura el papá (*coro*)
Ligia Elena está llena de felicidad.

Voz papá: Le voy a enseñar. Yo la voy a agarrar. Yo la voy a agarrar.

Voz mamá: Mire, doña Gertrudis, le digo que estoy . . . , a mí lo que
más me . . . a mí lo que más me . . . a mí lo que más me choca es que esa
malagradecida, yo pensaba que me iba a dar un nietecito con los cabe-
llos rubios, así como Troy Donahue, y viene y se marcha con ese tuza
[gentuza]. Ay, la juventud!
(*coro*)

[*Solo*: Ligia Elena, the innocent little society girl,
has run off with the neighborhood trumpet player.
Her father looks for her zealously,
everyone's talking about it,
and her mother asks anxiously where could she be.

Scoldings aren't good for anything, neither trips nor nuns
Nor the love promises that the little rich boys made her.
The note was so good that that humble trumpet made
That between agreements of eternal endearments she took off with
him.

Chorus: They have moved to a small room with little furniture,
and there they live content and full of happiness.
Meanwhile her sad parents ask where they failed
Ligia Elena and her trumpet player are loving each other.

Solo: Sweetly fly the days in that small room,
while in the luxurious mansions of high society,
other girls that know the bedtime story ask themselves
Oh, God, and when will my trumpet player arrive?

Chorus: Ligia Elena is content and her family is asphyxiated.

Solo: She took off with a neighborhood trumpet player (*chorus*)
They carried the little girl off in front of her father's eyes (*chorus*)
Where did we go wrong asks her mother (*chorus*)
Blacks are invading our white society (*chorus*)
Love made possible what money could not, sir (*chorus*)
What a good note it was that sounded that trumpet (*chorus*)
That racism thing, brother, is not cool (*chorus*)
Let me get her, her father swears to us (*chorus*)
Ligia Elena is full of happiness.

Voice of the father: I'll teach her. I'm going to go get her. I'm going to
go get her.

Voice of the mother: Look, doña Gertrudis, I tell you that I am . . . to me
what most . . . to me what most . . . what most chokes me is that that
ungrateful, I thought that she was going to give me a little grandson
with a blond little head, like Troy Donahue, and yet she comes and
goes with that crowd. Ay, youth!
(*chorus*)]

The *montuno* part of "Ligia Elena" becomes a musical space in which singers evoke and reproduce the conflicting voices of Latin American society, whether they are sexual, racial, or class-based. In "Ligia Elena," indeed, the song narrates the story of a young white girl from the upper class who falls in love with a poor black trumpet player. She elopes with him, while her parents suffer the shock of such events. The bourgeois logic of the racial inferiority of blacks underlies the colonized and colonizing ideal expressed by her parents, the deferred dream of having blonde, blue-eyed grandchildren just like Troy Donahue, and the expectations regarding a white, racially exclusive upper-class sector ("Se colaron niches en la alta sociedad"). Yet these very voices of the dominant sector are interspersed with antiracist utterances that construct a utopian, integrated society symbolized visually by the progeny of this interracial couple. Rubén Blades's early productions, of which "Ligia Elena" is part, have correctly been deemed as oppositional and radical in their critiques of Latin American society, but "Ligia Elena" also indicates the important role that salsa's call-and-response structure plays in a dialogic text. This plural ideological voicing allows for a reception and acceptance that crosses class and racial lines.

In contrast to Blades's overt oppositional stance in Ligia Elena, Willie Colón's famous song about AIDS, "El gran varón" (The great male) employs an ambiguous refrain concerning homosexuality: "No se puede corregir a la naturaleza" [Nature cannot be corrected]. This refrain reaffirms, simultaneously, divergent ideological stances regarding sexual orientation, contingent on how one defines "nature." The song narrates the tragedy of a young Puerto Rican man who endures a rigid upbringing by his father. He later moves to New York, where he lives as a homosexual and transvestite. This "gran varón" dies of AIDS in a hospital, alone and rejected by his father, who had different expectations for him. While the song as a narrative text clearly expresses compassion and sympathy for the gay man, the refrain suggests plural ideologies. The semantic polyvalence of the term *nature* leads to a potential multiple axis around the definition of homosexuality. On one hand, it establishes a counterpoint with the narrative song: the refrain could very well be voiced by the father; the patriarchal stance is expressed in the rigidity (imagery of a tree trunk) of its perspective. Males should obey the nature of their biologically male bodies and should function as males. According to patriarchal rule, the nature of man is to embody maleness, the phallocentric function, and to follow the rules of religion and society in its heterosexual path. Thus, according to the father's design for his son, AIDS is interpreted as the punishment for ignoring nature's (read patriarchal) sexual dictates.

A second reading would imply that homosexuality is an expression of our sexual nature, and therfore, any attempts to change or "correct" it are doomed to fail. This reading would reaffirm the sympathy and compassion of the poetic voice toward the AIDS victim, but most important is the ambiguity saturating the term *nature*, which invites the listeners to rethink and to deconstruct social values as such. It literally denaturalizes the concept of nature from itself, exhorting us to redefine sexuality and our bodies as social constructs ideologically constituted. The two musical examples shown illustrate the profound connections between the dialogism of salsa's lyrics and its diverse ideological voicings, a trait that has allowed salsa to be acceptable also within the dominant sector.

In addition to the eclectic syncretism of salsa, its soneo and call-and-response structure, I propose that the polyrhythmic basis of Afro-Caribbean music embodied in the clave—a rhythmic pattern of 3-2 or 2-3 set against a 4-beat measure and performed by the clave sticks—is an equally oppositional and dialogic element in salsa.[13]

First, the clave rhythm offsets and displaces, creating a tension between the basic beat and the clave sound, a sort of syncopated push and pull that proves surprisingly difficult to perform. Said tension, I argue, resists what Theodor Adorno has labeled the "rhythmic-obedient" behavior on the part of listeners, whose "response to music immediately expresses their desire to obey." Adorno's response analysis and his tenets regarding popular music in his essay "On Popular Music" are motivated by a preoccupation about individual freedom highly threatened by Nazism. Thus, for him, following a song's rhythm and marking its basic time units created associations with "coordinated battalions of a mechanical collectivity," with obedience, repression, and ultimately, dehumanization in the age of the machine.[14]

While salsa simultaneously represents the age of technology and machine-produced music (by its integration of synthesizers, electric pianos, and bass), its clave rhythm and its polyrhythmia resist the *unidimensional* reproduction of the basic time unit. This polyrhythmia forms the basis for a musical dialogism among the various instruments of the combo, the type of band usually associated with salsa music and Latin popular music. In contrast to the harmonization patterns of the orchestra, to its centripetal convergence in the instrumentation, and to the dominance of the melody line—the material and symbolic embodiment of musical expectations in the Western world and the bourgeois ego[15]—the combo or salsa band thrives on a simultaneous diversity of rhythms; on a melody line that is shared by the singer, the instrumentalists (as chorus), and the audience; and on arrangements that protect the independent creativity of each instrument.

It is true that much of salsa, like any genre of popular music, is based on certain melodic and harmonic formulas, a *standardization* of musical structures that, according to Adorno, leads to a false sense of *familiarity* in the audience and that ultimately, homogenizes and massifies their individuality into a set, standard response.[16] Yet within the context of Puerto Rican migration and cultural displacement experienced by U.S. Latinas/os, formulas and standardization represent very different, in fact, distinguishing values. The repeated melodies, rhythms, riffs, and instrumentation provide a sense of familiarity to the displaced community of listeners and an auditive, sensorial instance for reconstructing the cultural self and collective memory (as George Lipsitz has already documented in U.S. popular music[17]). As transitory as this experience may be, it counteracts the colonialist fragmentations with the past, with nation and homeland.

A Puerto Rican woman in southeastern Michigan who has felt very isolated from her island culture expressed the comfort triggered by the mnemonic elements of salsa music. After listening to a song by Willie Colón that reproduces many lyrical structures of the bolero, she reacted by saying that she had not really paid attention to the lyrics of the song, which dealt with a man asking of a woman total remembrance of his role as her sexual teacher, but that the listening experience—the musical sounds, notes, instrumentation, and melodic repetitions—had evoked in her a chain of sensorial associations and memories of her childhood in Puerto Rico: "No el significado, pero la música me recuerda a Puerto Rico. Tan pronto oí eso, podía oir las sábanas tendidas al viento. Y podía oler las flores en la noche en la isla, y podía ver a mi mamá. Me recuerda a Puerto Rico" [Not the meaning, but the music reminds me of Puerto Rico. As soon as I started listening, I could hear the sheets swaying in the wind. And I could smell the flowers at night on the island, and I could see my mother. This song reminds me of Puerto Rico].

These phrases, most revealing of the multisensorial associations that the act of listening provokes (listening, smelling, seeing) stand as a compelling testimony to the role of salsa music as a bridge between a trans- or dislocated present and a past home. Thus, the sense of familiarity that these formulas evoke for colonized peoples, such as Puerto Ricans and Latinas/os in the United States, should be valued differently from what Adorno's negative analysis presupposes. Adorno considered the enjoyment of repetition as "psychotic and infantile," an association clearly informed by his "pseudo-primitivist view of African American-derived music,"[18] but all music, as an art in and of time, is structured in repetition. Moving beyond Richard Middleton's own revisiting of repetition—"Why do listeners find interest and pleasure in hearing the same thing over again, and what kind of interest and pleasure are they?"[19]—the role of repetition in salsa music for U.S. Latinas/os needs to be framed within postcolonialism. These repetitions, both musematic and discursive,[20] cushion the break with a past erased by the colonizers and offer a sense of self and collective knowledge that allows an inside listener to establish a meaningful sense of the self in the world, as well as accumulated instances of cultural reaffirmation that wholly constitute cultural resistance. This important function of salsa is seen particularly in the U.S. Puerto Rican and Latina/o diaspora, as interpreted in continuity with the historical past of liberatory struggles that Angel Quintero Rivera has proposed.

Politically, then, the musematic repetition in call-and-response structures, the discursive repetition in salsa's intertextuality throughout the improvisatory soneos, and the performative expectations and values of the combo constitute the material embodiment of a plural, nonindividualist (read anticapitalist), yet free site of artistic expression, a multivoiced locus, musically speaking. The case of salsa music, then, invites music scholars to rethink theories of repetition, not just as structures that trigger individual pleasure or ego building but as a convergence of politics and pleasure—the pleasure of cultural mnemonics, of reconstructing the past and reconnecting it to the present through musical signifiers.

Mass Media and Salsa

The tensions between hegemony and resistance in salsa music stem basically from its modes of production and dissemination. For better or for worse and unlike its folkloric antecedents transmitted orally, salsa, like all contemporary popular music, is a part of mass culture.[21] The term itself illustrates the close relationship between the music and the recording industry. The label *salsa*, applied by Fania Records to Latin popular music in the United States, literally translates as "sauce" and suggests the spicy, hot elements needed for good Latin cooking and dancing. Tracing the trajectory of the term is a discursive process worth the effort, for it clearly reveals the underpinnings of salsa music as a tool for imagining social identity. Cubans and Puerto Ricans alike have disagreed with the commercial label employed by Fania All Stars. Yet while Guillermo Cabrera Infante traces the controversial and elusive term to Ignacio Piñeiro's authorship, Rafael Ithier, an original member as well as director and pianist of El Gran Combo de Puerto Rico, suggests that it is analogous to "soul" in the U.S. context. Izzy Sanabria, a Puerto Rican musical promoter in New York and founder of *Latin New York*, has been credited by many for coining the term in 1973 during his TV show, *Salsa*. He in turn credits the people who were using it to refer to the music and its rhythms. In addition, Max Salazar recognizes Cal Tjader for employing the term in his 1964 recording "Soul Sauce."

Rafael Cortijo in the past and many progressive Latinas/os nowadays have rejected this term for its colonizing and capitalist associations. As Jorge Duany has observed, the fact that the salsa label "has even been extended to the music of any 'Latin' country" is evidence of its homogenizing effects.[22] That salsa emerges as an umbrella term for an undifferentiated view of a diverse gamut of Latin musical genres unveils the capitalist efforts to erase Latin cultural specificity and to depoliticize much of its social and historical opposition.

Fania's attempts to create a larger market for salsa music was, ironically, the reason for its demise. The earlier film produced by Fania, *Nuestra Cosa* (Our Thing), portrays salsa as a music born from the jamming sessions on the street corners of the barrios in New York and reaffirms the close connections between the music and audience participation. Later, however, in order to sell this ethnic music to a mainstream market, Fania produced the film *Salsa*, problematic in its explanation of salsa's genesis as stemming from Africa via Hollywood. When CBS bought Fania's international distribution and production rights in 1976, Fania decided to "shift the tonic"[23] and produced two albums—*Delicate and Jumpy* (1976) and *Rhythm Machine* (1977)—that were total failures in sales. This attempt to "Americanize" salsa included taping the Latin musicians and then adding a set of drums, electric guitar, and the metals, muting the strident and aggressive sounds of salsa to gratify the different, softer tastes of a general population. The decline of Fania had already begun, despite their attempts to recover immediately afterward by hiring Rubén Blades as a singer. And while it is obvious that the music industry in the United States has benefited tremendously from the production and commercialization of Latin music, the relationship between the recording industry and the salseros' musical creativity is much more complex than a Manichaean view.

Cubans have systematically denounced salsa as a politically motivated commercialization and thus a dilution of Cuban rhythms and musical forms. However, it is also true that, as John Shepherd observes, "discourses constructed around the opposed notions of authenticity and commercialism have posed a considerable problem in understanding musical signification."[24] To reify salsa music as merely a victim or object of hegemony is virtually to preempt its powers for creativity, cultural resistance and reaffirmation, and possibly social change. And to sort salsa music as either "commercial" or "sociopolitical" is, again, another reifying practice that takes into account only the moment of initial production or the isolated text and that fails to consider listening practices and the larger sociopolitical context within which a musical performance is embedded.[25] As subsequent chapters will show, the production of meaning, the process of signification in cultural acts, cannot be traced uniquely to a fixed text but will vary according to an array of extra- and intratextual factors. Moreover, to identify one particular song as "commercial" and another one (usually Rubén Blades's) as "sociopolitical" is also to create a politically correct canon of "good" and "bad" music out of a complex and diverse sociomusical practice that resists such categorization. A Rubén Blades song may be a "good" song politically, but it is as much a commercial specimen of salsa as "Rhythm Machine," produced by Fania, or any of Eddie Santiago's pieces of erotic salsa.

Félix Padilla (1990) has proposed that "salsa music represents a social process mediated by forms of domination and resistance—that is, a process through which human agents constantly interact with, shape, and respond to objective forces which represent aspects of the broader social structure of the Latin music recording business."[26] He explains that while the "persisting competition that existed among recording companies contesting for the Latin music market" led to innovations in Latin music, simultaneously "the rise of a new class of Puerto Rican musicians . . . recognized the need to produce an alternative style to the popular Latin music of earlier periods which they perceived as being out of touch with the Puerto Rican barrio reality."[27] Thus, for Padilla, the dialectic between the hegemonic interests of the recording industry and the expression of resistance motivated by the social conditions of Puerto Ricans in New York explains the genesis of salsa. Ironically, the hegemonic interests of the music industry dovetailed then with the innovations necessary to voice the social unrest of the historical moment and the emerging ethnic awareness of Puerto Ricans in New York.

This does not suggest, however, that the strategies of the recording industry have not adversely affected salsa. As composer Willie Colón has noted, certain "códigos del mercado" [market codes] limit his creativity and experimentation. For instance, according to these market codes, many of which can be traced back to those established by Tin Pan Alley in the earlier part of the century, a song can last only four minutes, and this boundary, for Colón, seriously limits the possibilities of composing longer pieces and songs through which social issues could be portrayed in more profound and complex ways. In fact, Colón mentions the difference in popularity of certain of his songs based on this length criterion. Some of his long songs have been hits in Latin America, yet in the United States they have been basically ignored.[28]

Peter Manuel has convincingly shown that majors (major recording companies) and corporate conglomerates, such as Coca-Cola (previous owner of Columbia Records) and CBS, have exerted considerable pressure on New York City radio stations to devote more time to easy-listening and romantic pop ballads to the detriment of salsa's and merengue's popularity.[29] Singers like Julio Iglesias and José Feliciano "were given more airplay."[30] "Plugging" mechanisms that Adorno denounced in the 1940s are alive and well, as well as the payola practice: paying off disc jockeys for playing specific interpreters or songs. The political control of radio listening is effective when one considers that "98 percent of Hispanics in the United States listen to more than thirty hours of radio a week."[31] The monopoly of Anglo-owned corporations and the increasing trends toward "networkization" have facilitated this shift from salsa and merengue to easy listening and pop romantic ballads. The oligopolistic power of corporations and Anglo ownership of radio stations has successfully shifted the dissemination of Latin popular music, thus determining listening practices for Hispanic audiences.

Ironically, Manuel also documents the unflagging popularity of salsa and merengue in New York City's dancing clubs, in contrast to the pop romantic ballad of the manipulated radio formats. The centripetal, unifying, and homogenizing tendencies of the capitalist music industry are evident in these attempts to subvert and erase the centrifugal, plural, and oppositional textures and voices of salsa. An executive quoted by Peter Manuel was on target when he exclaimed that "the romantic ballad unifies the market, and salsa divides it."[32] It is clear, then, that salsa holds a socially "divisive/disruptive" potential (read oppositional) that the recording industry has not erased or neutralized yet, despite its best attempts. The fact that a corporate executive publicly attests to this power suggests that the oppositionality of salsa is neither a popular generalization nor a utopian desire on the part of progressive cultural critics.

Dancing to Salsa

Salsa is dancing music, and as such it escapes being disseminated only through the radio or the CD. Thus, while commercialization has definitely resulted in the production of trivial lyrics and in part has allowed salsa to become an object of passive listening or mere distraction, this music transcends reification by maintaining direct interaction with its audience and with the Latina/o community. The economic marginalization of salsa musicians, local groups, and younger bands obliges them to perform at private events such as weddings and family celebrations and in smaller Latin dancing clubs, thus maintaining a more direct contact with their local communities and audiences. Even big names such as Tito Puente and Willie Colón accept local gigs and perform for free at barrio street festivals. Celia Cruz also observes that most salsa gigs are limited to the weekends, since the Latina/o community, as a predominantly working-class sector, does not always enjoy the luxury of engaging in entertainment activities during the week.[33]

Like other forms of popular dancing, dancing to salsa may be analyzed by using Iaian Chambers's observations, such as: "the fundamental connection between the pleasures of the sound and their social realization in the libidinal movement of bodies, styles and sensual forms. It represents a social encounter, which can be a dance hall, a club, or a party, where bodies are permitted to respond to physical rhythms that elsewhere would not be tolerated; the moment when romanticism brushes against reality, and a transitory step out of the everyday can be enjoyed."[34]

Dancing to salsa music fulfills the roles outlined above, but these are informed by a very specific sociopolitical context. The observations of Latinas and Latinos interviewed for this study definitely support the escapist or cathartic function of dancing, yet this role is underlined by the class-based realities of this disenfranchised sector within the United States. Dancing to salsa music is, needless to say, a sensual experience; however, this sensuality is mediated constantly in various ways, whether defined and articulated by Latinas/os themselves or by cultural others. Finally, Chambers's observation of dancing as a "social encounter" is doubly significant given the socioeconomic and colonial situation of Latinas/os in the United States.

Edgardo Díaz Díaz's ethnographic study of a dance club in Austin, Texas, constitutes the most systematic study focused on the social meanings of dancing to an Afro-Caribbean musical repertoire.[35] Díaz's study "El repertorio de salsa en dos perspectivas genéricas" (The repertoire of salsa according to two gender perspectives) provides two important approaches to this sociocultural event. First, it analyzes the social values and meanings of the repertoire through a transcription of the musical selections that are codified according to issues of national identity, race, gender, class, and ethnicity. Díaz shows how musicians structure the order of songs performed, the flexibility of that order contingent on audience response, and the predominant role of salsa songs in that structuring, informed, in turn, by the various rhythmic speeds that each musical form represents. Thus, salsa songs begin and close each set, and merengues and boleros are interspersed throughout.[36] The musical transcript of the dance club reveals how dancing to Latin music constitutes a social event in which certain traditional values are reaffirmed and simultaneously inverted. For instance, musicians constantly reaffirm the various national identities of a pan-Latina/o audience, as particular songs from Puerto Rico, Colombia, Mexico, Cuba, the Dominican Republic, and Venezuela evoke expressions of national pride among individuals. Issues of racial affirmation of blackness and mulatto identity also come to the fore through songs such as "Moreno soy" (I am dark). Most visible, however, is the role of dances in creating a social space for negotiating gender roles and expectations. Díaz's analysis, for instance, of how women are objectified and represented in songs such as "La faldita" (The tiny skirt) and publicly alluded to as *traidoras* (traitors) by the MC is unique and central to our understanding of gender constructs dominated by a patriarchal society.

Most interesting in this regard are Díaz's observations about the double standards underlying the expected behavior of men and of women within the social space of the club. While going dancing has been defined as a cultural space where freedom and pleasure[37] are enjoyed beyond the social dictates of everyday life, Latino men enjoy a higher degree of freedom in publicly expressing sexual desire and erotic behavior than that accorded to women. In fact, men are expected to engage in drinking and to act out of control, whereas women have to behave in acceptable and contained ways, particularly when dancing. Thus, while going dancing establishes a space outside social dictates, normative and naturalized gender expectations still inform the different ways men and women engage in such pleasure and freedom and in the movement of their bodies.

José Limón's unique ethnographic approach to dancing to Tex-Mex music in a working-class night club called El Cielo Azul also reveals the power differentials that position men and women as they enter the space of the dance club. While Beatriz, Limón's key informant, revealed that she liked to dance and attended dances quite frequently, she also confessed that she doesn't "enjoy dances" because of the sexual expectations that men establish after dancing with women. "Usually she doesn't even get dinner, and *they* all want something," summarizes Limón.[38] Limón's key male informant, in contrast, asserts that "me cae chingos bailar" [I like dancing a fuck of a lot] (Limón's translation) and that he tries not to miss any weekend dances, an attitudinal discrepancy that suggests the ongoing objectification of women's bodies despite the carnavalesque, potential freeing of bodies that has been idealistically ascribed to dancing by cultural critics.[39]

Echoing the same dialectics between containment and freedom of women's bodies, in a larger, cultural context, salsa's polyrhythmia directly stimulates the centrifugal movement of our bodies. Despite articulatory efforts by producers and the entertainment industry to recontextualize salsa into concert music, to contain it into music to be *only* listened to, unidirectionally consumed as another commodity, salsa concertgoers will notice that whenever a Latina/o audience is present, there is dancing in the aisles and in any available open space within the confines of the theater or auditorium. This practice, consistently repressed by security guards for supposed reasons of safety codes, reveals, on the one hand, the profound relationship between salsa music, the cultural collectivity of dancing, and our bodies as social sites. On the other, it attests to Latinas/os' resistance to salsa's commodification through its strategic, physical insertion and cultural containment within the dominant spaces of concert halls and auditoriums.

Many Latinas and Latinos, particularly those in the United States, ascribe a social, cultural, and political value to dancing to Latin popular music. As José Limón asks himself in his ethnographic notes on dancing to Tex-Mex music, at this point I also ask "why pure dancing is political."[40] Yet unlike Limón's theoretical incursion, partly based on Randy Martin's analysis of art dance in New York and partly on his own rewriting of Jamesonian definitions of postmodernism from the vantage point of working-class Chicanas/os in South Texas, I choose to draw on the testimonies of Latinas in the United States as they accord their own meanings to this sociocultural practice within the framework of colonization and migration. While, in *Dancing with the Devil*, Limón more systematically discusses dancing to polkas in relation to "dance form as politics," he quotes Randy Martin when he asserts that dance "is a decidedly non-symbolic and non-signifying politics" and that dance acts as the artful and deeply satisfying production of a desire that, Martin says, is present but usually not acted on in society, "the desire to act politically."[41] In view of his previous discussion of postmodernity as it affects the personal, everyday lives of working-class Chicanas/os, Limón suggests that "this artful control over the effects of a negating, postmodernist climate is what Mexicanos achieve in their dancing."[42] For him, dancing to a polka is a "residual" element of Chicana/o culture culled from past traditions that offsets the dehumanizing effects of a late capitalism postmodernity.

Unlike Limón's ethnographic subjects, somehow muted by the overarching discourse of Jamesonian theory and by Limón's self-reflexive personal narrative, the voice of a working-class U.S. Puerto Rican woman from Detroit expresses the clearly conscious desire to act politically through dancing to Latin music: "I like to go to dances, yes, I like music at dances. The last dance that I went to was The Gran Combo's, and I liked it. . . . Yeah, it was nice! I was raised, yes . . . here in the U.S. But I was raised in a Latino environment. The food I eat is Latin, my music is Latin, my surroundings are Latin. So . . . I am Latina and since I was small I always loved that environment . . . and I won't give it up now nor when I get older. . . . dancing is part of my identity."[43]

Also revealing is the testimony of a middle-aged Mexican-American woman who viewed dancing as a cultural practice that differentiated her from her husband, an Anglo man who did not like to dance: "Cuando tengo un chance me escapo al Diamante Azul y ahí bailo. Antes de mudarme . . . Oh! sí . . . iba más seguido a los bailes. Sin mi marido, porque él es americano y no baila. Cuando voy a bailes me siento muy alegre" [When I have a chance, I escape to the Blue Diamond club and there I dance. Before I moved . . . oh, yes . . . I used to go more frequently to dances. Without my husband, because he is Anglo and he doesn't dance. When I go to dances I feel very happy]. For her, going dancing at El Diamante Azul in Detroit was meaningful not only as a practice that reaffirmed her cultural difference from that of her husband but as a gesture that simultaneously destabilized her gender-based dependence as a married woman, as the choice of the verb "me escapo" [I escape] clearly reveals. Moreover, this woman also commented on one occasion, when she went dancing with fifteen other women to celebrate her daughter's birthday: "Fuimos a un lugar donde había música . . . y éramos como quince mujeres. Estábamos bailando con una y otra, como locas . . . pero estábamos bailando [We went to this place where they played music . . . and we were about fifteen women. We were dancing with each other, like crazies . . . but we were dancing]. As Leslie Gotfrit observes regarding the contestatory value of women "dancing back," that is, dancing with each other on the dance floor of a systemic masculine and hegemonic space—the dancing club—this space is "appropriated for women's use," "exclusively for women's pleasure, control, and solidarity."[44] It is revealing, as well, that the Mexican-American mother refers to this experience as being "como locas" (like crazies), indeed locating themselves outside the boundaries of social rules and expectations, within a Bakhtinian carnavalesque space. The freedom afforded to these women by music and by the dancing space, although temporary, is profoundly meaningful as another strategy for gender survival and, even more, for an instance of gender bending in the absence of men.

The cultural self-consciousness and reflexivity about the value of music and rhythm among working-class Latinas/os threads through Willie Colón's testimony about the important emotional associations that he established through music and rhythms while growing up in a Puerto Rican barrio in New York. The rhythms and the presence of musical instruments at night and even during the day reaffirmed, in a most nurturing way, his sense of cultural identity. "The rhythms protected us," he observed in regard to the continuity of a collective sensorial experience articulated through the drumming on the streets every night.[45] In many cases, this political awareness cuts across class lines. Most of my Latina/o students in courses on popular music have reaffirmed the serious political value and cultural urgency underlying their identification with salsa music. This process of signifying, of producing meaning and reaffirming cultural identity and boundaries through the music, stands in sharp contrast to the controversial and much discussed "intoxicating" effects that some Anglo students have described to me in their intercultural experience of dancing to salsa music.

For many working-poor Latinos and Latinas, going dancing on a weekend night to the music of El Gran Combo de Puerto Rico or Las Chicas del Can or Eddie Santiago or Andy Montañez is not a limited or limiting form of "distraction"[46] or entertainment, as Adorno sees it but more clearly proposes a space liberated from the harsh realities of work and social injustice, that "transitory step out of the everyday" that Iain Chambers described. Four working-class Latinas in southeastern Michigan asserted in the interviews that dancing and music, together, allowed them to "forget" their worries, the "present," and any "problems." In fact, one woman clearly summarized this phenomenon by stating that when she was younger, in Latin America, she would go dancing "to escape from the poverty of every day" [para escaparme de la pobreza de cada día]. This need was so strong that, as she recounted, she was willing to be punished by her mother for attending dances without her permission. "Tres horas bailando para media hora de castigo" [half an hour of punishment for three hours of dancing] was worth her while.

Of course, neither this class-based motivation for musical entertainment, nor the young woman's defiance of family mores in order to socialize is exclusive to the Latina/o culture. Yet as a collective activity, for many Latinos and Latinas in the United States dancing symbolizes the recuperation of a national space and locus lost in the historical disseminations that migrations have represented. Within the social frame of cultural displacement and migration, dancing represents a time and a space for reaffirming culture through reenactments of those elements "lost" to the dominant culture: the use of Spanish lyrics, the racial familiarity, and the familiar sounds of a combo consisting of traditional instruments such as the güiro, bongos, tumbadora and maracas, instruments that take the audience back to their countries of origin and to the sounds of past social celebrations and daily life. Even for young upper- and middle-class Puerto Rican women who did not identify with this music while growing up in Puerto Rico, salsa becomes a cultural symbol once they "migrate," mostly to college life in the United States or as part of the "brain drain" phenomenon, crossing class and racial lines as they become "ethnified" or minority subjects within U.S. culture.

Thus, the dialectics between modernism and postmodernism that José Limón deploys in his analysis of popular dancing among Texas Mexicans are a dynamic force among the Puerto Rican women interviewed, for whom dancing is a clearly articulated political act. In fact, the modernist stance of unifying the past and the present, the "residual" tradition that Limón evokes, may be read in this context as a strategy of cultural survival and resistance and quite a creative one at that. The political value of dancing for Latinas/os may be connected to the strong, historical association of Afro-Caribbean music with dance. The collective significance of dancing, both in secular contexts and in religious rituals, has not been disrupted by migration nor colonization but rather reaffirmed. In light of the dwindling public spaces in major U.S. cities, *pistas de baile* (dance floors) surely serve as a substitute, even when the clubs themselves are privately owned.

While the practice of dancing to Latin popular music presupposes a phenomenology and a politics that need to be further explored, the desires and pleasures of the body as social site cannot be divorced from the colonial displacements that migration has created for many U.S. Latinas/os. For white women, as Leslie Gotfrit proposes, dancing to rock music at a club in Toronto is a contradictory cultural practice that can signify opposition to the systematic social repression of women's bodies and sensuality while it simultaneously signals a consent to hegemonic, heterosexist objectification of women's bodies. Comparatively speaking, in salsa the presence of the heterosexual couple on the dance floor marks a clear complicity with the social structures that perpetuate inequities in gender politics. For Latinas, however, while a soft bolero allows for erotic play and "the pleasure of unknown possibilities,"[47] this intimacy is established within the culturally significant larger space of the dance floor, which maps the ideal space of a cohesive cultural praxis, of solidarity.

Thus, two dialectic forces simultaneously characterize the bolero or other dance forms in which the independent heterosexual couple are intimately embraced or intertwined. If there is a sense of cultural solidarity created vis-à-vis outside forces, there is also, despite the surface appearance of the unity of the couple—in José Limón's poetic phrase, "como si fueran uno"[48]—an underlying gender conflict fueled by the gender-inflected domination of the male who "leads" and controls the woman's body. The centripetal bodily tension invoked by the Latin American romantic ballad, the bolero, may not signal resistance overtly; yet the musical sounds, the melodies and instruments together, activate, in Gotfrit's words, an "incredible longing" that is not only metaphysical or individually based, as Gotfrit deploys it here, but clearly political, as the Latinas' testimonies recorded above have affirmed.[49]

In contrast to the slow rhythms of the bolero, the centrifugal movements of a fast guaracha rhythm may serve as a liberating form of release, as a polymorphous sense of being in space, an experience of movement that is not exclusive to salsa dances (as Gotfrit states in her reference to dancing to rock music).[50] In a most poetic passage from *La importancia de llamarse Daniel Santos*, Luis Rafael Sánchez has described this contrast between the bolero and the guaracha, the two basic rhythms alternately performed by salsa groups. They encapsulate, in a musically symbolic way, the Bakhtinian tensions between the centrifugal and centripetal forces of cultural and discursive processes.

Opuestos que se armonizan las diferencias son el bolero y la guaracha. Y en el dinamismo de esa oposición el Caribe instituye su bandera—el Caribe suena, suena. Curváceo pronunciamiento o teoría y práctica del barroco es la guaracha. Inquieta por definición, incisiones prontas a las vueltas, acumulaciones eróticas que se esfuman mientras se formalizan: ahí está la guaracha. Lineal combinación que envasa su clasicismo y lo practica es el bolero. Quieto por definición, de ocurrencia bailable en la cuadrada eternidad de una loseta, sincrónica la tensión que lo embellece, acumulaciones eróticas que se concretan en una suspensión de fragilidades: ahí está el bolero. La guaracha es la cacería trepidante. El bolero es el festín del cazador y la presa. La guaracha abre el cuerpo, autoriza el desplazamiento, muestra en diligentes remeneos las partes más deseables, los tramos a humedecer, los estrechos a despulpar. El bolero cierra el cuerpo, prohibe el desplazamiento, reduce la rotación a la tentativa de una muerte vivificante. En la guaracha se extravierten las felicidades, las pasiones se ajotan de un bando y otro, se aleluyan el placer y el amor. En el bolero se recluyen las felicidades, los cuerpos se atesan y se atizan, se aleluyan el placer y el amor.[51]

[Opposites that harmonize their differences are the bolero and the guaracha. And within the dynamics of this opposition, the Caribbean hoists its flag—the Caribbean sings, it sings. Curved pronouncement of the baroque, theory and practice of the baroque, that is the guaracha. Restless by definition, elusive when persecuted like the will-of-the-wisp, incisions quick to turn around, erotic accumulations that disappear while they take on a form, that is the guaracha. Lineal combination that contains its own classicism and puts it into practice, that is the bolero. Still by definition, it can be danced within the eternity of a floor tile, with a synchronic tension that beautifies it, erotic accumulations concretized by suspended fragilities: that is the bolero. The guaracha is the vibrating hunt. The bolero is the feast of the hunter and hunted. The guaracha opens our bodies, it authorizes displacement; through diligent wiggling, it exhibits the most desirable parts, the sections to be wet, the straits to be pulped. The bolero encloses the body, prohibits displacement, reduces rotations to the intent of a life-giving death. In the guaracha, joys are extroverted, passions fly from one side to another, pleasure and love become aleluyas. In the bolero, joys are confined, the bodies are smoothed yet aroused, pleasure and love become aleluyas.]

The multiple pleasures of the text reside in the sensorial and rhythmical pleasure of Luis Rafael Sánchez's inverse images of the guaracha and the bolero, a pleasure parallel to the nonsignifying pleasures of the rhythms and sounds of the music itself and of the act of dancing. Sánchez revels in the erotic descriptions of both rhythms: the guaracha is the prelude, the hunt, and the bolero is the erotic consummation, the feast of the senses (although by itself it is also a prelude to sexual encounter). Yet within this glorified discourse of a heterosexual practice such as the bolero, Luis Rafael Sánchez subversively rewrites the heterosexuality of these dances with the word *ajota*, which suggests the underlying presence of *joto*, a derogatory word in Spanish that refers to gay men. This reappropriation of the heterosexual pleasures that salsa music offers suggests how writers like Sánchez and Vega, analyzed above, are appropriating popular cultural practices like dancing, and rewriting them with oppositional values that radicalize gender politics and the hegemony of heterosexual paradigms.

A scene in María Novaro's film *Danzón* (1991) elicits a differential rewriting of this dance from heterosexist dominant paradigms when Suzy, Julia's transvestite friend, asks her to teach her(him) how to dance the danzón. After rehearsing the basic steps, Julia teaches Suzy how to hold her, using the traditional heterosexual language of "la pareja." Julia asks Suzy to hold her "like a man"; "agárrame como hombre, que con los dedos yo me sienta que tú me mandes, me ordenas." [hold me like a man, so that your fingers make me feel that you are the one in charge, that you tell me what to do]. Yet Suzy cannot identify with the male role and asks Julia to teach her "like a woman" so that (s)he can understand. The aesthetics of the heterosexual couple, a code that Julia respects and in which she finds meaning, becomes, in this scene, null and meaningless. Julia's heterosexist discourse—"la pareja," "la dama," "como hombre," "lo bonito, lo sublime de la pareja"—is ironically juxtaposed to the visual markers of a man and a woman dancing, yet given Suzy's transvestism, it becomes a destabilized and doubly ironic image of a "couple." This ironic displacement is even more meaningful when we consider that it is only through dancing the danzón that Julia, throughout her life, had been able to express her own sexuality and desires as a heterosexual woman. Her observations to Suzy about the role of subtle eye contact during the dancing act, of that indirect, oblique eroticism that characterizes sexual dialogue and the aesthetics of the danzón, reveal Julia's agency and mastery in the erotics of the dance, a role exclusively activated in the parenthetical space of dancing with Carmelo Benítez, her dancing partner for six years, who mysteriously disappears at the beginning of the movie.[52]

In his poetry, Víctor Hernández Cruz has also explored the empowerment suggested in centrifugal dancing movements, from the recognition and acknowledgment of one's own power to the subversive sense of rhythm as "ammunition," as a disturbing transgression to the social order, analogous to what boom boxes, cocolos, and rappers have represented to the peace-loving middle-class.[53] As I have analyzed in a previous piece, the centrifugal movements of salsa dancing imply a going out of oneself, the creation of an alternative space, a state of mind that may function as therapeutic or political liberation. In the past, authorities were very well aware of these potentials, as the rumba, the drumming, and the merengue were prohibited in the colonial societies of the Caribbean.

Through the readings and rewritings of music by literary writers, the testimonies of Latinas and Latinos, and the deployment of a postmodern analysis of popular dancing as cultural practice, this interdisciplinary incursion reveals that to limit the values of dancing, as Adorno did, to a parenthetical space of nothingness or to a trivializing function of entertainment, is to elide the potential power of a social and collective praxis that creates "multiple pleasures" and that, depending on its subjects, may be profoundly meaningful or rather insignificant.

CHAPTER SIX

Cultural (Mis)Translations and Crossover Nightmares

✛

In her lucid analysis of "Women Dancing Back," Leslie Gotfrit refers us to dance as an activity that contests the split between "body and mind" that has ensued from the binary logic of Western culture. Unlike the mind, the body is "crucial to any oppositional politics," and dance allows for the possibility of "a re-integration of mind and body."[1] However, the general human and collective value of dancing, of course, is not exclusive to salsa music nor to Latin culture. I have stressed the importance of Latin dancing as cultural resistance and, following Víctor Hernández Cruz's poems, cultural acknowledgment; these functions are activated, for Latinas/os, within the complex colonial conditions under which they produce and consume culture.

Yet it seems that this "state of disembodiment," this radical fissure between body and mind that Gotfrit analyzes, informs Anglo constructs of salsa music. Perceptions by Anglos of Latin musical culture in the United States reveal an eroticized reading, a sort of tropicalization, that is not limited to the field of music but significantly recognizes the "human" aspect of Latina/o dancing vis-à-vis the presupposed technologizing and dehumanizing practices of contemporary Anglo popular music and of the Western world. A November 4, 1991, *Newsweek* article titled "Crossover Dreamers" concludes with such a view: "That is the sanctuary Latin music offers U.S. audiences—it is still played by human hands and danced by couples who can look into each other's eyes when they do it. Whether you like salsa or not, artists like Guerra have preserved more than just the mambo tradition. They've held onto a way of making music that the world is fast losing and would be much worse without."[2]

Fraught with historical confusion (Juan Luis Guerra performs more merengues and bachatas than salsa or even mambo) and conflating musical forms, nonetheless these observations identify a nostalgic, pretechnology stage of music that assumedly redeems salsa from the depersonalized musical practices of industrialized societies. This primitivist othering relies on strategies of depicting Latinas/os as figures that embody emotions, sentiment ("heart"), and magic (the article describes Juan Luis Guerra's erotic song "Burbujas de amor" as "magical realism"), thus continuing the discursive tradition of Anglo-constructed stereotypes and tropicalized representations of the regions and cultures south of the border.

Cultural (Mis)Translations

This discursive construct is not an isolated incident but emerges laden with historical instances of rewritings on the part of dominant institutions. U.S. adaptations of Latin American music erase, literally speaking, the political and cultural values of music and songs, replacing them with messages and themes that fulfill the needs of an Other, a culturally located listener or audience. A clear instance of this process is the English mistranslation and "adaptation" of one of Cuba's most famous exemplars of Afro-Cuban music, "Mama Inés," popularized as a *son* that expresses the collective subjectivity of black Cubans since the times of slavery. Issued as an "American adaptation" of "the greatest of all Cuban Rumbas," the 1931 English translation by L. Wolfe Gilbert clearly illustrates the conflation—rightly denounced by Leonardo Acosta—of diverse forms of Cuban music into "rumbas" (which later becomes the mambo and the cha-cha-cha), although the term was also used in Cuban *teatro bufo* to refer generally to all Afro-Cuban music.[3] It also stands as an instance of the systematic erasure of culturally and racially different voices:

> Aquí estamos to' los negros [Here we are all blacks]
> Que venimos a rogar [who come to ask]
> Que nos concedan permiso [that you permit us]
> para cantar y bailar [to sing and dance]
>
> Yo 'taba en casa de madrina [I was at godmother's house]
> Que ella me mandó a buscar [Cause she asked me to come]
> Que de doblar de la esquina [Right around the corner]
> Que ella vive en el manglar [She lives on the swamps]
>
> Ay mama Inés, Ay mama Inés, [Oh, Mama Ines, Oh, Mama Ines]
> todos los negros tomamos café [we blacks drink coffee]
> [Repeat]
>
> Nos vamos para el solar [We go to the land]
> donde están los negritos [where blacks live]
> a bailar el cangrejito [to dance a "cangrejito"]
> Te invito, vamo' a bailar [I invite you, let's go dance]

Ay mama Inés, ay mama Inés [Oh, Mama Ines, Oh, Mama Ines]
todos los negros tomamos café [we blacks drink coffee]

English version:
In Sloppy Joe's in Havana
I lingered quenching my thirst
I saw a dancer there
That was really where
I saw her first.

Such graceful beauty and rhythm
Had never come to my sight
She made me want to stay
Danced my heart away
Most every night.

Oh Mome Enez
Oh Mome Enez
They hum and strum that LA RUMBA for you

Oh Mome Enez
Oh Mome Enez
Though others come,
their LA RUMBA won't do

When I first saw this she-bango
I fell so hard for the tango
But now this brand new fandango's
got me like nothing got me before
Oh Mome Enez (*repeat*)
No Cuban rum like LA RUMBA for me

I'm deaf and dumb when LA RUMBA I see
Oh Mome Enez
My limbs get numb, oh LA RUMBA for me
Hawaiians dance in a crude way
The Africans in a lewd way
And though you dance in a nude way
Everyone loves your wonderful style
Oh Mome Enez
I'm blue and glum, dance LA RUMBA for me.
Oh Mome Enez,
They pay some sum, for LA RUMBA delight.
At first they think it's outrageous
And then they find it contagious
They spend their income and wages
Just to be in the spell of your charm.
Oh Mome Enez
And still they come for LA RUMBA and you.[4]

The voice of "todos los negros" that initiates this *son* establishes from
the beginning a collective subjectivity immediately heard in the "we" of
"Aquí estamos." Cuban blacks, slaves, emit a collective plea, the song itself,
to create a space in which to articulate their social and racial collective sub-

jectivity and their presence and agency in Cuban social history through their rhythms, songs, and dance.

This voicing, ironically, is exactly that: a constructed voice by Cuban composer Eliseo Grenet. This song is a tango-congo, according to Cristóbal Díaz Ayala, rather than a Cuban *son*, although in fact the former was heavily influenced by the *son* and by other Afro-Cuban musical forms. It developed in the 1920s, typifying blackness within Cuba's lyrical or musical theater, the zarzuela. "Mama Inés," indeed, was first performed by Rita Montaner in 1927's zarzuela titled *Niña Rita*; Montaner was a famous mulatta singer and actress whose performance was called "a scandal."[5]

This already mediated version of Afro-Cuban musical traditions, itself a rewriting of the Cuban *son*, assumes an additional layering in the "American" version that completely erases the presence of Afro-Cuban matriarchal culture iconized in the figure of Mother Inés. The song shifts from representing a culture of agency and reaffirmation in history, a collective subject, to becoming an eroticized female Other ("I saw her first / such graceful beauty and rhythm"), an object, who seduces the male, Anglo singing/ writing subject. Allegorically speaking, Cuba, like other countries south of the border, can be integrated into the U.S. mainstream only as politically neutralized difference and as a gendered, passive object at the service of U.S. needs and interests: the insistence of the dative in "play LA RUMBA *for me*" repeatedly reveals this hegemonic positioning on the part of the male Anglo subject. The fact that Desi Arnaz popularized this particular Cuban song throughout the United States in the 1940s and 1950s is partially explained, then, by the presence and dissemination of this earlier version in English, a text that in many ways may have justifiably invited many U.S. tourists to enjoy Havana as a space for tropicalized lust and pleasure.

In this light, the anglified "Mama Inez" embodies the ways in which popular music, as text, practice, and performance, produces ideology that has justified cultural and military imperialism. "And still they come," as the Anglo text summarizes in its closing, displaces the male *I* onto a plural presence that is inevitably allegorical of U.S. military interventions and invasions, not only of Cuba but of other Caribbean islands and Latin American countries. However, the Cuban influx of migrants in 1994, coupled with the Mariel exodus in 1980, may ironically be described as an inversion of that imperialistic phrase. Today's Cuban refugee crisis has transformed that "they" into a most heterogeneous and destabilized signifier.

The English translation, then, feminizes Afro-Caribbean popular music; that is, it erases the political, cultural, and racial collective subjectivities articulated in these songs and replaces them with an individualized expression of heterosexual desire that objectifies women as well as Cuba if read as political allegory. Anglo mistranslations such as this mute and render invisible the subaltern voices that speak through the music; these texts of resistance and articulations of cultural difference become politically innocuous texts as well as scripts for U.S. hegemonic desire.

Crossover Nightmares

The intercultural desire revealed in "Mama Inez" continues today, as the *Newsweek* article "Crossover Dreamers" suggests, regarding the power of Latin music to establish a strong following of Anglo listeners analogous to the Mambo "craze" during the 1950s. The attraction that some Anglos feel for Latin music, as Paul Emerson's case illustrates, still needs to be explored and explained in systematic ways. Emerson, a computer salesman in Detroit, was hailed in "Crossover Dreamers" as Juan Luis Guerra's ultimate fan. Rather than seducer, Emerson has been seduced by Latin American subculture and the rhythms of the Caribbean. He has learned Spanish as a result of his predilection for Latin popular music, and he has since moved to the Dominican Republic. Yet the tropicalization of salsa, its irrational embracing by cultural others, is also a result of mainstreaming efforts and co-optation on the part of the dominant sector. Is it a coincidence, for example, that the salsa of the 1960s and 1970s, a music performed mostly by working-class black musicians, was never really mainstreamed (Fania's commercial efforts came to a halt in the mid-1980s), but in the 1980s and 1990s names like Juan Luis Guerra, Rubén Blades, and Gloria Estefan, all white, middle- and upper-class, educated musicians, fill the headlines of *Newsweek*? The canon is revealing in and of itself, but even more meaningful is the fact that singers and groups that have had a major historical impact on Afro-Caribbean music—Patato, El Gran Combo, Andy Montañez, Ismael Rivera, Rafael Cortijo—are still strange names among the Anglo audience.

Don Michael Randel initiates his article "Crossing Over with Rubén Blades" with these same canonical issues, yet his conclusions are, at best, problematic. *Billboard* reported in 1987 that while El Gran Combo de Puerto Rico had been the "undisputed tropical leader in popularity, record sales, and world geographical musical diffusion," it "has never been a Grammy nominee."[6] Randel justifies this discrepancy by concluding that Rubén Blades's music offers innovation in its rhythms, lyrics, and arrangements, and thus the public recognition, rewards, and following among non-Hispanic and up-and-coming Hispanic audiences can be justified. In contrast, he analyzes one song by El Gran Combo de Puerto Rico, titled "Lírica borinqueña," from their 1986 album *Y su pueblo* (And their people).

He concludes that while this is a "very, very good" piece, it is also "very very familiar. And, indeed, this piece is in a way about its own familiarity. The singer sings that he writes typically Puerto Rican verse, Caribbean music from the land in which he was born, pretty music from his country. . . . This song evokes tradition, not novelty or modernity. It simplifies rather than complicates. It appeals to its largely urban audience in terms utterly foreign to that audience's daily experience but in terms of a familiar and comfortable tradition."[7]

I will not argue against Randel's positive assessment of Rubén Blades's innovative techniques in salsa's arrangements, accentual texts, and narrative songs. And while he is careful enough to recognize that Blades's songs "would not exist without El Gran Combo,"[8] the overarching effect of his analysis is to reduce the historical value of El Gran Combo's repertoire and musical contributions to salsa to one song (out of thousands that they have composed or interpreted). "Lírica borinqueña" may be deemed too traditional and pastoral for an urban audience, yet this song functions precisely to fulfill Rubén Blades's nostalgic refrain of his theme song in the film *Crossover Dreams*, one that evokes the inevitable return, whether physical or symbolic, to one's native country. This is a line that Randel himself quotes in his article.

The repetition of certain idyllic visions of Puerto Rico, as nostalgic or retrograde as they may be deemed by postmodernist standards, activates a specific need among colonized groups who have been displaced geographically and who have experienced the social traumas of shifting from rural to urban life or from one cultural space to another. In this view, Randel's article participates in the logic of the music industry, which has canonized Rubén Blades and dismissed other groups such as El Gran Combo de Puerto Rico. Yet the latter was the principal performer at Seville's Expo 92, and among Puerto Ricans it is not a traditional group but musical *tradition* itself (the group most representative of the changes that Puerto Rican urban popular music has witnessed throughout thirty years [1962–1992]). This counteracts Randel's simplification and undermining of the historical importance of El Gran Combo. Indeed, if one were familiar with El Gran Combo's concert tours throughout Latin American cities, U.S. cities, and Europe, one would evaluate their international renown differently.

Randel invokes a conversation with a Hispanic woman student at Cornell University who prefers Rubén Blades to El Gran Combo de Puerto Rico in support of his own analysis. Yet the author does not take into consideration factors of class positioning, racial attitudes, or gender awareness in his discussion of listener preferences and audience response.

Randel's article is a clear example of how scholarship has failed salsa

COMBO
RCSLP 2029/2030

SERIES 01498

El Gran Combo
De Ayer, Hoy, Mañana y Siempre

LADO A (2029)		LADO B (2029)		LADO A (2030)		LADO B (2030)	
1962-63 LA MUERTE (E. Farrai)	4:19	1967-68 MILONGA SENTIMENTAL (H. Manzi/S. Piara)	2:11	1972-73 JULIA (C. Carrizo)	3:29	1977-78 BUSCANDO AMBIENTE (T. Maldonado)	3:53
1963-64 ACÁNGANA (C. García)	3:45	1968-69 FALSARIA (M.T. Vera)	3:58	1973-74 LOS ZAPATOS DE MANACHO (R. Ithien)	3:37	1978-79 AQUÍ NO HA PASADO NADA (R. Anglero)	4:44
1964-65 OJOS CHINOS (K. Velez)	4:17	1969-70 PONME EL ALCOLADO JUANA (R. Ithien)	3:50	1974-75 LA SALSA DE HOY (R. Anglero)	3:37	1979-80 BRUJERIA (L. Borrego)	3:24
1965-66 EL CABALLO PELOTERO (B. Capó)	3:07	1970-71 POR EL PECHO NO (R. Ithier)	3:58	1975-76 VAGABUNDO (R. Giraldoz)	4:46	1980-81 COMPAÑERA MIA (V. Vergara)	4:24
1966-57 LA CALLE DOLOR (R. Rivera)	3:26	1971-72 DON GOYO (G. Arango)	4:02	1976-77 LA SOLEDAD (R. Anglero)	3:16	1981-82 EL MENU (P. Vazquez)	4:11

Grabado en Ochoa Recording, Ingeniero: P. Henriquez • Televicentro Sound, Ingeniero: P. Sanchez • Latin Sound Studios, Ingeniero: J. Fausty & D. Rodriguez
Tuxedos cortesia de El Chaleco • Fotos: Kurt Diaz • Producido por: Ralph Cartagena.

Members of El Gran Combo de Puerto Rico are shown on the back cover of their double album, *De ayer, hoy, mañana y siempre*, released by Combo Records Productions in 1982 on the occasion of their twentieth anniversary. Rafael Ithier, leader of the group, stands in the middle dressed in white. Courtesy of Combo Records.

music. It dismisses and ignores the real-life responses to music by its Latino and Latina audiences. It fails to account for issues of race, class, and gender in arriving at conclusions regarding reception and degrees of popularity. It homogenizes the multilayered and plural ideologies that constitute listener response to salsa, and it blatantly ignores the voices of working-class Latinos and Latinas in their own sociomusical practices. Randel does invoke the "reader or listener"[9] in a short discussion of how audiences use music "to construct meaning and their own identities,"[10] a discussion that is built on by Hayden White's theory of code-shifting in reception: "a dynamic process of overt and covert code shifting by which a specific subjectivity is called up and established in the reader, who is supposed to entertain this representation of the world as a realistic one in virtue of its congeniality to the imaginary relationship the subject bears to his own social and cultural situation."[11] While this Althusserian explanation of the importance of form in the constitution of subjectivities is extremely helpful in the study of popular culture's polysemic nature, it is also revealing that White's authority overshadows any need for further ethnographic surveying or for methods of study that would document the ways in which Latina/o audiences construct meaning and identity through music. By failing to take into account the historical and cultural specificities of popular music, its complex ideological sites, and the voices of those audiences that have sustained the music economically, Randel's scholarship becomes another problematic instance of the colonizing erasures that "Mama Inez" embodied earlier.

Thus, to speak about salsa as crossover music, as Randel's and other journalistic pieces do, is to monologize the complex ideological webs that such a music articulates in its production, composition, performing, and reception. It is more helpful, I believe, to think of crossover music in terms of audience configurations, needs, and reception practices associated with cross-cultural dynamics, or more accurately, with intercultural desire. "Crossing over" needs to be redefined beyond the validation of a musical performance by and to a hegemonic cultural sector as a gauge for judging musical popularity or "success." It becomes, for me at least, a result of the needs of an outside (Anglo) audience to reconcile Latina/o music with its own desires and values, as the tropicalizing phenomenon attests. In salsa and Latin music, only certain figures have been allowed to "cross over."

According to Randel, in the case of Rubén Blades, crossing over has been made possible by a new, emerging Hispanic audience "increasingly imbued with Anglo culture and energized by its very own political and economic aspirations,"[12] rather than "from an appeal to some new, largely Anglo audience."[13] While I agree that the sector of Latinas/os in the United States and throughout Latin America who prefer Rubén Blades is a young, upwardly mobile, professional audience, Blades's reception among Latinas/os has shifted throughout his career. However, he remains very popular among all class sectors, a factor that Randel fails to consider.

Additionally, Randel dismisses the fact that El Gran Combo is not the only salsa group popular among working-class Latinas/os; indeed, other artists, such Andy Montañez, the late Héctor Lavoe, and Oscar de León, dismissed by mainstream musical critics and the establishment, actually enjoy great popularity. Class and race boundaries, however, have limited their access to general Anglo audiences. El Gran Combo de Puerto Rico was formed as a branching out of Rafael Cortijo y su Combo, the all-black musical group that vindicated the bomba and the plena as popular music during the decades of the 1940s and 1950s and indisputably contributed to the formation of salsa music in New York. El Gran Combo, like its predecessors, gives voice to the needs, realities, and social experiences of the black urban working class, whether in New York or in other Caribbean cities. As such, the nasality of the singing, its diction, its themes, its humor, and its worldview may not necessarily coincide with middle- and upper-class Anglo values. Most Anglos, indeed, would enjoy the rhythms, as Randel's Latina student did, but would not engage with the narrative modes of the lyrics.

It is no coincidence, then, that Randel's sample, a Hispanic—not a self-named Latina—student at Cornell University, would dismiss El Gran Combo as insignificant in her life but would embrace Rubén Blades's "Decisiones." I would dare to hypothesize that for upper-class and aspiring middle-class young Hispanics, Blades's repertoire represents a safe, clean, white way of being political, as Blades himself has been an icon, throughout his own life, of the up-and-coming white Hispanic in the United States. His law degree from Harvard, his English last name (that could read in either Spanish or English), his growing fame as an actor in Hollywood, and his failed attempts at composing salsa in English ("Nothing but the Truth") already position Blades as an ideal musician for particular class sectors.

Manuel Cachán's analysis of Rubén Blades's ideological plurality is helpful in this discussion. While I have already expressed reservations about Cachán's rigid paradigms for salsa—as commercial and as sociopolitical—he acknowledges, nonetheless, the complex issues of reception that Blades illustrates. In his view, Blades's repertoire removes salsa music from the folkloric, tropical, and exotic view of "commercial" salsa, while his musical compositions and arrangements continue the oral traditions of popular culture in New York's barrios, as the song "Pedro Navaja" best exemplifies. Yet Rubén Blades's rewritings of oral tradition have been accepted and have achieved legitimacy precisely because he has conformed his literary discourse and style to elite literary criteria (his use of alexandrine verses, his rhyme patterns, and other stylistic nuances), thus achieving validation by the Latin American upper-class listener and/or reader. Ironically, Blades has played both fields, for he radically politicized the content of salsa songs while gaining stylistic acceptance by the social sectors he so ardently denounces in his music.

It is not surprising, then, that at a presentation during a Viva Chicago Festival in 1989, Blades apologized to the mostly working-class Latina/o audience for supposedly abandoning "el pueblo" in search of Hollywood fame. Such a stance reveals the tenuous and ambiguous role that he has held among working-class Latinas/os as a result of his real-life crossing over and his growing fame within the establishment and Hollywood. His two most recent collections, *Antecedentes* (1989) and *Caminando* (1991), were produced at a time when Blades's power was waning among his Latina/o audiences. They attempt to recover the Panamanian singer's earlier role as *the* political and oppositional voice among salseros, vindicating himself in the eyes and ears of the working-class U.S. Latino/a community.

U.S. journalism—like the "Crossover Dreamers" article—presents Rubén Blades side by side with Cuban-born musician Gloria Estefan, yet their respective successes among Anglo audiences stem from very diverse motivations and cultural positions. In contrast to Blades's ambivalence and double play with his audiences, Gloria Estefan has addressed from the beginning the expectations of a large, mainstreaming public. Her music is undoubtedly based on Afro-Caribbean rhythms, but the softer texture of her arrangements and sound and the English lyrics in her songs have brought Latin popular music to new levels of popularity among non-Latinas/os. Gloria Estefan, however, has never been labeled nor considered a salsa musician. She is a Latin pop singer and as such belongs within the tradition of pop ballads and soft rock, not under the rubric of salsa as it has been defined historically. Thus, comparisons between Estefan and Rubén Blades, for instance, seem rather forced, given the very different musical genres that they have performed.

Estefan's bilingual lyrics and her predominant use of English bring forth the value of language in delineating Latin(o) popular music and its role in drawing cultural boundaries. While Estefan's decision to sing in English and bilingually coincide with her views on the so-called universality of music and with her resistance to politicized music, her strategic move to produce *Mi tierra* totally in Spanish and in collaboration with important musicians such as Israel "Cachao" López and Tito Puente inserts her now into a larger tradition of salsa music that, with some particular exceptions (like "Pennies from Heaven"), has maintained its Spanish lyrics throughout a whole century. (The first Hispanic songs began to be recorded in the United States around 1906.)

The linguistic maintenance of Spanish in the production of salsa is quite impressive, given the pressures of a music industry interested in appealing to larger audiences. This persistent presence of Spanish, a subordinate language in any other social context in the United States, is not surprising in light of the demographic growth of Latinas/os in the United States and as another indicator of the oppositionality of salsa and its strong connections to the working-class Latina/o communities throughout the United States and Latin America. That the Japanese salsa band Orquesta de la Luz sings in Spanish reveals the profound connection of salsa to the Spanish language and its strong value as a marker of cultural identity, resistance, and affirmation.

Estefan's incursion into Spanish, like Rubén Blades's experiment with salsa in English, represent strategic linguistic shifts for marketing drives more than instances of an exclusively postmodern linguistic hybridity. Estefan's musical trajectory—particularly her production of *Mi tierra*—reveals the inverse pattern of the crossover performers who begin singing in Spanish to their own communities and then move on to mainstream audiences in English. During televised interviews and publicity regarding the production of *Mi tierra*, she candidly admitted that had she produced this type of traditional Afro-Cuban music earlier in her career, it would not have been that successful. Timing, of course, is significant, given the mainstreaming tendencies of salsa music in the United States since the 1980s.

Spanish in salsa brings to the foreground issues of cultural authenticity, a concept that has been blacklisted by many cultural critics and scholars in favor of the transnational and multicultural aspects of cultural productions. Any reference to authenticity reifies culture and fixes boundaries, so it may be relevant to bring up the fact that this term is too closely associated with nationalism and as such can only be rejected by our generation of scholars, particularly those of us in cultural studies. Yet this rejection, as Cuban musicologist Leonardo Acosta reminds us, may be another instance of colonization on the part of the metropolis. For years, the metropolis has critiqued the nationalism emerging from the colonized countries, yet it simultaneously appropriates these very nationalist-informed cultural expressions.[14] Thus, when authenticity is synonymous with nationalism, it is shunned from discussions of cultural studies and postmodernism. However, if we reconfigure this concept as a dialectical one rather than unilaterally—that is, as verb rather than noun,[15] as a process rather than as an inherent quality of a cultural product or artistic subject—then not only colonized groups can be deemed authentic or practice authenticity. The colonizer also is highly complicit in this process of social construction by attempting, from an outside location, to authenticate particular musical traditions, to give them validity, establishing them as true and genuine within the ideologies that can contain them. Thus, to *authenticate* from a hegemonic location is to give Latin popular music, or musicians, a constructed meaning that is inevitably different from those of the inside community. In other words, authentication can be understood as another instance of the discursive struggles over cultural meanings, identities, and power.

As academicians, it is too easy for us to reaffirm theoretically the values of multiculturalism and the collective nature of cultural authorship from the comfort and luxury of our daily lives as very well and not so very well paid professors. Nevertheless, these concepts are not just words but realities that hold material repercussions, strongly vital and central to Latina/o musicians who struggle everyday for a gig, yet whose music is now being performed by a David Byrne, a Paul Simon, or a Linda Ronstadt, who received "megabucks" for their multicultural productions. Willie Colón denounces the co-optation of salsa and Latin music by Anglo performers, and he points to the economic marginalization of Latina/o musicians and the highlighting of the mainstream musician as the "promoter of the culture." Indeed, he indicates the historical continuity of this phenomenon as he refers to the "Beatles redoing race music, Pat Boone covering Little Richard songs, and Elvis singing the blues."[16] Colón recognizes the fluidity of cultural productions and also acknowledges that in most cases appropriations did take place; as a result, "isn't it a shame that all these black musics were accepted only in a white disguise?"[17] The historical phenomenon of the acceptance of vernacular or ethnic musics, such as the blues, jazz, or salsa, contingent on their Anglo representations and performances, has been already probed and elucidated.[18] Yet by reaffirming the multicultural and collective authorship of popular culture, as Mackey has also observed, cultural critics can assuage these economic differentials and gaps in cultural authority, thus constructing, naively yet politically safely I believe, an ideal, egalitarian vision of multiculturalism and of cross-cultural communication in this society.[19]

Willie Colón, then, has rewritten the concept of crossover dreams (the title of Rubén Blades's first movie) into crossover *nightmares*. In a very brief but powerful note he denounces the negative economic repercussions of musical appropriations and the ensuing marginalization of Latina/o musicians. To theorize about multicultural authorship without including the economics of production and without taking into account the colonial status of Latina/o communities worldwide would mean failing to recognize the pervading colonization that these musical practices evoke. Postmodern theories stressing collectivity and shifting boundaries ironically also elide the principle of articulation, intricately bound to class differentials and central to the study of any form of music. Music itself is not a fixed object, mere content, but a series of patterns that are combined into new patterns and structures, semantically transvalorated. This mediation, as Richard Middleton describes it, always occurs in struggle.[20] Thus, class and race differentials must be embedded in discussions of popular music. If not, we reduce music to an idea, an abstract symbolism or metaphor, which it undeniably is; yet it is also intimately linked to a materiality, a political economy, and physical survival for real-life musicians. In this context, Willie Colón's concern about salsa's mainstreaming becomes significant: "What will we do when Anglo-Salsa becomes bigger than the music we have lived and liked for so long? When Latin America swings to Ronstadt and Simon in English and the Salsa Festival at Madison Square Garden is headlined by Byrne? When America says: Salsa? Oh, you mean like Paul Simon? How will it affect the Salsa genre when all its biggest stars are white and singing in English? Another way of not being able to love ourselves for what we are. Sour grapes or déjà-vu?"[21]

In the post–civil rights era, Latinas/os, African Americans, and other minority groups have reached a certain degree of access to cultural production and authorship, an access that, although limited, has carried financial remuneration and national visibility to some. Yet the value of cultural authority has been undermined simultaneously by the same intellectual projects that were meant to defend multiculturalism in the national sphere. Although the scenario that Colón portrays in the quote above is quite improbable because of the influx of immigration, the demographic growth, and the cultural pride of Latinas/os in the United States, the reality of cultural co-optation must be articulated for what it is, instead of being veiled and assuaged by well-intentioned cultural critics willing to ignore the material and economic realities that Latina/o musicians have confronted. In this last section, I have attempted to differentiate between a Rubén Blades and a Gloria Estefan for, indeed, each has crossed over (or has been crossed over, embraced) from very different sociomusical locations. Both have been conflated as "crossover" dreamers although, in fact, their respective receptions and audience configurations, their political positionings, and the kinds of music they compose are distinct from each other.

Yet Gloria Estefan and Rubén Blades share a symbolic value; they represent the whitening of salsa music that Anglo America desires to have racially, which is also part and parcel of its internationalization. Discussions of their music, such as Randel's and *Newsweek*'s, have failed to consider class and race factors as they affect the inclusion of certain musicians to the exclusion of others, perpetuating the tendencies of the mainstream to conflate all Latin(o) popular music as one homogeneous, tropicalized cultural expression. Through this postmodern, politicized, and decolonizing reading of salsa music as an appropriation, as object of intercultural desire, I hope to have brought to the foreground, as Nathaniel Mackey has observed about blackface minstrelsy, "a great deal regarding the obstacles in the way of genuine multiculturality or cross-culturality, a genuine, non-exploitative cultural exchange."[22] Like African-American music in the United States, salsa music has been transformed from "verb to noun," feminized and made passive, depoliticized in order to render innocuous its power for cultural differentiation.

This view about othering should not be read as a unilateral rejection of transnational exchanges; neither should it render null the internal power differentials and contradictions that salsa incorporates and exteriorizes within the Latino and Latina communities. Gender politics, in particular, have remained virtually unexamined in salsa; whereas salsa itself is feminized and rendered passive by the dominant Anglo forces, its privileging of the masculine at various intratextual levels—and intraculturally—must be deconstructed as well.

PART THREE

✠

DISSONANT MELODIES:
SINGING GENDER,
DESIRE, AND CONFLICT

✠

Theoretical Pretexts
Listening (as) Woman

✠

What follows here and in the fourth part of this book is an exercise both in *Listening Woman* and in *listening as women*, concepts based on critical discussions of women as readers informed by the convergence of feminist studies with reader-response theories.[1] In the context of popular music, however, reception does not embrace visual or verbal reading practices only but partakes in signifying practices through both individual and collective acts of listening, singing, and dancing. Any approach, then, to the ways in which salsa music textualizes the feminine through song lyrics cannot remain divorced either from real audience responses nor from other aspects of this music as sociocultural praxes. While "reading Woman" provides an initial conceptual framework for this study, it proves insufficient in its exclusively verbal dimension. Thus, it is imperative to translate this term, which emphasizes the verbal and the literary over the sonorous and aural, into a sociomusical act. The conscious, ambiguous ungrammaticalness of *Listening Woman*—it should read "listening *to* women"—suggests subtexts not only of previous scholarly discussions of issues of representation and textualizing practices but, moreover, about women as receptors and producers of meaning(s).

At first sight *Listen(Read)ing Woman* evokes the "images of women" methodology, a "resolutely thematical" criticism that, during the 1970s, proved "most forceful as a critique of the phallocentric assumptions that govern literary works."[2] Yet many analyses of this sort were, in practice, based on the simplistic assumption that texts "reflect" reality, thus leading to merely psychological or descriptive commentaries on female characters. In their attempts to uncover women's treatment as literary objects, many feminist critics implicitly reproduced this treatment, a flaw that was also, unfortunately, quite common in the context of Latin American scholarship on women.[3] As recently as 1988, Neyssa Palmer's analysis of female characters in the Puerto Rican narrative of the 1940s and 1950s exemplifies the dangers of this approach:

Todas estas vidas son trágicas, responden al mundo brutal e injusto que encuentran a su paso, sin otra alternativa que la resignación, pero no hay en ellas degradación moral alguna. Por el contrario, *el dolor las enaltece.* A través del proceder que develan como personajes, percibimos el profundo conocimiento que posee González *de la conducta y reacciones que observa la mujer puertorriqueña frente a la adversidad.*

[All of these women's lives are tragic; they respond to the brutal and unjust world around them; they have no other choice but to resign themselves, although there is no moral degradation. On the contrary, *pain exalts them.* Through their behavior as characters, we perceive González's (the author's) profound knowledge *of the behavior and reactions of Puerto Rican women in the midst of adversity.*] (my emphasis)[4]

The emphasized statements above illustrate the ways in which the hermeneutic practice elides the text as a literary construct and insists on a direct correspondence between fiction and reality, exercising what Toril Moi has termed "excessive referentialism."[5] Indeed, what Palmer does not take into account is that female representation and by and large any representation results from textualizing a myriad of factors such as gender, race, class, and ideology. She does not find a problem in defining a fixed gender identity for women as well as for men; she participates, in fact, in fixing women's identity, notably by naturalizing women's emotions and even ascribing patriarchal values to those emotions (e.g. "Pain exalts them").

Yet as a critical strategy, *Listening Woman* can supersede the simplistic representational assumptions that the above quotation illustrates. In reading women's representation in Latin popular music, *Listening Woman* entails "both the ways in which women are figured . . . and the ways in which such figuring gives representation its force by repressing female desire."[6] As Pamela Caughie implies, "Reading Woman" is synonymous with "reading what is not known in literature or theory,"[7] that is, reading the silences and filling in the gaps created by a male-centered perspective and phallocentric discourse. Thus, *Reading Woman,* as critical tool, always already implies an active agent within the (female) reader or listener who constructs meaning out of a text in differential ways; this dialectical relationship surfaces in the possible double readings of this signifier (woman as object, as in reading representations of women, and woman as subject, as in woman who reads).

While it is a given that gender makes a difference in reading as in listening, I am interested here in some of those differences but most interested in the ways in which those differences are produced in the text as well as through the process of the receptor(s) engaging the text (i.e., the song).

Moreover, to think of gender as sexual difference tends to duplicate essentializing, fixed definitions of the feminine as structurally differential (what is nonmasculine) or opposite to the masculine. Rather, as Cathy Schwichtenberg poses in "Reconceptualizing Gender: New Sites for Feminist Audience Research," gender must be posed "as a process of negotiation with culture rather than as the assumption of necessarily feminine qualities, attributes, or identifications."[8] While earlier in my work I had proposed a clearer distinction between *Listening Woman* and *listening as women*, a distinction that served me in structuring this interdisciplinary incursion,[9] I now doubt its phenomenological validity and thus have decided to merge both concepts with the use of the parenthesis, signaling the dialectics between both processes and their phenomenological indivisibility.

Although *Listening Woman* still serves to frame my discussion of women's representation by male salsa singers and composers, the meanings of and ultimately the power of those discursive constructions are not activated, nor do they assume force except at the moment of reception, through the very act of listening. Most thematic readings of popular music document songs and particular lyrics as unilateral expressions or simplistic, unmediated reflections of certain themes, ideas, or attitudes.[10] In contrast, this chapter strives to reproduce the tensions, conflicts, and multiple voices underlying the dialogic space of (hetero)sexual politics in salsa music. In this part of the book the analysis is limited to the voices we listen to in songs, but I ask the reader not to separate this textual analysis from the heterogeneous responses of both Latina and Latino listeners that will be presented in the next section. "Así Somos, Así Son," as I have titled Part Four, exemplifies the tension between the male-authored song "Así son" by El Gran Combo de Puerto Rico and the responses of Latinas who appropriate patriarchal lyrics to reconstitute themselves as active subjects of their own identity. The phrase "así somos," countered by a working-class Latina from Detroit after listening to this song, suggests that listening, like consumption, is not merely a passive behavior, an ideological consent but rather constitutes a potential instance of rewriting culture.

As a product of a male-dominated music industry and positioned as a commodity of a capitalist superstructure, salsa has led to women's exclusion from its arenas of production and composition. Salsa's repertoire is clearly marked by male voices that systematically privilege a masculinist perspective, a patriarchal ideology, and thus a phallocentric discourse. And while some female interpreters have been key figures in the development and popularity of salsa (e.g., La Lupe and Celia Cruz) and recently in that of the merengue (e.g., Sonia López; Milly y los Vecinos; Mayra, Celinés y Flor de Caña; Chantelle; and Las Chicas del Can), the younger women musicians who perform mostly texts written by men seem to enjoy the most visibility in the industry, thus reinforcing the music's monopolization by patriarchal perspectives and the male as writing subject. In spite of the fact that women singers invert the object of sexism as they sing patriarchal love songs and in doing so become acting subjects in control of their bodies, the seducers rather than the seduced; empower other women with specific visual cues as articulations of female subjectivity; and function as role models for their female audience, it is clear that female desire and female subjectivity are ultimately repressed in salsa intratextually and at times are outright invisible as well.

The locus, then, in which gender dialogism and sexual politics are played out is not only in women's songs but also in extratextual elements. Women's songs are the most self-evident arena for the articulation of female subjectivity, but we must also locate oppositionality and resistance in performative dimensions (as the figure of La Lupe clearly demands) and in women's responses to and rewritings of male utterances, whether literary texts (such as Luis Rafael Sánchez's hybrid literary rendering of Daniel Santos or Ana Lydia Vega and Carmen Lugo Filippi's stories) or the liberatory and alternative rewritings that Latinas themselves engage through the act of listening. These plural discursive sites destabilize, dialogize, and deconstruct the privileged male voices in Latin popular music. However, when we listen to lyrics, we listen to multiple articulations of desire and conflict that must be documented as well. This section brings together, in a sort of musicocritical medley, diverse lyrics and musical traditions—separated in many cases by either national boundaries or decades of historical distance—by which male and female voices have represented gender, conflict, and desire on our sentimental or affective culture.

CHAPTER SEVEN

Woman as Absence
Hetero(homo)sexual Desire in the Bolero

✛

Amor es un algo sin nombre que obsesiona
a un hombre por una mujer . . .
[Love is a nameless something that makes
a man obsessed with a woman . . .]
—Pedro Flores, "Obsesión"

A working-class Latina from Detroit acknowledged during my interview with her that "cuando estoy en un baile y escucho salsa, no le presto mucha atención a las palabras . . . pero cuando es un bolero sí le pongo atención" [when I go dancing, I don't pay much attention to the lyrics of salsa music . . . but when a bolero plays I do listen carefully to the lyrics]. This observation reveals her awareness that, as a member of a musical audience, she engages different listening strategies depending on the musical form she is hearing. Her musical competence leads her to listen more carefully to the lyrics of a bolero, the quintessential romantic ballad in Latin America, than to salsa songs. While she well enjoys the fast rhythms of the latter, it is the slow tempo of the bolero and the importance of both its lyrics and the voice of the singer that seduces her into listening closely.

Given the highly literary nature of this musical form, I will focus first on reading and analyzing bolero lyrics as a musical space in which Woman (or the feminine) is constructed mostly as absence, an absence that stimulates the expression and articulation of male desire through the text/song and through the act of singing. Despite the predominance of the male singing subject in this musical tradition, recent scholarship and postmodern fiction have successfully regendered the discourse of the bolero. Iris Zavala's essay "De héroes y heroínas en lo imaginario social: El discurso amoroso del bolero" and Luis Rafael Sánchez's *La importancia de llamarse Daniel San-*

tos, an original rendering of the male icon of guarachas and boleros both capitalize on the bolero's sublimated erotic discourse, subversively reinterpreting it as homoerotic rewriting. Although the bolero implies a different listening mode from that evoked by salsa, this romantic musical genre has been a central subtext of heterosexual love and an influential tradition that informs the discourse of desire and sexual politics in salsa music.

The origins of the bolero have been traced to Cuba at the turn of the century, more specifically to around 1885 and 1886. These years coincide with the historical emergence of the danzón, characterized by the habanera rhythm, which constitutes the rhythmical foundation for the bolero.[1] The late 1880s also mark the emergence of modernismo in Latin America, the neo-romantic revolution in poetic language and literature that represents the early stages of literary modernity. And as Iris Zavala has suggested, the idealizing, *preciosista*, abstract yet sensual and refined imagery and lexicon of modernismo informs the discourse of love embodied in the bolero.[2] Agustín Lara's composition "Mujer" illustrates the ethereal, idealizing and mythifying textualization of Woman as divine seductress, echoing Spanish romantic poet Gustavo Adolfo Bécquer's *Rimas* and the modernista leader Rubén Darío's poetic imagery of the feminine, a language that systematically renders woman as dematerialized, not real:

> Mujer, mujer divina,
> tienes el veneno que fascina en tu mirar.
> Mujer alabastrina,
> tienes vibración de sonatina pasional,
> tienes el perfume de un naranjo en flor,
> el altivo porte de una majestad.
> Sabes de los filtros que hay en el amor,
> tienes el hechizo de la liviandad,
> la divina magia de un atardecer,
> y la maravilla de la inspiración.
> Tienes en el ritmo de tu ser
> todo el palpitar de una canción.
> Eres la razón de mi existir, mujer.
>
> [Woman, woman divine
> in your look you hold the poison that seduces,
> Alabaster-like woman,
> you hold the vibrations of a passionate sonatina,
> you hold the scent of an orange blossom,
> the royal pose of a queen.
> You know about the filters of love,
> you hold a spell with your lightness,
> The divine magic of a sunset,
> and the marvel of inspiration.
> You hold in the rhythms of your being
> all the palpitations of a song.
> You are the reason for my existence, woman.][3]

In this text the male singing subject is, at once, creator of woman and her receptor as well. He constructs her as an ideal, a divine being superior to him and thus unattainable. The theme of unrequited love constitutes the central obsession in the bolero. She is goddess, witch, and fatal seductress (poison). She is, after all, the object of his unquenchable desire. And *el deseo* is, indeed, the main ideologeme of the bolero in Latin America, a desire that is played out musically and embodied in the "systolic-diastolic" movement of this musical form.[4] This tension musically emerges from the habanera rhythm and the syncopated double beat, suspending any resolution of sound and sentiment, prohibiting any pleasure in the sense of musical closure or endings and thus reflecting at the sonorous level the discourse of unrequited or unconsummated love that underlies the bolero. Desire is never fulfilled, always remaining as absence, never actualized into sexual or erotic pleasure. The interstitial location of language and the intermittence of presence and absence, then, continually inscribe desire both for singer and audience. The "absence" that becomes a "presence," as Iris Zavala argues, is mostly Woman, who becomes evoked and discursively present through the voice of the male interpreter.[5] Woman as sign of absence becomes present through language, through the act of singing, and through the bolero as performative act. The sensual evocation of the lyrics allows the heterosexual couple to give meaning to dancing and intimacy "in the squared eternity of a floor tile" as foreplay and anticipation of sexual pleasure.[6] As Agustín Lara's song "Mujer" suggests in its closing lines, woman holds in her own "rhythm" the "palpitations" of the song; that is, her body is always already the text for the male, as much as the song becomes the discursive space in which woman's body is inscribed.

The bolero, as constructed by Luis Rafael Sánchez in his rendering of Daniel Santos is, metaphorically speaking, the body of Latin America, in its transnational circulation and popularity. It is the music of "la América amarga, la América descalza, la América en español," of the masses who seduce, love, and desire in the midst of sweeping social changes, such as industrialization, urbanization, and transnationalism.[7] The bolero is the language of "exquisiteces" sung by all Latin Americans, a musical language that traverses social classes, generations, genders, and race boundaries, as Iris Zavala also proposes.[8]

Thus, the body of the bolero has been mythified as eternal, for its discourse of love transcends historical periods and crosses generational lines. In this sense, younger generations continually rediscover the traditional boleros of the 1930s, 1940s, and 1950s because those same lyrics and confessions of pain, love, solitude, and desire that their parents sang to each other while dancing continue to act as foreplay to their passion and as seduction itself. In the same way that my parents' generation sought meaning and intimacy in the voices of Tito Rodríguez, Daniel Santos, and Gilberto Monroig, young people today consume Luis Miguel's recent release, *Romance*, which includes a number of master love songs, from Roberto Cantoral's "La barca" to Gabriel Ruiz's "Usted." The popularity of Miguel's recording among young people exemplifies the continuous rediscovery of this music of love by younger generations of singers and interpreters.[9] Likewise, music critics have noted the ubiquitous presence and influence of the bolero in contemporary slow rock ballads and popular romantic ballads. Although many critics stress the qualitative difference among these musical forms, they value the traditional bolero over the contemporary love renderings, which they have deemed diluted and commercialized versions of the authentic bolero a la Agustín Lara or Tito Rodríguez.

The continental, eternal, and ubiquitous body of the bolero as sociomusical practice is closely linked to patriarchy and to its male-gendered voices and lyrics. Heir to the Western tradition of courtly love, boleros continue to articulate masculine constructs of the feminine, from the ideal and impossible woman to more universal archetypes, such as the woman seductress and witch, the femme fatale, the ungrateful woman who betrays the man's love, and the "lost woman," the latter image containing multiple meanings. For the Mexican singer Agustín Lara, known as the *flaco de oro* (the golden thin man) and mythified as the prototype of the bolero composer and bohemian interpreter, the prostitute, the sinner, and the "lost woman" constituted the inspirational muse for his boleros after 1930.[10] Indeed, titles such as "Perdida," "Amor de la calle," "Callejera," "Flor deshojada," "Arrabalera," "Cabaretera," "Si fuera una cualquiera," "Flor de arrabal," "Trotacalles," "Amor vendido," "Tú y tu vida," and others, systematically prove the centrality of the *mujer de la calle* as source of inspiration and object of desire for the male composer. The marginal location of the figure of the prostitute explains also the marginality of these love relationships, liaisons that usually reside outside legality, marriage, and family. While Mexican critics identify these titles as boleros specifically inspired by "las muchachas de la vida galante" [the girls of a licentious life] the image of the "lost woman" [la perdida] is not only informed by autobiographical circumstances and experiences but also branches out to any relationship in which the woman leaves the man. Moreover, this central structuring motif sheds historical light on the threatening values that urbanization brought forth to a Latin American patriarchal system in which wives, mothers, and daughters who worked outside the home literally became *mujeres de la calle* as they enjoyed increased access to the public sphere and to public spaces. These negative depictions of women represent, then, a defensive stance by men against the new public spaces inhabited by women who, as a result of urban migration, modernization, and their new role in the workplace, subverted the social values that restricted them within the household.

This patriarchal resistance also has been articulated in jíbaro music, as Chuíto el de Bayamón sings to men in "La mujer en Nueva York,"[11] admonishing them against migrating to the big city in the north where they risk losing their women to modernizing values and an increased degree of freedom:

> Singer, if you do not want
> To lose your woman
> Don't, don't sell your house
> To bring her to New York.
> Because even if things are worse there
> Here she'll take on bad ways
> She'll deceive you with another
> Maybe even your own friend
> And that's why I'm telling you
> That women go bad here.[12]

The male caveat against migration is seen as the descent from the purity of the rural homeland to the corrupting influences of the big city, modernization, and industrialization. Not exclusive to the bolero, this antiurban sentiment was voiced throughout the 1930s, 1940s, and 1950s in various forms of popular music, as well as in the literature about migration emerging from island writers. As late as 1963, René Marqués' drama *La carreta* epitomized this discourse about the tragic consequences of migration and urbanization on the family unit. Most important, the playwright locates the progressive moral degradation of urban life, moving from the countryside to San Juan to New York, in the figure of the virginal daughter-become-prostitute. This larger discourse on women, migration, and urban life, not coincidentally produced during the most important decades of the bolero, allows us to read between the lines those lyrics that have been mostly rendered as individual voicings of love, desire, and loss.

Pedro Flores's bolero titled "Se fue" (She left) encapsulates the centrality of woman's absence for the heterosexual male subjectivity, an absence that might also be read as the result of social displacements:

Se fue para no volver	[She left never to return
Y mi pobre corazón	And my poor heart
Se enfermó de ausencia.	Fell ill from her absence.
Ahora que estoy convencido	Now that I am convinced
Que nunca jamás volverá	that she will never return
Ahora yo sé lo que sufre	Now I know the suffering

| quien pierde su felicidad. | of those who lose their joy. |
| Se fue para no volver. | She left never to return. |

Se fue para no olvidarme	She left not to forget me
Como no podía odiarme	For she could not hate me
Se fue para no volver.	She left never to return.
[*Repeat*]	(*Repeat*)
Ahora que he de padecer	Now that I shall suffer
Por la ausencia de ese amor	Because of this absent love
Yo no sé qué voy a hacer	I don't know what I will do
Con mi pobre corazón.	With my poor heart.[13]
	(*Repeat last stanza*)]

This beautiful and highly emotional bolero, interpreted by Daniel Santos through the unique modulations of his sensual, deep voice, represents the lyrical simplicity by which the "words about absence seduce us into a presence," as Iris Zavala suggests regarding the motif of absence, of unrequited and frustrated love. Here the male singing subject expresses what were once the requirements of courtly love: the suffering caused by the beloved's indifference or outright rejection manifests itself as physical illness, fever, *corazón enfermo* (ill heart), and so on. This metaphorical malaise, however, should be explained beyond the individual realm and recontextualized within the conditions of modernization in which the absence and abandonment of women of the domestic sphere distances and diminishes men's patriarchal power and control. This "illness," indeed, bemoans the ways in which urban migration destabilizes patriarchal power, as Chuíto's refrain suggests when he concludes that in New York, "aquí la mujer se daña."

Dialogically singing/speaking, women boleristas have presented their *propia versión* (own version) of love relationships and of gender politics. Sylvia Rexach, the renowned Puerto Rican composer of boleros, responds to separation with a movement away from the man and from the relationship, toward the freedom of the open space:

Es tarde ya	[It is late already
por qué has venido tú ahora . . .	Why have you come now . . .
Es tarde ya,	It is late already,
pues ya han pasado varias horas.	too many hours have gone by.

Es tarde para comprender	It is too late
qué es lo que yo siento,	to understand what I feel,
Ya no se puede jugar	You can no longer play
con mis sentimientos.	with my emotions.

Es tarde ya pues hace rato	It is too late since
que te fuiste.	you left long ago.
Fíjate bien que fuiste tú	Remember, you wanted it
quien lo quisiste, vida.	this way, dear.

Es tarde y yo no vuelvo	It is too late
a brindarte tesoros a ti.	and I will not again
Es tarde y me esperan	bring you treasures.
me voy por ahí.	It is late
	and they are waiting for me
	I will walk around.]¹⁴

This feminist text expresses the desire of the woman subject to be liberated from a past relationship. It is too late, she says, for her to accept either his love or his return. This implies that the male lover has come to her asking for her continued love. She rejects this proposal, answering that it is too late, a "tarde" that not only refers to their failed relationship but also to the night, the nocturnal environment of boleros. Her willed exit from his life is expressed in the line "yo no vuelvo a brindarte tesoros a ti" and is even more defiantly uttered in the last line, where she exits his life and his feelings in order to enter the life of others: "me esperan." "Me voy por ahí" expresses her will to enter that open social space, transgressing the enclosed limits placed on women in Latin American society. She expressly leaves at night for an undefined destination, to a space ("por ahí") of unknown others, despite the social repercussions she implicitly will suffer; that is, she will become a "perdida" according to male social dictates.¹⁵

Even in this purest and most sentimental of musical forms, the fact that love is structured around conflict, vengeance, accusations, and metaphors for war should not be surprising given the struggles for power in which men and women have engaged. In "Ahora no," Lolita de la Colina reaffirms that the separation between lovers is not necessarily destiny, as many boleros would see it, but rather willed by women.¹⁶ The young Dominican singer Sonia Silvestre's own "Yo quiero andar" (I want to walk) voices the need for women to define their own path in life through the motif of walking. For her, life is like the night, a long voyage of experiences that she wants to embark on, while the implicitly male *tú*, the beloved, prefers the stagnant relationship based on possession and oppression. The refrain, which states that the man wants to sleep and the woman wants to walk, additionally suggests sexual intercourse and the female singing subject's reversal of the missionary position, which signifies female passivity and male activity and domination. The predominance of metaphors of mobility—open spaces, exits, and doors—signals women's need to articulate independence and freedom from oppressive (hetero)sexual relationships.

This emphasis on free movement also contests, in a larger social domain, not only the boundaries of the domestic sphere imposed on women but also the rigid disciplines and limitations of bodily movements, gestures, and comportment imposed on a feminine body by society's standards. Acceptable feminine movements, in contrast to men's, are systematically more centripetal and rigid, unwittingly expressing a sense of closure. A loose woman, in contrast, is constructed as such precisely because her "looseness is manifest not only in [her] morals, but in [her] manner of speech, and quite literally, in the free and easy way she moves."[17] The expression "loose woman" itself suggests a violation of those societal and patriarchal norms of movement that women across diverse cultures have internalized to one degree or another.

It is also apparent that women boleristas have appropriated negative constructs of the feminine and deployed them against men through their songs. A good example of this is María Greever's "Maldición Gitana" (Gypsy curse) which in many respects rewrites the woman-as-witch construct that permeates the male bolero, as in "Infortunio" by Don Fabián.[18] In "Malagueña salerosa" (Charming Malaga woman) the male singer repeats: "Que eres linda y hechicera"[19] [You are beautiful and bewitching]. Maria Greever mimics the male-defined discourse of female *brujería*, and transforms the male subject into the object of women's purported destructive energy.[20]

The separation motif is central to most boleros. A common narrative figure is that of the abandoned male singer/interpreter who drinks and sings alone to forget his romantic misfortunes. Gilberto Monroig's interpretations and performances likewise were visually constructed around the bohemian male subject who drinks and smokes while singing about the absence of his beloved. Daniel Santos's album cover for *El inigualable* (A man unequaled) depicts the bohemian, masculine space of a bar with such signifiers as a bar table covered with drinks and a lone male figure smoking a cigarette (see illustration on page 134).

This ubiquitous smoke, like references to shadows, rain, and fog, suggests a metaphysicality that transcends the material world. These interstitial, blurred, and even ethereal signifiers visually remind us of the passage of time, the past and the present, which the discourse of love itself attempts to mediate through a *carpe diem* philosophy. For instance, Tito Rodríguez's interpretation of Alberto Cortez's song, "Un cigarrillo, la lluvia y tú" (A cigarette, the rain, and you) significantly locates the lover, the *tú*, within those spaces of ambiguity.[21] This "estar/no estar" cannot be resolved; the singing subject revels in the dialectic tension between absence and presence, and it is, according to Zavala, through the "palabras sobre la ausencia" [words about absence] that we are seduced into presence.[22] The absolute promises of "siempre" and of eternal love, the negative and painful recognitions of that "nunca" accompanying unrequited love and the loss of the beloved, are reaffirmed by the smoke enveloping us all in the nocturnal, chiaroscuro spaces of bohemian life.

It has been said that the bolero says it all. The overwhelming affective intensity and absoluteness of its lexicon, the cathartic nature of its songs, the pain and the nostalgic desire underlying these musical utterances have been constructed as a totalizing text. Yet we must question who speaks through boleros or perhaps most important, whose voices have been heard or rather "filtered" through the discourse of love. The following discussion embraces an aperture in regendering the bolero proposed by both Iris Zavala and Luis Rafael Sánchez in two provocative readings that subversively rewrite the bolero as discourse of homosexual desire.

René Campos clearly indicts the bolero as an exclusively male cultural territory, a denouncement that is at once true and not totally so. Indeed, we may speak of the *discurso boleril* as predominantly masculine in the ways in which it articulates the desires and experiences of a particular heterosexual male subjectivity. However, a blanket statement such as Campos's renders invisible the central contributions of women as composers of boleros. Popular pieces such as "Bésame mucho" by Consuelo Vázquez, "Esta noche la paso contigo" by Laura Gómez Llanos, Monna Bell's "Recuerdos de Ipacaraí," Emma Elena Valdelamar's "Mucho corazón," and María Greever's "Cuando vuelva a tu lado" are just a few samples of the great popularity and dissemination of women-authored boleros, however consistently they have been articulated by male singers.

If it is true that men, for more than a hundred years now, have been able to articulate their desire for women through the language of boleros and through their rhythms,[23] then it is precisely through this discourse of desire and love that the masculine becomes destabilized. Its boundaries, like the iconic cigarrette smoke of bolero performances, are blurred with the sentimental, affective language that has been ascribed to women historically. The singer of "Fichas negras" (Black chips) sings to woman's "perversity,"[24] and in "Infortunio," woman is deemed "fatal," leading the lover/singer to an eventual, symbolic death of his emotions.[25] René Touzet, in "Conversación en tiempo de bolero," (Conversation to the bolero beat) suggests that indeed the male appropriation of the language of sentimentality is based on the prerequisite silencing of woman. The singing subject explains that the bolero is a dialogue that men have to sing only because women cannot be spoken to.[26] José Alfredo Jiménez's *boleros rancheros*, (in)famous precisely for their misogynist and patriarchal stance, also reveal the maculinist strategies of men in silencing the woman through seduction and eroticism.[27] This overt articulation of power differentials during sexual interaction reveals the dominance of the male over the female in songs generally considered liberatory because of their erotic content. It also points out the underlying violence that informs male desire even within presumed consensual relationships.

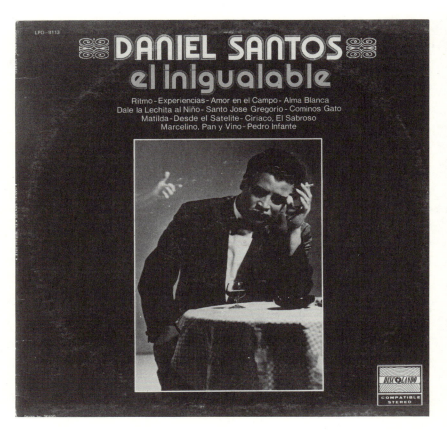

Album cover for Daniel Santos's *El inigualable*, released by Discolando Records, Venezuela, illustrates the typical pose of a man, represented by boleros, sitting alone and sad at a bar or table and smoking a cigarette. The hand on the left suggests a woman singer as well as a shooting gesture. Designed by Drago Artistic Designs. Courtesy of Orlando Bru.

"Amanecí en tus brazos" partly illustrates the strategic synecdoche produced by male desire to which the female, the beloved, is subjected. Beyond the absolute yet ambiguous and open-gendered *tú*, the beloved, or the object of desire, is systematically alluded to mostly through her parts, yet very infrequently, if at all, as a whole subject who thinks and feels.[28] Like the canonical Petrarchan love lyrics, male desire focuses on the woman's lips, eyes, and mouth.[29] Similarly, Agustín Lara's "Arráncame la vida" (Tear out my life): "porque al fin tus ojos / me los llevo yo"[30] [because, at the end, I steal your eyes] constantly provides the listener with a fragmented vision of the human being. Indeed, the most central metaphor for love, *corazón* (heart), suggests the compartmentalization of the woman or the beloved into one of her bodily organs or parts as a prerequisite for its possession. "To say 'heart' has meant to say everything," René Campos reminds us.[31] Ironically, it is the totalizing metaphor for possessing the female emotional and affective life. Yet this patriarchal synecdoche is not mere rhetoric but rather an articulation of a form of "psychic alienation" or "psychological oppression" to which women have been subjected.

Sandra Lee Bartky reviews three categories of oppression by colonialist regimes as identified by Frantz Fanon: stereotyping, cultural domination, and sexual objectification. A central process in both sexual objectification and racial denigration is fragmentation, or "the splitting of the whole person into parts of a person which, in stereotyping, may take the form of a war between a 'true' and 'false' self—or, in sexual objectification, the form of an often coerced and degrading identification of a person with her body."[32] Bodily parts become representative of the whole or "reduced to the status of mere instruments" for the satisfaction of male desires and fantasies. Most poignantly, though, it is the pervasive degree to which women are represented synecdochally in popular music that gives these patriarchal discursive strategies such immense social power. While it may be argued that the close-ups of the mouth, the eyes, the hands, and the body in general in the tradition of the bolero constitute a central element of its sensuality and become the iconic core of its eroticizing force, the overarching presence of the fragmentation of the female in other musical forms across cultures attests to this transnational patriarchal power. Moreover, it continues to represent the female as mere body, as physicality, constructs that have been deployed historically to justify economic exploitation of women and of peoples of color as well.

In this "libidinal economy" articulated by the bolero, male desire seems to have the upper hand. However, the fissure lies in the act of singing, of uttering a language that has been ascribed socially to the feminine. Sentimentality, emotion, pain, love, and loss remain circumscribed to the space of the feminine, to the domestic and personal, intimate sphere. In that sense, perhaps, the bolero has been inherently feminine, although this does not imply that it is a cultural production that belongs to women. René Campos observes that, within the conventions of the bolero, "the man can reveal himself as sensitive and emotional in a sanctioned form that does not threaten his masculinity."[33] The fact that men can assume the feminized language of the affective realm without being cast as feminine themselves attests to a most central patriarchal function of this musical form. These lyrics obviously provide a safe locus for male catharsis and for the male *grito* (scream) repressed in the public sphere; as Tito Rodríguez sings in "Nuestro balance" (Our Balance), the singing male screams unwillingly, opening up his heart.[34]

To confess that his heart has been "opened," implying not only catharsis but also a wound, vulnerability, and pain, socially goes against the grain of masculinity in Latin American societies. Octavio Paz identified this gendering of the masculine through the image of the Mexican mask, that is, in the hermetic nature and contained self-disclosure of the affective realm expected from men.[35] As Daniel Santos sings about singing, "porque el que canta, dice mucho y sufre poco, porque el que canta olvida su dolor"[36] [for he who sings says much and suffers little, for he who sings forgets his pain]. Singing boleros, then, is an alternative discourse to masculinity in Latin America. It has served, in public performances as well as in the intimacy of living rooms and bedrooms, as a language for self-disclosure and emotional healing that can be uttered only in the fictive space of the stage or in the intimate space circumscribed by the (hetero)sexual couple. This explains, partly, the privileged place that the bolero holds in the opinion of some Latino men interviewed.

This romantic *sensibility*, as Lawrence Grossberg defines it,[37] is mostly valued by Latinas/os as a positive discourse about heterosexual relations in which women are held in high esteem and respected, in contrast to the disrespectful and machista language of salsa. For instance, a twenty-eight-year-old Puerto Rican male interviewed for this study preferred Gilberto Santa Rosa's romantic salsa songs to salsa erótica because Santa Rosa's songs "present it [desire and sexuality] in very nice ways," "eliminating some of the negative erotic themes and putting eroticism in a more positive way." This male listener makes a valid distinction between salsa romántica, sentimental songs and love ballads informed by the lyrical discourse of the bolero, and salsa erótica. The latter emerged during the 1980s as a commercial attempt to revitalize salsa in face of the growing popularity of the merengue. It is characterized by open, erotic references to sex, orgasms, and lovemaking. One of its major interpreters and early representatives is Eddie Santiago.

Salsa erótica has had a significant following, and it opened the doors for speaking "the erotic" in a culture that has traditionally deemed this a taboo. However, salsa erótica has been created mostly by male composers and interpreters, except for the recent incursions of Cuban-American Albita Rodríguez, who in fact sings to homoerotic desire. In addition, a twenty-five-year-old Puerto Rican mentioned his predilection for "la música de los tríos y los boleros viejos" [music by trios and old boleros]. He equates, in fact, the discourse of desire of the bolero with Latin masculinity: "Nosotros los latinoamericanos somos locos hablando del amor y de estar enamorados y de sufrir por el amor y el amor es el pan de la vida, y sufrir por una mujer, eso es parte de nosotros" [We, Latin Americans (men) go crazy talking about love and about being in love and about suffering for love and "love is the bread of life," and to suffer for a woman, that is part of us].

This male predilection for the bolero, obvious in the intertextuality with boleros that underlie his description, [38] reveal boleros as "marked writing," what Hélène Cixous has defined as phallologocentrism "hidden or adorned with the mystifying charms of fiction"—of lyrical melodies and idealizing language in this case.[39] Thus, male listeners identify this affective language as theirs, as a sort of gender capital, simultaneously evincing that this language of the bolero actively constructs masculinity in Latin America. Moreover, they express a predilection for such a discourse on love on the basis of what they consider positive images of women and of erotic desire. This preference testifies to the seductive power of the lyrical tone that the bolero deploys, the "marked writing" that feminists have identified. The observation above also reveals the naturalization of the male as victim, "both used and abused by the female," as René Campos also comments in vindicating the bolero as an inversion "of the male-female relationship in its traditional, patriarchal context."[40] Two contradictory values in gender politics dovetail here. While the affective and emotional language of the bolero allows men to communicate and express themselves in the affective domain, becoming a liberatory value in the context of social boundaries, the construction of the male as woman's victim dangerously positions women as the object of male aggression, revenge, or violence, converging, in fact, with the more overtly misogynist discourse of salsa and other forms of popular music.

The particular case of a Latina from Detroit exemplifies this double-edged potential:

y mi novio se pasaba cantándome esa canción. . . . El me cantaba esa canción a mí como si él la hubiera escrito para mí. Es según él, como el refrán "el que tiene una mujer que la atienda, si no que la venda," Que significa el que tiene una mujer que la atienda sino que busque otra. Y yo le digo, ¡Pero coño! ¿Yo soy la mujer que tú estás atendiendo o soy la otra? ¿Qué tú quieres decir con eso? ¿Qué es lo que está pasando? Y él me dice, no pero si yo no quise decir eso. Y yo le digo que por qué me dice eso con tanto empeño si yo voy a mí misma y yo sé que puedo seguir pa'lante muy bien.

[my boyfriend used to sing that song to me. . . . He sang it as though he had written it for me. According to him, the song is like the proverb "he who has a woman needs to take care of her, if not he should sell her," which means that if a man doesn't take care of his woman, he should find another one. And I say to him, shit! Am I the woman that you are taking care of or am I the other one? What do you mean by this? What's going on? And he says to me, no but I did not mean to say that. And I say to him, then why do you sing that to me with so much insistence if I am my own person and I can very well continue to move on independently?]

As this Latina reminds us, although boleros represent an alternative, liberatory space for Latin American men, it is also deployed by these men as a strategy for possessing and controlling the women in their lives and for maintaining their socially invested power in (hetero)sexual relationships.

The simultaneous and multiple gender forces at work in the bolero as sociomusical practice are not bound to masculinity. Like any other sociomusical practice, the bolero, as cultural text, is also open to regenderings and productions of meaning that move well beyond the heterosexist boundaries implicit in their authorship and lyrics. In her provocative and central piece on the bolero, "De héroes y heroínas en lo imaginario social: El discurso amoroso del bolero" (About heroes and heroines in the social imaginary: The discourse of love in the bolero) Iris Zavala stresses throughout her analysis the structural discursive apertures that characterize the bolero's central signifiers, the *yo* and the *tú*. Depending on the receptor's own sexual identity and that of the singer or interpreter, the poetic *I* or "semiotic subject" constantly shifts sexual identity and is internally "plural" and exchangeable in its gender value. The ambiguity and open-ended gender of the *yo* and the *tú* (particularly in Spanish, where the system of inflections makes it easy to change the gender of adjectives, verbs, and subjects) allows for a regendering or a rearticulation of the utterance.

For Zavala the communicative triangle *emisor/mensaje/receptor* (speaker/message/receptor) is continuously destabilized as to gender inflections. This discursive analysis has vast implications, for it would render invalid or at least incomplete an analysis of women-authored boleros in contrast to male-authored ones. Zavala, however, is prompt to indicate that whereas male-authored boleros are clearly inflected as masculine given the references to women as "perdidas," "hechiceras," and so on, she finds in women-authored boleros a larger degree of gender "aperture" (ambiguity) than in men's texts. Thus, I have refrained from engaging in any analysis of male versus female boleros except for positioning them in dialogue and contestation with/against each other as I did above. What is significant is the centrality of the singer's sexual identity and of the act of singing through which the text is gendered with his/her voice and body. The presence of the audience, the listener or receptor, in this semiotic triangle further complicates fixing gender values on to these texts. How does a heterosexual female listen to a bolero authored by María Greever but inflected in the masculine (as they mostly are) and sung by Tito Rodríguez? What about Agustín Lara's sentimental tirades about his *perdidas*, who become *perdidos* in the voice of Toña La Negra, who interpreted most if not all of his compositions? What meanings are produced among lesbian and gay interpretive communities that continue to consume boleros as texts that articulate desire between homoerotic lovers? Gender, then, is always already destabilized in this particular musical sensibility given the open-gendered nature of the *yo* and the *tú*, a linguistic recourse that has characterized love poetry throughout the Hispanic tradition.

If Zavala's article hints at the structural possibilities for homosexual rewritings of boleros, Luis Rafael Sánchez places the figure of Daniel Santos—the Don Juan of Latin America, the icon of masculinity and Latin machismo—within a sexual discourse of ambiguity that rewrites boleros (as well as guarachas) as articulations of homosexual desire. *La importancia de llamarse Daniel Santos* (The importance of being called Daniel Santos) (1988) is a consciously crafted, ambiguous, and ambivalent text that explores sexuality, power, class, masculinity, and machismo through the eponymous figure of Daniel Santos and through the intertextual presence of bolero and guaracha lyrics, both of which constitute a most heteroglossic and polyphonic text in Puerto Rican literary tradition. The music destabilizes the ideal positioning of the bourgeois, elite reader, proposing instead a more democratic act of reading popular cultural texts in their juxtaposition with references and allusions to high culture—Shakespeare, Homer, Darío, Neruda.

A truly postmodern instance of cultural and discursive hybridity, *La importancia de llamarse Daniel Santos* deploys bolero lyrics as cultural utterances that allow exploration of gender identity and sexual politics in the Caribbean, in Mexico, and throughout Latin America. There is a constant tension between the commonality of boleros and guarachas and their singular value as a class-based cultural production that emerged among the urban proletariat. Since the 1930s, bolero lyrics in particular have appealed both to the romantic sentimentality of "the bourgeois macho of Garden Hills," the "Crema," as "to the male from Barrio Obrero and the lumpen, the "Mierda." In the words of Luis Rafael Sánchez, "Daniel Santos postula una genitalia interracial, transnacional" [Daniel Santos proposes an interracial, transnational genitalia]. Bolero and guaracha lyrics function as a link to the macho sensibility, the *vivir en varón* (living as a male) that informs, like a unifying thread, the textual totality of the book. The "impossible dialogue" among social classes in Latin America is achieved within the locus of bolero lyrics, for these have a common attitude toward women. Resentment and dependency, idealization and accusations, love and hate are but some of the contradictory and ambivalent attitudes that unify Latin American men from diverse and opposing social origins in a discourse of gender-based solidarity. In other words, the bolero and Daniel Santos discursively and thematically map a continental geography of male desire throughout Latin America.

La importancia de llamarse Daniel Santos also finds a major subtext in Oscar Wilde's *The Importance of Being Earnest*, a dramatic work that similarly explores the ambivalence of identity, the possibilities of double identities, and the mask that destabilizes the concept of a unitary, coherent identity. This Wildean subtext invites a rereading of the Latin American male as an embodied text defined by an inner tension, the *estar/no estar* no longer framed between man and woman but between two gender identities, the masculine and the feminine, a blurring of gender that we have already located in the bolero's internal possibilities for discursive regendering.

While *La importancia de llamarse Daniel Santos* proposes itself as a fictional biography of the (in)famous Puerto Rican singer Daniel Santos, who died on November 28, 1992, the text itself is not only fictional dialogue and stories nor invented ethnography. It also includes one of the most radical critiques of machismo penned by a Latin American writer. Luis Rafael Sánchez indicts "el macho, machería y machismo" and subversively rereads the figure of Daniel Santos and his repertoire as a locus of decentered sexual identity. Daniel Santos is ubiquituous and eternal, like the boleros that he sings, and these characteristics are indeed informed and mediated through the subtextual figure of Don Juan, who, in his attempt to seduce numerous women, escapes unicity and incarnates multiplicity.[41] Thus, Daniel Santos is not only a singer but an embodiment of the macho's polyphonic condition per se, a decentralized ego that traversed Latin America, multiplying his seed, his image, and his name—literally disseminating himself—throughout the continent.

The eponymous patriarch of Latin American sentiment and desire, pleasure and love, Daniel Santos also becomes the object of desire and the enunciative locus of a male homosexual gaze/voice. As icon of desire and of pleasure realized, Daniel Santos serves as a locus of a free erotic play that Luis Rafael Sánchez surreptitiously associates with homosexual desire. The dialogue among Cuban "locas" (queens), which concludes with references to "Lágrimas negras" ("Black tears"), allows us to see Daniel Santos and his musical pleasures from the perspective of an ideal gay audience. The author's monologue on gayness, or *locura*, in New York City and the erotic description of a male body in "Los mil y un tic del macho" ("The thousand and one ties of a man"), a discourse that evokes pleasure in the hetero-(homo)sexual gaze of the reader, whether man, woman, or both, suggest this Wildean hidden identity at play.

"Los mil y un tic del macho" is an ambiguous description, a double discourse on the male body. It is a critique of the macho physique, of hard bodies, of the male body as performance and of machismo as performative act. The ambiguity of this performance is linguistically constructed in the anaphoric patterns of the phrase *parecer varón* (to look like a male), an utterance that signifies both machismo as performance and an articulation of homosexuality as a histrionic act. The description also revels in the pleasure of the narrator's gaze as he meticulously describes the body parts of this *varón*, gazing down the male body like a gradual, eroticizing striptease that concludes with a gastronomical discourse on the *güevo* (testicles). The final passages of this second section, "Vivir en varón," which demythifies machismo, are framed by the song "Somos diferentes" (We are different), the bolero that originally sang to heterosexual relations and that Orquesta de la Luz has appropriated to sing to cultural difference. Here, Luis Rafael Sánchez rewrites these lyrics within the context of difference in sexual orientation. Lines such as "tenemos que olvidarnos de este amor / porque un amor así no puede ser" [we have to forget about this love / because a love such as this cannot be] are no longer bound to heterosexual relations but now suggest, after the homoerotic discourse that precedes it, the articulation of homosexual desire as restricted by dominant morals and values.

The final section of this hybrid book concludes with a scene reminiscent of the Garden of Delights yet localized in the outskirts of San Juan, Puerto Rico, in a mountainous area called El Verde, to which a number of young people escape, playing "hookey" from their schoolday routine. The voyeur/narrator revels in witnessing, without being seen, a moment of lovemaking between a girl and her young male lover, a scene framed by popular music, including the pop version of Beethoven's Fifth and some boleros sung by Santos. The glorifying reaffirmation of free sensuality, pleasure, and eroticism—coded in the mountains where *cimarrones* (maroons) found liberty on the margins of the city—becomes a sort of erotic utopia outside the boundaries of social etiquette, sexual mores, and rules. "Todo lo llenas tú, sexualidad, todo lo llenas"[42] [Sexuality, you fulfill everything, you fulfill everything] closes this text of pleasure, indeed of multiple pleasures, desires, and decentralized eroticism that proposes a re-writing of Daniel Santos as the ultimate icon of machismo, into a figure who embodies and incarnates (homo)sexual desire (or at least who evokes it). The *gay saber* (gay knowledge) or *gaya sciencia* (gay science, poetry) that Iris Zavala mentions as a set of historical knowledges involved in the emergence of the bolero[43] has been fictionalized in Luis Rafael Sánchez's text of sensual and (homo)erotic liberation. In the words of Puerto Rican poet Jorge A. Morales, "cada cual tiene su bolero" [to each his or her bolero].[44]

CHAPTER EIGHT

Patriarchal Synecdoches
Of Women's Butts and Feminist Rebuttals

✛

La Sonora Matancera, Cuba's most famous *septeto* (septet) whose singers included Daniel Santos, Celio González and Celia Cruz, popularized a hit called "Las muchachas" (The girls) during the 1940s and 1950s.[1] Analogous to the Beach Boys' hit "California Girls," "Las muchachas" maps women's bodies as national or continental geography. Whereas in "California Girls" the Beach Boys celebrate the free-spirited, outdoor character of West Coast Anglo women, the Sonora Matancera expresses a male predilection, not without its own alternative nationalist overtones, for the Cuban woman from Havana, Matanzas, or Santiago.

The enumerative structure of these lyrics presents an ideal (national) body that is a composite of the various best "parts" of the female types from various Latin American countries. Illustrating the pervasiveness of the synecdoche in musical textualizations of the female, the ideal woman in "Las muchachas" represents the continental body of Latin America, embraced by the polyphonic subjectivity of a Don Juan or a Daniel Santos— "I love them all." Indeed, after naming a preference for Cuban women— "No, no, pero cuando veo a una habanera toda la sangre se me alborota. Y si yo veo a una matancera entonces sí que boto la pelota" [No, no, but when I see a woman from Havana, I get agitated. And if I see a woman from Matanzas, then I really get excited]—the male singing subjects conclude that they want to "dance" with them all. This pluralizing of Woman (Woman as multiplicity) not only maps the geography of a Latin male gaze and desire, but most centrally, it delineates a Don Juan subjectivity whose desire and libidinal economy are never static nor totally satisfied.

"Las muchachas" illustrates the predominance of the male gaze and masculine desire in Afro-Caribbean music and in salsa, one that fetishizes the woman's *caderas* (hips) as a signifying locus of (often political) pleasure. The mulatta, in particular, has been constructed as an antinomy to the Beach Boys' ideal of a blonde, thin California girl. Certainly, as Puerto Rican writer Edgardo Rodríguez Juliá exemplifies in his beach chronicle titled "El veranazo en que mangaron a Junior" (The great summer when Junior was arrested), the aesthetics of the ideal body in Latin America is culturally and racially marked.[2] In a narrative voice that resonates with salsa's phallocentric language, Juliá chronicles a beach festival in Punta Salinas, Puerto Rico, and establishes *el gufeo* (humorous signifying) as a communal ritual based on a culture of male pleasure, gaze, and desire. Both observer and participant, the narrating subject, a journalist, positions himself as a voyeur in the utopian and carnavalesque space of a salsa festival at the beach. The underlying *mirada definidora* (defining gaze) structures and constructs this text as a sexual performative act, contiguously relating musical and erotic performance. In one passage the author describes the musical performance by Junior Moonshadow as a series of gestures of phallic penetration, ejaculation, and aggression that equate sex and music as performance (not unlike Eddie Santiago's provocative movements of penetration staged throughout his singing appearances). The text itself traces the male desire through gaze into an erection and an orgasmic discourse that concludes in an almost postorgasmic descent. As the narrator's defining gaze identifies "tres ricuras de hembras con buenos muslos y mejores nalgas" [three tasty females with good thighs and even better butts],[3] the sounds and discourse of Cuban rumbas serve as intertext to the male experience.

Edgardo Rodríguez Juliá's fixation with the female "butt," inscribed throughout his work in narratives like "Una noche con Iris Chacón,"[4] is reaffirmed in the lyrics of salsa and Afro-Caribbean musical traditions, whose songs and cuts continue to position the Caribbean mulatta as the embodiment of rhythm, movement, and erotic pleasure. Orquesta Aragón's "Tan Sabrosona," authored by Rafael Lay and Richard Ergües, is structured around a male voice/gaze that addresses the mulatta woman: "mi negra no te molestes si te dicen sabrosona / por ese andar que tú tienes / tan tremendo y retozón" [my black woman, don't get upset if they call you tasty / because of the way you walk / so tremendous and playful].[5] Clearly, this visual erotic fixation on the hip and pelvic movements of the mulatta woman is phallocentric. Yet the historical and political implications of this discursive, patriarchal gaze have not been examined systematically. When Cuban male singers cry out, "mira prieta sabrosona / conmigo vas a acabar" [look, tasty dark-skinned woman / you are destroying me], they do so not only because of a male vagina dentata anxiety nor because their hypererotization of the dark female body poses a threat to their own

The album cover for *Latinissimo: The New Xavier Cugat Orchestra*, released in 1994 by the Madacy Music Groups, Quebec, Canada, shows three women's butts painted with tropicalized motifs, illustrating the ongoing representation of Afro-Caribbean and Latin American music as women and the prevalence of patriarchal synecdoches in the discourse about music.

sexual power. Such male utterances suggest that the mulatta not only threatens masculine psychosexuality but also disrupts the ordered masculine political and national body. As Vera Kutzinski intimates in her analysis of the mulatta figure in Cuban poetry,

For what the mulatta, unlike the ideology of mestizaje, represents is not a stable synthesis but a precarious and tenuous multiplicity, "a concentration of differences," of "insoluble differential equations." The mulatta indexes areas of structural instability and ideological volatility in Cuban society, areas that have to be hidden from view to maintain the political fiction of cultural cohesion and synthesis. The key signifier of such instability and volatility is the nonwhite woman's body conceived as the site of troubling sexual and racial differences. As much as this site has

One of the opening photos in Umberto Valverde and Rafael Quintero's book about women salseras in Cali, Colombia, *Abran paso: Historia de las orquestas femeninas de Cali* (Centro editorial Universidad del Valle, 1995) provide an example of patriarchal synecdoches in men's discourse about women and music. Photo by Fernell Franco. Courtesy of Umberto Valverde.

all the attractions of a mythic place of intellectual and psychological refuge and "epistemological consolation" in a society like Cuba, it is simultaneously feared as the locus of potential change, disruption, and complication.[6]

As Kutzinski also observes, the literati of Cuban white male poets have represented the mulatta as "pure rhythm," thus commodifying blackness and erasing issues of race and racist social practices from their political and social implications. What Kutzinski is suggesting, then, is that by fixating on the mulatta body and particularly on her hips as a locus of desire and pleasure for the Cuban male subject, poets and musicians systematically detract attention from racist practices in Cuban society. However, what is ironic in this synecdochal erasure is that it is precisely the black woman's hips, her pelvis, and her genitalia, her vagina, that have been subjected historically to racism through rape and sexual violence. This displacement, then, is one of signifieds: by trivializing her hips *only* as a rhythmical and musical pleasurable entity, then Caribbean patriarchy can erase from the body of the mulatta any traces of violence and racist practices for which it has been responsible throughout history.

It is also true that during colonial times black music and rhythms were considered, by the colonialist regime, a sign of racial inferiority. Indeed, Afro-Caribbean music was seen as an infantilizing practice, a sign of puerility, according to Fernando Ortiz.[7] In this light, then, depictions of mulatta women dancing, engaging in rhythmical movements, continue to inscribe a gender- and race-based inferiority, an infantilization of women and an emptying out of their rational power. Also evident in the title "Las muchachas," it has a particular impact on women of color in the Caribbean, a construct that continues to be embedded in our contemporary social relations.

As a painful reminder of the historical continuity of these patriarchal constructs, in one of my short escapes to bookstores in Ann Arbor I ran into one of the many new anthologies on the cultures of Latinos and Latinas. Entitled *Currents from the Dancing River* and edited by Ray González, well known for his previous editorial ventures, this anthology opens with a piece by Enrique Fernández, a cultural essay titled "Salsa × 2," powerfully located as the opening pages to the rest of the anthology.[8] Like Antonio Benítez Rojo's *The Repeating Island*, Fernández's essay illustrates the contemporary utility of discursive patriarchal tendencies.[9] Spanish-born Cuban-American writer and journalist Fernández, who has become the Latino spokesperson for the *New York Times*, proposes food and sexual pleasure as the essential icons and motifs that distinguish Latinos from non-Latinos. He invites the (Anglo) reader to "hear my music, eat my food, you are mine, you are me."[10] This highly charged utterance reduces the complex history of U.S. Latinas/os and of Latin America to the sensorial realm of sound and taste, thus displacing the cultural agency and historical variability of our social complex. By emphasizing sounds and tastes, cultural pleasures in which Latinas/os undoubtedly engage as much as any other cultural sector does as part of its traditions, the author depoliticizes and neutralizes the oppositional and heterogeneous community values that both music and food represent for us.

The intercultural desire that Fernández plays with in this cultural "come on"—eat my food, you are mine—implies a masculine voice whose desires are to "possess" the Other (the female Anglo, of course) through the seductive power of Latin popular music, of salsa picante, and of course, of his own words. The depoliticizing, deracializing, and dehistoricizing effects of this cultural incursion are evident in his reading of the famous Dominican merengue "El negrito del batey." He accents the male voice that expresses the pleasure of dancing with a tasty, black woman—"me gusta bailar medio apretao / con una negra bien sabrosa" [I like to dance a bit tightly with a very tasty black woman]—as an illustration of the intense pleasure of music and food central to Latina/o culture as Fernández constructs it here. Significant, however, is the author's erasure of, and neglect to engage in, the politics of slavery to which the song alludes from the beginning: the black male voice complains about hard physical labor and humorously suggests that work was invented by God for the ox and the animals, not for human beings, a contestatory utterance against the exploitations of slavery and the dehumanizing and animal-like practices to which slaves were subjected. In this context, dancing as a signifying cultural practice reveals the spaces of resistance and pleasure that the slaves carved for themselves as rituals for survival.

The affirmation of dancing, then, needs to be framed within the larger history of slavery in the Caribbean rather than as a mystified, essentialized expression of a Latina/o erotics. Echoing Tomás Blanco, Enrique Fernández goes on to explain the use of the word *negrita* among Caribbean Latinos as a term of endearment, in contrast to the "ugly violence" of the word *nigger* in the United States, even when the latter is uttered by African-Americans themselves. And "what about the 'negra bien sabrosa,'" Fernández continues, "the yummy Negress the singer wants to dance the sideways step of the merengue, holding her good and tight?"[11] In response, the male writing subject continues to perpetuate the phallocentric language about Latinas that has historically objectified black and mulatta women as objects to be cannibalized, ingested, totally possessed, and intellectually invalidated. An ironic twist is that the discourse of "gastronomic sexuality" that Fernández reproduces contains a measure of sadism as a language of devouring, a violence that he denies in Latin American racial relations. Fernández's paraphrase of what he incorrectly considers essentially Latina/o—the erotic "comerte" culminates in a Spanish interjection, "¡Ay, qué rico!" which suggests that sexual climax is intimately linked to its articulation in Spanish.

Spanish, then, is rendered as a language "unabashed in lovemaking" and also truly immersed in violence and conquest in Latin America, not in the United States. Fernández proposes, in a sort of erotic cultural utopia, that it be considered "our finest Hispanic heritage."[12] In his view the intensity of love and sensorial pleasure that marks all Latino experience (notice that I did not inflect Latino as female) is the answer to that Anglo Other's "sensory vacuum," which he also constructs in an essentializing way. Fernández, then, strategically essentializes Latino culture as a utopian, eroticized alternative to Anglo America's puritanism-based repression of the sensual and the disciplining of the bodies. Many of his assumptions remain questionable: the discursive repetitions of a masculinist and phallocentric subject that favors male gaze and desire while eliding the experience of black, mulatta, and Latina women—the discursive tradition of an eroticized Latin America that "feeds emotionally" her Male Other, the United States, and the first world countries in exchange for economic dependency, a macrocosm of the husband-wife domestic relationship.[13]

This "gastronomic sexuality" contaminates the verbal discourse of writers like Enrique Fernández and Edgardo Rodríguez Juliá and continues to be deployed in Latin popular music, particularly in that icon of the *negra sabrosa* from which a constellation of male desires emanate within Latin American cultural history. The discursive referent of woman as *sabrosa* (tasty) is coupled with the essentializing references to her rhythmic skills.

In the case of Orquesta Aragón's song mentioned above, the textual power of the adjective is multiplied by the suffix *ona*, as in *sabrosona*, thus hyperbolizing the value of woman as an object to be consumed, possessed, and cannibalized.

This particular construct is systematically deployed in the Dominican merengue and continues to be activated in the Dominican bachata, Latino rap, as well as in salsa music.[14] In the merengue the strategy of the double entendre, the linguistic pun, continues to veil this gender-based discursive violence as humor and play to avoid censorship. In an early article on the merengue, Catherine Guzmán mentions "Caña brava," composed by Toño Abreu in 1918, as a cut that "broke all records of popularity." "Caña brava" illustrates the strategy of masking sexual desire through metaphors of food, taste, and appetite: "Caña dulce / caña brava / dame un gajo / de tu caña" [Sweet cane / brave cane / give me a piece / of your cane], a metonymic language in which the sugar cane stands for the woman's body.[15] Despite the phallic shape of the sugar cane, the caña contains a multiplicity of social and historical allusions—the plantation system, the exploitation of women slaves, the sweetness of the cane, and the hard physical labor entailed in its harvesting—that serve to create a text open to various interpretations and associations.

In one of the most popular merengues in history, "El sancocho prieto" (The dark stew), the hungry male singing subject addresses an implied female *tú*, asking her to serve him some savory dark stew. The "sancocho prieto" is openly equated with the color of the woman's skin, thus suggesting not only that a mulatta or black woman is the object of his desire but in the economy of gender, that it is the dark-skinned woman who serves the male his food as she also becomes the food to be served: "El sancocho prieto / color de tu carne / tú tendrás que darme / porque estoy hambriento" [The dark stew / the color of your skin / you will have to give me / because I am hungry]. Moreover, these lyrics reaffirm the expected role of women as the "emotional feeders" of the rest of the family, a role that, as Sandra Lee Bartky has pointed out, continues to indicate women's oppression within the domestic role despite advances in the workplace.

Gerardo's rap hit "Rico Suave" (Tasty soft) consistently plays with the metonymic relations between woman and food—this time "sushi." El General's hits "Te ves buena" and "Las mujeres de San Diego" and even Juan Luis Guerra's "Woman del callao" textualize this male oral desire for consuming woman.[16] However, in the context of the Dominican Republic, Deborah Pacini argues that the popularity of bachatas "de doble sentido" [double entendres] during the 1970s and 1980s also needs to be explained in socioeconomic terms. While there were "economic rewards for producing this type of song," these bachatas were heavily criticized "as immoral and indecent" by the dominant sector. Thus, the bourgeoisie censored working-class texts while sanctioning other forms of sexually explicit materials.[17]

This systematic continuity has contributed to naturalizing male desire for race- and gender-based synecdoches and to the tacit acceptance of representations of women as sale and commodity. When Edgardo Rodríguez Juliá states that Puerto Rican men have been "programado[s] atávicamente para la apreciación, distinción y metafísica del trasero"[18] [programmed, like atavars, toward the appreciation and distinction and metaphysics of the butt], he is indeed justifying this process of naturalizing a fixation that is ultimately a convergence of racism and misogyny. He is explaining it as an atavism, the traces of an ancestral characteristic that fixes sexist behavior and practices throughout history and that precludes and denies any value to women's historical cultural agency or to the impact of feminism in Latin America. In this regard, Edgardo Rodríguez Juliá's proposal of the beach festival as a utopian, carnavalesque space in which erotic freedom is coupled with musical performance and with dancing, fails to create a more democratically gendered text. To the contrary, it offers a highly phallocentric discourse that naturalizes the power of the male subject to construct the female according to his own needs and desires. To reduce the complexity of women as human beings and social entities to the image of the *cadera*, of the butt, is to perpetuate, textually speaking, the history of economic and sexual exploitation of women of color in the Caribbean, as well as their metonymic subordination to a mere corporeal part.

African-American women rappers, like Queen Latifah and Salt'n Pepa in "Shake Your Thang" "assert their right to express sexual desire and to control their own bodies" in the production of their feminist videos.[19] By reappropriating female bodies as signifiers of resistance to oppression (I say reappropriating because women are appropriating the male appropriation of their own bodies), they are able to imbue different, feminist meanings to the female body, meanings produced by women themselves that present women in control of their own bodies. In this light, Fransheska's merenrap entitled "Menéalo" (Shake it or move it) is also addressed as a woman's contestatory response to objectifications of the female body.[20] She deploys her own body's erotic movements and rhythmic modulations, as she says, to consciously fuel the eroticizing discourse about Fransheska that colors reviews about her music and her performances. In other words, by inverting the agency of said eroticization, Fransheska assumes more control of her body as a signifier as well as displacing the control of the journalists to represent her as a locus of pleasure and desire.

Given the demonizing process by which Latin American women were chastised for dancing during colonial times—"Niñas que vais bailando / Al infierno vais saltando" [Girls who dance / jump directly to hell][21]—that is, for being the objects of a patriarchal repression of the sensual, Fransheska's "re-buttals" of these social constructs of the feminine are as historically significant as they are contemporaneously relevant. When Fransheska associates her eroticized movements as a prelude to sexual intercourse, a decision made by the woman herself, she also suggests the power of the female eroticized body over the male. She moves, she says, so that she can overpower the male gaze that continually objectifies her as mere corporality. The power of the female body over masculine will is indeed the origin of that consistent ambivalence that men express about women in the bolero, a fear that as "seductresses" women, with the "charms" of their bodies, will eventually destroy the masculine ego, displacing the power of the phallus as central signifier.

Much like Fransheska's reappropriations, Latina rapper Lisa M's "Flavor of the Latin" also culls cultural constructs of Latinas/os as erotic, sensorial beings in order to reaffirm her presence as a Latina rapper.[22] This interlingual song serves as her introduction to audiences both in Puerto Rico and on the mainland. She identifies herself as 100% Latina, evoking the trope of women as food as well. Verging on self-advertising, however, this cut is constituted by the constant refrain that echoes throughout: "Flavor of the Latin," always sung in English by a male voice in the background and asserted by a subsequent "Sí." The song concludes with a political affirmation of Lisa M's ethnicity: "I'm Puerto Rican and proud." Again, this particular song illustrates the blurred ideological boundaries of this type of discursive strategy: by appropriating, deploying, and repeating these cultural formulas—the Latina *con sabor*—the text takes on multiple possibilities for signifying. Lisa M locates herself and her music as centrally Latina, thus inviting a particular audience. Simultaneously, however, the text leaves open fissures through which intercultural assumptions about gender may be reaffirmed, utterances that in fact may have been consciously deployed as marketing strategies.

This gesture of reappropriation, much like Las Chicas del Can's minimal dress on stage, introduces, nonetheless, an ideological and gender-based ambiguity as to the possibilities of the readings and reactions it evokes. As Sylvia Walby summarizes in *Theorizing Patriarchy*, there has been substantial disagreement as to whether it's a "sign of resistance for women to display and exert their sexuality or incorporation into a patriarchal system or whether it's both simultaneously."[23] This point brings home, to Latin American culture, even deeper implications, given the highly contested aesthetics of the feminine among Latina and Latin American women who choose to use bright colors, high-heel shoes, and tight dresses. The self-eroticizing impulse assumes for Latinas a cross-cultural meaning, for it conscientiously diverges from the Anglo feminist paradigm of effacing female sexuality from their own bodies by resisting the dictates of the fashion industry and of society, by choosing not to wear makeup or dresses and indeed by creating an androgynous style that would blur the boundaries between the feminine and the masculine as social constructions and impositions on individuals.

Latinas who have chosen to self-eroticize their bodies through the prominence of makeup should be interpreted in the context of cultural resistance and affirmation as well as in the larger framework of gender relations in Latina/o societies. For many Latinas, the poetics and politics of self-erotics is a material, physical, and clearly visual way of opposing the sexual repression of the female, which is heavily inflected by a Catholic patriarchy. To "look" like a *puta*, to perform in this sense, should not be read, as many Anglo feminists have done, as an assimilation of the social dictates of what it takes to be feminine but rather as a repossession of one's own body away from the higher social powers, such as parents, church, and society. Anglo feminists like Sandra Lee Bartky, for instance, argue against the idea that "the preservation of a woman's femininity is quite compatible with her struggle for liberation," finding such feminism "incoherent." In a convincing discussion on the ways that modern patriarchy has created "subjected and practiced" bodies out of women's made-up, thin, beautiful, and sexy bodies that are unattainable except through denying one's own needs—what she also calls "the female body as spectacle"[24]—she argues that these patriarchal strategies cut across race and class differences and that the overarching influence of the media and advertising affects women from all groups and racial sectors.

However, Bartky does not consider that patriarchal structures and cultural histories are not identical everywhere and what for Anglo America is the ideal beauty—the thin, tall bodies—for the Latin gaze, both male and female, signals deficiency, not beauty. Indeed, wider hips and fuller bodies have been generally established as ideal aesthetic standards for women, although the influence of U.S. media also has had its impact throughout Latin America and within U.S. Latina/o communities. As in Judith Ortiz Cofer's poem "So Much for Mañana," the voice of a Puerto Rican mother admonishes her daughter, who has been living too long in the United States, to gain some weight because "men here like their women with some weight."[25] The rap song titled "La gordita" (Dear little fat one) by Santi y sus Duendes, also illustrates the different cultural values circulating among

Latin American societies regarding the female body, although once again the dominant male perspective continues to focus on the female body as source of pleasure. At the beginning the singer wants to praise "gorditas," who have been excluded from praise and attention in media and popular culture. But then the text becomes another instance of the objectification of women, as the singer alludes to the pleasure he derives from touching his "gordita's" rolls and folds.[26]

In some ways, then, the "tyranny of slenderness" is not necessarily deployable among Latinas, although the use of makeup, as we have seen, definitely marks femininity in our culture. What may be sexual subordination in Anglo America's obsession with the female body, in Latin America takes on different forms of repression and "disciplining"; thus, the self-eroticizing of many Latinas and Latin American women may not indicate exclusively an internalization of patriarchal codes and expectations nor a false consciousness among Latinas but strategies of reappropriations that symbolically allow women to be in control of their own bodies.

However, it is important also to acknowledge the fissures of such performances which, like other forms of cultural texts, may be read in multiple ways. While reappropriating one's sexuality becomes a significant political practice at the individual level, within the larger, public space of the stage it may assume double-edged ideological repercussions. It could signal even stronger displacements of phallocentric power and of the power of the male to control the female body, given the physical distance, the hierarchies of the higher stage over the audience, and the already contested yet at times still functional dichotomy of the performer (producer) versus the audience (receptor). Simultaneously, it may systematize, formalize, make public, and unwittingly naturalize the objectification of the female body in the eyes of a misogynist audience.

Toña La Negra's interpretation of "La Negrita Concepción" is an interesting performance in this regard.[27] While the song may have been written by a man—Cuates Castilla—Toña's own vocal rendering of the mulatta or the negra suggests a self-ironic appropriation of her own body as a mulatta in Mexico. That Toña sings "La Negrita Concepción," in contrast to a male rendering of that same text, imbues the lyrics with a potential feminist revisioning. La Negrita Concepción is described as a famous rumbera who moves in extraordinary ways: "Hay que ver cómo se mueve . . . Ay mamá qué tembladera . . . Cómo mueve la cintura" [You have to see how she moves . . . Oh, woman, what shaking . . . How she moves her waistline]. The centrality of her body as the locus for centrifugal movements and the fixation of the male gaze on that movement reaffirm Kutzinski's analysis of the instability and volatility that the mulatta body brings to harmonious paradigms of nation. Yet Toña's interpretation also emphasizes the refrain "Esta negra es una fiera / que no tiene domador" [This black woman is a beast / without a tamer]. If read literally, this is clearly problematic as a primitivist construct of black women as beasts, a construct historicized in and through the institution of slavery. Yet from a feminist perspective and as sung by Toña La Negra, this refrain simultaneously alludes to the independence of the black woman, to her oppositionality and resistance as a "fiera" without a "domador," a tamer, or one who controls her.

Within the strong, brassy sounds of the mambo rhythms that frame the lyrics, the name Concepción is meaningful, directing us to the female black body as the origin of mestizaje and mulatismo in the Caribbean and ironically to the figure of the Virgin. It becomes a reaffirmation of the power of the mulatta to control her own life and her own body, to be the sole agent of her rhythmical movements, and to reject any possibilities of being owned by the masculine other, as the references in the song to the *marinero* and the *cocinero* clearly reveal. In the voice of Toña La Negra, whose very name marks the racial centrality of her figure in Mexico, "La Negrita Concepción" possibly becomes, in the eyes and ears of women and blacks, both a feminist contestation to the male gaze and a racial vindication of blackness as historicized gestures of resistance, oppositionality, and liberation.

CHAPTER NINE

Singing the Gender Wars

✠

Yo la mato o pide perdón [Either I kill her or she apologizes].
— Daniel Santos, "Yo la mato"

The increased mobility and integration of Latin American and Puerto Rican women into the work force and their growing access to the public spheres has had a destabilizing impact on the power of patriarchy in Latin America. New gender values and subjectivities among women have indeed resulted from their massive incorporation into the labor force. It is these new attitudes that conflict and clash with the traditional values that continue to instill "an ideology of inequality."[1] In fact, contemporary sociological studies in Puerto Rico have shown that the longer a woman works outside the home, the more likely that her attitudes will change.[2] Concomitantly, as women's gender expectations change and become more profound and long-lasting, the attitudes and practices of traditional males and of patriarchal society become more resentful and reactionary.

Such resentment can be traced through the historical development of Latin music. The bolero, for instance, gained much popularity during the 1930s, precisely at the moment when industrialization and urbanization in Latin America drew large numbers of women to work outside the home. In response to such changes, the *discurso boleril*, with its euphemistic and elegantly veiled expressions of courtly love and ill hearts, accused women of men's problems: "Usted es la culpable."[3] Yet this type of accusation simultaneously revealed male dependency on women's love and presence, that ubiquitous "no puedo vivir sin ti" [I can't live without you] that permeates this musicolyrical tradition. Thus, through a centripetal language of refinement, harmony, idealization, and nostalgia, the bolero continues to articulate those conflicts between men and women that have followed social and economic changes since the turn of the century.

Following the tradition of the guaracha in Afro-Caribbean music, with its popular diction, masculine and phallocentric perspectives, and a burlesque, parodic tone articulated from marginalized positions, salsa music emerged in New York City's Latin barrios during the 1960s and 1970s. It then shifted toward a more aggressive, warlike articulation of (hetero)sexual relations in Latin(o) American societies than the bolero had sung about. As a syncretic sociomusical practice, salsa exhibits a heterogeneous array of conceptions of the feminine. While centrally integrating the amorous discourse of the bolero and its obsession with the absent or lost woman, salsa presents more heterogeneous subject positions regarding women. For instance, it draws from the merengue's puns about woman as object to be consumed and cannibalized, as well as its idealized images of mothers, young women, and daughters and its passionate confessions of love. Also prominent in salsa's lyrics is the dualistic construct of the promiscuous, sexually superendowed black woman or mulatta, on the one hand, and the pure, sexually unattainable virgin/mother figure, on the other.

These configurations are not exclusive to salsa, for they abound in the literature of Hispanic countries as well as in the folklore and literature of other Western cultures.[4] As Sander Gilman has pointed out, the building of stereotypes "perpetuate[s] a needed sense of difference between the 'Self' and the 'object,' which becomes the 'Other.' Because there is no real line between the Self and the Other, an imaginary line must be drawn; and so that the illusion of an absolute difference between self and Other is never troubled, this line is as dynamic in its ability to alter itself as is the self."[5] This basic need, Gilman argues, leads to the construction of what Stephen Pepper has called "root metaphors," that is, "a set of categories which result from our attempt to understand other areas in terms of one commonsense fact."[6] By establishing analogical values between real life experiences and the world of myths, stereotypes establish associations that may entail either "negative images" or "positive idealizations."[7] It is at these two poles, indeed, that women are positioned and represented within Hispanic culture.

Yet during the 1970s and 1980s, salsa music was characterized by quite disturbing articulations of violence against women and of (hetero)sexual conflict consistently framed as metaphors of war and physical struggle. In part, this is not suprising, given the poetics and politics of a musical movement born in the war zones of Anglo society and whose aesthetic—harsh brass sounds, loud volume, polyrhythmia—reproduced the noises, the harsh realities, and the environment of life in the urban barrios.[8] In this light, salsa music has constituted a cultural public space for voicing gender conflict among Latin men and women, establishing a sort of (hetero)sexual politics in the ways in which "the discourses which comprise it [reproduce] a struggle equivalent to that experienced socially by its readers."[9] Yet while an ideal "equivalent" articulation of sexual politics would necessarily be dialogic in its formulation, salsa music remained mostly male-dominated and patriarchal in its perspectives during those years. In this sense, salsa seemingly has precluded any apertures for gender dialogism or plurality. Yet the 1980s and 1990s have witnessed a gradual growth in the participation of women in this musical culture, accompanied by shifting practices not only in composition but also in reception and in signifying acts.

Thus, throughout this analysis, male articulations of violence and gender conflict will be consistently dialogized by those voices of women singers who utter both male- and female-authored lyrics and who engage in a musical war against males by inverting sexist textualizations about women and "singing back" to men as objects of their diatribes. These women's lyrics are constituted by the same metaphors of war and violence that men have deployed against women throughout history. This musical stance, however, does not necessarily entail constituting a female subjectivity through music; rather, it suggests a more reactive position that duplicates the fixed binaries of gender roles imposed by Western systems of patriarchy.[10] While Anglo American feminism may dismiss these songs as sites of gender oppression, in my opinion they must be understood and appreciated within the cultural, social, and historical contexts of heterosexual relations in Puerto Rican society. These lyrics are valuable insofar as they eloquently articulate the struggles of Puerto Rican women and Latinas in the process of empowering themselves by contesting the dictates of a strong patriarchal system. Moreover, they collectively constitute musical spaces for oppositionality and contestation by recognizing, addressing, and appropriating masculine and misogynist discourse in popular music.

The problematic issue has not been so much the content of female songs but the fact that women's music has remained marginalized and invisible from the musical industry. Accordingly, my intent in this section is to bring together, and against each other, songs and lyrics that have been part of our cultural repertoire but that in isolation have not been read or listened to as a dialogic discourse on gender. By creating a critical collage of both male and female voices, we may be better able to identify gender conflict as a distinct social and cultural issue that has, in many ways and in many societies, been veiled or repressed, both in the name of feminist and social liberation and by the forces of patriarchy. The value of popular music in this respect is tremendous, for collectively it has carved a public as well as personal space in which to argue about male-female relations in Latina/o societies.

While violence in salsa music has been identified as two types—the arbitrary violence of the barrio and the more productive and sanctioned revolutionary violence of political revolutions in Latin America—violence against women has been excluded from most discussions of this music. A couple of isolated scholarly articles and journalistic incursions into gender issues have remained, at best, marginal in systematic analyses of this sociomusical practice.[11] Yet like many other forms of popular music—country western, rap, and rock and roll come to mind—salsa's negative textualizations of women should not be exclusively seen as an overarching indictment of Latina/o culture nor of Latin(o) men but as one of many forms of patriarchy that cross cultural boundaries. In fact, analyses of other forms of U.S. popular music since the 1930s reveal analogous female prototypes in their lyrics: women are goddesses, virgins, witches, and gold diggers.[12] Scholarly studies of gender representations in African American music also have identified these systematic figurations of the female, which rap music has intensified in the politics and poetics of the postindustrial ghetto.[13] What gives meaning, then, to these blanket representations are the specific sociohistorical, cultural, and racial contexts in which these are deployed and activated by and for particular audiences.

A tension exists for me, as a Latina scholar, regarding the implications of this particular analysis. To present this internal gender critique of salsa music to outside audiences has meant taking the risk of reaffirming stereotypes of Latin(o) machismo and thus of Latin(o) men's putative primitive and violent ways. Given the danger of the crosscultural implications of this analysis, I feel compelled to argue that misogynist violence and gender conflict in salsa must be part of an examination of larger structures of patriarchy and of phallocentric discourse that cross national and cultural lines. At the same time, salsa must be understood within the particular social experiences of disenfranchisement, oppression, and marginalization to which many Latinas/os and Latin Americans have been subjected. It is evident, as I write, that some of the most aggressive expressions against women in salsa are by now receding. Historically, then, salsa documents some shifts in gender conflict and sexual politics, shifts particularly seen in the language and in the forms that patriarchy takes, although this does not imply that salsa is not misogynist nor patriarchal any longer, as many Latino men have told me.

Robin Kelley's piece on gangsta rap has been helpful in thinking through this tension. As a feminist scholar, I am committed to denouncing violence against women in all contexts, and clearly this has been a central motivation in this book. Yet by exclusively focusing on Latino male misogyny, as Robin Kelley argues about black males, it would "deflect attention away from the larger crisis, thus serving to soften the blow of patriarchal backlash and separate black youth [Latinos] from dominant discourses — which is precisely one of the functions of 'Othering.'[14] Indeed, the social tragedy of domestic violence is not the exclusive domain of peoples of color nor of the proletariat, as many have constructed it in a displacing logic, but reflects the human victimization that ensues from capitalism in its most dehumanizing modes. As bell hooks has eloquently stated, in the context of an advanced capitalist society, men, disempowered and controlled by "the economic needs of capitalism,"

are fed daily a fantasy diet of male supremacy and power. In actuality, they have very little power and they know it. Yet they do not rebel against the economic order nor make revolution. They are socialized by ruling powers to accept their dehumanization and exploitation in the public world of work and they are taught to expect that the private world, the world of home and intimate relationships, will restore to them their sense of power which they equate with masculinity. They are taught that they will be able to rule in the home, to control and dominate, that this is the big pay-off for their acceptance of an exploitative economic social order. By condoning and perpetuating male domination of women to prevent rebellion on the job, ruling male capitalists ensure that male violence will be expressed in the home and not in the work force.[15]

Thus, hooks concludes, men find that the home and the family can function as a "control situation" where they can retaliate and not suffer the consequences of acting violently. This cycle of violence is systematically condoned and celebrated by U.S. society, in the media, in parenting practices that equate punishment with love, and in the global context of militarism, war, and foreign interventions. Thus, late capitalism's impact on U.S. patriarchy, doubly felt in Puerto Rico's economically dependent society, frames and explains violence against women as another instance of how violence permeates a society based on "the Western philosophical notion of hierarchical rule and coercive authority."[16] In colonized Latino societies such as Puerto Rico's, the male becomes a mediating representative of the same oppression as that represented by the colonialist regime.[17] In this context, misogyny and violence against women in salsa music during the 1970s and 1980s is not altogether surprising. It cannot be used as evidence of the primitivism or machismo of working-class Latino males in the barrio. Rather, gender violence in salsa music must be read as an articulation of the multilayered and contradictory relations of power and marginalization experienced by Latinos and Latinas whose daily lives were marked by under- and unemployment, economic disenfranchisement, racism, cultural marginalization, and violence on the part of social institutions, government, and the judicial system.

A clear historical antecedent to the gender wars in salsa music is the

Cuban *son*. Ignacio Piñeiro's original cut, titled "Castigador," a *son ha-banero* interpreted by the Septeto Nacional, illustrates the transhistorical and overarching dimensions of this warlike, heterosexual discourse.[18] While the song begins with a dialogue between the poetic *I*, the singer, and the so-called *castigador* (castigator), later the two voices merge into an undifferentiated voicing of misogyny. Initially, the singer addresses the castigator, asking him to be more humane, to have a child's heart for her and to "tener piedad" [have pity] on those females who ask him for his love. Yet the castigator replies, "Que se muera" [Let her die], and his gendered violence becomes the dominant voice throughout the rest of the song. The refrain and chorus of male voices repeat, "castígala, castígala" [punish her, punish her], and the song closes with a male voice that asks, "Entonces yo qué debo hacer" [Then, what should I do?]. The castigator and singer's voice responds with a call to punish the woman with physical domination and violence: "la cojo por el pelo, le doy . . . la maltrato mucho [I grab her by the hair, I hit her . . . I mistreat her a lot]. The song finally closes with a male scream of victory over his subordinated and destroyed victim.

Sixty years later, the Puerto Rican conga player Sonia López recorded the song "Castígalo" (Punish him), a feminist inversion or reversal of the misogynist violence of Piñeiro's earlier *son*.[19] She begins the song by reiterating the female's subordinate affective position in relation to the man, who smiles at her and delights in her suffering. The female singer asks the male to look at her trembling lips, as she confesses that she is "dying" for him. But then she invokes the power of the saints and of the Virgin in particular and asks them to punish him so that he will return to her, "llorando y suplicando" [crying and pleading] in an ideal fantasy that he will submit to her and ask her for her forgiveness. Illustrating the contradictory and multilayered roles that religion affords women in Latin American culture, this invocation to the divine realm is constituted as the state of romantic utopia whose verbs and signifiers remain the realm of the future and the subjunctive, as hypothesized reality.

Most powerful in this song, as in Piñeiro's gender attack, is the repetitive nature of the refrain. Sonia López's reiteration of the imperative utterance, "Castígalo, castigador," reminiscent of the ideology behind the literary Don Juan's eventual damnation in hell, makes up most of the song. It has the potential for becoming an empowering refrain for women listeners by articulating the anger and resentment against the men in their lives. In a feminist ironic turn, López's rendition inverts the subject/object dichotomy that songs like "Castigador" had already inscribed in the collective unconscious of Caribbean audiences. "Castígalo, castigador" is a clearly gendered utterance against men who practice violence, domination, and even emotional abuse of women. Although contained within the linguistic domain of an ideal, it strongly pronounces a female desire for revenge. Indeed, like the epigraphs selected for this section, the hypothetical nature of these utterances seems to characterize women's discourse in this context. Their revenge against men, particularly the physical violence articulated as a strategy against misogyny, are usually uttered as desire, as possibility, as hypothetical reality, rather than as fact. While a Daniel Santos naturalizes the male will to destroy woman in "Yo la mato" (I (will) kill her) by adding popular speech codes such as "Oye, qué cosas tiene la vida" [That's life], women's songs, like Lisa M's "Ingrato," close with reaffirming female desire, doubly deferred by two verbs of desire, to kill him back. She swears she wishes she could kill him.[20]

Las Chicas del Can is a female merengue group well known for controversial dress codes and performance gestures (one of their album covers contains the group dressed in black leather bikinis around a motorcycle) and the high-pitched voices that purportedly infantilize them. One of their songs, "Celoso" ("Jealous man"), is a feminist cut that presents physical violence as a form of revenge against the jealous male. Like most songs on the album *Explosivo*, "Celoso" was written for the group by their producer, Wilfrido Vargas, a factor that makes it difficult to trace gender ideology only through authorship.[21] In this case, the lyrics clearly present a female subject who denounces the repressive behavior of an extremely jealous male to whom she has lost her freedom. The song tells the story of a love relationship that goes sour after the man physically abuses the woman. Now, the singer says, it is her turn. Since he mistreated her, she now explodes full of anger and takes on the offensive in beating up the man. As if responding to Johnny Ventura's old merengue "Dale un palo," Las Chicas del Can deploy the same metaphor of "dar palos," one that is eroticized in the Dominican Republic but seemingly used in this song as physical revenge against oppressive men. The singer states that the jealous man needs to be beaten on the head, his ribs, and on his knees. The double reading of this metaphor, "dar palo," nevertheless accords a certain ambiguity to its signifiers, which may undermine the readings of the song as a feminist revenge. In other words, there is a simultaneous play between the desire to take physical vengeance on the male oppressor and the erotic suggestion of the female placating his erotic needs and desires.

"Esta noche o nunca," a popular song throughout Latin America, reveals the relationship between male sexual desire and woman's submission to his needs. By equating male needs with the will of God, the singing subject assumes the omnipotence of a divine being that women obligatorily have to obey. Tonight or never, "esta noche o nunca," is his final ultimatum.[22] And indeed, this ultimatum, which belongs to a vast repertoire of popular songs throughout Latin America, is tragically echoed in an estimated 60 percent of heterosexual couples in Puerto Rico who fall victims to domestic violence or sexual abuse.[23] Whether due to alcohol, drugs, jealousy, or violent tempers—reasons cited for male-induced violence on their female partners[24]—the tragic proportions of patriarchal violence against women cannot but suggest that lyrics such as Daniel Santos's "Yo la mato" or Ignacio Piñeiro's "Castígala" have had powerful effects on both male and female listeners.

Psychoanalytically, the tendency for men to need to differentiate and individuate themselves from their mothers by objectifying an Other and by emphasizing rigid boundaries between Self and Other has led to their denial of the Other as subject. Yet their violence against their subordinated Others only intensifies the contradictions of their dependency. As the song "La cárcel de Sing Sing" articulates: "yo tuve que matar a un ser que quise amar / y que aún estando muerta yo la quiero / al verla con su amante a los dos los maté / por culpa de esa infame moriré" [I had to kill the being I wanted to love / even dead I still love her / when I saw her with her lover I killed them both / because of that vile woman I will die].[25] In this master-slave relationship, the male subject, the master, discovers that "if it completely devours the other . . . or controls the other . . . it can no longer get what it wanted from the other," that is, the recognition of the self on which we depend.[26] The male subject negates the object's own subjectivity by trying to control her, thus failing to sustain the source of his much-needed social recognition. This contradiction, embedded in any Hegelian master-slave relationship, has been the underlying tragedy in the convergence of passion and violence, of crimes of passion. Indeed, given the culturally sanctioned macho behaviors that have continued to characterize male-female relations in Puerto Rico, it is not surprising that domestic violence was only recently, as of 1989, considered a crime punishable by law. And not coincidentally, the music industry continues to plug songs that naturalize violence against women, whether physical, sexual, or psychological.

A central form of violence against women in popular music is the very basic speech act of name-calling, of insults and vituperative language, what we may deem as discursive terrorism or violence through words.[27] This strategy of offense, quite commonplace in popular songs, powerfully fixes negative perceptions of women as traitors, dishonest, pretentious, vain, gossipy, and liars and as bandoleras, dishonest golddiggers who love men only as a means to economic survival. Again, I would argue that the destructive impact of this type of discursive terrorism on women's self-perceptions cannot be denied, given the substantial amounts of time Latinos and Latinas spend listening to music and to the radio in particular. Moreover, studies have shown a major discrepancy between the way that Puerto Rican women practice their autonomy and gender values versus their condemnation of other Puerto Rican women as "passive," a gap that may be explained by the internalization of patriarchal discourse on women's perceptions of other women.[28]

An older Latin American man once commented to me, in a sort of nostalgic tone, that he was disappointed at the way that contemporary music, including salsa and pop romantic ballads, sang to love relationships. He was seduced by the old language of the traditional bolero, and in many ways he was mourning that loss. He was right in perceiving a shift. In salsa music, particularly, the language of love has changed its tone from a lyrical, idealizing one about separations, conflicts, eternity, and unrequited passions to a more aggressive, material, and cynical attitude toward heterosexual relations.

In stark contrast to the "simple" lyrics of the above-mentioned bolero "Se fue," the salsa song, "Oprobio," composed by Rafael Hernández and interpreted by El Gran Combo de Puerto Rico, reveals the different tone and perspective that the male singing subject assumes with respect to the woman's absence and the breaking up of the relationship.[29] While both texts open with almost identical lines—"Ya se fue, ya se fue;" [She already left] and "Se fue" [She left]—the lyrics of "Oprobio" unfold into a diatribe against the woman and a concatenation of insults justified by the act of her leaving, by her *abandono*. It is a farewell to woman, yet one not colored by the bolero's nostalgia, love, nor even painful acceptance but rather marked by an almost self-parodic attitude toward love and the particular relationship in question. The male singing subject begins by thanking God that she left, since after all, "ya ella no me [le] servía" [she was of no use to me], thus poking fun at the traditional heart-breaking and affective discourse that the bolero opened up to the male subject. More poignantly, these opening lines define the woman's absence as relief rather than loss. She is constructed as an object of consumption, as a commodity for the male, a value that has overarchingly been recorded in advertisements, media, religion, and social institutions. By objectifying her and reducing her to mere function of service, pragmatism, the male singer feels no need to mourn his loss.

The song "Oprobio" then continues to say good-bye to the woman through an enumerative structure of insulting and negative adjectives and epithets. She is bandolera, pretenciosa, saco de trampa, bochinchera, orgullosa, lengüetera, caprichosa, vanidosa, buchipluma, zalamera. These are all epithets that construct woman as dishonest, vain, cruel, treacherous, a sack of tricks, gossipy, and easy-tongued. Collectively, the common tenor is that of woman as a treacherous signifier, a slippery, shifting sign impossible to decode, a social and discursive image that permeates men's perceptions of women. Yet these accusations against women are conditional, contingent on women's submissions to their needs and desires. Women are treacherous golddiggers and plain bad when they do not satisfy men's sexual desires and needs.

Héctor Lavoe's song "Bandolera," composed by Víctor Cavalli, epitomizes discursive violence against women.[30] This cut lasts nine minutes, thirty-two seconds (quite extensive for a recorded version), and can be considered problematic if we take into account the fact that its misogyny is expressed the minute the song begins. "Bandolera" is entirely an ennumeration of derogatory comments about women, finished off with an expression of physical abuse. The male singer warns her: "te voy a dar una pela / pa que aprendas a querer" [I will beat you up / so that you learn to love], followed by a piano solo and the brass instruments, followed in turn by the onomatopoeia of physical abuse: pow, pow, pow . . . Te vuelvo a dar, te voy a dar pa' que aprendas" [pow, pow, pow . . . I hit you again, I'll hit you so that you learn]. Again, the bandolera title reinforces the image of woman as dishonest, a liar who was "born to fool others." In fact, love is described early on in the song as a social construct that has failed because of the lack of trust between men and women: "Por eso yo no creo en el amor, yo creo en mí, yo sé de mí, yo sé vivir" [That is why I do not believe in love, I believe in myself, I know about myself, I know how to live].

These lines establish a male egocentric subject location that precludes any possibility for emotional reciprocity or communion with others. The male singing subject cynically deconstructs love as another social gimmick, another act of treason and lies, another form of oppression. The only sort of consistency and reliability that he can imagine is in solipsistic self-knowledge. The rest of the song, like "Oprobio," constitutes a defensive concatenation of insults and a series of utterances of physical violence and abuse against the bandit-woman, othered and objectified.

The Bandolera and the Economics of Love

Me buscaste en los bolsillos,	[You searched my pockets,
me tumbaste la cartera	you emptied my wallet
Y esa va a ser la razón	And that is why
Porque te voy a pegar . . .	I will beat you up . . .]

The final stanza of Héctor Lavoe's "Bandolera," above, reveals the economic and material motivations behind this discursive violence. The female is deemed as a bandit woman, a Latina version of the golddigger, because throughout the relationship she has depleted the man of his financial possessions. "Me buscaste en los bolsillos," sings Lavoe to his beloved bandolera. This figure, commonplace in salsa music, is drawn from a topical repertoire rooted in old Hispanic and European legendry. The emergence of this female figuration significantly marks sociohistorical periods of men's preoccupation with economic and material survival. In the United States of the 1930s the golddigger emerged precisely as a musical symbol that allowed men to reconcile the economic hardships of their period with the threatening values and competition that "the feminization of American culture, particularly in the sphere of work" constituted.[31] Similarly, in African American rap "welfare queens making babies or golddiggers who use their sexuality to take black men's meager earnings" are common prototypes of the black woman, given the dismantling of the black male as the main family provider.[32] Thus, for the Latino male subject who has experienced the economic marginalization of New York barrios during the 1970s and 1980s in particular, the bandolera construct functions as a symbol or icon that allows men to reconcile these shifts in economics and the deflation and undermining of the traditional Hispanic values of masculinity and of the macho as the honorable father who always and unconditionally provides for his wife and his children.

Much more revealing, however, is the resemantization of the figure of the bandolera since its early historical emergence. The phenomenon of banditry has been common to Europe since the medieval times, and there exists a particular legend in Galicia, Spain, about a bandolera named Pepa La Loba. Orphaned from a very young age, Pepa is a female version of the Spanish *pícaro*, or rogue, throughout her youth, a subject marginalized in mainstream society and thus a locus of resistance in many ways. She is unjustly imprisoned for the murder of her protector, and she eventually escapes jail dressed in the clothes of the priest who came to her cell to confess her. She takes revenge on the real murderer by killing him and allowing him to be devoured by wild dogs. Later, her life is that of a runaway, an outcast, a woman on the margins of society. She robs and steals with the help of her *bando*, all men. It is said that she would dress up as a man and paint a mustache on her face. She became an object of terror throughout the whole county. In another version, she became the lover of an older male who later abandoned her for a younger woman. Pepa leaves his house without any resistance. Later she returns and kills him, his new lover, and all of their children.[33]

A legendary figure like Pepa La Loba and other bandoleras merit a new reading as protofeminist characters. Pepa transgressed the social norms of femininity in quite radical ways: she cross-dressed, thus blurring the fixed gender boundaries of her own female body and of her sexuality; she killed men, thus assuming behaviors and actions—violence, aggression—that have been socially relegated to the order of the masculine; and she avenged herself on the man in her life who was responsible for her unjust imprisonment in one version and for her betrayal in the other. Contemporary salsa songs and Latin popular music reconstruct this bandolera figure from the masculine perspective, that is, from the subject position of the male who has loved a woman and who is afraid of becoming the object of her anger and retaliation. This figure clearly articulates male fear of women's agency, anger, and strategies for survival. It allows men to express the fear of their own vulnerability in the face of changing gender roles and, concomitantly, to displace this fear onto women, accusing them of these shifts and of the uncomfortable position of men as potential victims and objects of aggression or violence.

The threat of the bandolera is not exclusively economic but affective as well. The bandolera in salsa not only steals money but also steals the man's heart, his love. In a poem entitled "El bandido robado" from Galician folklore, the male bandit himself is the object of a robbery: a woman has stolen his heart![34] Salsa songs such as Pedro Conga's "Ladrona de amor" (Thief of love) and Rubén Blades's "Ella se esconde" (She hides) express man's double-edged fear and desire for female seduction: "¡Qué bandolera que eres tú! ¡Qué raquetera en el amor! ¡Me has enredado en tu revulú y me has robado el corazón!"[35] [What a bandit you are! What a liar in love! You have involved me in your mess and you have stolen my heart!]. The bandolera myth, then, unfolds and branches out into various other textualizations. First, the man accuses the woman of stealing his property during the love relationship, the most literal rendering of this figuration; second, the woman is accused of stealing the man's heart; and third, an inversion of the previous constructs is that of women defined as merchandise or property to be acquired, as commodities and value for men, either through marriage or through sexual intercourse. Clearly illustrated in Rubén Blades's recent cut, "Ella se esconde," again the common tenor in all of the above discursive constructs of the feminine is the lack of trust, man's vulnerability, and woman as slippery signifier, difficult if not impossible to decode. The treacherous woman, a product of the romantic construct of Woman as Mystery, ramifies into metaphors of witches and witchcraft. Bandits, traitors, and witches, women in Latin popular music, as in other musical traditions, are sexual objects and treacherous signifiers, "hiding behind the corners of her smile," as Rubén Blades's song consistently reiterates.

Latina singers have not remained passive nor mute with respect to these characterizations. Son de Azúcar, an all-women's Latin music band, sings back to the male fear of the female. In "Devoradora," the female singing subject appropriates the construct of the woman as "devoradora," a beast ready to devour man, to castrate him and ultimately consume him.[36] With humor and self-irony, these lyrics reaffirm those gender-based fears: "Me dicen que soy piraña / que soy mujer araña / porque todo lo que veo / sin excepción lo devoro" [They tell me I am a piranha / a woman spider / because I devour without exception / everything I see]. Yet as the song develops, that irony unfolds onto a feminist reaffirmation of women's strategies for seducing men and thus for disempowering them: "Devoro con la mirada / soy mujer muy liberada / los atrapo con besitos / y aquí me caen rendiditos" [I devour with my gaze / I am a most liberated woman / I trap them with kisses / and they fall here all subdued] or "Y no es que yo sea coqueta / sino una mujer completa" [It's not that I am flirtatious / but a complete woman], in fact correcting the negative prototype of animal-like powers—"Y no es que sea una piraña / y no es que sea mujer araña" [And it's not that I am a piranha / nor a woman spider]—and transforming it into a positive power as a woman: "pero sí sé que conmigo / todos los hombres se amañan . . . todos los hombres me adoran" [but I know that with me / all men settle down . . . all men adore me].

In other words, this text attempts to correct and revalorize the negatively laden seductive powers of women from a fear-founded image of irrational, destructive potential—the masculine version—to that of a "complete" woman who, by her own virtues as thinking, feeling, and developed human being, is then attractive to men. While the text continuously deploys signifiers that evoke the negative prototypes—she speaks of her poison and of herself as a "domadora"—the concluding question leaves the song open to multiple readings: "¿Devoradora yo?" [I, devourer?]. Again, female oppositionality in these songs seems to be structured in double discourses that allow multiple, ambiguous readings. Simultaneously, however, this open-ended text also allows for the possibility of couples to engage in discussing whether woman is *devoradora* or not. The ironic final question, in other words, may ignite potential discussions around this gender-based discourse.

While I have not identified any songs that specifically appropriate the figure of the bandolera from a feminist perspective, a number of Latinas have definitely contested men's discursive terrorism against women, singing back analogous strategies of psychological oppression. Milly y los Vecinos, a merengue group, sings to/against men's own strategies for masking their patriarchy and oppressive behavior with women. In "Ese hombre," they denounce the Latin(o) macho who has fathered numerous children, comparing him to a "viento" (wind) that blows away flowers and that kills "ilusiones" (illusions) with pain.[37] Analogous to Ana Lydia Vega's story "Letra para salsa y tres soneos por encargo" (Lyrics for salsa and three endings ordered), this song deflates and dismantles the masculine discourse of a Don Juan who seduces women and later abandons them. The repetitive refrain compares the man to "las chicharras" (cicadas) who make a lot of noise but ultimately offer nothing. In addition, the song enumerates other accusations that unveil the falsity of the image of a man as provider in the reality of financial need. While the song serves as a caveat for other women, it also deconstructs the masks, strategies, and discourse used by men to seduce women into satisfying their own needs and desires. In other words, men are also treacherous, slippery signifiers.

La India, the Puerto Rican salsa singer from the Bronx who combines the singing styles of a Celia Cruz and an Ella Fitzgerald, a sort of R&B sonera, also performs a song entitled "Ese hombre" on her CD *Dicen que soy* (They say I am).[38] Also a song that serves as a caveat for other women, the text begins by bursting the bubble. The man who appears "gallant" becomes a plurality of negative traits: he is really a fool, selfish, capricious, vain, insensitive, arrogant, and a host of other epithets. The enumerative strategy, that "enumeración caótica" that served too well the democratizing and human poetics of a Pablo Neruda, has been deployed in popular music as the central structural recourse for singing the gender wars. Indeed, women singers have been inverting the object of men's discursive terrorism as an initial strategy of resistance against misogyny and patriarchy.

Nonetheless, this recourse fails to elucidate or to articulate a discourse that illuminates the multiple modes of constituting female subjectivity. It is a recourse that is limited insofar as it duplicates the dualist, binary oppositions of gender identity that have plagued women with the inferior end of the axis. It leaves no aperture for new and radical ways of being female and of being male, that is, for blurring those rigid boundaries and for discussion of not only gender roles but also multiple forms of sexuality and sexual orientation. By enumerating the negative characteristics of either men or women, coupled with the mnemonic value of repetition and refrains as well as of music itself as a temporal art, Latino and Latina singers nonetheless have articulated the conflicts between men and women that continue to characterize heterosexual interactions in our societies.

Celia Cruz's defense of women, such as in "Las divorciadas" and "Que le den candela" (in her more recent recording, *Irrepetible*),[39] Milly y los Vecinos's "Ese hombre" (1991), and Sonia López's "Castígalo" are examples of cuts that speak in defense of women within heterosexual relations. Yet the lyrics of these songs establish gender in dualistic, oppositional terms—male versus female—that clearly denote the traditional "battle between the sexes." While Anglo American feminists may dismiss these songs as samples of gender oppression, in my opinion they must be understood within the cultural, social, and historical contexts of (hetero)sexual relations in Puerto Rican society. These songs are valuable insofar as they eloquently articulate the struggles of Puerto Rican women and Latinas to empower themselves by contesting the dictates of a strong patriarchal system. Although in the United States feminist scholars have moved beyond this paradigm of male-female interaction, for many U.S. Latinas and Latin American women their reality with men is beleaguered by outright conflict and even physical violence. The fact that Lorena Bobbitt became a popular heroine overnight among Puerto Rican women and that a new word — *bobitazo* — began circulating with innuendos of potential female revenge, indicates that (hetero)sexual interactions are very much associated, culturally and socially at least, with images of conflict and metaphors of war.

Songs such as the ones mentioned above partially allow women to name their desire for the recognition of their own power as subjects. By rejecting this "battle between the sexes" as a paradigm that fixes identity, Anglo feminism elides the very real social tensions between men and women, in any culture or society, whose personal interactions may be embedded in conflict and even violence. It may be a coincidence, for instance, that in the past ten years Puerto Ricans have listened to these women's songs as well as mobilized to create laws against domestic violence and physical abuse by men, yet this coincidence is a significant one indeed.

An alternative to these monologic strategies of inversion is that proposed by Lisa M and other rappers who perform dialogic lyrics in which both men and women speak to heterosexual relations. In "Tu Pum Pum," both Lisa M and Santy articulate a sort of dialogue that partly constitutes a parody of gender stereotypes and partly enunciates an alternative to heterosexual relations.[40] The text begins with a reference to "el pum pum," the onomatopoeic utterance that alludes to the woman's hip movements, in the voice of the man. He asserts that her sensuality and her body are not going to kill him, a parody itself of earlier traditional discourse of love and of erotic hips. Santy also makes a self-reference to his height — he is "chiquito," short — which goes against the grain of an ideal masculinity as determined by mass media but which in fact reevaluates this masculinity from a more Latino-centered reality, that is, that Latino men tend to be shorter than the Anglo media portrays.

The song then becomes a "battle of love" — (*batalla de amor*) — between these two voices. While Lisa M refuses to be seduced by him, Santy continues to try to convince her that short men are good and honest and that he is indeed "a general." She replies that if he is a general, she is a captain, and that her strategy of war is to invert his own discourse of power. She then does precisely that by calling on the subtexts of the Don Juan discourse and that of "Las muchachas": she says she will marry any man, regardless of his Latin American nationality, as long as he is big and speaks Spanish.

These musical gender wars also have signaled certain shifts in patriarchal strategies for dominating women. While the discourse of the 1970s and 1980s was characterized by discursive battles of love in which physical violence, anger, revenge, and vituperation framed male-female interaction, more recent songs indicate a shift in the modes in which patriarchy is articulated. El Gran Combo's song "Psicología"[41] encapsules what Sandra Lee Bartky, in her Foucaultian reading of modern forms of female repression, has called the "modernization of patriarchal power."[42] According to Bartky, "Foucault has argued that the transition from traditional to modern societies has been characterized by a profound transformation in the exercise of power." In contrast to the deployment of older forms of power, centrally embodied in "the person of the monarch,"[43] in modern society "power has now become anonymous,"[44] yet by its very own diffusion away from the monarch or the church it has been relocated in the process of the formation of the individual subject, that is, into subjectivity itself. Modern power, then, is exercised through "faceless, centralized, and pervasive" ways, through new institutions, such as bureaucracy, welfare, correction, production, and education.

For women in particular, these shifts in power have translated into a subsiding of traditional forms of regulation, such as the traditional family role (the Husband and Father) and the church's (the Divine Individual, the priest), thus giving way to the modern forms of patriarchal power, those values of femininity and of the female body as spectacle, as a certain "style of the flesh," that are internalized by women across class, culture, and racial lines. "Normative femininity is coming more and more to be centered on woman's body—not its duties and obligations or even its capacity to bear children, but its sexuality, more precisely, its presumed heterosexuality and its appearance."[45] Foucault's image of the Panopticon, then, is doubly significant for women in modern times; as they internalize values of beauty and of femininity, they become the self-policing gaze of their own bodies.

Yet most significant is the emergence of psychology as a cultural and individual terrain in which patriarchal power is articulated. Foucault in fact exemplifies the modernization of power in the historic institutionalization of modern psychology and sociology as a "new knowledge of the individual" is required. Shifting from traditional forms of coercion such as physical abuse and what could be deemed domination through the domestic, El Gran Combo's song "Psicología" traces how Latino men have been forced to rethink, adapt to, and negotiate women's new social roles, not altogether surprising given the fact that one can trace shifts in Puerto Rican social and cultural values in the past thirty years through their repertoire.

The male singing voice begins addressing the social myth that "women are difficult": "Muchos dicen que la mujer es un ser difícil de manejar," an opening line that reiterates the social function of popular songs as interventions in the production of cultural myths, assumptions, and values. The reiterative use of "dicen que" [it is said, people say] in many salsa songs frame these texts as such, as cultural interventions that actively function to reaffirm and reevaluate traditional ways of thinking. In this particular case, El Gran Combo's male singer, through a text composed by Chico Alejandro, responds to this particular patriarchal assumption of a female character essentialized as "difficult." In response to this social construct, the song articulates a "recipe"—of course, created by men—that offers more efficient ways of dealing with women. Addressing his male counterparts, the singer shares this recipe, in an inversion of the feminine discourse of cooking and domesticity, with his male listeners. This is a recipe that has been successful, "siempre ha funcionado," thus revealing the modern and more efficient, cleaner ways of holding control over women.

The male singer then gives numerous caveats to other men. Since domination through machismo is no longer viable nor socially acceptable—"en vez de usted bregar a lo macho / le da mejor resultado bregar con psicología" [instead of dealing a lo macho / dealing with psychology gives better results]—men need to strategically use psychology, that new, modern knowledge of the self, to maintain control over their female partners. Indeed, the song presents alternatives to explicit conflictive situations, such as taking her out to a restaurant when she burns the beans or speaking softly to her, uttering "sweet words," or taking her out to the movies; but ultimately there is no aperture toward an equality of power between both. What "Psicología" reveals is a shift in the signifiers of patriarchal power, not a profound equalization of men and women in their personal relations. For the male singer and composer of "Psicología," this newfound knowledge of women and their ensuing shift in behavior toward them is their only alternative to maintaining superiority, ultimately a tactic for patriarchal survival.

When the singer advises the use of psychology "para que puedas vivir bien cómodo" [in order to live comfortably] or says that the man needs to convince his woman "con un ardor sensual" [by sensual passion], unequal power relations remain untouched, and the song is as patriarchal and repressive of female desire as the previous salsa songs about bandoleras and even the boleros that silenced women with a kiss. While many Latinos have informally argued with me that salsa music is no longer as misogynist and patriarchal as it was during the 1970s, this reading of "Psicología" proves otherwise. Any shift toward more humane and less violent modes of gender interaction is a positive development in itself. Yet the unfortunate fact remains regarding the subject position of the male: he is in control of the musical discourse and of its production, composition, and distribution. By virtue of this inequality within the music industry, music interventions still perpetuate a masculinist discourse of the female and the feminine.

CHAPTER TEN

Singing Female Subjectivities

⊹

Postmodern critics and feminists have identified a new era of women's participation in high and low cultures. This is clearly evident, for instance, in the emergence of "women-identified music" recording studios in the United States, a countermovement that arose against the misogynist lyrics of rock and roll.[1] However, the creative and political presence of women composers, producers, and performers in the terrain of Latin popular music is not as evident as their transformative role in other arts like film production, theory and criticism, narrative, and poetry. This is not to say, however, that women have not participated in the composition or performance of Latin music. To be rendered invisible is not synonymous with a lack of agency. A closer look at histories of Latin American popular music, particularly in Cuba, Puerto Rico, and Mexico, attest to the pervading presence and agency of women not only as singers but also as composers.[2] "Babalú," the Cuban song interpreted by Miguelito Valdez and later popularized on television by Desi Arnaz in the 1950s, was composed by Margarita Lecuona.[3] The bomba titled "Maquinolandera," deployed by Rosario Ferré in the short story of the same title, was composed by Margarita Rivera, Ismael Rivera's mother, more familiarly known in Puerto Rico as Doña Margot. As seen earlier, the textual female subjectivity in the plena "Mamita, llegó el Obispo" possibly indicates a woman's authorship veiled under the anonymity imposed by the institution of folklore. These few examples only begin to tell the story of women's agency and authorial power in popular culture, an issue that claims urgent historical documentation.

This historical veiling, moreover, has been coupled with the discriminatory practice of restricting women's participation to that of mostly vocalists, rather than opening up other roles such as instrumentalists, composers, arrangers, and most important, directors of groups. The major exception to this pattern is the emergence of eleven all-female salsa bands in Cali, Colombia, since 1990. According to Umberto Valverde and Rafael

Quintero,[4] this phenomenon was made possible by the central importance of dancing in Cali's urban culture, which historically has offered women access to music and has created a demand for musicians. Most important, I believe, is the presence of institutions of training in musical and popular cultural arts such as the Instituto Popular de Cultura, the University of Valle, Bellas Artes, and the Academia de Música Valdiri. In addition, the success of these performers has been attributed to their keen sense of discipline and professionalism, a result, in turn, of their position as women in a male-dominated industry. Lise Waxer, currently living in Cali, is completing ethnographic work on Cali's women salseras and is playing in an all-female Latin jazz band called Magenta.

Rayda Cotto, a black Puerto Rican musical director, performer, and composer, argues that these boundaries are racially marked as she calls into question the persistent whitened images of women in musical events and televised performances.[5] As Cotto notes, black Puerto Rican women have less access to these roles than do their white counterparts. Generally speaking, women's absence from the stage is also a result of their lack of access to the public space of the street, where younger musicians receive their training by participating in informal jam sessions. A "decent woman," says Latin society, does not belong in jam sessions nor in the masculine spaces of nightclubs, touring, and cast parties. The fact that Latinas have historically achieved more prominence as vocalists than in other musical roles suggests a process of containment in their professional development and opportunities. Women singers are allowed to perform onstage as long as they sing the words of others and as long as, in some cases, they play to the desires and fantasies of a male audience whose gaze continues to objectify female bodies. Such is the case of Las Chicas del Can, a female merengue group whose repertoire is wholly penned by men and whose stage presence and dress also seem to be defined according to masculine dictates of female objectification. While it is true that this group has had some impact on Latina fans, mostly by serving as role models for those younger women who aspire to sing and perform, I find no ideological ambivalence in the ways that they invite their audience to objectify their bodies.

Yet authorship by women, as essential as it is for the articulation of female subjectivity in popular music, should not by itself mark an exclusive space for the transformation of sexual politics. Celia Cruz's ever popular performance of "Usted abusó" (You abused me), the bossa nova Brazilian theme she interpreted with Willie Colón, possibly had a more profound liberatory impact on Latinas than many women-authored pieces. "Usted abusó" articulates, from the abused victim's point of view, an accusation or indictment against the abuser in the heterosexual couple; the open-ended use of the second-person singular *usted* allows for either male or female performances and for the indictment of either sex. The performance of a song, despite the sexual identity of its author, can indeed be "gendered," both by performer and audience, depending on the performer's own sexual identity and voicing. Celia Cruz's performance of "Usted abusó" changed the original message of the song from that of a male diatribe against a woman to that of a feminist anthem against sexual abuse and domestic violence.

Many young women's groups, particularly in the merengue tradition, appear rather bland in their potential to divest patriarchal lyrics. Their songs, characterized by the oppositional stance between the sexes, either reproduce patriarchal and misogynist textualizations of women or instead refrain from engaging female subjectivities. In fact, the strongest presence of Latinas in popular music—Ana Gabriel, Yolandita Monge, Lisette and Ednita Nazario—is in the romantic pop ballad, a genre informed by the traditional bolero. This constitutes a historical extension of the patriarchal practice of containing women within the generic boundaries of "lyrical" forms of artistic expression. To sing to and about love from an individual viewpoint is much more socially acceptable and politically innocuous than to sing about those social issues that characterize salsa's thematic repertoire, such as migration, national identity, class, race, and gender itself. And while it would be essential to document the possible apertures and fissures through which these women singers resist and subvert their own location as enunciators of the "romantic," the weight of tradition, formulas, and standardization within the genre of the romantic pop ballad undermine the potential for women to radicalize gender constructs in more systematic ways.

However, emerging salsa singers such as La India, Olga Tañón, and Albita are gaining popularity fast, appearing in major events, and receiving important national recognition.[6] A substantial portion of their repertoire is composed by them or by other women, although they also perform traditional cuts in Afro-Caribbean music. What distinguishes their performances from those of other groups is the highly oppositional content of many of their songs, their control over the production and composition, and the degree of performativity, mostly in the case of La India and Albita, which destabilize fixed notions of gender. These emerging figures indicate an important shift toward a growing female visibility in U.S. and Puerto Rican salsa scenes.

Yet this is not altogether new. A generation of women—mostly Cuban, Puerto Rican and Mexican—whose own compositions, performances, and bodies together have powerfully contested the patriarchal dictates within

Latino and Latin American culture has hardly received any scholarly attention. Singers who emerged in the 1950s and 1960s, such as Toña La Negra in Mexico, Ruth Fernández and Mirta Silva in Puerto Rico, and Celia Cruz and La Lupe in Cuba and the United States, represent women who in diverse ways opposed, resisted, and transformed Afro-Caribbean music into a space from which female subjectivities could emerge. Most of these women, whose racial identities significantly were either black or racially mixed, appropriated the musical theatrical stages as well as the radio and television airwaves as public spaces for articulating the historical visibility and agency of Caribbean women in Latina/o culture. Like Rafael Cortijo y su Combo in Puerto Rico, Ruth, Celia, Toña, Mirta, and Lupe contested, by their racially marked presence, the predominance of whiteness in the media. They also served as role models and pathbreakers for more contemporary performers. While these women's performance styles, musical repertoires, and artistic personalities were unique and very different from one another, together they constitute an important generation of women singers and musicians whose historical impact is yet to be examined and whose histories, both personal and musical, are yet to be written.

Toña La Negra, born María Antonia Peregrino, Veracruz's most salient woman performer, specialized in interpreting boleros written by such male composers as Agustín Lara, Pedro Flores, and Rafael Hernández, among others; and although she did perform boleros authored by women, such as Mexican composer María Greever's "Cenizas," she could quite easily be seen as an interpreter of men's words. However, the modulations of her voice and her almost matriarchal presence contributed to the inclusion of the Caribbean cultural heritage among Mexican listeners. The popularity of tropical music in Mexico was not only because of the presence of a Mambo King like Pérez Prado nor the recordings of Benny Moré but also because of Negra's vindication of Afro-Caribbean compositions, rhythms, and textures. Her stage name—La Negra [The Black Woman]—reveals her strategic racial self-objectification or essentialization, a racializing gesture that exhorted Mexican audiences to accept the African heritage of the Caribbean coast as a central element of their culture. Some of her most famous hits—"Oración Caribe," "Noche Criolla," and "Veracruz"—sing to the geocultural spaces of an Afro-Caribbean Mexico that has remained marginal to a historical social imaginary invested in its indigenous, pre-Columbian past and in its very rigid European mestizaje. Moreover, the impact of one of her most popular songs, "Angelitos negros" (Black angels) (composed by Andrés Eloy Blanco) was felt all over Latin America. Its text denounced the colonialist, Eurocentric, and whitened paradigms in the visual arts that have prevailed throughout Latin American high culture:

Pintor nacido en mi tierra	[Painter, born on my land
con el pincel extranjero	holding a foreign brush
Pintor sigues el rumbo	Painter, you follow the path
de tantos pintores viejos.	of so many painters in the past.
Aunque la Virgen sea blanca	Even though the Virgin is white
píntame angelitos negros.	please paint little black angels for me.
Que también se van al cielo	For all the good blacks
todos los negritos buenos.	also go to heaven.
Pintor, si pintas con amor	Painter, if you paint with love
¿por qué desprecias su color?	why do you reject their color?
Si sabes que en el cielo	If you know that in heaven
¿también los quiere Dios?	God also loves them?
Pintor de santos de alcoba	You, who paint saint figures
si tienes alma en el cuerpo	if you have a soul
¿por qué al pintar tus cuadros	why is it that in your paintings
te olvidaste de los negros?	you forgot the black ones?
Siempre que pintas iglesias	Whenever you paint churches
pintas angelitos bellos	you paint beautiful angels
pero nunca te acordaste	but you never remembered
de pintar un ángel negro.[7]	to paint a black angel.]

Through Toña la Negra's voice, the urgency of examining the arts from the perspective of racial exclusion took on a strong personal tone. Throughout the song she exhorts listeners to recognize the black cultural and historical legacy in Latin American culture. Much before the emergence of multiculturalism in the United States, although simultaneous to the civil rights movements and the nationalist Chicano and Nuyorican movements on the mainland, the circulation of this song denounced the Eurocentric underpinnings of religious icons and of the visual arts throughout Latin America and the exclusion of the nonwhite elements from the representations of the divine. The contradictions of colonization and the systematic erasure of the colonized from representation itself, both of which have marked the history of Latin American arts, literature, and music in its relational dialectics with Europe, are expressed in the opening verse: "Pintor nacido en mi tierra / con el pincel extranjero" [Artist born on my land / holding the foreign brush]. The potential impact of this song on race relations throughout Latin America is evident in the fact that even the Argentine Libertad Lamarque popularized it as the theme song for a movie of the same title.

Mirta Silva, on the other hand, began her career in the 1930s in Harlem, where she began composing songs when she was sixteen. She recorded in New York and was a member of Grupo Victoria, directed by Rafael Hernández, whose many compositions she also interpreted and recorded.

It is believed that she composed more than one thousand songs, although most music journalists stress the fact that "she interpreted guarachas and composed boleros." This emphasis signifies a naturalized dichotomy between the genre of the guaracha as a nonfemale text and the bolero as the quintessential expression of sentimentality and thus femaleness.[8] Notwithstanding these discursive associations that have framed women's contributions to popular music, Mirta Silva irreverently contested the particular image of the sentimental female. In the 1950s she hosted and produced a TV musical program, "Una hora con nosotros," which featured the contemporary musicians and artists with whom she shared the stage. She appeared in radio shows and frequently traveled to New York to perform for the Puerto Rican community. In 1953, for instance, she performed alongside Felipe Rodríguez in New York, and in 1957 she appeared with Lucho Gatica and others in the Teatro Metropolitan.

The publicity for these shows reveals another aspect of Mirta's public persona, one that was constructed by popular epithets. She was warmly known as La Gorda de Oro (The Golden Fat Woman) because of her weight and large body structure; La Bomba Atómica Puertorriqueña (the Puerto Rican Atomic Bomb) was also deployed to advertise her performances as well as La Vedette Que Arrolla (The Sweeping Vedette).[9] All these epithets play on her body size (*gorda*, which translates into a potential and explosive, subversive power of her performances; *bomba;* and *arrolla*), her comedy, and her singing. This combination of physical presence and performance style created a unique effect for her audiences. Mirta Silva was not the sensual, sleek vedette that Latin America saw in Tongolele, nor was she a motherly, tender figure. Through her irreverent humor, singing style, and physical overendowment, she self-parodically subverted popular expectations of the delicate, fragile, and even sexy female singer. Although matronly, she was not at all a maternal figure but rather more of an androgynous image on television, her body and voice a social space of conflicting gender expectations.

Among this group of women singers, La Lupe represents, for me, the most feminist and radical as a performer of Afro-Caribbean music. Born Lupe Victoria Yoli in Santiago, Cuba, the young Lupe worked as a teacher and also sang as member of a trio called Los Tropicuba.[10] Interestingly, critics writing about this early period of her career have chosen to stress the ways in which her musical performances radically departed from the expected behaviors for a female singer. It has been said that her then-husband, also a member of Los Tropicuba, commented after her first performance that he "thought she was having an epileptic fit,"[11] a parodic comment that indicates the transgressive style that has characterized her singing and stage presence since those beginnings. She was indeed fired from the trio, and she did indeed divorce her first husband. She then went on to sing in La Red, a club where she polarized the audience into those who were "addicted" to La Lupe and those others who could not stand her.[12] Most revealing, however, is the possible symbolic value that her defiant and unique style of body movements and gestures posed during the late 1950s, when Cuban society was experiencing its transition into socialism:

> . . . además de que es una inteligente y sensible cantante, cuando quiere, hace en público lo que inconscientemente casi toda Cuba tiene ganas de hacer en aquellos momentos: gritar, llorar, arañarse, morderse, quitarse los zapatos, decir malas palabras, en fin romper de alguna forma la terrible tensión que la transición de revolución a socialismo exige día a día y hora a hora, de cada ciudadano. La Lupe es un espejo de los tiempos y como tal, triunfa, y un buen día del año 1961 se va también de Cuba

> [. . . besides being an intelligent and sensible singer, when she wants, she achieves in public what almost all of Cuba unconsciously felt like doing at that time: screaming, crying, scratching and biting themselves, taking off their shoes, swearing, that is, releasing in some way the terrible tension that the transition from the revolution into socialism had demanded day by day, hour by hour, from each citizen. La Lupe is a mirror of those times and as such, she triumphs, and one day in 1961 she also leaves Cuba].[13]

If musicologist Díaz Ayala explains her success in the cathartic role she may have played in Cuba during the beginnings of socialism, César Miguel Rondón defines her role in Afro-Caribbean music as the singer who made Tite Curet Alonso's compositions famous. Thus, La Lupe's value can be defined only in relation to male musicians, in this case, the Puerto Rican composer of salsa, Catalino "Tite" Curet Alonso, whose "La Tirana" (The tyrant woman) became equated with La Lupe as its interpreter.[14] According to Rondón, "a partir de 'La Tirana,' Curet Alonso se convertiría en el más extraordinario de todos los cantores de la circunstancia amorosa en el mundo de la salsa" [after "La Tirana," Curet Alonso would become the most extraordinary of all singers (composers) of love in the world of salsa].[15] This is yet another instance of the strategies of gender exclusion exerted by otherwise progressive critics and writers.

Nevertheless, Rondón also recognizes the historical importance of La Lupe in the initial stages of the development of salsa as a musical tradition in New York. Indeed, her particular and unique style of singing, her voice, "gritona, desordenada y falta de respeto" [screaming, disorderly, and disrespectful], marked the emerging differentiations between traditional Cuban music and the new sound of New York salsa. La Lupe embodied and voiced the "otro elemento, el del canto marginal, hiriente, algo descuidado, lleno de esas mañas y esos trucos que jamás soportó el ortodoxo del canto caribe" [other element, that of the marginal song, wounded, somehow disheveled, full of tricks and habits that the orthodox Caribbean song never assumed].[16] She represents the bridge between the big band sound and the barrio, inscribing in her performances as well as in her modulations that "grito de guerra" that salsa has represented as the music of marginalized sectors.[17]

Despite her genealogical importance in salsa, La Lupe (also known as La Yiyiyi) found herself by the 1970s on the margins of this already emerging salsa industry. Rondón explains this invisibility as a result of the fact that her role in that transition had already taken place,[18] confirming a patriarchal assumption that women's role in music is to pave the way for male singers. It is essential, however, to indicate that the galvanizing force of the male presence in the development of salsa as a musical tradition and its insertion into the music industry must have had tremendous repercussions in La Lupe's own trajectory as a salsa singer. The systematic ways in which La Lupe has been constructed as a singer in relation to a man—to Tite Curet Alonso and particularly to Tito Puente, with whom she recorded and sang—are quite evident in our perusal of reviews, histories of salsa, and newspaper clippings. Unlike Celia Cruz, whose musical success has multiplied in the United States as a symbol of the transnational latinization of this country, when La Lupe died in 1992 at the age of fifty-three, she was virtually ignored by her past audiences. After her career dwindled in the 1970s, she moved to Puerto Rico and later returned to New York, where she experienced a series of personal tragedies and later became an active Christian. While her obituary note in the *New York Times* traces and details the personal tragedies that beset La Lupe until her death in 1992, there is no acknowledgment of the feminist impact of her lyrics on salsa music nor of the subversive, radical performances of this woman who, ironically, gave voice to the urban, warlike, and male-gendered modulations of salsa.

Theatrical scripts and dramatic performances already are recovering La Lupe's life and work, signals of Puerto Rican and feminist attempts to recover untold history.[19] Yet it is also important to examine how, in fact, some of her key songs contributed to a female subjectivity that differed radically from the binarisms and dualistic discourses that have prevailed in salsa music concerning heterosexual relations. If "La Tirana" is the textual product of a male composer, it nevertheless describes the persona of a woman who sings to a man, contesting historically negative textualizations of the feminine. The song begins by underlining the perspective that informs these social constructs via an irony masterfully uttered in the sarcastic smirks and laughter that La Lupe interjects at precise instances:

La Lupe: En Algo Nuevo was released in 1980 by Música Latina International. It includes "Soul Salsa," in which La Lupe raps in Spanish. Photo courtesy of Víctor Gallo and Sonido Inc.

Según tu punto de vista	[According to your point of view
Yo soy la mala.	I am the wicked one.
Vampiresa en tu novela	A vampiress in your novel
La gran tirana.[20]	The great tyrant.]

The deconstructive stance, already at play in the first line, suggests that the equation woman equals evil is a construct motivated by the man's subjective point of view, by his situatedness. This bolero continues to reflect on and develop the centrality of perspective in social interaction, thus proposing an ironic reading and tone to the reiterative refrains: "Según tu punto de vista / Yo soy la mala / La que te llegó hasta el alma / La gran tirana" [According to your point of view / I am the wicked one / The one who penetrated your soul / The great tyrant]. While the antagonic discourse of love is ever present in this song—"el día en que te dejé / fui yo quien salí ganando" [the day I left you / I won the battle], a line to which the crescendo effect reaffirms the strength and power of the woman's victory—the text ultimately proposes a deconstructive reading of gender constructs, a feminist and progressive stance that is consistent with Tite Curet Alonso's other salsa compositions.[21]

Presenting reality as subjective perception rather than as a rationally based, monologic representation, "Puro teatro" (Pure drama), also composed by Curet Alonso, became one of La Lupe's most popular hits.[22] Indeed, many of us may remember this song as the closing musical number in Pedro Almodóvar's film, *Mujeres al borde de un ataque de nervios* (Women on the verge of a nervous breakdown), not an arbitrary selection given precisely the poetics of parody and performance that both the film and the song articulate. The well-known opening line of the refrain— "Teatro . . . lo tuyo es puro teatro" [Drama . . . you are pure drama]—may have spoken to many women listeners who have deployed similar tactics in their affective interactions with cheating men. If life is a stage, as the first line of the song proposes, the woman subject reasserts her own *des-engaño* (disillusion) regarding her man's performative strategies to keep her from knowing the truth about him. Thus, the song suggests that the man does not have to resort to drama, to perform, since he is the embodiment of a performance—all lies and drama, a shifting signifier that the woman cannot read. She speaks of his "dolor barato" [cheap pain] and how lying is the perfect role for the man, since, after all, "esa es tu forma de ser" [that is your way of being]. By blurring the boundaries between performance and personality, the woman singer dismantles, as Ana Lydia Vega and Carmen Lugo Filippi do in their story, the performative tactics of men that assure them a power differential in their affective relationships with women.

That the woman is well aware of these performances is clear from the beginning of the song: "Ya conozco ese teatro," "Mentiste serenamente / Y el telón cayó por eso;" "Perdona que no te crea / Me parece que es teatro" ["I already know that drama," / "You serenely lied / And thus the curtain fell," / "Forgive me for not believing you / I believe it is all drama"]. The text's deconstructive process becomes doubled within the tradition of intertextuality that has characterized salsa music. In "Puro teatro," La Lupe refers to her own songs. In indicting the male for his lies, she reminds him by speaking with a highly charged sarcasm, "Y acuérdate que según tu punto de vista yo soy la mala" [and remember that according to your point of view, I am the evil one], referring the audience to her other hit, "La tirana." Coupled with the nondiscursive yet highly emotional interjections and gestures characteristic of her style, these types of seemingly marginal utterances are central to the reading and signifying processes that the song provokes. Indeed, it is in the performance aspects of La Lupe's singing, not merely in the text, that a different female subjectivity is presented and simultaneously articulated. Throughout her career, La Lupe defied gender stereotypes and expectations. Onstage, she would take off her shoes and would throw them at the audience, she would play with the boundaries of so-called decency and indecency in her body movements, she would dress "to kill" with an accentuated style of makeup usually associated with "putas," and she would voice the physical sounds of sexual desire and erotic energy through the moans and groans invested with the sexual politics of the private and the public. It is in this radical and aggressive performance that we can fully understand and locate the transgressive and radical importance of La Lupe in the process of ascribing gender in salsa music.

In fact, while it is true that Curet Alonso's texts do not articulate the misogyny and patriarchal discourse that other salsa songs may exhibit, it is in one of La Lupe's own compositions in which one finds one of her most transgressive performances (at least aurally). In "Canta bajo,"[23] she combines English and Spanish to articulate erotic desire and sexually explicit gestures through a dialogue with the bass instrument. While she begins urging the bass to sing for her, she augments the degree of explicitness of her desire by alluding to touching the bass and putting her fingers in it. This quite particular song is, again, accompanied by moans, kisses, and oral gestures that create a very erotic and highly suggestive experience for the audience.

In view of her marginalization from the salsa industry, La Lupe asserted her authority as a central voice in the making of salsa as Latina/o music. In another of her original cuts, "Dueña del cantar," the Cuban singer wastes no time acknowledging the centrality of her figure and voice in salsa.[24] In the world of *el sabor*, that is, of salsa music, she is the owner of salsa, she asserts. Utilizing poetic enumeration, La Lupe reasserts the centrality, ownership, and authority that the industry itself failed to recognize and capitalize on. It is ironic—or perhaps consciously orchestrated—that in the opening commentaries to the song, La Lupe reminds listeners that "estamos en la familia de Masucci," thus explaining her own location as a member of one of Fania's "family" of major salsa interpreters and instrumentalists. Thus, the song can be read as an oppositional response to that particular economic relationship with Fania that eventually pushed La Lupe out of circulation as a major salsa star. When she sings that she is *the* voice and the owner of song, and the chorus repeats "dueña del cantar" to her in the *son montuno* section, she is in fact symbolically asserting the right of women singers and of female voices to be equally heard and integrated into the salsa canon.

Much like the unacknowledged economic contributions of women's domestic work and mothering, La Lupe's style of singing, her repertoires, her performances, and her presence have been sorely neglected by the industry and critics alike. That she transgressively eroticized herself as a feminist act of resistance possibly remains one of the most central motivations behind the masculine silencing to which she was subjected.

PART FOUR

✝

ASÍ SOMOS, ASÍ SON:
REWRITING SALSA

✝

Listening to the Listeners
An Introduction

✠

Así son, así son las mujeres. Así son, así son cuando se quieren.
[Such, such are women. Such are women when we love them.]
—El Gran Combo de Puerto Rico, "Así son"

Así somos. Somos atrevidas, ya no somos tan cohibidas, tan dejadas.
Ahora ya hacemos lo que queremos . . . podemos dejar a los hombres.
[Such are we. We women are daring, we are no longer inhibited, submissive.
Now we do what we want . . . we can leave men.]
—A Latina after listening to "Así son"

El Gran Combo de Puerto Rico, the very institution of salsa music [la institución de la salsa] as a Puerto Rican man reminded me, released their record album entitled "Aquí no se sienta nadie" in 1979.[1] Out of the hundreds of albums they have recorded in their thirty years of existence, this particular record, released during the group's golden age, contained many songs that would mark their privileged role in molding the salsa canon. Cuts such as "Brujería," "Más feo que yo," and "Así son" became musical staples in everyday life on the island during the late 1970s and early 1980s. These songs were played on the radio and "en las patronales y en fiestas y en vivo" [at the patron saints' festivities, at parties and at live concerts].[2] As one young Puerto Rican man observed, "todos los números de ese disco pegaron, todo el mundo los cantaba, en la radio todavía se escuchan de vez en cuando" [all the songs became hits, everybody sang them, still today we can listen to them on the radio]. Moreover, he insisted that "cualquier cosa que esta gente toque le gusta a la gente" [whatever El Gran Combo would play, people would love it].

El Gran Combo's tremendous popularity, evidenced in the pervasive social circulation of their songs, is particularly illustrated in the cuts from

Aquí no se sienta nadie. "Así son" serves as an ideal case study of the articulation between the local and the transnational, marking the shifts through which popular culture—the aural, the visual, and mass media—have become the central markers of cultural literacy in Latin America. As Jean Franco has noted, in these times of postmodernist globalization, "the small scale and the local are the places of greatest intensity."[3]

"Así son" embodies the processes of signifying, the semiotic circulation and the multidirectional flow of signifieds that characterize the life story of any cultural text. The song was an immediate hit after its release; both men and women have sung its lyrics and danced to its rhythms and musical arrangements. The open-ended nature of its refrain—*así son*—has allowed multiple interpretations to be constructed throughout the years and across diverse interpretive communities within Puerto Rico and its diaspora. Indeed, the phrase "así son," although uttered and developed throughout the song as a male diatribe against women, was appropriated by Puerto Rican feminist writers Ana Lydia Vega and Carmen Lugo Filippi in their short story "Cuatro selecciones por una peseta" as a vindictive parody of men as listeners and consumers of popular music.

From a different structural location, across the stage perhaps, Latinas who are active listeners and consumers of salsa music continuously rewrite patriarchal and misogynist salsa texts. They engage in "productive pleasure," which allows them as culturally bound receptors the opportunity to produce meanings and significations that are relevant to their everyday lives.[4] As the second epigraph of this section shows, a cultural text like "Así son" does not embody semantic closure, nor is it limited to its gendered genesis. Rather, it becomes, by means of its circulation across plural contexts, a cultural text that triggers diverse and even contradictory and conflicting meanings in and among its receptors.

Many scholarly readings of popular music silence listeners by assuming how they will or will not react, and in doing so, they impose on the "masses" the most "correct" or "liberatory" interpretations of cultural texts. In contrast, my intent here is to integrate the voices of Latinas and Latinos in a collage of significations, memories, desires, disagreements, affect, and pleasures—what Lawrence Grossberg has termed "affective economies"[5]—that partly constitute the cultural and gender semiotic space of salsa music. As a recent incursion into audience research suggests, "any critical theory of audiences within democracy must address the monopolization of communications and the cultural strategies necessary to ensure audiences the right to move from being listeners to being speakers."[6] Indeed, this silencing of the so-called masses still characterizes most analyses of popular culture, even some framed under a cultural studies rubric.

Moreover, female desire and will within the terrain of salsa music are multiply repressed by scholarship (as well as by other institutions) as they emerge from the masses, from women, and in this case, from a subordinate cultural minority in the United States, Latinas. Scholars such as Andreas Huyssen assume that the "gendering of mass culture as feminine and inferior," a social, political, and aesthetic project that originated in the late nineteenth century, has become obsolete with the decline of modernism and with the increasingly "visible and public presence of women artists in high art, as well as the emergence of new kinds of women performers and producers in mass culture."[7] In reality, the public presence of Latinas in salsa has been minimal, their voices, meanings, and impact on cultural thought marginalized at best. This silencing and systematic erasure pertains not only to performers, who indeed enjoy a certain degree of visibility in the media, but mostly to consumers, who are perhaps the most central subjects in the constellation of signifying agents that populate the locus of meaning.[8] It is not a coincidence, as Tania Modleski argues, that philosophers and thinkers have historically rendered the masses feminine because of "the mute acquiescence of the masses to the system—the silence of the majority." Just as women have been equated with a lack of articulation and language, the feminized masses have been located "outside of meaning, outside of language and of representation."[9] Doubling this historical phenomenon, scholarship has also trivialized the role of popular music and popular culture, constructing the nature and texture of its texts as not sophisticated enough, too simple, too facile. This "disgust at the facile" is analogous to societal aversion toward the social construct of the "easy woman."[10]

With women and popular song lyrics, as signifiers, thus trivialized and reduced to univalent objects of consumerism, salsa songs are multiply precluded from assuming a major role as oppositional cultural and social voices. Condescending attitudes toward popular music and the concomitant superficial readings of it are signs of the persistence of the modernist "great divide" between high art and mass culture. Moreover, this trivializing actualizes class prejudices. By equating popular music with "easy listening," elitist scholars undervalue the economic and cultural realities of the working class from which this music arises. In these multilayered marginalizations, Latina listeners, particularly those from the working class, remain muted—not because they have nothing to say about salsa music (which they love and with which many identify as strongly as men do) but rather because of the elitist scholarly disdain that has not recognized the central role that Latinas play in the longevity of this particular musical tradition.

In this light, Part Four strives to vindicate the everyday practice of listening to salsa music as an active process of struggle over discourse and meaning. Within the context of Latina/o migration, listening to salsa music becomes a reaffirmation of a minority culture within the United States, and as such it may inspire a sense of stable identity and "home" for Latinas/os, however temporarily experienced. Salsa music as a sociocultural praxis also serves to create a space in which to articulate conflicts, constructs, and attitudes toward gender and (hetero)sexual relations. This multiplicity of roles, constantly shifting according to class, race, generation and age, migration, location, values, and personal experiences—that is, according to the listening subject's own positioning—suggests that music as a cultural text always already moves beyond its written signs and that, like the act of reading, it can never be listened to twice in the same manner. To judge salsa music only from the point of view of gender politics, that is, to reject it as *música machista* (sexist music) is to ignore the complex semiotic directions that any musical text may travel and thus embody. It also assumes that Latinas are passive listeners or compliant consumers of the music, an Adornian-constructed audience that placidly accepts these antifemale messages. The ethnographic work in the following chapters tells a very different story, even a story about differentiating as a social act. It illustrates the very real role of women as "cultural producers" insofar as they activate the "circulation of meanings" that constitutes popular music as cultural praxis.

CHAPTER ELEVEN

Así Son

Constructing Woman

✠

The male-centered discourse of the song "Así son" originates from the conjunction of two musical traditions: the bolero and the salsa. As in the bolero, in many salsa songs the woman's absence functions as the pretext for the expression of man's desire.[1] El Gran Combo's song, "Así son," clearly fits within this discursive tradition:

> Tintineo de copas, chocar de besos
> humo de cigarrillos en el salón
> El Gran Combo que toca sus melodías
> y gente que se embriaga con whisky y ron.
>
> Yo que me desvelo por tu cariño
> Tú que me desprecias, ay, sin compasión.
> Andas como una loca por las cantinas
> Brindando a todo el mundo tu corazón.
>
> *Coro*: Así son, así son las mujeres
> Así son, así son cuando se quieren.
>
> Tú me dejaste a mí
> Pero pensando que yo era pobre
> Y te pasas por ahí
> pero cambiando oro por cobre.
>
> *Coro*: Así son, así son las mujeres
> Así son, así son cuando se quieren.
>
> Alcé mi copa de vino
> Para brindar por tu ausencia
> Sé que nunca me quisiste
> y ya que el amor, ya no tiene esencia.
>
> *Coro*: Así son, así son las mujeres
> Así son, así son cuando se quieren.
>
> Pero eso mira yo no creo más en quereres
> por eso mira no te quiero que mira María Mercedes, no no no
> Pero cuando se quiere de veras, señor,

Mira yo quiero quererte, pero que ahora a mi manera
Pero que mira, pero que a mí me pasa lo mismo que a usted
Pero que mira cómo son, que mira cómo son. . . .

Coro: Así son, así son las mujeres
Así son, así son cuando se quieren.

[Cups clinking and the sounds of kissing
cigarrette smoke inside the room
El Gran Combo playing its songs
and people getting drunk on whisky and rum.

I am sleepless for your love
You reject me, mercilessly
You go around the bars like a fool
Offering your love to all.

(*Chorus*): That's the way, that's the way women are
that's the way they are when we love them.

You abandoned me
thinking that I was poor
and now you go around
exchanging gold for copper;
(*Chorus*)

I raised my cup of wine
to toast to your absence
I know you never loved me
since love has no essence
(*Chorus*)

That is why, look, I don't believe anymore in loves
that is why, look, I don't love you, look, Maria Mercedes, no no no,
For when one really loves,
Look, I want to love you, but my way now
But look, I'm going through the same as you
But look at the way they are, look at the way they are. . . .
(*Chorus*)]

The song's opening references to drinking, music, and sexuality occur within the male locus of a bar or nightclub, a space in which the male singer/subject can cathartically enunciate his accusations against "his" woman, who has left him and is acting *loca* (crazy), offering her love to others. Moreover, the metatextual allusion in the first stanza to El Gran Combo itself "playing their songs" underlines the masculinity of the singing space as well as of the song's lyrics and voice. The space of the nightclub is framed by a marginal hypersensuality in which women can participate only as "prostitutes," "offering [their] love to all." Not coincidentally, this is the same figuration accorded by the male singer to his ex-lover. Thus, the man's first characterization of the woman he loves is a negative one; she is a traitor to his love, whereas he is her victim. The syntactic contiguity between the reference to drinking and the male singer's suffering after having been abandoned signals, again, the multiple cathartic functions of the various textual spaces evoked: the nightclub, the acts of drinking and singing, and the song itself. The first stanza implicitly refers its listeners to the figure of the bandolera. The economics of love once more become the male rationale for female abandonment. In the eyes of the male singer it is obvious that she left him "thinking that [he] was poor," but ironically, she has gone on to other men of less financial resources ("pero cambiando oro por cobre").

This affective ambiguity appears in the final stanza of the song as well as in the *montuno* section, the improvisatory verses in which the singer culls previous bolero verses—"a mí me pasa lo mismo que a usted" [I suffer like you]—to inform the present text. While the singer expresses cynicism toward love and relationships, he still insists that there is a real way of loving, that it is possible to have an ideal, productive relationship, although that ideal is molded and defined "his way," which is also clearly articulated in Willie Colón's "Cuando fuiste mujer." In light of his failure to maintain his will, the *montuno* closes with the reiteration of the chorus line, that open-ended utterance that allows listeners to construct "the way women are."

A Literary Rewriting

The refrain to "Así son" is the epigraph and subtext to Ana Lydia Vega and Carmen Lugo Filippi's short story "Cuatro selecciones por una peseta."[2] The story's ironic subtitle identifies the bolero as the subtext to both "Así Son" and the story itself: "Bolero a dos voces para machos en pena, una sentida interpretación del dúo Scaldada-Cuervo" [Bolero in two voices for suffering males, a sincere interpretation by the duo Scaldada-Cuervo]. While this statement takes its rhetoric from the bolero tradition, it also subverts the rhetoric by using it to contest that tradition. The "two voices" allude to the collective authorship of Vega and Filippi, as well as to the opposition between male and female voices. The reader is introduced to two female writing subjects who speak and who speak doubly. On one level the story is about four Puerto Rican men, Eddie, Angelito, Monchín, and Puruco, who meet at a bar to express their anger at the women who have either abandoned or betrayed them. On another, the "sentida interpretación" [sincere interpretation] of the subtitle suggests a hidden perspective, a double talk through which the reader is alerted to alternative meanings and subversive interpretive strategies. *Sentida* would be literally translated as "felt" and only derivatively as "sincere," "honest," or "sentimental." However, it is clearly related to *estar sentido* (to be hurt or angry), a phrase that at first glance would seem to apply exclusively to the male protagonists. Yet in the context of a piece of writing by two female subjects, this phrase suggests an angry or spiteful motivation for the writing itself. We could thus read the subtitle and the story as an expression of vindictiveness toward men or at least as an attempt by these authors to see and define men from a woman-centered perspective.

The "four selections" correspond to the diatribes uttered by the four protagonists against "their" women as well as to the songs they select on the jukebox. A closer analysis reveals, however, that the men's words and the songs' lyrics continually contaminate each other. The men do not always speak in their own words but sometimes in those of song lyrics like the famous Latin American bolero "Usted" by Gabriel Ruiz—"Usted es la culpable de todas mis angustias, de todos mis quebrantos" [You are to blame for all of my suffering, for all of my pain]—in addition to lyrics from salsa, tangos, and rancheras. Notably, all of these musical genres articulate a patriarchal ideology in which women acquire value as women only when they love a man or allow themselves to be loved by a man. As El Gran Combo repeatedly sings in "Así son:" "Qué buenas son las mujeres, qué buenas son cuando quieren," which doubly translates to "women are so good, so good when they want to" as well as to "women are so good, so good when they love [you]." Its corollary, "Qué buenas son cuando se quieren" [Women are so good when you love them], clearly reaffirms the hegemonic masculine definition of a woman's value contingent on her affective relational position to the male.

The words men use to construct women are the semantic and ideological link between the popular songs quoted in the short story and the *quejas* (complaints) of the story's four male protagonists. Eddie wanted his wife to be a nurse/slave to his mother; when she left the house for an hour, he beat her up. Because Monchín allowed his wife to go out to work, he "lost" her to unions and politics. Puruco was sensitive enough not to go out to bars frequently but instead had his friends over every night and expected his wife to serve him dinner and to wait on his friends. As for Angelito, well, he never married at all. Their misogynist diatribes reflect a discrepancy between male perceptions of women's roles and how their wives may have perceived themselves (not explicitly present in the story but suggested in their decisions to leave). These men were threatened not by so-called inherent female traits but by the economic and emotional independence that these women were gaining through work or through the consciousness of their own conditions as women within an abusive marriage.

Is this short story and the popular music it draws on, a realistic gauge of social reality in Puerto Rico? According to statistics, Puerto Rican women are abandoning men. During the 1980s, almost 50 percent of marriages ended in divorce. This rate is rising, not always because women are being unfaithful or treacherous, as the songs suggest, but because they are no longer tolerating men's double standards. While 71.6 percent of divorces in Puerto Rico have been filed by women, 41.9 percent of divorced women interviewed in a study revealed that they had petitioned for divorce because of their husbands' extreme authoritarianism or infidelities.[3] Thus, it would not be unfounded to argue that one of the strategies of gender discourse in salsa is to invert reality, turning it upside down and accusing women of men's resistance to adapt to women's changing social roles. As a group, Puruco, Monchín, Eddie, and Angelito constitute a symbolic microcosm of Puerto Rican men's entrenchment in traditional gender roles within the context of social change.

The four diatribes of these men may be read as textualized forms of "productive pleasure." Their respective *quejas* are interspersed with snatches of lyrics from salsa, boleros, tangos, and rancheras: "Qué buenas son las mujeres qué buena [*sic*] son cuando quieren"; "Túuuuuu, sólo túuuuu"; "Usted es la culpable de todas mis angustias."[4] References to tangos and rancheras complete the repertoire of patriarchal lyrics: "no hay como un tango pa olvidal" [there is nothing like a tango to help me forget] and "Los acordes de una ranchera matahembra sobrepoblaron el aire" [the chords of a female-killer rancher overpopulated the air].[5] Such song lyrics and musical references offer these four working-class Puerto Rican males a form of catharsis and a patriarchal paradigm with which to reconstruct and give meaning to their own life experiences. The men actually produce meanings from the songs but only from those lyrics that are relevant to their position as men who have been abandoned by their wives or lovers. In "Cuatro selecciones por una peseta," the four characters iconize a gendered interpretive community constituted by working-class Puerto Rican males who listen to certain popular songs that reaffirm and naturalize their socially mandated masculine behavior.

Viewed in this light, Latin popular music serves as a code or a language for those who lack one. Eddie, Angelito, Monchín, and Puruco consistently depend on the codes of popular music to define their otherwise repressed affective experiences as well as to construct women in relation to their feelings. As mass media products, these lyrics (in this case, disseminated by the *vellonera*), provide the men with a language for catharsis, for expressing and relieving their emotions. As "emotional type listeners," they react to sentimental music by attaining a "temporary . . . awareness that [they] have missed fulfillment." This music "permits its listeners the confession of their unhappiness," yet their catharsis is illusory. The music is not truly liberating since it actually "reconciles them by means of this release, to their social dependence."[6] Ironically, the emotional type of listener believes that he or she is escaping an unhappy reality by means of this music, as in the story's last line: "No hay como un tango pa olvidar" [there is nothing like a tango to help me forget].[7] However, these listeners are participating in a pattern of social dependence by indiscriminately accepting this musical discourse as personally relevant. While they may pose as authors of their own gender discourse, these four men are, as the story seems to suggest through an Adornian stance, passive receptors who internalize and mimic these ideological messages. Their position may, in fact, be read as analogous to the colonial situation of Puerto Rico, in which U.S. capitalist hegemony continues to control mass media programming and advertising.[8]

Through irony, parody, and strategies of inversion, "Cuatro selecciones por una peseta" dismantles the constructions of women in Latin popular music, particularly in salsa. Here, the representation of the feminine as absence, as in Willie Colón's "Cuando fuiste mujer," becomes superimposed on a representation of the Puerto Rican male as one who lacks a language of his own and the necessary cultural and gender codes to deal with his repressed emotions: "Cuando calló Jaramillo el silencio era un bache de lágrimas machamente contenidas" [When Jaramillo stopped talking, silence was a puddle of tears restrained in a macho way].[9] In addition, the story's ironic positioning of these four men inversely reconstructs the discursive image of the muted, passive masses as masculine rather than feminine. The double discourse of the title further suggests that the "selecciones" to be listened to, or consumed, are not only the musical ones but the four men's diatribes. The cumulative effect of the ironic, tongue-in-cheek tone of the feminist narrative voice and the parodic distortions of male discourse at the level of the signifier, indicate that this short story is not about women, as the epigraph seems to suggest, but ironically about men. By the end of the story, the reader has gathered that (1) Eddie, Puruco, Monchín, and Angelito have been unfaithful to their wives and/or are still dependent on their mothers, (2) are not politically savvy, and (3) are quite naïve about each other as friends. "Así son, así son los hombres cuando no los quieren" [such, such are men when they are not loved] summarizes what the story is really all about: two women writers (and readers) deconstructing male discourse and behavior.

Toward a Feminist Politics of Listening

A traditional incursion into music and literature would have ended here. Yet after examining Vega and Filippi's story, many questions and contradictions remain regarding the complex dialectics of ideology and pleasure that this particular song, and salsa as a sociocultural practice, bring to the foreground. For instance, where are the feminist listeners in salsa music? Why do Latina listeners like Vega and Filippi, and I, enjoy salsa as much as we despise and oppose its misogyny and patriarchal constructs of women? Are those of us Latinas who are consumers of salsa "to be regarded as aberrant 'feminine' readers or participants in 'masculine' culture," to quote Cathy Swichtenberger, because of our complicity and participation in a misogynist and patriarchal cultural production?[10] Can this "consumption of even 'incorrect' content have a progressive political effect at some level, under some circumstances, to some end," as Wahneema Lubiano also proposes?[11] How do Latinas in various class locations listen to salsa, and what does this music mean in their lives? How does salsa acquire meaning for Latinas in the United States, and how is gender dissonance negotiated vis-à-vis salsa's central role as a marker of culture within our postcolonial conditions?

Wary of essentializing gender as opposing difference, I am not so much interested in contrasting women's listening practices against men's. However, a larger view of the complexities of the listening process is possible when the ethnographic work embraces a diversity of socially and gender-located subjects. Thus, interviews with Latino men, while not as extensive as those with women, have helped to identify certain differences in listening to two songs—"Cuando fuiste mujer" and "Así son"—differences that I hope will not lead to generalizations about both men and women but will indicate divergent approaches to these songs and to salsa in particular. To examine the (hetero)sexual politics of salsa, the ways in which the "discourses which comprise it reproduce a struggle equivalent to that experienced socially by its readers,"[12] we must consider the dialogic textures and cross-disciplinary spaces of feminist responses to the masculine monologism of most of these lyrics. Simultaneously, we must consider the ways in which many Latinas/os may reaffirm the gender politics, the power differentials between men and women, that the songs themselves enunciate.

Ethnographic interviews with eighteen Latinas and eight Latinos in Detroit and Ann Arbor, Michigan, reveal the active role of both men and women listeners in giving meaning to salsa.[13] These interviews clearly show that despite the minimal participation of Latinas in the music industry, Latinas, as a specific audience, have learned to appropriate this masculinist music for various purposes in their own lives. The sense of "productive pleasure" that they enjoy as a result of their listening practices allows them to invest salsa with liberatory meanings for them as working-class women or as women of color. It allows Latinas to negotiate power differentials with the men in their lives, whether they come from upper-class professional families or from a working-class background. In addition, Puerto Rican men who have grown up on the island clearly articulated a high level of literacy about the music, the groups and interpreters, and the historical evolution of salsa that was absent in the women's responses. For instance, they commented on specific musical arrangements, rhythms, instrumentation, the historical impact of certain songs, and the development of salsa music. This suggests, in fact, that Puerto Rican men identify at a higher degree with salsa music as a masculine tradition, as a musical repertoire that mirrors their own experiences, their language, and their values and perceptions as men. It also reaffirms the greater access to knowledge about the music industry itself, about the *farándula* (singers and musicians), and about the processes of music production that men tend to enjoy more than women do. In the words of a Puerto Rican male, growing up in Puerto Rico meant playing the trombone and emulating the trombonist of El Gran Combo, among others, as his role model. For women, this was hardly the case.

Of the eighteen women interviewed, nine were born in Puerto Rico; two in Mexico; one each in Colombia, El Salvador, and Venezuela; two in Chicago; and one in Detroit. All, however, were raised in the United States or have spent more than five years in this country. Four Latinos were born in Puerto Rico, one in El Salvador, one in Colombia, and one in Venezuela. Three of them have lived in the United States for more than five years. The others came to the United States within the past three or four years to study. Besides the experience of migration, what is common to all of these Latinas and Latinos is that they are familiar with salsa and have identified themselves as listeners and consumers of this music.

On the new bases of their social location and degree of engagement with salsa, I identified two groups among the women interviewees: the University of Michigan (UM) group, which consisted of ten Latina students (two graduate students and eight undergraduates) and the Detroit group (eight working-class Latinas). The UM group was definitely younger in median age represented (twenty-one years), as opposed to the Detroit group's median age of thirty-five, a difference that in some cases accounted for more literal readings of the songs on the part of the younger group. Five of the eighteen women were married and thirteen single, an important factor that allows for a higher frequency of musical practices, particularly going dancing, among the latter group.

Among the Latinos, the median age represented was twenty-nine. Four were single and three married. This group consisted mostly of Puerto Rican and Latin American young men who have come to the United States to study. Only one respondent, age fifty-one, was not a student.

A clear division arises when looking at class variables among Latinas. While the UM group consisted of two students from working-class backgrounds (the two graduate students), the other eight Latina students came from families with two professional parents. These class differences, I argue, account for some clear contrasts in terms of their valoration of salsa, that is, their acceptance or rejection of the songs that we played for them. Class divisions definitely informed the different responses of these two groups to our question: Who is your favorite salsa group or singer? Four of eight working-class women mentioned El Gran Combo de Puerto Rico as one of their favorite musical groups, or even *the* favorite, whereas none of the UM group even mentioned this all-black, all-male band. Rubén Blades, Juan Luis Guerra, and Luis Enrique competed for first place in the young UM women's hearts. While Rubén Blades was singled out for his political songs and profound lyrics, both by upper-class Latinas and by many of the Latino respondents from various class origins, Juan Luis Guerra was equally lauded for his "very poetic songs and [for being] very sexy" as well as for his "danceable rhythms." However, the women in the Detroit group seemed to add more qualifiers to their musical choices. As a Rubén Blades fan said, "His songs are based on reality." And an Eddie Santiago fan added that although she liked his songs, she wasn't happy with the images of women they portrayed. A fan of El Gran Combo immediately mentioned this group because its language and words were very much what she had grown up with in Puerto Rico; she identified them as "more folkloric."

I mention these examples to anticipate some very clear class divisions that emerged from the interviews more prominently among the women than among the men, thus informing the degree with which working-class women feel much more engaged in this music than do the UM students. These brief examples begin to point to a process of naturalizing song lyrics that seems more prevalent among the younger upper-class Latinas. Their working-class counterparts told me that while they may identify very closely with salsa music, this cultural identification does not preclude their critique of gender representations. The UM group, as I will discuss later, also rejects the masculinist discourse of salsa but with very different motivations.

For the Latinos interviewed, as a group, their position on salsa music seemed much stronger than that of the group of Latinas. "La escucharé por siempre porque es parte de mi vida" [I will always listen to it because it is part of my life] concluded a twenty-five-year-old puertorriqueño, not coincidentally the most musically literate of all interviewees. The apparent omniscient presence of salsa in their lives also illustrates the higher degree of exposure, access, and participation of males in this musical culture: "As far back as I can remember, it was always there," commented another Puerto Rican young man. Some remembered listening to salsa since they were babies or since they were quite young, either six or eight years old, at parties. One remembered first listening to salsa "on a bus in Cali" when he was about seven years old, thus attesting to the prevalence of this music in everyday life and as an overarching cultural signifier throughout public spaces. Another Puerto Rican man remembered becoming a salsa fan when he entered high school, a case analogous to the Venezuelan student who entered this culture through school parties and dances as his upper-class professional parents did not listen to salsa music in their home. Yet, as the following comment reaffirms, salsa music was everywhere, permeating the lives, values, and emotions of men and women in Puerto Rico: "Salsa is part of the culture; one grows up listening and dancing to salsa and merengue. If it's not playing on the radio, it plays on the neighbor's radio; if not, somebody plays it on the streets, or it plays in the stores as part of their advertisement."

One twenty-eight-year-old puertorriqueño confessed becoming "addicted to this stuff" after he arrived in the United States. Growing up in Puerto Rico he was more of a rockero, although he did listen to salsa with political content. When he migrated to the United States as a student and met his present wife, he "started to miss the music" and began to buy it, influenced by his wife's avid interest in salsa. While salsa was "ever present" in Puerto Rico and one could take it for granted as it were, in the United States it was compelling for him to become a conscious consumer of this music in order to be able to listen to it. On the island, inversely, he would listen to salsa in public spaces—the beach festivals, *las patronales*, public events—and would "have to" buy tickets to attend rock concerts.

Most Latino men articulated "an ideology of authenticity" as fans of salsa music. Like rock fans who distinguish between authentic and co-opted rock music, these middle-class cocolos repeatedly constructed a difference between "good" and "bad" salsa, which, in their words, refers to political, progressive songs, on the one hand, and commercial cuts on the other.[14] While many of them included El Gran Combo de Puerto Rico as one of their favorite groups, this acknowledgment was qualified by characterizing El Gran Combo as "fun," "graciosos," a humorous musical group whose "social" messages were differently valued from the larger, more serious political messages of Rubén Blades or Willie Colón. These men accentuated the revolutionary nature of Rubén Blades's lyrics because they find in his music "un llamado, una invitación a que escuches el mensaje" [a call, an exhortation to listen to the message]. In addition, for a Colombian male who used to be a rockero, Rubén Blades became the symbol of a Pan-Latino "internationalist latinoamericano message," his repertoire speaking to the heterogeneous cultural locations of latinoamericanas/os as they become ethnified, become U.S. Latinas/os.

Indeed, these observations among the men indicate a preference for Blades's anticolonial songs without rejecting El Gran Combo's importance in popular culture. Indeed, the underlying dichotomy constructed by these men is not so much based on class or race identities, as it is among the women, but rather on the diverse modes of listening that these different repertoires trigger in the consumers. It was interesting that the men identified two types of salsa music: first, danceable music; then, songs for listening. El Gran Combo's repertoire has been systematically categorized as danceable music, and thus the listening quotient has been reduced. Consequently, the lyrics of their songs are "lost" or diluted by the listening context in which they are played. Blades's songs, on the other hand, exhort the listeners to pay attention to the words of the song, to the "message," as much as to the musical arrangements, the rhythms, and the harmonies. While historically Blades vindicated and enhanced the literary quality of salsa songs, it is not arbitrary to state that El Gran Combo's repertoire has been trivialized as entertainment, as light music to be danced to but not taken seriously. Perhaps this reveals not so much an inherent inferior value in their songs and music, as Randel attempts to convince us, but rather a class and racial displacement by which the black working-class group constitutes the buffoon figure, the comic role that is merely entertaining and does not need to be taken seriously. Scholarship, however, should address the need to document not only the historical development of salsa music through El Gran Combo's musical repertoire but also the social changes in Puerto Rico that are definitely articulated in their lyrics.

While most of the women from both groups first listened to salsa as young children or adolescents, the working-class women very clearly traced their first memories of salsa to their mothers. One woman observed the following:

Yo me recuerdo que nosotros visitábamos mucho a la familia y ellos eran mayores, y la ponían y entonces yo la escuchaba . . . la oía también y me gustó. Pero no me recuerdo . . . tenía que ser desde que era bien chiquita . . . como desde que era baby. La escuché desde que nací. Sí, la escucho mucho, todas las mañanas, en mi casa, es que como mi mamá lo pone al amanecer de Dios, yo lo escucho. Y . . . sí, a mi mamá le gusta mucho la salsa.

[I remember that we often used to visit our relatives and they were older and they would play it and thus I would hear it. I would also listen to it and I liked it. But I don't remember . . . it must have been when I was real little . . . like since I was a baby. I listened to it since I was born. Yes, I listen to it often, every morning in my house; since my mother plays it in the early mornings, I listen to it. And . . . yes, my mother likes salsa very much.]

Another woman recalled how she and her family would drive to church listening to salsa music in the car. "My mother," she added, was a "vieja salsera" [an old female salsa fan]. A third woman also associated salsa with her mother, as she remembered that although she was not allowed to go to dances, her mother transmitted her love of salsa to her: "Sí, mis padres eran muy estrictos. No había razones religiosas envueltas . . . mi mamá, le voy a decir: mi mamá ella siempre cuando cocinaba se ponía a bailar. Siempre estaba cocinando y bailando y cocinando y bailando. Yeah! I know, like you say, that when you are having kids waiting for you . . . it is the only way to survive" [Yes, my parents were very strict. Not for religious reasons . . . my mother, I'll tell you: whenever my mother was cooking, she would always start to dance. She was always cooking and dancing and cooking and dancing]. These voices reaffirm the central importance that mothers have in the passing on of cultural and national traditions. They simultaneously reveal, however, that a male-produced, strident urban music such as salsa can function as a source of relief and catharsis for housewives and mothers. Salsa is distraction, entertainment, escape, but it has also been appropriated as a tool of survival for many Latinas confined to housework and child rearing. Indeed, an interviewee once mentioned that the fast rhythms of salsa were a wonderful way to get her in the mood to clean her house.

While the university women also began to listen to salsa at a relatively young age, none of them associated the music specifically with their mothers, a significant difference that marks a particular identification with salsa as a racially and class-marked cultural possession. While 60 percent (6 of 10) of the UM group responded that they had first listened to salsa in preadolescence and adolescence (possibly by attending social events and dances and as participants in youth culture), three other women mentioned that they had been initiated as salsa listeners during early childhood; one non–Puerto Rican woman discovered salsa when she moved to Ann Arbor to study. There is, in fact, a substantial difference between the responses from the Detroit group, which showed a stronger degree of engagement and identification with the music, and the UM interviewees, who as a group tended to feel more detached from it.

The frequency with which Latinas listen to salsa seems also to be marked by class location. Seven of the ten UM women listen to salsa "de vez en cuando" [sometimes], "casi nunca" [almost never], or "muy poco" [very seldom], in sharp contrast to the responses from the Detroit group: "In the mornings when I clean," "almost every day," "every day," "when my Cuban boyfriend comes to see me," and "at home while I cook to get inspired and feel more relaxed." This quantitative and qualitative difference suggests thinking about these groups as different interpretive communities. If, as Janice Radway postulates, an interpretive community can be defined as "larger collections of people who, by virtue of a common social position and demographic character, unconsciously share certain assumptions about reading (listening) as well as preferences for reading material,"[15] the responses to two particular salsa songs will reaffirm that class differences produce separate interpretive communities. As their responses suggest, what working-class Latinas "do" with salsa music seems to be much more active engagement, with more social significance, compared to their upper-class counterparts.

Key questions that signaled the different degrees of engagement with the music between the groups were whether they had listened to the two songs before and whether the songs reminded them of anything. None of the UM Latinas had ever listened to Willie Colón's "Cuando fuiste mujer," and only one, not coincidentally from a working-class background, attested to having had listened to "Así son" before. It is true that two songs should not be used exclusively to gauge levels of familiarity with such a diverse and broad musical canon. However, such responses do suggest, in general ways, that upper- and middle-class Latinas are not fans of salsa in the same ways as Puerto Rican men (regardless of class background), who spoke of their high degree of engagement with the music, its performers, and its repertoire; nor do they experience the affective engagements that the Detroit women expressed throughout their interviews. This gap in salsa literacy reaffirms the strong sense of identification that exists between certain social sectors and this music of black, working-class origins. While Puerto Rican men seem to exhibit the strongest identification with salsa as "their" culture, working-class Latinas also claim it as a cultural product that emerges from their class location.

The tendency of postmodern approaches to salsa would be to highlight the plural locations and the transnational impact of this music—its internationalization and multicultural performance and productions—perhaps diminishing its local meanings, the value of having a particular music identified or associated with a specific social sector. From that perspective, salsa nowadays would be definitely losing value and meaning among the Puerto Rican working class. In contrast, what the ethnographic data suggest here is that although salsa continues to move toward multiaudiences and multilocations (in terms of race, class, gender, and national and transnational boundaries), that movement has not undermined the strong sense of cultural identity that salsa provokes among working-class individuals. This distinction also has class-based implications that contest prevalent ideas about salsa's universal values and its power to integrate listeners from all class and racial locations. I have previously spoken to salsa's value as a marker of pan-Latinity in the United States; it is essential to examine the different processes and structured locations from which diverse individuals give meaning to this music.

Class-based differences among the Latinos seemed to emerge in less salient ways than among the women, partly because the class origins among the men were more homogeneous. Four of the men came from professional, middle-class families, but only one, from Venezuela, grew up in an upper-class environment. That Latino commented that his family "never played salsa music" at home, illustrating the efforts at racial and class differentiation that are still prevalent among a large part of the Latin American bourgeoisie. In fact, my own upbringing on the island was characterized by my parent's denial of salsa's social or cultural value. They never played it at home, instead spending Sunday afternoons listening to albums from Broadway shows such as *Oklahoma*, *Annie Get Your Gun*, and *Showboat* and to classical music, repertoires that allowed them to distinguish themselves from the more "vulgar" tastes of *el pueblo* in the service of social mobility. The Colombian male who identified himself as having grown up in the upper-class sector in Mexico commented that he had learned to appreciate salsa in the process of his own deterritorialization. While in high school in Mexico, he did not listen to this music because it was considered a tropical, working-class music. Instead, the ideal in that youth sector was the U.S. rock and disco music that was emulated by Mexico's white youth, the professional middle-class and bourgeoisie already socialized into colonialist patterns of consuming culture. However, it would be a simplistic generalization to state that all upper-class families reject salsa. As a young Venezuelan woman from upper-class origins observed: "desde siempre en mi casa ponían salsa" [since always in my home we played salsa]. It is essential to note the diverse individual tastes and pleasures that are represented within any particular class.

The ethnographic discourse among the eight males is further characterized by a persistent effort to distinguish diverse listening practices based on "education." As young Puerto Rican men socialized in traditional gender roles, some of them explicitly recognized that their formal education, both at the University of Puerto Rico and at University of Michigan, had transformed the values and attitudes they brought to the music as male listeners. Six of the eight respondents clearly disagreed with the way that Willie Colón portrayed women in his song "Cuando fuiste mujer," and they all saw the patriarchal tenets of El Gran Combo's "Así son" as a problematic representation of women. Yet the differentiations constructed around these readings and around their own subject positions as "educated," "politically correct" Latinos have interesting and significant implications.

This marked tendency among the male UM students from Puerto Rico branched out into particular distinctions: (1) the past forms of traditional listening and their present listening practices as sensitive, educated males; (2) their disagreement with and opposition to machismo in the music versus the complicity of other, less educated Puerto Rican or Latino men who may participate in these misogynist ideologies; (3) locating salsa songs such as Willie Colón's and El Gran Combo's historically as the prevalent mode during the 1970s and as examples of "erotic salsa," thus displacing machismo in salsa from contemporary repertoires such as Gilberto Santa Rosa's songs and romantic salsa (versus erotic salsa). Such strategies of displacement and projection may be motivated by the negotiations of class identity with which they may be experimenting as they shift their social status from that of their parents toward a more privileged position as young U.S.-trained intellectuals and professionals, that is, their need to create boundaries between their family's socioeconomic origins and their newly constituted social status. As some of them commented, the construction of salsa music only as machista music also has affected the ways that Anglo women unfairly perceive them as Latinos. Thus, they expressed a constant desire to displace, diachronically and synchronically, salsa's phallocentric repertoire onto cultural, social, and historical spaces separate from their own present location as "educated Latinos."

Moreover, as ethnographer, I need to ask myself to what extent is the respondent's critical attitude merely a function of the fact that the ethnographer places them in a situation where they are required to be critical?[16] The fact that one respondent kept asking the interviewer, "What do you want me to say?" suggests, at least overtly in his case, a self-consciousness as interviewee that undoubtedly affected his conscious responses during the process of the interview. Comments such as "These songs are not really good examples of salsa" or "I hope that these songs are not all that will be used in this research" indicate, in fact, a preoccupation with the study's cultural and gender repercussions for the men.

Constructing Woman as Text

To textualize the female, that is, to construct gender identity and the feminine through language, is partly established through the deployment of a cultural symbolic economy, that is, a collection of multiple signs that trigger desire, fear, aggression, and love.[17] We have already analyzed, in

Part Three, some figurations of the feminine, such as the inscription of woman as absence, the synecdochal violence of patriarchal language, and the discursive terrorism that projects gendered social constructs based on anger, fear, and a defensive sort of aggression. Yet, salsa songs, as cultural and social texts, also constitute the linguistic and discursive space in which the male writing/singing subject can concretely articulate the nature of womanliness, of the feminine. This power to represent the female Other, to speak for her as it were, within a lyrical, musical text that masks any sort of overt violence and that indeed projects itself as an expression of love and desire, needs to be examined and deconstructed as well.

A discourse analysis of a song by Vilma Planas and Héctor Garrido and interpreted by Willie Colón titled "Cuando fuiste mujer" better illustrates this most subtle form of gender construction.[18] How does the singing/writing subject construct Woman as song, as text? The lyrical melody and harmonies informed by the bolero and its apparently "romantic" words establish its condition as "marked writing," what Hélène Cixous has defined as phallologocentrism "hidden or adorned with the mystifying charms of fiction [in this case, of lyricism]."[19] This is precisely why I chose this text as an object of analysis. Not only do its lyrics exemplify gender construction at its best, but also its musicality, the slow tempo, and its lyrical tone created a catchy melody for me. I found myself humming this song over and over again, indeed having been wonderfully and dangerously "seduced" by this patriarchal musical text.

CUANDO FUISTE MUJER

Conmigo aprendiste a querer y a saber de la vida
Y a fuerzas de tantas caricias tu cuerpo formé.
Tu rostro de pálida seda cambió sus matices
Se tiñó de rubor cuando fuiste mujer, fuiste mujer.

Sentía tu cuerpo temblar sin la noche estar fría
Sentía tu cuerpo vibrar en la noche que ardía.
Sintiendo el gemir de tu amor que me dio su tibieza
Hice mío tu amor cuando fuiste mujer, fuiste mujer.

Quiero que tú sigas siendo niña
aunque en tu alma seas toda mujer
quiero que tu alma y la mía
se unan por amor formando un nuevo ser.

Quiero que tú nunca más te olvides
de tus sentimientos, de tu forma de ser
Quiero que recuerdes para siempre
el momento aquel en que te hice mujer
y fuiste mujer y eres mujer.

Coro: Quiero que tú nunca más te olvides
Solo: No te olvides del amor que compartimos debajo de la

luna cuando dije entre mí como esa mami no hay una
Coro: Quiero que tú nunca más te olvides
Solo: Que conmigo aprendiste las cosas de la vida esa noche te juro nunca se me olvida
Coro: Quiero que tú nunca más te olvides
Solo: Quiero que tú sigas siendo niña aunque en tu alma seas toda una mujer
Coro: Quiero que tú nunca más te olvides
Solo: que tu alma y la mía se unan por amor formando un solo ser
Coro: Quiero que tú nunca más te olvides
Solo: Mi recuerdo te desvela, soy el ansia que te llega nunca podrás olvidar lo que te enseñé
Coro: Quiero que tú nunca más te olvides
Solo: Pregunta por ahí quién es el que te ama siempre he sido yo, en la vida hay amores que no pueden olvidarse, como nuestro amor
Coro: Quiero que tú nunca más te olvides
Solo: En una noche encendida tú me entregaste tu cuerpo yo te di todo mi ser . . .
Coro: Quiero que tú nunca más te olvides
Solo: Cómo temblamos de alegría, yo jamás me olvidaré

WHEN YOU BECAME WOMAN

With me you learned to love and to know about life
And I molded your body with the power of my caresses
Your pale silk face changed its hues
You blushed when you became a woman, a woman.

I felt your body trembling when the night was not cold.
I felt your body vibrating in the ardent night.
Feeling your moaning love that offered me warmth
I made your love mine when you became a woman, a woman.

I want you to remain a little girl
even though in your soul you are all woman
I want your soul and mine
to fuse in love and form a new being.

I don't want you to ever forget
your feelings, your way of being.
I want you to always remember
that moment when I made you a woman
and you were woman and you are woman.

Chorus: I don't want you to ever forget
Solo: Don't forget the love we shared in the moonlight when I told myself there's no other woman like you
Chorus: I don't want you to ever forget
Solo: That I taught you about life that night I swear I'll never forget
Chorus: I don't want you to ever forget
Solo: I want you to remain being a girl, even though you are a woman in your soul

Chorus:	I don't want you to ever forget
Solo:	I want your soul and mine to fuse in love and to form a new being
Chorus:	I don't want you to ever forget
Solo:	You cannot sleep thinking of me, I am the anxiety that you feel, you could never forget what I taught you
Chorus:	I don't want you to ever forget
Solo:	Ask others who could love you, I have always loved you, in life there are certain unforgettable loves, just like our love
Chorus:	I don't want you to ever forget
Solo:	In this ardent night you surrendered your body, I gave you my whole being
Chorus:	I don't want you to ever forget
Solo:	How we both tremble with joy, I will never forget . . .

The male singing subject addresses *tú* (you), the implied woman and lover, from the position of master. She acquires her knowledge of love and of life, and indeed, her life itself, only through him. The syntactic position of "conmigo" [with me] as the first word of the song establishes the foundational position of the male subject as her first and primary teacher: "conmigo aprendiste a querer y a saber de la vida" [with me you learned to love and to know about life]. She is like the blank page on which his pen(is) inscribes his desire. She is text; he is author. The reference in the third and fourth lines to her blushing face, full of desire, underscores this interpretation of woman as lack, as absence. Her desire fills a gap due to lack of knowledge and inexperience. Sexual intercourse with the master is the bridge between her emptiness and her presence, however imperfect this presence may be for her (however tinged with shame, "rubor"). The male singer further articulates his desire for possession and appropriation when he confesses that "hice mío tu amor" [I made your love mine], thus reinforcing the masculine *Yo* as the agent that possesses.

In the recurring theme of remembrance and the memory of her first sexual experience ("quiero que recuerdes para siempre" [I want you to always remember]), he ascribes eternity to the transitory nature of the encounter. Through the romantic construction of "nunca más te olvides" [don't forget me], the male subject appropriates for himself not only her love and her selfhood, which are also defined by him, but their effects on her, his traces that will endure throughout her whole life.

Sexual intercourse and phallic penetration are equated with his formation of her: both symbolize her initiation into womanhood and being. A causal logic underlies the polysyndeton: "el momento aquel en que te hice mujer y fuiste mujer y eres mujer" [that moment when I made you into a woman and you were woman and you are woman]. This gender contouring, reminiscent of the myth of Adam's rib, is earlier revealed in the second line when he suggests that her body was shaped by his caresses. Yet the contradictions of his love surface in the opening phrase of that line: "Y a fuerzas de tantas caricias tu cuerpo formé" [And I molded your body with the power of my caresses]. Although clearly meant to be read figuratively, these *fuerzas* relate to *caricias*, with *caricias forzadas* (forced caresses) reemphasizing the male's power over the female body, his authority to shape it and thus to mold her. The power relations suggested in this line reflect the underlying violence and the suppression of female desire on which the (hetero)sexual politics of salsa are based.

Woman's desire in this song is far from being hers. It is a sexuality imposed from the outside, from the man's sense of power over her body, identity, and life. While female desire is alluded to once by the male voice, it is never self-defined but rather marked precisely by the absence of any female voice. Masculine desire, in contrast, is overdetermined in the anaphoric structure of the verses, notably the "quiero" that continuously reiterates itself behind the mask of "eternal love." The dialectics of oblivion and remembrance also allow male power to be reiterated. The structure of the refrain, the *estribillo*, reflexively articulates the song itself as a memory of the male singer/composer's agency and of his powerful role in the woman's development.

Yet the master's desire entails a central contradiction. While he expects eternal remembrance as her master and the author of her womanhood, he does not truly desire her to be a woman. He will eventually be made expendable as her master if and when she achieves maturity as a woman. Thus, the male singer/subject qualifies female potential: it is only her "soul" that develops into womanhood, not her body. He needs her to remain childlike, although he aspires to a spiritual union between souls. The metonymic cluster of body/child/soul/woman is repeated at the end of the song during the *montuno* section, in which the singer improvises on the preceding verses. Because of the improvisatory freedom of this section, the *montuno* may be read metaphorically as the sexual unconscious of the male singing subject. In Colón's *montuno*, he sings "tú me entregaste tu cuerpo / yo te di todo mi ser" [you surrendered your body / I gave you my whole self], illustrating the phallic reduction of the woman to the female body, a sexual metonymy that objectifies women as Woman and is counterposed by the male subject to his own selfhood as totality or wholeness. The last line of the song, "jamás yo me olvidaré" [I will never forget] turns the male subject into an agent of memory. However, the mutuality between the man and the woman suggested by this last utterance has already been undermined and rendered untenable throughout the song by the previous assertions and reiterations of his will. This last line perhaps unveils the underlying motivation of his will to be remembered by his lover forever as a possible displacement of his own need to remember himself in the role of master. The text of the song, as musical and sonorous repetition through time, serves as a vehicle for such remembrance, eternalizing indeed a specific moment that is no longer real.

Listening to Willie Colón

As a Latina remarked in an interview, any of these salsa songs or boleros that deal with male-female interactions can indeed evoke discussions and dialogues that allow listeners to reflect on and reimagine their own realities and their own relationships. The role of popular songs in constituting a cultural and social locus or space in which gender roles, gender identity, sexuality, and conflict can be signified and articulated dialogically becomes perhaps the most positive contribution of popular music to everyday life and to social issues. Thus, the political correctness or incorrectness of popular culture does not reside in its texts nor in the industry or conglomerates that produce them but, most important, in the active cultural praxis of listening and rewriting in which the "masses" or audiences, despite the Adornian insistence on their passivity, constantly engage. Structured interviews may represent an artificial medium by which to gauge listening practices but they also may be strategically deployed by the ethnographer as a carefully constructed locus in which listeners may speak to these practices.

None of the ten UM Latinas liked Willie Colón's rendition of "Cuando fuiste mujer." A number of them liked its rhythm, clearly distinguishing between the rhythm, the music, and the singing on the one hand and the problematic lyrics on the other. Likewise, for all except one of the Latinos interviewed, the lyrics of the song were rejected and the rhythms and musical arrangements were mentioned as their only source of listening pleasure. However, unlike the women, Latinos reaffirmed the unique value of the song's musical arrangements, to which they spoke in much more musically specific ways:

Musically, its great, great trumpets.
Tiene mucho cuero y tiene una parte al final en que se calla, no hay coro y hay mucha música [there's a lot of conga and there's a part at the end in which the singer stops, there is no chorus, and there's a lot of instrumental music].
La combinación del piano y los trombones es bien característico de Willie Colón [the combination of the piano and the trombones is very characteristic of Willie Colón].

The song did not evoke many personal memories among the UM Latina group. For four of the ten interviewees, Colón's song did not trigger any associations or memories and when it did, these were related to the sexist attitudes they had personally encountered. The song reminded one woman of Latina/o dances at the university, and two others were reminded of how men only think of themselves and never of women's needs. A Mexican American woman compared this song to Mexican music "pues es increíblemente machista y sexista" [because it is incredibly machista and sexist]. She continued: "También, cuando [ella] conocía a algún muchacho pues [ella] no quería a alguien que fuera así. La canción trata a la mujer de una manera muy anticuada que la mujer es virgen y él se siente orgulloso de eso. Le da mucha importancia a la virginidad de la mujer" [Also, when I would meet some guy, I knew that I didn't want someone like that. The song treats the woman in a very antiquated way, that the woman was a virgin and that he is really proud of that. It gives too much importance to the woman's virginity].

A Puerto Rican graduate student commented that this song reminds her of "power relations in Puerto Rico, since the singer treats the woman like an object or like his property." While all the women rejected this song for its obviously phallocentric discourse, their responses also revealed class conflict among them. Some women in this group associated the song's machismo with working-class males:

Porque Willie Colón le da un enfoque muy machista. El no es estúpido, porque ¿qué se cree él? Se cree superior en todo sentido de la palabra. . . . Me acuerda que los salseros tienen generalmente una mente sucia y enferma. Siempre tienen que cantar del sexo y de cosas eróticas, como todas las palabras usadas eran muy eróticas.

[Willie Colón gives this song a focus that is too machista. He is not stupid, what does he think he is? He thinks that he is superior in all senses of the word. . . . I remember that salseros generally have a dirty and sick mind. They always have to sing about sex and erotics, like all the words that they use are very erotic].

When asked if she thought that this song reflected the way men perceive women, she replied, "Algunos hombres, no todos tienen la mentalidad antes mencionada" [Some men, although not all think this way.]

Another female respondent distinguished between "algunos hombres" [some men] who are machistas and her father and husband, who are not: "Ni mi papá ni mi esposo son así" [Neither my father nor husband are like that]. These responses suggest the women's desire to erase themselves as victims of machismo (as daughter and wife), their othering of machismo onto those outside their affective domain, and their hesitance to analyze their own participation in this structured behavior. Correspondingly, these comments reflect a classism veiled under a feminist stance. While ascribing misogyny to the working class, these women elevate themselves and the men around them above the reality of gender oppression. They are not victims, possibly because they assume that education has freed them from these behaviors and attitudes that they can only define as a result of "ignorance" and "disease." These responses are analogous, in many ways, to the strategies of displacement that characterized Latinos' responses to salsa music in general.

Of the eight Latinos interviewed, the song evoked memories for only two. For these two puertorriqueños the song triggered associations with other salsa cuts dealing with the same theme—a man constructing a woman, molding her into a sexually knowledgeable person. Yet, despite these associations, they consciously questioned the validity of this discourse: "Although I like the song, I have a problem with the message that she was not a woman until she met him . . . this is the type of song that I won't pay much attention to, I'll keep going." "Hace unos años yo iría por la calle cantando esa canción. Pero ahora no" [Some years ago I would have walked down the street singing that song. But not now].

While the first respondent explained that his political disagreement with the song would motivate him to engage in discriminatory listening that ignored cultural texts that do not validate his conscious values, the second subject distinguished between his assumed active participation in the masculinist discourse of the song in the past and his present disavowal of it, a differentiating logic that characterized many other male responses.

Most Latinos rejected the masculinist and patriarchal perspectives and language associated with salsa erótica; however, one male felt an unqualified pleasure in listening to Willie Colón's song: "la letra es muy bonita y el acompañamiento musical es de un músico . . . muy bailable . . . puedes escuchar todos los instrumentos que acompañan" [the lyrics are very beautiful and the musical accompaniment is that of an artist. . . . very danceable. One can hear all the instruments that accompany this song]. Unlike the rest of his male counterparts, this respondent characterized it as "a beautiful song," "a romantic song" that in fact he "would dedicate to [his] wife." A reading of this sort may be categorized as naïve, given the absence of a discursive deconstruction or questioning on his part. That he does not identify the song as an illustration of "marked writing" is not surprising, given the overall male predilection for the bolero tradition that has been identified earlier. As another Latino remarked, "Sólo en un bolero o en un vals, en las canciones románticas, no se ve ese menosprecio hacia la mujer" [Only in a bolero or in a waltz, in the romantic songs, one does not see this devaluing of women].

If these men tended to characterize the discourse of (hetero)sexual love in the romantic ballad as less patriarchal, it is because they have not unveiled the subtleties of this form of marked writing. Thus, the first respondent's reading is not necessarily naive or politically contradictory but consistent with a masculine predilection for the romantic ballad. In fact, he defined this song as "romantic," whereas most other men categorized it as an example of the salsa erótica songs of the late 1980s. In this sense, this respondent demonstrates an accurate perception of the bolero-like, lyrical, and romantic musical discourse, structures, and arrangements of "Cuando fuiste mujer," the same elements in the vocalizing, instrumentation, and lyrics that seduced me into humming it and playing it repeatedly in my car and at home. Revealing a most sensitive reading of the song's language, another male respondent added that in fact the song would have been much more seductive had the impositive *quiero* [I want] been replaced by the "more romantic use of *quisiera*" [I would like to], which is "una petición, un deseo" [a wish, a petition]. For him, the *quiero* seemed too intransigent, forcing the man's will on the woman and thus not allowing the song to project itself as a romantic text.

What the first respondent explains, then, is that given the positive homage that this song pays women, it does not reflect men's attitudes at all. Moreover, he calls for men to assume a more romantic attitude toward love and toward women. He identifies the positive value of the song in its poetic language; thus he observes that "la lírica es más depurada" [the lyrics are more stylized] in this text than in many other salsa songs. However, a final comment reveals a different perspective: "la letra no es tan políticamente correct ya uno estando en Michigan" [the lyrics are not so politically correct now that I'm in Michigan], he reminds himself parenthetically after responding to the song. This last comment about other possible ways of reading the song is a partial acknowledgment that his dominant discourse, however, remains within the patriarchal logic of men constructing women, of valuing their virginity and sexual lack relationally and inversely proportionate to their own sense of superiority over the female. His experience of migration, of cultural displacement, and of education have perhaps afforded him new possibilities of reading cultural texts, as most of the men reaffirmed throughout their interviews.[20]

Another interviewee also acknowledged certain contradictions in his reception to "Cuando fuiste mujer." His identificatory stance was the strongest among the men, for he felt the song was "close to home, that's how I used to feel" and it reminded him of "one relationship in the past." In fact, "trying to capture that moment makes it a great song—that energy" and adds to the value afforded to the song itself. Simultaneously, though, he recognized the problem of sexism in the lyrics, yet he also acknowledged the complex processes of consuming popular music in which we all participate: "It's sexist, but that doesn't mean I won't buy it or I can see myself saying those words 'te entregué todo mi ser'" [I gave you my whole self]. Unlike other Latinos who tried to disassociate themselves from machista music, he recognized his affective engagement and participation in this patriarchal discourse in spite of his ideological dissidence toward its semantic aspects and gender politics. Thus, he envisioned himself enjoying the pleasures of the song, its music and rhythms, without paying much attention to the words: "I imagined myself dancing to this song. I could block out the words. I can see it being part of a good night." Despite the limitations of the interview format, the song triggered in him fantasies about a romantic evening during which he would establish some sort of intimacy with his partner. When he adds that he could "block out the words" in order to assert his difference in gender politics, he is enunciating a traditional romantic fantasy produced by the numerous images of heterosexual love and seduction that bombard us in our everyday lives.

Unlike both the UM Latina and Latino groups, the Detroit women afforded this song a myriad of meanings and values. Of seven who responded to this particular question, four stated that they had listened to this song before, either at somebody else's home or as part of their musical collection. Moreover, the song reminded some of them of people and places associated with the specific instance when they had first listened to the song: "me recuerda la casa de mi hermana porque ahí fue que la oí" [it reminds me of my sister's house because that's where I heard it] or "me recuerda a mi hermano que le gustaba mucho salsa y era muy alegre" [it reminds me of my brother who liked salsa a lot and was very lively]. Only one respondent did not experience any memories; most found that it evoked some meaningful person, place, or event (including Puerto Rico, the island) as they listened to this song.

For one young Puerto Rican woman, this song tells her life story. She was involved with an older man for eleven years, and as she put it, "he was the one who made me a woman." "It hit home," she concluded as she explained why she liked the song:

Me gusta . . . porque dice de cómo yo me crié. . . . Yo estuve con un puertorro por once años, en fin . . . él fue el que me hizo mujer. So, si . . . esa canción me llega a mí. Hasta el extremo porque yo era una niña y él me hizo mujer. Ahora no estamos juntos pero que . . . it hits home. Básicamente dice, tú sabes . . . qué es amor. Y hay sentido detrás de la música.

[I like it . . . because it talks about how I grew up. . . . I was involved with a Puerto Rican man for eleven years, in fact . . . he made me a woman. So, yes . . . this song reaches me. Extremely so because I was a little girl and he made me a woman. We are no longer together but . . . it hits home. Basically it says, you know . . . what love is. There's meaning behind the music.]

This quotation illustrates how musical discourse—"me hizo mujer" [he made me a woman]—contaminates the choices of words and the ways that listeners speak about their own life experiences. The comments also suggest that in fact men are not the only ones that may identify with this masculine experience and that, as another Latino suggested, it depends on whether the memory of the relationship was a pleasurable, positive one for the woman or a negative one.[21] The memories of this woman in particular are positive as she reaffirms the structures of patriarchal dependency in which she developed. Yet it is interesting to note that what seems valuable to her, as a migrant Latina, is that this man "que [la] hizo mujer" was a "puertorro" [a Puerto Rican], a subtle comment that illuminates the political, national, and cultural value that she ascribes to this past relationship. While I did not probe further into this, perhaps her reference to being "made a woman" involved not only sexual knowledge but also political awareness of herself as a colonized subject. I dare to suggest this because throughout her interview she exhibited the strongest degree of political awareness of all the Detroit women, and the language and personal discourse she used to speak about her choices were systematically linked to her cultural identity as a Puerto Rican woman, as her earlier comments about the politics of dancing showed.

Other readings revealed more oppositional rewritings that fulfilled the needs of the female subject. The song reminded another respondent of the differences between living in the United States and in Puerto Rico. She alluded to perceiving Latinas on the mainland as much more independent of men, mostly because they were financially independent. She thus related the end of the relationship, which the male singer continues to resist through his insistence on *el recuerdo,* to women's new status and options. Listening to the song allowed this woman to reflect on how women, particularly herself, negotiate their dependence and independence and their sense of autonomy in relationships:

porque en mi situación si . . . ellos se quieren hacer los más grandes. ¿Qué se creen ellos? We have a mind too. Aunque allá en Puerto Rico eso es más o menos verdad porque los hombres son los que trabajan y las mujeres se quedan en la casa haciendo lo que sea. Pero aquí es diferente. La mujer . . . se atiende sola. Como yo, que vivo sola y me atiendo sola. Sí, mi novio piensa así. En el principio yo no decía nada pero yo estaba viviendo antes que él y me estaba ganando la vida sola. Y esto es una ventaja. Es verdad que yo estoy enchulada de él y no puedo vivir sin él pero yo no estoy para estar detrás de él porque él hizo todo conmigo. It's not like that. Financially, I was single before I met him. Y si él te echa a la calle, yo ya tengo de qué vivir.

[because in my experience, yes . . . [men] want to make themselves the most important. Who do they think they are? We have a mind too. Although, over there in

Puerto Rico that is somewhat the truth because men are the ones who work and women stay at home doing whatever they may do. But here it is different. The woman . . . takes care of herself. Like me, I live by myself and take care of myself. Yes, my boyfriend thinks this way. At the beginning I didn't say anything, but I had a life before he came along and I was earning my own living. And this is an advantage. It is true that I love him and that I can't live without him, but I'm not about to place myself beneath him just because he's done everything with me. It's not like that. Financially, I was single before I met him. And if he throws me out on the street, I already have a way to take care of myself.]

For this woman, Willie Colón's song is not about virginity nor about becoming a woman sexually. It is about differentials of power between men and women; it helps her clarify how she can balance two contradictory aspects of her own relationship, the emotional dependence that she feels toward him—"no puedo vivir sin él" [I can't live without him]—and the autonomy that she enjoys as a woman who works to earn her own money. This financial independence allows her the possibility of leaving him if the relationship becomes perverted by his dominance or abuse and provides a personal vision that she can survive with or without him. Most revealing, however, is her self-construction as an independent woman in contrast to the women on the island who, according to her, remain at home and are too dependent on their men. The island/mainland dichotomy, a differentiating gesture analogous to the one seen in Latinos' responses about male values, allows her a sense of empowerment not possible for those other women whom she perceives as more "traditional" than she is.

In a wonderfully feminist response to "Cuando fuiste mujer," a young Latina thought about her sister growing up to be a woman and her own process of also becoming a woman. Yet in her evocations she never alluded to the mediating presence of any man. She changed the status of woman as object in the song to her sister and herself as subjects of their own lives: "It reminds me of my sister . . . you know, just watching her grow up. And both of us. You know, just seeing her grow up and then seeing myself as she grows up and then wanting to be just like her. Yes, she is older than me and I've seen her grow into a woman . . . and I'm doing that right now." In this response, she replaces the Male as Master with her older sister as a role model for her own female development. At a later point she established the difference between a male subject position and that of a woman singing subject, although her final observations reveal the residual traditional values that still contain or modify her thinking: "He is just thinking about how he saw it, and not just what we went through when we were growing up. If a woman was singing this, she should get into a lot more stuff. Explain what goes on . . . like her personal story. When she grew up, she did this and that. She should talk about her sister, how she was in school, what was every day like. And when she got older, she met somebody, she got involved with him, and became a woman . . . and how she realized that."

Although this response initially strives to establish the possibility for salsa songs to sing to female subjectivity and confirms the need for women to participate actively in popular music as composers and producers, the final details about this imagined female experience—very similar to her own life—conclude with the same discourse and images borrowed from Colón's song: "she got involved with him and became a woman." The systematic degree, among both male and female listeners, to which the words of the interviewees were contaminated by the musical lyrics is not surprising, given the temporal immediacy between song and response that characterized these utterances. However, it also reveals the power, ideologically marked by each song, of popular music to inform the very words that we deploy in speaking about our own lives. Thus, salsa music accords a particular discourse about gender identity, (hetero)sexual relations, sexual politics, and sexuality that is unconsciously internalized by both male and female listeners. However, while the above comment proposes a female perspective that may suggest a "feminist" stance, it is also true that a Latino man also commented on that very possibility. One male respondent stated that, "si quizás debió haber sido cantado por una mujer y hubiese sido expuesta en distinta manera" [perhaps if it had been sung by a woman . . . it would have been performed in a different way], showing that both men and women listeners are aware of the gender positioning that informs musical performances and texts. However, the young Latina managed to replace the dominant male subjectivity with two female subjects who look to each other as role models and to displace any masculine presence in the constitution of her and her sister's bodies and minds.[22]

Another Latina pointed to the contradictions in the messages that society gives young women: at the same time that sex is a taboo subject within Latina/o culture, it permeates the popular songs that Latinas listen to everyday. Other feminist rewritings of the song include sporadic observations on the *mujer/niña* (woman/girl) binary that the song establishes. Even if a woman is no longer a virgin, one Latina argued, she should still be able to behave like a little girl if she wants to. In her response, she strategically chose the subordinate element of the *mujer/niña* dyad, her infantilization, as a metaphor for a desired autonomy. While she agreed with the way that the song speaks about women—"Me gustó . . . el ritmo y lo que dice de una mujer" [I liked . . . the rhythm and what it says about a woman]—she qualifies her reading by explaining that behaving like a little girl can represent a form of rebellion against social norms:

Pues lo que yo oí es que algunas muchachas después que sean mujeres, no pueden actuar como una nena chiquita, tú sabes, it's still hard. . . . Y después que uno . . . you know . . . el que dice que después que un hombre y una mujer hacen el amor, que la mujer entonces es una mujer. Pero I don't think that it is true. Because . . . yo ahora mismo tengo veintidós años, pero I'm a little girl. Tú sabes, y eso es lo que la canción dice, no es que a uno la van a mirar diferente . . . eso es así y tiene que respetarla. Y puede ser una niña whenever she feels like it. You know . . . eso me gustó.

[Well, what I've heard is that once girls become women, they can no longer act like little girls, you know, it's still hard. And after you . . . you know . . . that saying that after a man and a woman make love, the woman becomes a woman. But I don't think that it is true. Because . . . I am twenty-two years old, but I'm a little girl. You know, and that is what the song says, it's not that people will look at her differently . . . that's the way it is and they need to respect her. And she can be a girl whenever she feels like it. You know . . . I liked that.]

These spontaneous comments again constitute a discursive space in which this particular listener reflects on the impact that female development has on the code of behaviors imposed on women. Like Judith Ortiz Cofer's writing on how young women are more societally repressed once they've begun to menstruate,[23] this Latina reaffirms the possibility of continuing to enjoy the freedom that they were allowed as children, particularly in the movement of their bodies. In contrast to the Latinos and UM Latinas, who underscored the gender politics of this song by focusing on the man's power to mold women's sexuality, most Latinas from Detroit minimized the power of the male singer and rewrote the meaning of these lyrics from their own perspectives and their own life experiences. This feminist recourse, which I have earlier called *listening as women*, balances out the power differentials between the dominant presence of male singing and writing subjects in popular music and the multiple women listeners whose life experiences and gender locations are being systematically repressed and excluded in the texts they receive.

CHAPTER TWELVE

Así Somos
Rewriting Patriarchy

✛

Patterns of listening to El Gran Combo's song "Así son" show different ways of producing meaning, not only between men and women but also between the Latinas from the University of Michigan and those from Detroit. These differences in listening practices, as individual engagements in cultural semiotics, do not by any means reveal essential differences between how men and women listen to popular music. In fact, there are a number of strategies for reading and producing meaning that overlap all three interpretive communities. The significant difference between men and women in their qualitative responses to the musicality of such songs, to music as an industry, and to its processes of production signal the "structured secondariness" in which women are located in the cultural space of salsa music, that is, the existence of "a whole alternative network of responses and activities through which [women] negotiate their relation to the sub-cultures [in this case salsa] or even make positive moves away from the sub-cultural option."[1] That is, while working class Latinas may speak about salsa music as a central part of their everyday lives, they do so through tactics of appropriation, rewriting, and countervaluation. Indeed, they recontextualize the music and transform its social value to best fit their own needs and desires.[2] They did not share the Puerto Rican male fans' detailed knowledge of the music's social impact nor of each musical group's development nor of the particular song's historicity. (I suspect that had I interviewed the wife of one of the Puerto Rican students in Ann Arbor, she might have proved an exception to this. Also, I have not included in these samples the numbers of individual women who are musicians themselves and whose knowledge and participation in producing salsa would offset these results). I am not trying to suggest here that Latinas are not active participants in sociocultural praxes nor that they do not belong in or to salsa. Rather, I am suggesting that their political, gender-based location as women does indeed exclude them from developing a musical competence in the fullest sense of the word.

In contrast to Willie Colón's relatively monologic voice in "Cuando fuiste mujer," El Gran Combo's "Así son" combines a patriarchal ideology, voiced through the persona of the singing, abandoned male, with a polyvalent, open refrain, "así son," which opens the text to a myriad of readings, valorations, and rewritings. Indeed, the open-ended nature of the refrain, in conjunction with the rest of the text, which is quite specific about heterosexual relations, allows listeners to negotiate between the textual hegemony of the stanzas and the freedom accorded by its potentially polyvalent refrain. Interestingly, one Puerto Rican man identified the social situation framed within "Así son" as directly mimetic of social reality in Puerto Rico. His comments suggest that this song could well serve as a mirror of individual experience for men, as a text by, for, and about men's repressed affective domain. The song reminded this interviewee of his father's restaurant: "[H]e had a jukebox, and I remember when he would serve alcohol in the restaurant men would come to drink after having fights with their girlfriends, play this same type of song, feel sorry for themselves in a corner, and then leave. . . . I know specifically my cousin, who would go to the restaurant, he would get drunk and complain, 'Women, look how they are, look how they pay you back.' This same cousin is now happily married today and is a loving father and husband, so his views possibly changed."

This observation semantically links this particular salsa song, Vega's and Filippi's short story, and the tremendous popularity of the song in Puerto Rico throughout the late 1970s and early 1980s. The above image is not merely an image but a real historical and personal event that marks gender identity in terms of the space (the restaurant with the jukebox), the discourse (diatribes against women), and the affective and emotional states experienced (anger, loss, and depression) as a result of (hetero)sexual conflicts. That the interviewee even identified a particular individual, his cousin, as a participant in that socially gendered practice, suggests the commonality of that masculine ritual. However, in contrast to Vega and Filippi's story, where four men suffer in each other's company, the event described above is a solitary one. The solidarity central to the fictional version is foremost a narrative recourse that allows multiple masculine discourses to be deconstructed simultaneously. However, it may constitute a form of negotiation between the individualist ritual of men and the more feminine forms of catharsis in which women engage, such as talking to friends. However, given the social value of *el viernes social* among Puerto Rican men, the collective dialogues of Eddie, Puruco, Monchín, and Angelito are not far from the socially engendered rituals that mark the beginning of the weekend on the island.

Furthermore, what this continuum reveals is the powerful discursive role that music plays in inscribing a particular ideology among its listeners. The theme of this song was indeed identified as "very prevalent" on the island. Another Puerto Rican man recalls: "y yo recuerdo que como todo el mundo lo cantaba, después decían 'sí, es verdad, así son las mujeres' pero yo no estoy tan seguro que quien dijera eso lo creían, no creo, 'pero muchacho, es verdad, así son las mujeres, como la canción de El Gran Combo,' así decían" [. . . And I remember how everyone would sing it, then they would say, 'yes it's true, that's how women are,' but I am not so sure that those who said it believed it, I don't think so, "but brother, it's true, that's how women are, like the Gran Combo song," they would say]. He later qualifies this observation by adding that they did not sing all of the lyrics seriously, yet they quoted the title and the refrain. To separate, as he did, the song from the refrain, could be a response to the textual dichotomy of the particular versus the general, of the closed text and the open-ended utterance. Yet this signals an important listening strategy that separates and accentuates the parts of the complete song that are socially and historically relevant, those lyrics indeed from which larger social meanings can be produced, from less significant ones. While the repetitive and brief nature of refrains indicates that these are the elements of a song most remembered and repeated, rearticulated in the collective unconscious of a particular cultural sector, the refrain "así son" offered both male and female Puerto Rican listeners a musical utterance from which emerged a multiplicity of responses that would construct and complete its ideology. When asked whether this song in any way reflected the perceptions that men have of women, and vice versa, another male interviewee reaffirmed that gender differences in popular culture are in fact inscribed within this type of generalizing discourse: "sí, en general escucharás que las mujeres son así, no específicamente como él [the singer] lo dice, pero sí en general que las mujeres hacen esto y esto por esto y lo otro" [Yes, in general you will hear that women are this way, not exactly as the singer says it, but yes in general that women do this and this for this and the other reason].

The ideological and discursive contiguity and continuity between the refrain and the social language about gender identity, again evinces the circulation of popular songs and of their language within and among (male) listeners. Notwithstanding the circularity of this relationship—the "así" in the song is in fact a reflection of the popular behavior, of the "folklore"—the open utterance ideally lends itself to its popular deployment as language about gender relations:

Pues la gente dice así son las mujeres y los hombres dicen así son las mujeres y las mujeres dicen así son los hombres, los hombres son de tal manera, los hombres son locos, y los hombres dicen las mujeres son locas, yo no las entiendo, y en ese sentido, cuando se dice "así son las mujeres," ya se entiende, hay una cuestión en la cultura popular que las mujeres son de cierta manera, y uno no se puede dejar llevar, tiene un marco de referencia de cómo las mujeres actúan en ciertas situaciones, pero de nuevo no me estoy refiriendo específicamente a esta canción.

[Well, people say that that's how women are and men say that that's how women are, and women say that that's how men are, men are this way, men are crazy, and men say that women are crazy, I don't understand them. And in this sense, when one says, "that's how women are," it's already understood. In popular culture women are assumed to be a certain way, and one cannot allow oneself to be carried away by them, there's a frame of reference about how women behave in certain situations, but again, I am not referring specifically to this song.]

Notwithstanding the final statement, in which the interviewee distances himself from the ideology of the song, the fact is that he reaffirms the cautionary function of this salsa song and of its masculinist discourse for male listeners. "Ya se entiende" [It's already understood], he asserts, establishing complicity between the patriarchal message that the refrain articulates and the needs of male listeners to understand that refrain as a very specific caveat against making assumptions about the women in their lives. The "ya se entiende" unveils the communicative circuit or process by which patriarchy continues to reassert itself, by which consent is effected.[3] Essentializing gender difference is very much part of this interviewee's discourse when he concludes that "pero obviamente son de una manera al igual que los hombres son de otra manera" [but obviously they are the same in the same way that men are the same], a statement that he qualifies with caveats about the dangers of generalizing and about the need for statistical data that will reaffirm these assumptions. As a student in the social sciences, his discourse fluctuates between the rational discourse of his academic discipline (and the recognition that these differences are products of diverse processes of socialization in men and in women) and the values and visions that he articulates throughout, which represent an ideological continuity with that patriarchal "popular thinking."

An altogether different semantic route was taken by a non–Puerto Rican Latino who valued the open-ended nature of the refrain as an expression of men's and women's vulnerability in relationships and of those aspects that one cannot control, a sort of determinism that somehow participates in the essentializing mode of defining gender as difference: "Así son . . . is an open thing. There's always some thing different, I like that . . . many people share that they cannot control a relationship, they can try, but . . . that's how women are, and that's how men are, and you move on, así son cuando se quieren, that's the way it is, it's miserable, it's good." What is common, then, among these male responses is the overarching role that the song plays in allowing Latinos to work out and reconcile themselves to the affective dissonance that they may experience when a relationship fails and, most particularly, when a woman leaves them, a circumstance that destabilizes the socially sanctioned centrality of the male ego. Most dangerous, however, the listening process activates an essentializing logic with respect to gender that undergirds the song, the language about gender, and the social assumptions about a fixed identity or way of being that remain at best unchallenged.

Nevertheless, the consent to this patriarchal logic articulated among these Latinos is not as clearly unilateral as the "orthodox version" of this concept portrays. Rather, the men's engagement in listening and responding to this song illustrates a process of "partly negotiating their adaptation and place within the dominant culture." Consent is practiced as a "negotiated complicity" rather than a direct, unquestioning compliance with the values of the dominant system.[4] Although from very different socially structured positions than those of Latinas, these men also experience ambiguities in their engagement with salsa, contradictions between the semantic aspects of the music, its ideology and gender-related messages, and the affective realm, the pleasures that they derive from it as a cultural and masculine reaffirmation of their historic selves.

As a result of this gap or contradiction, many Latinos engage in a process of displacing the patriarchal or "traditional" gender values of these songs onto other social sectors or cultural spaces. As some of the above responses suggest, the Puerto Rican students recognize a shift in the ways that they define gender and locate themselves in relation to women. One, for instance, mentions that "nuestra educación nos lleva a entender y prestar atención a los mensajes" [our education leads us to understand and pay more attention to the messages], an observation that reveals a process of differentiation concomitant with the achievement of higher educational levels and social status. In this sense, he believes that his attention to Rubén Blades's political messages are a direct result of the critical skills that he has developed through schooling, problematically implying that those listeners who are not "educated" will enjoy Blades's songs only because his "canción es linda" [song is pretty]. To the contrary, the interview with the Latino who has not undergone formal education in the United States shows that political readings and concerns are not necessarily correlated to educational level.

Similarly, another Latino distinguished between his own disagreement with the gender ideology of "Así son" and the assumed consent of other groups, whom he did not identify except as "others": "en la mayoría de los casos, en ciertos grupos, yo creo que es el caso en muchos grupos, ellos le dan la razón" [In most cases, among certain groups, I believe in many groups, men agree with the song]. Like the Detroit woman who established an opposition between the traditional women on the island and the more independent Latinas on the mainland, a number of Latinos located these patriarchal ideologies as a tradition in their countries of origin but not necessarily in the United States: "tema tradicional de nuestros países, y también en este país hay gente que piensa así" [It is a traditional theme in our countries, and also in this country there are people that think in this way].

Others argued that these changes are informed not only by education but also by age, generation, and indeed by the process of migration:

["Así son"] es más vacilón que otra cosa, está generalizando aunque cuando la escucho no le doy pensamiento a la letra . . . hay un poquito de la cultura nuestra en la canción; está generalizando aunque ha ido cambiando, hay un elemento machista. . . . De una generación hacia arriba, [la canción] sí reflejaría en términos generales las actitudes de los hombres, en sus refranes, etc., aunque tratan a sus mujeres con mucho respeto. En mi generación, yo diría que se ve menos, con las amistades que yo estoy, [amigos] puertorriqueños, también el elemento de la educación, todos han ido a la universidad y han sido challenged y han modificado sus ideas, no comparten esa idea del Gran Combo.

["Así Son" is more play than anything else, it is generalizing, although when I listen to it I don't think about the lyrics . . . there is a little bit of our culture in this song; it is generalizing; although our culture has been changing, there is still an element of machismo. . . . The song might reflect the general attitudes of the men from a previous generation, their proverbs, etc., although they treat their women with a lot of respect. In my generation, I would say that one sees less of this, in the friendships that I have, among Puerto Rican friends, also the element of education, they've all gone to college and they've been challenged and they've modified their ideas, they don't agree with el Gran Combo.]

After this observation, the interviewee attempted to quantify in percentages how many men of his generation versus his father's generation still hold traditional patriarchal values. He estimated that 60 percent to 70 percent of his generation, at all levels of education, may share the views articulated in El Gran Combo's song, while he believes that 80 percent of his father's generation holds these traditional views. It was surprising that his first estimate was so high in lieu of his prior comments. And while the quantitative estimates are not as important as his own perceptions of these gradual shifts in gender ideology and behavior, overall his assessment tends to illustrate a more realistic view of gradual, slow, ideological shifts. Also revealing are his initial comments regarding the trivial nature of the song's message, "más vacilón que otra cosa," an attribute that minimizes the song's serious impact on gender ideology while also underestimating his own internalization of patriarchal ideology.

A Latino born in El Salvador shared his own perceptions of different gender ideologies, attitudes, and behavior between those Latinos in El Salvador and Mexico and those who, like him, have transformed their everyday behavior and gender attitudes as a result of their cultural displacement:

Yo he aprendido en este país que tanto el hombre como la mujer tiene que hacer partes iguales. . . . En El Salvador [el refrán es] "en mi casa mando yo" . . . para el hombre latinoamericano venir a este país tiene que venir a aprender y dejar el machismo a un lado y eso es lo que enorgullece al hombre latinoamericano, especialmente los mexicanos; yo conocí muchos mexicanos que son muy machistas.

[I have learned in this country that men as much as women have to play equal roles. . . . In El Salvador (the proverb is) "I rule in my house" . . . for the Latin American male to come to this country, he must come to learn and to leave machismo behind and machismo is what gives self-confidence (or pride) to Latin American men, especially Mexicans; I've met many Mexicans who are very sexist.]

Neither education nor generational differences account for this man's self-perceived shifts in gender ideology but rather the need to share the housework and the role of income producer with his wife and his older children in order to survive economically as political refugees in this country. Although he admits that even in El Salvador he changed diapers and helped with the housework, he also distinguishes the pervasiveness of machista behavior in Latin American countries from those machista practices sanctioned in the United States. Obviously, economic structures have informed such transformations in gender roles and in the ideal patriarchal identity of the male as the main provider for the family.

Finally, the observations by another Puerto Rican–born student at University of Michigan summarize this process of displacing machismo:

Hace seis o siete años atrás, yo hubiera cantado sin ningún problema, y ahora entiendo porque he pasado por un proceso de aprendizaje de ciertas cosas, entiendo que eso sería ofensivo a ciertas personas, no las cantaría frente a una mujer. . . . Pero simplemente por el hecho de que me parecen canciones joviales no las veo como malas tampoco.

[Six or seven years ago, I would have sung it without any problem, and now I understand since I've gone through a process of learning about certain things; I understand that it would be offensive to certain people. I wouldn't sing it in front of a woman. . . . But because I think of them as happy songs, I don't see them as bad either.]

This statement encapsulates the receptive ideological ambiguity that some men experience in listening to salsa's patriarchal lyrics. While their ideological dissidence is clear to them, they still justify these songs because "parecen canciones joviales" [they seem happy songs] or as a Latino remarked, because they are "más vacilón que otra cosa" [more joking than anything else]. For these listeners, the humorous and trivial textures they present as a reflection of popular culture in Puerto Rico are a source of affective pleasure for them when they listen to "Así son" in the United States, away from the public spaces in which these types of songs may be taken for granted.

As they generally identify a gap between the semantic and the affective, between ideology and pleasure, these Latinos also note how they, as listeners, try to reconcile this contradiction by participating in selective modes of listening practices, what we may call discriminatory listening. Within this practice, they erase or undermine those elements that may cause ideological dissonance—in this case, the lyrics—and stress the musical aspects (the rhythm and the musical arrangements) and the song's value as cultural reaffirmation. This strategy allows them to engage in their respective productive pleasures, including memories of growing up in Puerto Rico, enjoying its rhythm and dancing to the song, and discerning the musical specificity of its arrangements:

No puedo negar que me crié con ella y me gustaba, que te traiga los recuerdos . . . con la nota al calce del tema de la canción, que todas las mujeres son malas y traicioneras, que no es así.

[I can't deny that I grew up with it and that I liked it, that it brings me memories . . . in terms of the theme of the song, that all women are bad and traitors, it's not that way].

People do not necessarily consume these songs and agree with the message, se disfruta por el placer y no tanto por la letra . . . ¿hasta qué punto uno está meditando sobre lo que la canción dice? No creo que eso sea el caso.

[People do not necessarily consume these songs and agree with the message, one enjoys them for the pleasure and not so much for the lyrics . . . to what degree is one paying attention to what the song says? I don't think that that's the case.]

Yo tengo grandes problemas con las generalizaciones . . . Creo que si el estribillo "Así son las mujeres" estuviera en la letra de la canción y no en el estribillo, sería mucho más aceptable.

[I have big problems with the generalizations . . . I believe that if the refrain, "That's how women are," were in the text of the song and not in the refrain, it would be much more acceptable.]

Me gustó. . . . El Gran Combo es mi grupo favorito, el soneo de los cantantes, Jerry es el que más me gusta, los vientos, el ritmo, el cencerro, lo oigo y me dan ganas de bailar. . . . El soneo va con el ritmo, la voz va a la par con ese acompañamiento musical.

[I liked it. . . . El Gran Combo is my favorite group, the improvisation of the singers—I like Jerry the best—the wind instruments, the rhythm, the cowbell; I listen and feel like dancing. . . . The improvisation goes with the rhythm; the singing goes together with the musical accompaniment.]

A mí me gusta la canción, no el tema en específico pero en general la música.

[I like the song, not the theme in particular but the music in general].

As a consequence of this gap between the music and the lyrics, consumers strategically choose specific listening modes and social contexts in which to engage a particular song:

This song is one to be played at a party and danced to . . . women would repeat the lyrics, dance to it but the analysis of it, they would object to it.

Ese es el tipo de canción que la gente no le presta mucha atención a la letra, la gente le gusta bailarla, bueno a lo mejor "así son las mujeres" es lo único que la gente escucha, no es que la gente no escuche la letra, tú puedes cantar algo simplemente y no darle ningún pensamiento a lo que está detrás de esa simple letra que tú estás escuchando.

[This is the type of song in which people don't pay much attention to the lyrics, people like to dance to it, well maybe "Such are women" is the only thing that people hear, it's not that people don't hear all the lyrics, you can simply sing something and not think about it or about what's behind these simple lyrics that you are listening to.]

A Latina from Detroit observes: "Pero porque la sepas cantar no quiere decir que tú compartas esa opinión. . . . Es como los muchachos y muchachas de quince ó dieciséis años . . . que le gusta la canción por el ritmo y no por lo que dice." [But just because you know the words, it doesn't mean that you share that opinion . . . It's like fifteen- or sixteen-year-old boys and girls . . . they like the song for its rhythm and not for what it says].

Both men and women consistently referred to this mode of discriminatory listening as a practical tactic that allows them to enjoy the music without semantic dissonance. These observations speak to the need for scholars to identify the various types of listening practices that are deployed by particular audiences and molded by the spaces in which music is received. The Latina who mentioned (in Part Two) that she tends to listen to bolero lyrics more than to the texts of a salsa song is attesting to the ways in which the musical form itself always already prompts a process of emphasizing particular elements while subsuming or nullifying others. In addition, the particular social context also influences listening modes. At a party, talking to others and listening to music as background or while dancing, music may be received secondarily as a background staple that sets the ambience or as background sounds to other cognitive activities. Driving a car, for instance, where music can be played in the illusory personal space bounded by the windows, illustrates the limitations of listening with which we are bound in our musical reception. Restraining us from dancing and from engaging in the most direct forms of physical and corporeal rhythmical movements and pleasures, the car, however, has become, in the context of U.S. Latinos, a mobile urban space of cultural production that allows us to recover (temporarily) our particular cultural specificity within the broader landscape of homogenized cities and public spaces. I cannot but allude to the personal pleasure and emotional high that I myself experience when I play salsa music inside my 4×4 on a snowy, cold morning on my way to work at the University of Michigan. That repeated experience, which becomes a rhythm in itself, a performance for no particular audience, contributes to a much desired sense of cultural stability in my own experience of migration and displacement.

On the other hand, the fact that these songs are played at parties and dances does not always preclude the impact of their lyrics. A Detroit Latina remembered that "Así son" started a heated discussion about sexual roles at a Christmas party. Her story suggests that listeners do pay attention to the lyrics during parties and that women do actively disagree and articulate their own dissonance with the subordinate positions in which these lyrics place them:

Esto ["Así son"] me recuerda un día pa' las Navidades que una amiga . . . una amiga que nosotros tenemos que decimos que es como prima nuestra que estaba oyendo esto y se dio unos traguitos, you know. Y eso se le subió a la cabeza y discutió con el marido. Porque estaban hablando de esta canción, y a mi cuñado le gusta mucho la salsa . . . y ella ya estaba un poquito ennotada y empezaron a discutir. Y ella decía que eso no es verdad . . . y el esposo decía que sí. Y ella empezó a discutir y creó un conflicto por lo que la canción decía.

[This reminds me of a Christmas party when a friend . . . a friend of ours that we say is like a cousin, was listening to this song and having a few drinks, you know. And the drinks went to her head, and she had a fight with her husband. They were talking about this song, and my brother-in-law likes salsa very much . . . and she was already a little drunk and they began to fight. And she was saying that it wasn't true . . . and her husband was saying that it was. And she began to argue and created a conflict over what the song was saying.]

This brief narrative demonstrates the potential of popular music to create spaces for dialogue and even conflictive confrontations about its messages. The fact that this woman was a bit drunk when she confronted the patriarchal ideology of the song and thus also challenged her own husband's gender ideology suggests that perhaps not all women are willing to sacrifice the pleasures of parties, music, and dancing, spaces meant for collective sharing and for friendship, to confront and address ideologies that affect them in their everyday lives. Among my friends and those people that I interviewed, I have noted much resistance against the violation of the potential pleasures to be enjoyed in these spaces of entertainment and "escape." In this regard, the level of unconscious consent to the discourses being articulated by salsa music is much higher than in other cultural and social contexts.

While both the male and female respondents engaged in these forms of selective listening practices, it is also essential to examine the different aspects of the song that each group attended to. The different gender politics at work in listening to "Así son" may be located in the elements of the narrative that were remembered by men and women, as well as in what they "did" with these ideologically charged motifs and plots. Although all the Latinos explicitly disagreed with the song's representation of women and its generalizing statements about women's behavior, they consistently offered very literal and consensual readings of certain elements of the song that reaffirmed the very gender ideology they believed themselves to be critiquing.

For instance, most men emphasized the negative image of the (absent) woman as she is portrayed by the singing subject: "la mujer como golddigger" [woman as golddigger]; "ella aparece materialista" [she seems to be materialistic]; "como si todas las mujeres fueran como prostitutas yo creo que es equívoco . . . ya que habla del vino, del cigarro, de calles, entonces eso es a lo que se refiere, a prostitutas" [It is incorrect to assume that all women are prostitutes . . . the song talks of wine, streets, and so that's what it is referring to, prostitutes]. The first two statements reveal a most literal reading of the woman as *bandolera,* and although the word itself does not appear in the song explicitly, its subtextual presence is clearly identified by these male listeners, revealing their familiarity with this discursive tradition. In the third observation, the male listener constructs the woman as prostitute based on the conjunction of three symbolic elements—wine, smoking, and the public space of the street—which she has transgressed as exclusively male spaces or behaviors.

Synthesizing the information from the song itself, particularly the line that reads "brindaste a todo el mundo tu corazón" [you offered your heart to everybody] another male listener summarizes the male singer's source of pain and suffering: "Este es un individuo que esta mujer lo dejó y después esta mujer está por ahí, tú sabes, con otros hombres, que para él esos hombres son menos que él . . . olvídate . . . no todas las mujeres te dejan a ti y se van con veinte mil más" [this is an individual who was abandoned by this woman, and then this woman is over there, you know, with other men, and these other men are less than him . . . forget it, not all women leave you to be with twenty thousand other men].

Unable to verbalize the word *puta* or *prostituta,* this male respondent periphrastically defines the woman as such, not only through his silencing of these signifiers but also through his numerical hyperbole in a sort of Caribbean baroque poetics, referring to the men this woman has supposedly seduced. By pluralizing or exacerbating what in the song was only suggested metonymically through the image of the "corazón," the listener has reaffirmed, identified with, and justified the emotional pain of the male singer and his diatribe against this particular woman. By also emphasizing the element of competition among males ("esos hombres son menos que él"), he also engages the masculine subjectivity that the song articulates through these particular allusions, metaphors, and ideologemes. He has indeed completed the patriarchal narrative in the song through strategies of foregrounding and hyperbole.

Positioned differently from the Puerto Rican men interviewed, most Latinas from the UM group were not familiar with "Así son" by El Gran Combo, except for one respondent, again the working-class Puerto Rican woman who remembered having listened to it in Puerto Rico. The significant degree of unfamiliarity with this song among the UM group reaffirms the possible process of configuring diverse salsa repertoires and canons that delimit different class sectors. None of them liked the lyrics or the message, although six of them did attest to receiving pleasure from the music, the voice, and the rhythm of the song. It was interesting to note that one woman disliked the song because "es medio viejita" [it's a bit old], thus favoring salsa of the 1990s over the 1970s canon. Yet this observation also suggests that this Latina, like most of the Latinos, was able to locate this particular song historically, a form of salsa literacy that she did not share with the others.

These Latinas did not associate significant personal or intimate experiences with the song. If anything, most Latinas identified this song as one of many articulations of patriarchy framed within song, film, and discourse. The song reminded them of "el machismo del hombre" [male sexism], of "una canción mexicana que es muy sexista y machista, es muy parecida" [a Mexican song that is very sexist and machista]; of "las películas en que ponen a los hombres en unas barras para así 'llorar sus penas' [those movies that picture men at a bar, crying over their suffering]. These three associations identify the song's patriarchal ideologeme as well as other cultural expressions of patriarchy similar to those identified by Ana Lydia Vega and Carmen Lugo Filippi in their short story, where the men cry away their sorrows by singing not only salsa songs but also rancheras.[5] A Latina did associate this song's patriarchal discourse with a repeated personal experience: "las veces en que muchos muchachos me dicen que no entienden a ninguna mujer, que todas son iguales" [those times that men have told me that they don't understand women, that we are all the same]. In this case, she realizes that "Así son" is part of a masculine discourse that constructs women in derogatory ways, a locution characteristic of the young men she has known who have consistently articulated this construct of the female, possibly in relationship to her own person.

What the UM Latinas found in "Así son" was definitely the sexism articulated by the male singer. Whereas most of the Latinos accentuated the figure of the absent woman, Latinas focused their attention on the icon of the male sitting at a bar:

Esta canción refleja que el hombre no es muy seguro de sí mismo pero no refleja el modo de ser de la mujer.

[The song shows that this man is not very sure of himself, but it doesn't reflect anything about the behavior of women.]

La mayoría de los hombres, cuando están borrachos desahogando sus penas piensan que eso es así. Pero no todos los hombres piensan así porque no todos son iguales.

[The majority of men, when they are drunk, unloading their problems, think that it is this way. But not all men think this way because not all men are the same.]

Los hombres a veces ven a la mujer como un mero objeto. Mientras que las mujeres tienen otras metas, otras responsabilidades, y según lo que ellas se propongan, eso lo pueden lograr.

[Sometimes men see women as mere objects. While women have other goals, other responsibilities, and depending on what they set themselves to do, they can achieve it.]

. . . desprecia a la mujer, está generalizando a la mujer.

[. . . it devalues women, it generalizes about women.]

Together, these observations resist the patriarchal constructs of women as they are sung by El Gran Combo. Yet they also exhibit a variety of perspectives regarding the disjunction between text and reality, between song and experience. For some, the song reaffirms male anxiety while it silences the female perspective. For one Latina, the male voice and perspective should not be used to generalize all men; another respondent argued that men objectify women, whereas women see themselves in very positive ways. Thus, while the productive moment in this case tends to vary from voice to voice, there is a consistent gesture of detachment from the text, a disagreement with and a distancing from the location of the male voice, from the context in which it was fictionally produced—the bar or nightclub—and from the whole narrative and discourse developed therein.

In sharp ideological contrast, the Detroit women immediately and consistently associated the discourse and figure of the male singer with the men in their lives. Most important, however, they inverted the negative view of women and rewrote it to produce meanings that would reaffirm their growing sense of autonomy as women and as Latinas. Unlike the Latinos who reaffirmed the negative figurations of the absent woman in "Así son" and the UM Latinas who collectively distanced themselves from that reality, most Detroit Latinas reconstructed this absent woman into a figure that signified positive, liberatory values for them in their everyday negotiations with the men in their lives as well as in the process of defining themselves and reimagining their relationships.

Unlike the UM Latinas, who mostly voiced detachment from the male singer and his discourse, all but two of the Detroit women produced meaningful associations as they listened to the song. Some associated the song with memories of their youth and of the centrality of music in their lives, creating an instance of remembrance that led to nostalgia for their countries of origin:

Cuando yo era joven y que he ido a los bailes y muchos de ellos no podía ir porque mi mamá no me dejaba.

[When I was young and used to go to the dances and I couldn't go to many of them because my mother would not allow it].

Bueno, el ritmo que yo oigo en las trompetas y en los timbales. Me recuerda mucho a mi hermano. Mi hermano siempre se pasaba cantando y haciendo como los timbales. Y me recuerda en el carro de casa, en el carro de él, que siempre ponía la salsa y yo miraba por la ventana y veía el paisaje. Me pone triste en sí porque extraño el país.

[Well, I can hear the rhythm in the trumpets and the timbales. It reminds me a lot of my brother. My brother always used to sing and imitate the timbales. And I remember our car at home, his car, in which he would always play salsa and I would look out the window and watch the scenery. It makes me sad because I miss my country.]

Other women clearly identified the male personae of "Así son" and its concomitant patriarchal discourse with men they have known:

Sí, me recuerda a algunos hombres que conocí, que siempre están hablando, expresando así de la mujer. Me recuerda a hombres salvadoreños que conocí, mexicanos también.

[Yes, it reminds me of some men that I once knew, that they would always talk this way about women. I remember Salvadoran men that I knew, Mexicans too.]

Me recuerda a los cubanos. Los cubanos son bien buenos. Ellos te mantienen, te ayudan y todo, pero son unos descarados. Creen que mientras más mujeres tengan, más machos se sienten. Entonces a ellos le gusta esta canción . . . porque se dan cuenta de que ellos son unos descarados y que las mujeres, para darle por la cabeza a ellos, hacen lo mismo. Pero eso es mentira porque yo soy una que le gusta estar con un hombre nada más. Entonces, él se va a estar con otra, mientras está conmigo. Y eso me hace sentir muy mal, como si yo fuera una cualquiera. Pues yo en ese caso voy y busco otro para hacerle lo mismo . . . aunque ellos no lo vean así. Pero las mujeres, como somos tan "naive," somos tan "gullible," nos creemos esas cosas sin pensar que eso nos daña la reputación. Por eso es que los hombres escriben canciones así.

[It reminds me of Cubans. Cubans are very good. They take care of you, they help you and everything, but they are a bunch of impudents. They believe that the more women they have, the more macho they will be. Thus, they like this song . . . because they realize that they are a bunch of impudents, and that women do the same thing to get back at them. But that isn't always true, because I am the type of woman who only likes to be with one man. Then, he goes after another woman while he is with me. And that makes me feel really bad, as though I were just anyone. Then, in this case, I went and looked for another man, to get back at him . . . although men don't see it that way. But, women, because we are so naive, we are so gullible, we believe that we can do this without realizing that it will damage our reputation. That's why men write songs like this.]

The Detroit woman who associated the song with Cuban men—in particular with her Cuban boyfriend—appropriated this diatribe against women and turned it against men, a strategy that is analogous to what Ana Lydia Vega and Carmen Lugo Filippi achieve in their parodic portrayal of Puerto Rican men listening to music at a bar.[6] This inverting, a common feminist recourse similar to the process of countervaluation that Limón has proposed and that Radway explains, is also prevalent in songs interpreted and composed by women. If a woman is a *castigadora*, then the women sing to the *castigador*. If she is the *mala*, then he is the devil. In this case, "Así son" reminded this Latina listener "of Cuban men," whom she characterizes as "wonderful but *descarados*," an inversion of negative modifiers that she had identified previously in the voice of the male singer as he constructed women: "the male singer generalized about women accusing them of being *descaradas*." She thus reads male diatribes against women as projections of men's own sexual promiscuity and of the machismo value of measuring their masculinity by the number of women they have possessed, a characteristic discourse of the Don Juan figure.

In her response, this woman examines the conflictive struggle between men and women over sexuality and power. She does not condone multiple partners for a woman as a means to punish men's Don Juan behavior. Indeed, she judges women who engage in these moves as gullible or naive, that is, those who have internalized the power games that males have set up. Simultaneously, she is quite sensitive to issues of *reputación*, the Latina/o cultural value of others' perceptions that is so influential in self-definition. *El qué dirán* [what would others say?] becomes, in her mind, a central reason for not engaging in these moves for sexual power. This woman continues to employ these songs, their lyrics, and the listening act itself as a space for reflecting not only on her own issues of dependency and autonomy (recall the first line regarding how men support a woman and take care of her financially) but also in general for reflecting on the sexual politics between men and women.

The textual image of the woman who enters a bar or a nightclub and is therefore "easy"—"y te portas como una loca . . . ofreciendo a todo el mundo tu corazón"—is also inverted and rewritten by these women listeners. They rewrite this construct into a positive image, into the woman who is independent, who likes to enjoy herself without a man necessarily:

Porque yo te digo . . . yo voy a barras. Antes tomaba, pero ahora es para oir la música . . . para bailar. Para hacer lo otro pa' eso me quedo en casa. Si llegué sola, me voy sola. Si llegué acompañada, me voy acompañada con esa persona, no con alguien diferente. So, en un sentido a mí no me gusta la canción porque no todas las mujeres son así. . . . Los hombres están mal al asumir que todas las mujeres son fáciles si están en una barra.

[Because, I'll tell you . . . I go to bars. Before, I used to drink, but now I go to hear the music . . . to dance. To do that "other thing" I stay home. If I go alone, I leave alone. If I arrive with a companion, I leave with that person, not with someone different. So, in a sense, I don't like this song because not all women are like this. . . . Men are wrong in assuming that all women in bars are easy.]

In this case, the above Latina reasserts her right to transgress the male space of the "barra" and to dance or drink without being constructed only as a sexual object, an easy woman. She stresses the positive aspect—the fact that she can enter a bar, with or without a man, and enjoy the music or a drink. What is most interesting is the absence of any emphasis on the negative constructs of women, neither the prostitute nor the easy woman; rather, the narrative is read as reasserting the will of real women like herself despite the sexist discourse to which they may be subjected.

That these readings definitely reflect personal issues in these women's lives has also been quite clear throughout these interviews. The woman who most sharply rewrote the *estribillo* "así son" into a feminist utterance—"así somos"—spoke about her own experience in leaving her husband and then returning. This memory, evoked by "Cuando fuiste mujer," continued to reappear as a tenor to her responses and to inform the productive pleasure that she experienced from these two salsa songs. After listening to "Así son," she responded by saying: "El estribillo está bien . . . así somos. Somos atrevidas, ya no somos tan cohibidas, tan dejadas. Ahora ya hacemos lo que queremos . . . podemos dejar a los hombres" [The refrain is good . . . that's the way we are. We are fearless, we are no longer so restrained, so passive. Now we do what we want . . . we can abandon men].

She then continued to recall her own experience of leaving her husband. While it was not an easy decision for this middle-aged Mexican woman, the separation led to a profound transformation in her relationship with her husband. Her strategy as a listener and speaker to change the verb *son* into a personal, collective *somos*, marks a clear instance of how listeners reinterpret specific lyrics, transforming them and literally rewriting them to be able to identify and seek pleasure and reaffirmation in their life situation. For her, the *estribillo* is now appropriated by a collective voice of women who have stolen the language of the masculine lyrics and thus completed the open-ended utterance with adjectives and traits that reaffirm women's autonomy, growing sense of independence from men, and power in decision making. The *nosotras* implicit in her response may be read as an ideal, utopian view of women's freedom to *hacer lo que queremos* (to do what we want); through this utterance she has scripted the history of her decision to leave her husband. Her "podemos dejar a los hombres" enunciates the power that she now feels after having resolved that conflict in her own personal life. She reasserts, then, the possibility of risk taking, of making decisions that may be difficult at first but perhaps productive in the long term. She has resisted the literal reading of the woman as a traitor and instead has reconstructed the autonomy that every woman should feel in her interactions with the men in her life.

A central listening strategy among these Latinas, which constitutes an ideological feminist opposition to the ways that men completed this song, is that of filling in women's silenced or repressed desires or feelings. Because in "Así son" we hear explicitly only the male voice, his perspective, and his discourse, both the Detroit and the UM women listeners fill in the gaps with those motivations, feelings, reasons, and perspectives that a male-authored text may repress or ignore. Some women qualified the idea that the male singing subject is drinking because he was abandoned, with the idea that "pero por algo lo habrá de haber dejado" [she must have left him for a reason]. Thus, they immediately invoke the motives of the woman absent in the text. The fact that she left him shows "women's independence from men," another Latina suggested. A UM Latina commented that, "when a woman leaves a man, usually the man hasn't treated her well. . . . Women respect themselves while men treat them like objects." Moreover, they identified the underlying motivation of these patriarchal figurations of the *bandolera* and of affective betrayal: "cuando una relación con una mujer no le ha ido bien, piensan de esta manera" [when the relationship with the woman is not good, then they think this way].

Converging in this feminist listening strategy, both groups of Latinas recognized the oppressive maneuverings of patriarchal discourse, as men continue to construct, generalize, and define all women. By stereotyping women, male singers deny them their individual subjectivity, their agency, their identity. Latina women listened to salsa songs, but they also spoke, and in the process of speaking they resisted, opposed, and actively rewrote the words, images, and textualizations from which they dissented. In addition to their gradually growing presence onstage or as musicians and composers, Latinas thus claim their agency in salsa music as consumers and listeners, as a gendered audience across the stage, on the dance floor, and on the receiving side of their stereos, CD players, or radios, consistently transforming these otherwise monologic texts into productive moments in their everyday lives.

The interviews presented here clearly exemplify popular culture as "a particular historical place where different groups collide in transactions of dominance, complicity, and resistance over the power to name, legitimate, and experience different versions of history, community, desire, and pleasure through the availability of social forms structured by the politics of difference."[7] Indeed, by selecting two particular songs and documenting the heterogeneous responses, the contradictory productions of meaning, the various gestures of resistance and opposition, and the plural degrees of consent to the dominant ideologies experienced by diverse social and gendered groups within the larger Latino/a community, I have called attention to the complexities of the productive moment within a cultural community. While the Latinos interviewed explicitly dissented with the patriarchal persuasive modes of the lyrics, they simultaneously revealed anxieties about their own shifting gender values as Latin American men.

Upper-class and middle-class Latina students at UM, on the other hand, tended to distance themselves from the sexist and patriarchal ideologies that they locate in working-class men and in the urban spaces associated with that particular sector. Their detachment and relatively lower degree of productive pleasures may suggest a feminist awareness of sexism in popular music, but these gestures of distancing are clearly associated with the class-based logic of locating that patriarchy in the working-class male sector. Indeed, there was a general and implicit refusal to participate affectively in the musical culture of salsa, which they may have deemed, from their dominant bourgeois gaze, "a surrender to the moment, the fun of the event, or the horror of the vulgar."[8] However, it is also significant that as young professional migrants in the United States, their structured location as listeners or consumers of salsa music, like those of the Latino interviewees, has shifted toward a higher level of participation as consumers and listeners. Thus, the productive becomes for them an important moment in the process of cultural reaffirmation.

The Detroit women also experienced a high degree of ideological dissent to the patriarchal and misogynist views articulated in these songs. Yet because El Gran Combo's music speaks to the experiences of the working class, they exhibited, at the same time, a higher degree of affective and social engagement with the music than did UM Latinas although to a lesser degree than that expressed by the Puerto Rican men. As working-class women, these interviewees consider salsa music a central part of their everyday lives. Thus, they highlighted those class, racial, and social aspects of the music that enhance their understanding of their cultural circumstances as U.S. Latinas. However, they also demonstrated, among the three groups, the most active and dynamic degree of the productive. That is, they *listened as women* by rewriting and transforming the otherwise monologic, masculine lyrics into songs that reaffirmed their self-image as autonomous, independent Puerto Rican or Latina women.

This study proposes the existence of various interpretive communities within the larger world of Latino and Latina listeners. This, in turn, suggests the configuration of different canons within salsa that speak to the values, realities, and perspectives of various class, racial, and gender groups. The processes of listening to salsa songs and producing meanings relevant to everyday life are not fixed either; these tend to shift according to the listening context and musical space. Latinos and Latinas, like other musical audiences across cultures, engage in strategies of emphasis, discrimination or selection, erasure of dissonant ideologemes, and completion of the perspectives or narrative elements silenced or repressed by the dominant ideologies inscribed through language.

These heterogeneous listening practices cannot be fixedly associated with particular class sectors, as previous studies of culture seem to suggest. Pierre Bourdieu, for instance, defines "the cultural forms of dominant bourgeois groups" as "the celebration of formalism, an elective distance from the real world, with all of its passions, emotions, and feelings," a "celebration of stylized detachment." On the other hand, the "productive moment of corporeality" is consistently located by theorists in the popular sector, which refuses "to engage in social practices defined by an abstract rationality."[9] Here, the implicit binaries of reason versus emotion and physicality, located in the class duality of the bourgeois versus the working class, undergirds both Bourdieu's and Henry Giroux's otherwise important discussions. The above multiple responses to salsa songs allow us to acknowledge that working-class women indeed engaged in more profound discussions and more sophisticated strategies of gender and cultural negotiation and semiotic production than did their upper-class counterparts, partly because salsa is a cultural expression that speaks to their class reality and cultural displacement. They theorized about independence and autonomy, about machismo, about economics in late capitalism, and about migration and displacement. Their engagement with the music was not limited to an unconscious, preverbal act of physical pleasure that precluded any sort of intelligent or rational analysis. These women clearly acknowledged the political value of dancing to salsa in the United States as much as they renounced the patriarchal tenets that repress their desires and perspectives in the articulation of (hetero)sexual relations.

Thus, processes of the productive are not as fixedly class-bound as has been suggested. To conceptualize fluid, structural locations in society with respect to cultural texts and semiotic production allows us to appreciate the complex, at times contradictory, and ever changing meanings that we constantly produce in our interaction with cultural texts and systems. The fact that upper-class Latinos and Latin Americans also engage in listening to salsa music for diverse reasons and that the pleasures of "decolonizing the body" through the act of dancing to salsa have become even more politically relevant as a result of migration demonstrate the processual nature, the historicity and the personal complex of each individual's history that inform the moment of the productive. The Puerto Rican men who may have sung and consented to patriarchal lyrics on the island are no longer willing, at least consciously, to participate in this dominant ideology. Yet they enjoy a higher degree of identification as male salsa fans, cocolos who constantly negotiate their privilege as males and their objectification as Latinos in the United States through the pleasures of listening, dancing, and singing to salsa.

These processes of musical reception have also made salient the centrality of differentiation as an integral part of constructing individual, cultural, and social identity. The politics of differentiation throughout these interviews varied according to the affective, social, and educational location of the speaker. For some U.S. Latinas and Latinos it was important to create a boundary between themselves and those perceived by them to hold traditional values in the insular society, a construct that validates the transformations that they themselves have undergone in their own socialization. Many Latinas from professional families felt a need to differentiate themselves from machismo that motivated them to displace it onto the working-class male, a classist and racist generalization revealed in their interstitial comments about how not all men are the same. The fact that many UM Latinos also shared the need to separate themselves from the larger culture of machismo as a result of their education speaks to the power differentials inherent in the process of constructing difference as a step in reaffirming identity. That machismo is a cultural practice and ideologeme always displaced onto otherness was clearly illustrated throughout these interviews.

Salsa music, then, becomes the cultural locus through which gender politics, sexuality, and cultural identity are continuously defined and redefined, contested, negotiated, and ultimately, even internalized. These interviews are but some selected instances of the profound complexities at work in the dialectics of ideology and pleasure, in the inexorable gaps between the semantic and the affective, that make popular music, in this case salsa, such a unique space for scrutinizing the culture and politics of gender.

Afterword

✠

Throughout this book, I have identified and analyzed discursive traditions in the terrains of Puerto Rican music, literature, and culture that have served to legitimize and naturalize the asymmetries of power between men and women and have led to what Anglo feminist critics of mass media have termed the "symbolic annihilation" of women.[1] The feminization of Afro-Caribbean music, a process traced to the late nineteenth century in Puerto Rico, continues to circulate in U.S.-dominant representations about salsa music; an English translation of a Cuban song and journalistic representations about Anglo desire for Latin rhythms and dancing reveal the inter-cultural underpinnings of this process. Eroticization also informs the almost omnipresent motifs and voyeuristic metaphors in various Caribbean cultural texts about the mulatta and her rhythm, illustrating that this discourse is not only the exclusive result of either patriarchy or colonial encounters but is also historically linked to the racialized histories of the Hispanic Caribbean islands.

I am aware, however, that discourse analysis poses the risk of conflating everything into discourse, thus eliding the dialogic tensions between producers and consumers of music and the historical specificity of the musical forms and traditions discussed here. Thus, to denounce patriarchy or to engage in content analysis about the representations of women in Latin(o) popular music is not enough at a time when we now define popular culture as sites where diverse social sectors negotiate meanings and where power struggles are enacted. As this book has demonstrated, the patriarchal ideology behind an image like the dancing mulatta shifts, depending on the politics of the singing subject. As I have shown in Part Three, when women singers, as subaltern subjects in a male-dominated industry, appropriate this imagery, its oppressive value is transformed into a rhetorical weapon for resisting those masculinist ideologies.

Released in 1994, the song "Calypsos," written and arranged by Wild

Mango, the multicultural women's group from the Bay Area of San Franciso, reveals how the icon of the dancing mulatta can also suggest a homoerotic reading or, at the very least, the reaffirmation of women's sensuality unmediated by a male perspective.[2] This is the result of women's growing participation in the music industry as producers, composers, and arrangers. It is also, of course, defined by the sexual politics of the group members. What has been otherwise a problematic icon in male-authored texts is mediated here by an introductory text in French in which the figure of the moon suggests a homoerotic gaze and desire, thus implying to listeners that the gaze on the mulatta could be that of other women desiring women. Most interestingly, the oppositional value of this cut also resides in the very intersection or crossroads of a multicultural production such as *Made in Mango*, a recording characterized by the combination of various rhythms associated with Latin America, Arab cultures, and of course, the Trinidadian calypso.

In the 1990s, I would argue, the continuing dominant trend toward salsa romántica seems to exemplify another instance of feminization as I have discussed it in this book. This time, however, feminization is evident in the industry-induced hegemony and canonical status of bolero-informed songs about individual heterosexual relationships. Most of the new salsa interpreters in the 1980s and 1990s, both men and women, invariably sing to and about love, in contrast to the more heterogeneous thematic repertoire of salsa figures from the 1970s. While Olga Tañón's 1994 release, *Siente el amor*, includes only love songs, Celia Cruz's *Irrepetible*, released the same year, includes songs about (hetero)sexual relations, mostly in defense of women, such as "Que le den candela" and "La guagua." In the latter, she defends women's rights to travel in city buses without being touched by men, while in the highly political "Cuando Cuba se acabe de liberar," she visualizes a utopian return to Cuba after the fall of Fidel Castro.[3] Willie Colón's 1993 release, *Hecho en Puerto Rico*, presents love songs such as "Idilio," an interesting fusion of salsa romántica with the lyrical language and versification of *décimas jíbaras*. This song plays on the market for love ballads while simultaneously reaffirming national identity for Puerto Ricans. A song such as "Buscando trabajo" addresses the economic difficulties and unemployment that Latinos face in the age of globalization and dwindling job security for workers, and "Atrapado" narrates the life of a drug dealer in a song that denounces U.S. materialism.[4]

A cursory view of this shift in repertoire suggests that salsa romántica has become the dominant genre needed by younger interpreters to establish themselves in the late 1980s and throughout the 1990s, although it has not undermined at all the diversity of genres and topics that singers such as

Celia Cruz and Willie Colón have consistently presented. Moreover, Wilson Valentín's current research suggests that the resurgence of the salsa canon from the 1970s, as evidenced by the increased consumption of "classic" salsa both on the island and in New York, shows that Latina/o audiences look for and consume music that is socially and politically relevant to their times, even when the industry does not produce such lyrics. The phenomenon of memorializing Héctor Lavoe, in particular, speaks to the agency of the public in defining what is meaningful in the 1990s.[5]

The romantic tendency in the Latin musical canon also should be analyzed systematically from a hemispheric perspective, given the globalizing and transnational processes that inform it. As Néstor García Canclini observes, globalization entails "the planetary functioning of an industrial, technological, financial, and cultural system whose headquarters is not in a single nation but in a dense network of economic and ideological structures."[6] The insertion of salsa musicians in the ever-more privatized culture industry may then "neutralize the autonomous development of the field," as García Canclini observes for the visual arts in Latin America.[7] In this context, the fusion of salsa with classical music illustrated in the joint concert of Gilberto Santa Rosa and the Puerto Rican Symphony Orchestra on May 23, 1996, is highly significant. Art music met popular music in Salsa Sinfónica, a performance held, ironically, at the Centro de Bellas Artes (never named after Rafael Cortijo) and partly sponsored by the Banco Popular de Puerto Rico and American Airlines.[8] This concert illustrates the growing mainstreaming and symbolic "whitening" of salsa in Puerto Rico and confirms my discussion in Part Two about the process of articulation. In the 1990s this shift may have been facilitated by the feminized (i.e., depoliticized) tunes of salsa romántica that more easily converge with the musical traditions of a symphony orchestra.

The concert's repertoire reveals the way in which love songs and ballads mediate between art and popular music. A review by Sara del Valle indicates that the first part of the concert was characterized by an initial instrumental medley of nationalist songs about Puerto Rico: the danza "Verde Luz," "Soñando con Puerto Rico," and Rafael Hernández's "Preciosa."[9] This beginning, warmly received by the audience, offered a strong sense of national reaffirmation, which was followed by a sequence of Gilberto Santa Rosa's most popular interpretations of love ballads and salsa romántica, including Albita's "Qué manera de quererte." The second part of the concert, according to the reviewer, broke the stiffness and formality of Santa Rosa's performance in the first part. This duality between the stiff elegance of the first part and the more "popular" style of the second signals how the concert symbolizes a postmodern attempt to blur the boundaries between high and low art. The second part, indeed, was characterized by extramusical elements that inserted the concert into the language of mass media: live puppets, a video screening, and a live appearance of local television personalities who accompanied Gilberto Santa Rosa singing a capella the hit "Conciencia"(Conscience). While it is true that symphony orchestras, such as the Boston Pops, have long performed popular songs, this particular concert is significant for the ways in which the icons and technology of mass media are being integrated into the hallowed spaces of a concert hall in the Centro de Bellas Artes.

It is also highly reminiscent of Néstor García Canclini's concept of *hybrid cultures* in Latin America, where heterogeneous icons, symbols, technology, and cultural practices, derived from different historical periods and cultural traditions, converge in cultural practices that articulate our vexed relationship with modernity. Salsa music, in many ways, is itself a hybrid cultural site. In it, old Afro-Caribbean rhythms continue to be deployed in musical compositions that reflect modern technologies of sound and postmodern preoccupations with urban life, cultural displacement, and gender relations. Angel Quintero Rivera's argument for the need to recognize the historical continuity of maroon culture as it survives in the modern, urban music called salsa converges with Canclini's emphasis on how modernity encompasses multiple historical temporalities and heterogeneous cultural traditions.

In terms of gender politics, salsa romántica has created, ironically, an aperture for a growing number of women interpreters, partly because of the tacit social assumption that it is more acceptable for women to sing love ballads and partly because by the 1990s women in Latin America have had more access to musical training, instrumentation, and the public sphere in general. Emerging new voices, such as Deddie Romero and Olga Tañón from Puerto Rico, Trina Medina from Venezuela, Miriam y las Chicas from the Dominican Republic, Cuban-American Albita Rodríguez, and the eleven all-women salsa groups from Cali, Colombia, have rendered invalid the myth of the exceptional status of Celia Cruz as the only woman in an all-male musical industry. Things have changed substantially since Jeremy Marre produced the documentary *Salsa! The Latin Music of New York and Puerto Rico*, filmed in the early 1980s. He then asked Ralph Mercado, a music producer, why there were so few women singers in the Latin music business except for Celia Cruz. Mercado replied: "I don't know, I guess there just hasn't been that many around,"[10] thus naturalizing and accepting as inevitable women's systematic exclusion from salsa productions. Today, such a reply would not be valid.

While some women singers in the 1990s—Deddie Romero and Olga

Tañón—interpret mostly salsa romántica, their very presence as interpreters accords a much needed woman's perspective to the discourse about
love and heterosexual relationships. Together, their lyrics continue to engage in a battle between the sexes, yet some of this struggle is articulated in
a language less strident than salsa from the 1970s contained. Salseras in the
1990s sing about not tolerating abusive relationships, as in Deddie
Romero's cut "No llores, no vuelvo," or about taking the initiative to leave
the man, as in Olga Tañón's "Hablando sola." Besides her songs about
exile and nostalgia for Cuba, Albita Rodríguez, in *No se parece a nada*
(1995), sings love songs with openly erotic lyrics that can equally suggest
lesbian love and homoerotic as well as heterosexual desire. Composed
mostly by her and Julia Sierra and musically informed by Afro-Cuban
rhythms and musical forms, her songs articulate more radical, feminist perspectives that can speak to diverse sexual orientations. "Qué manera de
quererte," the opening song and one of the most popular cuts, seems to
speak about passion as it simultaneously proposes "other" ways of loving.
Her song "Solo porque vivo" strongly denounces the social intolerance
that she has experienced as a lesbian, although there is no mention of homosexuality in the text. Thus, Albita's music illustrates how women composers are a necessary element in the development of alternative, feminist
perspectives in popular music, although her songs reveal the necessary
compromises and containments that popular musicians have to make in
order to be "acceptable" by larger audiences.

Obviously, this book does not constitute a historical work on the role of
women as agents or subjects in the production of Latin(o) popular music.
Readers interested in a history of women in salsa music may have been justifiably frustrated by the absence of such sequential narrative in this book,
as I was during the process of writing by the lack of historical documentation on women salseras. Painfully aware of this scholarly need, however, I
have referred to all the women that I have identified in my own readings
and research and in my own discoveries as a consumer of music. Although
the politics of distribution are still unfortunately tilted in favor of men,
major distributors such as Sony have had an important role in making
more women salseras visible in the 1990s. The need for documenting
women's participation in salsa and other forms of Latin(o) popular music
is, undoubtedly, urgent, and scholars of popular music and cultural studies
should address this very important dearth in our production of knowledge. I look forward to Lise Waxer's doctoral dissertation on women
salseras in Colombia and to future interventions in this area.

Although limited in scope, the audience research that I present in this
book is a contribution to studies of reception and consumerism in the field

of Latin(o) popular music. Quantitative approaches are always helpful and allow us to document, empirically, what and how much music is being sold. Surveys help us confirm processes of canon formation as well as the historical and ideological shifts that scholars identify in popular music. They may also allow us to study interesting discrepancies between what conglomerates "plug" in commercial radio and what consumers like to listen to in their private sphere, such as while driving, during parties at home, at work, and as background to other social activities.

Yet qualitative approaches, oral histories, interviews, and ethnographic work are even more urgent, given the historical silencing of the "masses" in scholarship, even in studies that attempt to explain them and to vindicate the agency of the popular sector. Scholarship has constructed women as passive consumers, and they are seen, implicitly, less apt as producers of meaning. However, the responses from working-class Latinas that I analyze here reveal a strong engagement, both affective and intellectual, with the gender politics of the songs. While the Puerto Rican men interviewed showed more access to information about the music, the musicians, and the musical industry, the working-class women went further than the men in rewriting the texts, appropriating them, and reimagining themselves in their social and affective relationships. Thus, Part Four, "Así Somos, Así Son: Rewriting Salsa," posits that women, as consumers of popular music, are active subjects in their role as listeners, rather than the passive consumers that industries perhaps expect them to be. Consumption, then, cannot be seen exclusively as a unidirectional process of subordination but rather as a cultural practice in which individuals, groups, and institutions negotiate cultural identity and social, class, and racial meanings, as well as naturalizing or contesting gender relations.

Néstor García Canclini has identified the need for studies of cultural consumption in Latin America, precisely in order to determine "of what use culture is to hegemony," "to verify from what patterns of perception and understanding their audiences are related to cultural goods, and even less so what effect their everyday conduct and their political culture generate."[11] Likewise, Jesús Martín Barbero has insisted on recognizing that there are different sets of "cultural competence" that live on "in the pool of cultural images that nourish the growth of different social protagonist identities such as women or youth"; he argues that these competencies are then "activated" by cultural practices, such as watching television. He calls for qualitative studies that could be described as "watching with the people" and that allow us to "examine the 'stories,' the life stories, that people recount and that they recognize in their viewing of television."[12] Barbero's call, however, limits itself to an exhortation, while Canclini's methodology, informed by the exigencies of the social sciences, does not present directly the voices of those surveyed in his study of museum audiences. We need to continue to tease out the complex, diverse, and not always politically correct negotiations between consumers and their cultural texts in order to develop more profound understandings of hegemony as domination by consent. However, to achieve this, we need to validate and utilize the cultural competencies of the very heterogeneous audiences that continue to remain on the margins, those same cultural producers that have been silenced despite our best democratic intentions.

Notes

✝

Preface

1. Elmer González's article on Deddie Romero "Desde Borinquen" (*Latin Beat*, September 1994, 10), begins precisely by discussing women's lack of visibility in the circulation of salsa music, particularly in radio programming. Likewise, Franz Reynold, in "Ritmo: La música de hoy" (*Latin Beat*, September 1994, pp. 18–19) initially frames his article by denouncing how "the nurturing of quality female singers and songwriters appears to be a low, or no, priority" (18) and how Latinas still remain "musically enshrined in boleros, bachatas, and baladas," that is, as inspiration rather than as authors.

2. This gender-marked invisibility does not reside exclusively in the symbolic realm but affects the economic circulation of women's musical productions. That is, practices of distribution and marketing for women's CDs are much more limited than for men's, as my own research experience revealed. I want to thank the staff at Schooolkid's Records in Ann Arbor, Michigan, for their help in locating many of the Latina women's CDs.

3. A similar representational tension is played out in Umberto Valverde and Rafael Quintero's recent publication, *Abran paso: Historia de las orquestas femeninas de Cali* (Cali, Colombia: Universidad del Valle, 1995). While this book constitutes a first and important ethnographic documentation on the phenomenon of women's salsa bands in Cali, the male gaze behind the photographic texts subtly (and not so subtly) undermines the authorship and subjectivity of the women's voices as they are articulated throughout the interviews.

4. Ibid., 6.

5. I analyze these difficulties in more detail in Part Three of this study.

6. See Tricia Rose's contribution to "A Symposium on Popular Culture and Political Correctness," with Manthia Diawara, Alexander Doty, Wahneema Lubiano, Tricia Rose, Andrew Ross, Ella Shohat, Lynn Spigel, Robert Stam, and Michele Wallace (*Social Text* 36 [fall 1993]: 1–39).

7. Adalberto Aguirre Jr., "A Chicano Farmworker in Academe," in *The Leaning Ivory Tower: Latino Professors in American Universities*, ed. Raymond V. Padilla and Rudolfo Chávez Chávez (Albany: State University of New York Press, 1995), 25–26. See also Sonia Saldívar-Hull, "Chicana Feminisms: From Ethnic Identity to Global Solidarity," in *Feminism on the Border: Contemporary Chicana Writers* (Berkeley: University of California Press, in press).

8. See Deborah Pacini Hernández, *Bachata: A Social History of a Dominican Popular Music* (Philadelphia: Temple University Press, 1995), 158–72.

9. See Ariel Dorfman and Armand Mattelart, *Para leer al Pato Donald* (Val-

paraíso, Chile: Ediciones Universitarias, 1971); Néstor García Canclini, *Transforming Modernity: Popular Culture in Mexico*, trans. Lidia Lozano (Austin: University of Texas Press, 1993), and *Hybrid Cultures: Strategies for Entering and Leaving Modernity*, trans. Christopher L. Chiappari and Silvia L. López (Minneapolis: University of Minnesota Press, 1995); Jesús Martín-Barbero, *Communication, Culture and Hegemony: From the Media to Mediations*, trans. Elizabeth Fox and Robert A. White (Newbury Park, Calif.: Sage Publications, 1993); and Beatriz Sarlo, *El imperio de los sentimientos* (Buenos Aires: Catálogos, 1985).

10. In "What's Left of the Intelligentsia? The Uncertain Future of the Printed Word," *NACLA* 28 (September–October 1994): 16–21, Jean Franco traces how the literary intelligentsia in the past had acted as the "voice of the oppressed," mediating for the popular sectors and acting as "advocates of social change." Now, with the advent of mass culture and new technologies of communication, and with the ascendancy of the visual image and of popular music over the printed word, writers and intellectuals are forced to redefine their aesthetics, forms and genres in order to reach a larger public. A more nostalgic and troubled defense is posited by Beatriz Sarlo in her article, "Argentina under Menem: The Aesthetics of Domination," in the same issue of *NACLA*, 33–37, in which she analyzes how Carlos Menem's image and politics have in fact been mediated and controlled by what could be called a televisual ethos. In her analysis, she concludes with an exhortation for the return of the intelligentsia in defining nation: "Intellectuals—especially Left intellectuals—can play a decisive role in producing new ideas about how the media can be used in a democratic, reflexive, imaginative and transparent manner. Certainly, these new ideas would confront an enormously concentrated power" (37). However, what she fails to note in this programmatic call is the power of the intelligentsia itself (in which she clearly participates), to exclude nonacademic Others from processes of cultural production and naming.

Part One: The Danza and the Plena
A Literary Prelude

1. See Magdalena García Pinto's interview with Rosario Ferré in *Woman Writers of Latin America: Intimate Histories* (Austin: University of Texas Press, 1988), 81–103, regarding the reception of this story. For an assessment of the historical and aesthetic impact of the journal *Zona de carga y descarga*, see Juan Gelpí's *Literatura y paternalismo en Puerto Rico* (San Juan: Editorial de la Universidad de Puerto Rico, 1993), 171–82. Gelpí enumerates a series of countercanonical strategies deployed by this collective, one of whose editors was Rosario Ferré: a collage format that rejected the monologic texture of earlier journals, a constant search for new modes of representation, inclusion of feminist texts, a forum for theoretical reflection on the crisis situation of Puerto Rican literature, and significant book reviews that revealed the experimental and radical positions of the collective. The journal was published for a period of three years, from 1972 to 1975.

2. Sandra Messinger Cypess observes that this short story "has received much critical scrutiny because it epitomizes the exploration of the image of women from a feminist perspective." See "Tradition and Innovation in the Writings of Puerto Rican Women," in *Out of the Kumbla: Caribbean Women and Literature*, ed. Carole Boyce Davies and Elaine Savory Fido (Trenton, N.J.: Africa World Press, 1990), 84.

3. See Rosario Ferré, "¿Por qué quiere Isabel a los hombres?" in *El coloquio de las perras* (San Juan, P.R.: Editorial Cultural, 1990), 111–15. An English version (not translation) of this essay appears in *The Youngest Doll* (Lincoln: University of Nebraska Press, 1991), 147–51.

4. One of the most lucid analyses of Ferré's *Papeles de Pandora* is Ivette López Jiménez's "*Papeles de Pandora:* Devastación y ruptura," *Sin nombre* 14 (October–December 1983): 41–52, in which the rupture with bourgeois ideology is identified as a central tenet of Ferré's writings. Also of interest are Margarite Fernández Olmos's "Luis Rafael Sánchez and Rosario Ferré: Sexual Politics and Contemporary Puerto Rican Narrative," *Hispania* 70 (March 1987): 40–46, and "From a Woman's Perspective: The Short Stories of Rosario Ferré and Ana Lydia Vega," in *Contemporary Women Authors of Latin America: New Essays*, ed. Doris Meyer and Margarite Fernández Olmos (New York: Brooklyn College Press, 1983), 78–90. María Inés Lago-Pope, "Sumisión y rebeldía: El doble o la representación de la alienación femenina en narraciones de Marta Brunet y Rosario Ferré," *Revista Iberoamericana* 51 (July–December 1985): 731–49, also focuses on a feminist analysis of both characters. Lorraine Elena Roses, in "Las esperanzas de Pandora: Prototipos femeninos en la obra de Rosario Ferré," *Revista Iberoamericana* nos. 162–63 (January–June 1993): 279–87, proposes a reading of the two female characters as a case of hysteria, as defined in psychoanalysis, and also suggests a bisexuality in the erotic desire of each other. Luz María Umpierre's early article, "Un manifiesto literario: *Papeles de Pandora* de Rosario Ferré," *Bilingual Review* 2 (May–August 1982): 120–26, had already suggested a lesbian reading of the same. Juan Gelpí, *Literatura*, 161, also observes that the (homo)erotic pleasure that the story evokes as a result of the mutual discovery of each other's body has hardly been identified by critics. Feminist approaches, then, have suggested a number of analyses of both women: as self and other in terms of class, race, and social identity and, more radically, as a portrayal of lesbian desire. Also see Lucía Guerra Cunningham, "Tensiones paradójicas de la femineidad en la narrativa de Rosario Ferré," *Chasqui* 13 (1984): 13–25.

5. López Jiménez, "*Papeles*," 43.

6. Gelpí, *Literatura*, 1–16.

7. Henry Giroux, *Border Crossings* (New York and London: Routledge, 1992), 119.

8. I will use the term *hegemony* based on Gramsci's work. For a clear, basic summary, cf. Dominic Strinati, *An Introduction to Theories of Popular Culture* (New York: Routledge, 1995), 165–71: "a cultural and ideological means whereby the dominant groups in society, including fundamentally but not exclusively the ruling class, maintain their dominance by securing the 'spontaneous consent' of subordinate groups, including the working class, through the negotiated construction of a political and ideological consensus which incorporates both dominant and dominated groups" (165).

9. See Arcadio Díaz Quiñones's introductory essay, "Tomás Blanco: Racismo, historia, esclavitud," in Tomás Blanco, *El prejuicio racial en Puerto Rico* (Rio Piedras, P.R.: Ediciones Huracán, 1985): 15–91; "Recordando el futuro imaginario: La escritura histórica en la década del treinta," *Sin nombre* 14, no. 3 (1984): 16–35; Angel G. Quintero Rivera also has analyzed this phenomenon from a historical perspective in chapter 4 of *Patricios y plebeyos: Burgueses, hacendados, artesanos y obreros: Las relaciones de clase en el Puerto Rico de cambio de siglo* (Rio Piedras, P.R.: Ediciones Huracán, 1988).

10. Susan McClary, in *Feminine Endings: Music, Gender, and Sexuality* (Minneapolis: University of Minnesota Press, 1991), 3–34, identifies five levels in which music and gender intersect: (1) musical constructions of gender and sexuality, (2) gendered aspects of traditional music theory, (3) gender and sexuality in musical narrative, (4) music as a gendered discourse, and (5) discursive strategies of women musicians. My interest in examining how the danza and the plena have been feminized relates to McClary's fourth category of study, that is, looking at how music and musical forms themselves have been gendered as "feminine."

11. Lucía Guerra-Cunningham, "Tensiones paradójicas," 22, critiques Ferré's underlying phallologocentric structure, which she considers prevalent in her short stories. Our intertextual and interdisciplinary approach will help to elucidate this issue.

12. Judith Butler, *Gender Trouble: Feminism and the Subversion of Identity* (New York and London: Routledge, 1990), viii–ix.

Chapter One: *A White Lady Called the Danza*

1. See Samuel R. Quiñones, "Otra versión sobre el origen de la danza puertorriqueña," *Revista del Instituto de Cultura Puertorriqueña* 9, no. 30 (1966): 5–7, for his proposed analogies between the danza and the medieval cantigas. Also see Cesáreo Rosa-Nieves, "Los bailes de Puerto Rico," *Revista del Instituto de Cultura Puertorriqueña* 65 (October–December 1974): 14–18, and Marisa Rosado's anthology *Ensayos sobre la danza puertorriqueña* (San Juan: Instituto de Cultura Puertorriqueña, 1977); the latter includes Salvador Brau's essay as well as two important pieces on the danza by Amaury Veray. Peter Manuel, in "Puerto Rican Music and Cultural Identity: Creative Appropriation of Cuban Sources from Danza to Salsa," *Ethnomusicology* 38, no. 2 (spring/summer 1994): 249–80, argues that the Puerto Rican danza is essentially a Puerto Rican appropriation of the Cuban contradanza, a process of "resignifying" Cuban music that according to Manuel is also evident in jíbaro music, bombas and plenas, tríos, and salsa music.

2. I have used the 1974 edition published by the Instituto de Cultura Puertorriqueña, San Juan, Puerto Rico. *El Gíbaro* is a typical *cuadro de costumbres* about Puerto Rico, first published in Barcelona in 1849. A second augmented edition appeared around 1882–83 with a prologue by Salvador Brau, and in 1949 a modern edition, annotated by Antonio Torres Morales, appeared, with revised orthography. The present edition is a "facsimile of the original"; it includes graphics and drawings that were not part of the original but were culled from press vignettes.

3. Amaury Veray, "Vida y desarrollo de la danza puertorriqueña," in Rosado, *Ensayos*, 24.

4. See Sander Gilman, *Difference and Pathology: Stereotypes of Sexuality, Race and Madness* (Ithaca, N.Y.: Cornell University Press, 1985), and "Black Bodies, White Bodies: Toward an Iconography of Female Sexuality in Late Nineteenth-Century Art, Medicine and Literature," in *Race, Writing and Difference* (Chicago: University of Chicago Press, 1985), 223–61.

5. See Vera M. Kutzinski's *Sugar's Secrets: Race and the Erotics of Cuban Nationalism* (Charlottesville: University Press of Virginia, 1993), particularly the first chapter, "Imperfect Bodies," which traces the inscriptions of the mulatta in nineteenth-century Cuban poetry as an overdetermined site of sexuality. Indeed, as Kutzinski reaffirms, "to speak of black female sexuality here is somewhat redundant since the body of the dark complexioned woman appears to be the only available site of female sexuality in nineteenth-century Cuban literature. White women, that is, those of known 'purity of blood' and hence of social standing, were, almost by definition, exempt from such sexualization" (30). In Puerto Rico representations of female sexuality and race also express this phenomenon.

6. Salvador Brau, "La danza puertorriqueña" in *Disquisiciones sociológicas y otros ensayos* (Río Piedras: Ediciones del Instituto de Literatura, University of Puerto Rico, 1956), 189–206.

7. Janos Marothy, *Music and the Bourgeois, Music and the Proletarian* (Budapest: Akademiai Kiado, 1974), locates the transition from collective forms of music to those informed by an emerging capitalist mode of production and the en-

suing bourgeois ego, individualism, in the Renaissance (16). In the Puerto Rican context, Edgardo Díaz Díaz has analyzed the social practice of dances at the turn of the century in his article, "La música bailable de los carnets: Forma y significado de su repertorio en Puerto Rico (1877–1930)," *Revista Musical Puertorriqueña* 5 (January–June 1990): 3–21. He analyzes the shift between figure dances, such as the contradanza, and the independent couple dances, such as the waltz, as a reflection of the tensions between dwindling monarchic values of social order and "aristocratic ceremoniality" and those of an ascending Creole bourgeoisie, expressed through an individualist spirit.

8. Braulio Dueño Colón, "Estudio sobre la danza puertorriqueña" in Rosado, *Ensayos*, 14–22.

9. Díaz Díaz, "La música," 15.

10. Veray, "Vida y desarrollo," 25.

11. Brau, "La danza puertorriqueña," 198.

12. Veray, "Vida y desarrollo," 23.

13. Brau, "La danza puertorriqueña," 199.

14. Ibid., 200.

15. Ibid.

16. Colón, "Estudio," 17.

17. Angel Quintero Rivera, *Music, Social Classes, and the National Question in Puerto Rico* (Rio Piedras: University of Puerto Rico, Centro de Investigaciones Sociales, 1987), 29–39.

18. Mariana Valverde, *Sex, Power and Pleasure* (Philadelphia: New Society Publishers, 1987), 150.

19. Brau, "La danza puertorriqueña," 205. See also Quintero Rivera, "Music," 221.

20. Peter Manuel, "Puerto Rican Music," 252. As Manuel later adds, "The rise of the danza became linked with the emergence of this naturalistic hacendado proto-bourgeoise" and its "independence movement" (253).

21. Brau, "La danza puertorriqueña," 204.

22. John Storms Roberts, in *The Latin Tinge: The Impact of Latin American Music on the United States* (New York and Oxford: Oxford University Press, 1979), considers Louis Moreau Gottschalk (1829–1869) "the most celebrated and well-documented mid-century example of Latin influence on American music" (27). More recently, Federico A. Cordero reevaluted the influence of Gottschalk on Puerto Rican music in "Sitial de honor de Louis Moreau Gottschalk en la historia de la danza puertorriqueña," *Claridad*, 7–13 September 1994, 29.

23. Brau, "La danza puertorriqueña," 205.

24. Ibid., 206.

25. Ibid.

26. Juan Flores, "Cortijo's Revenge: New Mappings of Puerto Rican Culture," in *Divided Borders: Essays on Puerto Rican Identity* (Houston: Arte Público Press, 1993), 92; also published in Juan Flores, George Yúdice, and Jean Franco, eds., *On Edge: The Crisis of Contemporary Latin American Culture* (Minneapolis: University of Minnesota Press, 1992), and in *Centro de estudios Puertorriqueños bulletin* 3 (spring 1991): 8–21. Hereafter, references to this essay will correspond to the *Divided Borders* edition and pagination.

27. Quintero Rivera, *Music*, 229.

28. José A. Balseiro, "La danza puertorriqueña," in Rosado, *Ensayos*, 13–14.

29. Margot Arce de Vázquez, Laura Gallego, and Luis de Arrigoitía, eds., *Lecturas puertorriqueñas: Poesía* (Sharon, Conn.: Troutman Press, 1968), 29–31.

30. Antonio S. Pedreira, *Insularismo* (San Juan: Biblioteca de Autores Puertorriqueños, 1942), 41–42.

31. Ibid., 197.

32. See the following critical readings about Pedreira: Juan Flores's *Relectura de Insularismo e ideología burguesa: Nueva lectura de A.S. Pedreira* (Rio Piedras, P.R.: Ediciones Huracán, 1979) and the English version in his *Divided Borders*; also Juan Angel Silén's *Hacia una visión positiva del puertorriqueño* (Rio Piedras, P.R.: Editorial Edil, 1970) and Juan G. Gelpí's *Literatura y paternalismo en Puerto Rico* (San Juan: Editorial de la Universidad de Puerto Rico, 1993).

33. John J. Johnson, *Latin America in Caricature* (Austin: University of Texas Press, 1980), documents in chapter 3 the gendering of the United States as male and of Latin America as female. Refer also to Ruth Glasser, *My Music Is My Flag: Puerto Rican Musicians and Their Communities, 1917–1940*. (Berkeley: University of California Press, 1995), in which she documents how in the 1920s and 1930s "many members of this [wealthier] class equated North American music with Puerto Rico's economic and social progress" (39) and how this colonial assumption affected musicians and their canon. Refer also to Peter Manuel, *Popular Musics of the Non-Western World: An Introductory Survey* (New York and Oxford: Oxford University Press, 1988), 22.

34. Peter Manuel, "Puerto Rican Music," 255. Here Manuel interprets Pedreira's characterization of the danza in *Insularismo* as positive: "The danza embodied the best aspects of Puerto Rican character—gentility, mildness, and aestheticism—the very qualities threatened by vulgar, crass, commercial, and naturalistic Americanization."

35. Susan McClary, *Feminine Endings: Music, Gender, and Sexuality* (Minneapolis: University of Minnesota Press, 1991), 11.

36. Peter Bloch, *La-Le-Lo-Lai: Puerto Rican Music and Its Performers* (New York: Plus Ultra Publishers, 1973), 41. See also Alejo Carpentier's observations about Ignacio Cervantes's Creole danzas as "feminine" in *La música en Cuba* (Mexico City: Fondo de Cultura Económica, 1972), 226.

37. Doris Sommer, *Foundational Fictions: The National Romances of Latin America* (Berkeley: University of California Press, 1991).

38. Adela Rivera Montalvo, *San Germán y La Borinqueña: Himno de Puerto Rico* (San German, P.R.: Insertco, 1986), 11.

39. Sandra Messinger Cypess has denounced the invisibility of women writers in the nineteenth-century literary canon in Puerto Rico, including Lola Rodríguez de Tió, Luisa Capetillo, and María Bibiana Benítez. See "Tradition and Innovation in the Writings of Puerto Rican Women," in *Out of the Kumbla: Caribbean Women and Literature*, ed. Carole Bryce Davies and Elaine Savory Fido (Trenton, N.J.: African World Press, 1970) 77. Ruth Glasser, *My Music*, 27, identifies the nationalistic value of this version but fails to mention its female authorship.

40. Loida Figueroa, "María Dolores Rodríguez y Ponce de León; y Bonocio Tió y Segarra," *Claridad*, 18–24 November 1994, 16–17.

41. Cypess, "Tradition and Innovation," 77.

42. Rivera Montalvo, *San Germán*, 5.

43. Ibid., 7.

44. Quintero Rivera, "Music," 34.

45. Fernando Ortiz, in *La música afro-cubana* (Madrid: Ediciones Júcar, 1975), 17, differentiates *metalepsis* from *metástasis*, the latter a process of musical transvaloration across class lines. The case of the danza can be seen as an illustration of both phenomena.

46. Top Hits Records and Tapes D-2134, 1981.

47. For an overview of Puerto Rico's colonial history, see Edwin Meléndez and Edgardo Meléndez, eds., *Colonial Dilemma: Critical Perspectives on Contemporary Puerto Rico* (Boston: South End Press, 1993).

48. Mapeyé, *Criollo y más*, TeleCumbre LP-2002, 1986.

Chapter Two: A Sensual Mulatta Called the Plena

1. Tomás Blanco, "Elogio de la plena," *Revista del Ateneo Puertorriqueño* 1, no. 1 (1935): 97–106.

2. Juan Flores, "Bumbún and the Beginnings of la Plena," *Centro de estudios Puertorriqueños bulletin* 2 (spring 1988), 16. Hereafter, references to this article will be cited from Flores, *Divided Borders: Essays on Puerto Rican Identity* (Houston: Arte Público Press, 1993).

3. Francisco López Cruz, *La música folklórica de Puerto Rico* (Sharon, Conn.: Troutman Press, 1967).

4. Flores, "Bumbún," 88. See also Ruth Glasser's account of the origins of the plena in *My Music Is My Flag, Puerto Rican Musicians and Their Communities, 1917–1940* (Berkeley: University of California Press, 1995), 171–77.

5. Flores, "Bumbún," 88.

6. Ibid., 87.

7. Cuban musicologist Leonardo Acosta, in *Música y descolonización* (Havana, Cuba: Editorial Arte y Literatura, 1982), 167–75, maintains that the dichotomy between anonymous and individualized music is illusory and frequently "arbitrary," for anonymous is any musical piece whose author is unknown to folklorists and musicologists. He thus calls for a revision of the term *folklore* and also illustrates how, in one Latin American context, folkloric music has been consistently identified with a particular author or composer (175).

8. Flores, "Bumbún," 85.

9. Edgardo Rodríguez Juliá, *Puertorriqueños: Album de la Sagrada familia puertorriqueña* (Madrid: Editorial Playor, 1988), 36.

10. Flores, "Bumbún," 89.

11. See Juan Flores's discussion of the controversy concerning Rafael Cortijo and his music in the naming of the new Fine Arts Complex in San Juan and how it elicited previous social constructs of Puerto Rican identity, in "Cortijo's Revenge," *Centro de estudios Puertorriqueños bulletin* 3 (spring 1991), 8–21. Hereafter, references to this article will be cited from Flores, *Divided Borders: Essays on Puerto Rican Identity* (Houston: Arte Público Press, 1993).

12. Glasser, *My Music,* 177.

13. From the oral tradition. I am thankful to Joe Díaz, arranger and collector of Puerto Rican music, for his generosity in providing me with a copy of the text and a musical arrangement. Some sources identify the bishop as Irish, whereas another source (documented by Ruth Glasser, *My Music,* 175) testified that he was from Spain.

14. Rosario Ferré, "Una conciencia musical," in *La escritora hispánica,* ed. Nora Erro-Orthman and Juan Cruz-Mendizábal (Miami, Fla.: Universal, 1990).

15. Edgardo Rodríguez Juliá, "Llegó el Obispo de Roma" in *Una noche con Iris Chacón* (San Juan, P.R.: Editorial Antillana, 1986), 11–52.

16. See Ruth Glasser's discussion of the history of plena in New York, in *My Music,* 177–90.

17. Jorge Pérez Rolón, "La plena puertorriqueña: De la expresión popular a la comercialización musical," in *Centro de estudios Puertorriqueños bulletin* 3 (spring 1991), 52. This article is a condensed version of a longer, unpublished piece titled "La bomba y la plena puertorriqueña: Sincretismo racial o transformación histórica-musical?" which the author generously shared with me.

18. Flores, "Bumbún," 85–86.

19. Pérez-Rolón, "La plena puertorriqueña," 53.

20. Ibid., 54.

21. Néstor García Canclini, *Las culturas populares en el capitalismo* (Mexico: Nueva Imagen, 1982), and the English translation, *Transforming Modernity: Popular Culture in Mexico*, trans. Lidia Lozano (Austin: Universtiy of Texas Press, 1993).

22. Ruth Glasser, *My Music*, 186–90.

23. Pérez-Rolón, "La plena puertorriqueña," 54.

24. Flores, "Bumbún," 86.

25. Peter Manuel, *Cassette Culture: Popular Music and Technology in North India* (Chicago: University of Chicago Press, 1993). Manuel's analysis documents the new democratic uses of cassette technology among northern Indians and ensuing changes and functional shifts of music. Thus, when Leonardo Acosta, in *Música y descolonización*, chapters 2 and 3, portrays the commercialization of Cuban popular music in the United States as a unidirectional process of capitalist colonialism, he excludes the potential reappropriations of technological developments that musicians have historically practiced in the continuous dialectics of co-optation and resistance. For a lucid analysis of the latter, see Tricia Rose, "Soul Sonic Forces" in *Black Noise* (Hanover, N.H. and London: University of New England Press, 1994).

26. Edgardo Rodríguez Juliá, *El entierro de Cortijo* (Rio Piedras, P.R.: Ediciones Huracán, 1983).

27. Flores, "Cortijo's Revenge," 98.

28. Ibid.

29. José Luis González, "El país de cuatro pisos" in *El país de cuatro pisos y otros ensayos* (Rio Piedras, P.R.: Ediciones Huracán, 1984), 30.

30. Rodríguez Juliá, *El entierro de Cortijo*, 70–71.

31. Rodríguez Juliá, *Puertorriqueños*, 36.

32. Rodríguez Juliá, "Llegó el Obispo de Roma."

33. Michel de Certeau, *The Practice of Everyday Life* (Berkeley and Los Angeles: University of California Press, 1984), 35–37.

34. Rodríguez Juliá, "Llegó el Obispo de Roma," 13.

35. At the risk of reducing the ideological complexities of any musical form, there seems to be consensus among musicologists, cultural historians, and critics that the plena has been an important cultural expression of resistance and a tool for the critique of the government, the church, and the bourgeois in Puerto Rico and on the mainland. Refer to Ruth Glasser's more recent discussion on the "social stigma" of this musical form in *My Music*, 173–77.

36. Flores, "Cortijo's Revenge," 98.

37. Tomás Blanco, *El prejuicio racial en Puerto Rico*, ed. Arcadio Díaz Quiñones (Rio Piedras, P.R.: Ediciones Huracán, 1985).

38. Ibid., 107.

39. Ibid., 113.

40. Ibid., 129–30.

41. Blanco, "Elogio de la plena," *Revista del Instituto de Cultura Puertorriqueña* 22 (July–Sepember 1979): 39–42.

42. See Juan Flores's critique of organic metaphors for national identity in "Cortijo's Revenge," 98.

43. Arcadio Díaz Quiñones, Introduction to Tomás Blanco, *El prejuicio*, 63.

44. Ibid., 77. See also Vera M. Kutzinski's discussion of the same phenomenon in Cuba in *Sugar's Secrets: Race and the Erotics of Cuban Nationalism* (Charlottesville: University Press of Virginia, 1993), 147–48, her analysis of Gustavo Urruitia's *Sunday Literary Supplement* to *Diario de la Marina* entitled "Ideales de una Raza," and of Urruitia's constant efforts to emphasize "how much better race relations were in Cuba" in contrast to the United States.

45. Blanco, "Elogio de la Plena," 42.
46. Ibid.
47. Ibid.
48. Ibid.
49. Sander Gilman, *Difference and Pathology: Stereotypes of Sexuality, Race and Madness* (Ithaca, N.Y.: Cornell University Press, 1985), 223.
50. Ibid.
51. Ibid., 228.
52. See Manuel Moreno Fraginals, "Cultural Contributions and Decultura-tion," in *Africa in Latin America: Essays in History, Culture, and Socialization* (New York: Holmes and Meier, 1984), 11–12. He proposes that the concrete, material conditions that slaves experienced, particularly the absence of women, explain the erotically laden language in black cultural expressions. He thus contests hyper-eroticism as an essential trait in blacks, explaining it as a result of inhuman conditions. I would go a step further and contest Moreno Fraginal's own assumptions about black cultural expressions as quantitatively different from those of other racial groups, assumptions that elide the primary role of the Eurocentric gaze as the central perspective, the norm by which others are measured.
53. Quoted by Debra Castillo in *Talking Back: Toward a Latin American Feminist Literary Criticism* (Ithaca, N.Y.: Cornell University Press, 1992), 162.
54. Frantz Fanon, *Black Skin, White Masks*, trans. Charles Lam Markmann (New York: Grove Press, 1967). In chapter 2, "The Woman of Color and the White Man," Fanon analyzes the desire of black women for white men as an articulation of their internalized colonialism and racism, a desire, indeed, for "lactification," for whitening the race. Ironically, Fanon's male reading of Mayotte Capecia's *Je suis Martiniquaise* dovetails inversely with Tomás Blanco's portrayal of the Puerto Rican woman as the carrier of prejudice. For both, woman betrays her own race and culture.
55. Blanco, *El prejuicio racial*, 130.
56. Alejo Carpentier, *La música en Cuba* (Mexico City: Fondo de Cultura Económica, 1946), 141.

Chapter Three: Desiring the Racial Other

1. Rosario Ferré, "Cuando las mujeres quieren a los hombres" in *Papeles de Pandora* (Mexico City: Joaquín Mortiz, 1976), 29; translated by Rosario Ferré and Cindy Ventura. See also, in English, "When Women Love Men," in *The Youngest Doll* (Lincoln: University of Nebraska Press, 1991), 135.
2. Edgardo Rodríguez Juliá, "Respeten, que hay damas," in *Puertorriqueños: Album de la Sagrada familia puertorriqueña* (Madrid: Editorial Playor, 1988), 54.
3. Ibid., 55.
4. Ibid., 56.
5. Also see Mariana Valverde's analysis of the virgin/whore duality in *Sex, Power and Pleasure* (Philadelphia: New Society Publishers, 1987), 157–58: Women "are offered only two basic forms of desire as possible models": to become the object of male desire and to repress her own sexual desire and identify with the "higher self-less ideals of nurturing and mothering." Yet as Valverde concludes, "The content of the fallen woman's desire is different from the Madonna's, but the form is the same. Both women mobilize a vast reservoir of psychological and physical energy *in the service of male desires*" (emphasis mine).
6. Elizabeth Grosz, *Jacques Lacan: A Feminist Introduction* (London and New York: Routledge, 1990), 128–29.

7. Rodríguez Juliá, "Respeten," 55.

8. Ferré, "Cuando las mujeres," 26; "When Women Love Men," 133.

9. From the oral tradition. Acknowledgments are due to Joe Díaz for a written version of these lyrics. The translation is mine.

10. Ferré, "Cuando las mujeres," 26, "When Women Love Men," 133.

11. Ibid.

12. See René Girard's *Deceit, Desire and the Novel: Self and Other in Literary Structure*, trans. Yvonne Freccero (Baltimore: Johns Hopkins University Press, 1965).

13. Valverde, *Sex*, 38.

14. Ferré, "When Women Love Men," 143.

15. Lorraine Elena Roses uses the reference to blood throughout the story as the basis for an interpretation of the text that we consider a misreading. According to her, the blood appears as an indication of a physical attack on the part of Isabel Luberza by which La Negra is wounded. Such a reading reaffirms her thesis about the prototypes of the hysteric and the sorceress as the basis for the characters, thus invalidating the emancipatory and democratic effect of the final fusion between the two women. The allusions to blood in the story, in my opinion, are doubly significant: on the one hand, as signifiers of race and racial difference, and on the other, as images that merge with the red nail polish, thus suggesting the association between eroticism and death. Lorraine Elena Roses, "Las esperanzas de Pandora: Prototipos femeninos en la obra de Rosario Ferré," *Revista Iberoamericana* 162–63 (January–June, 1993): 270–87.

16. Sandra Cypess, "Tradition and Innovation in the Writings of Puerto Rican Women," in *Out of the Kumbla: Caribbean Women and Literature*, ed. Carole Boyce Davies and Elaine Savory Fido (Trenton, N.J.: Africa World Press, 1990), 84.

17. Debra Castillo, *Talking Back: Toward a Latin American Feminist Literary Criticism* (Ithaca, N.Y.: Cornell University Press, 1992), 159, 164.

18. Ferré, "When Women Love Men," 138–39.

19. Ibid., 136.

20. Juan G. Gelpí, *Literatura y paternalismo en Puerto Rico* (San Juan: Editorial de la Universidad de Puerto Rico, 1993), 157.

21. Elizabeth Grosz, *Jacques Lacan*, 65.

22. Ferré, "When Women Love Men," 145.

23. See the definition of *tongonear*, derived from *tongo*, in Fernando Ortiz, *Glosario de afronegrismos* (Havana: Imprenta El Siglo XX, 1924), 461. Ortiz traces the word to "la intromisión del sufijo *ng*, que tras una aféresis (con-to-ng-oneo) hace nacer de tal guisa dicha voz de otra: *contoneo*, que le es sinónima, aunque sin el sentido burlón de aquella degenerada" [the intromission of the suffix *ng*, that through apheresis (con-to-ng-oneo) gives birth in such a way to the other's voice: *contoneo*, is a synonym, however without the chiding meaning of that degenerated term].

24. See Margarite Fernández Olmos, "Desde una perspectiva femenina: La cuentística de Rosario Ferré y Ana Lydia Vega," *Homines*, 8, no. 2 (1984–85): 303–11.

25. The strategies of erasure and of silencing the black presence within the Puerto Rican upper class at the turn of the century are unveiled in Rosario Ferré's short novel, aptly titled *Maldito amor* after the title of a well-known danza by Juan Morel Campos.

26. Tomás Blanco, *El prejuicio racial en Puerto Rico*, ed. Arcadio Díaz Quiñones (Río Piedras, P.R.: Ediciones Huracán, 1985), 40.

27. See Vera M. Kutzinski, *Sugar's Secrets: Race and the Erotics of Cuban Nationalism* (Charlottesville: University Press of Virginia, 1993), 164–68.

28. Ibid., 76.

29. See Deborah Gray-White's analysis of analogous racial constructs in the U.S. South in "Jezebel and Mammy: The Mythology of Female Slavery," in *Ar'n't I a Woman? Female Slaves in the Plantation South* (New York: W. W. Norton, 1985), 27–61.

30. A meaningful comparison here is Manuel Ramos Otero's short story, "La última plena que bailó Luberza," published side by side with Ferré's story in *Zona de carga y descarga* and reprinted in *El cuento de la mujer del mar* (Rio Piedras, P.R: Ediciones Huracán, 1979), 47–68. While both texts probe the social and erotic power of Isabel "La Negra" Luberza, Ramos Otero's fictional version of this prostitute is informed by religious references, including santería; the language of dreams and death; and significantly, the masculinization of Isabel as an "omniscient being, a dictatorial figure close to García Márquez's "Mama grande."

31. Ferré, "Cuando las mujeres," 40.

32. Valverde, *Sex*, 43.

33. Ferré, "¿Porqué quiere Isabel a los hombres?" in *El coloquio de las perras* (San Juan: Editorial Cultural, 1990), 150.

34. Castillo, *Talking Back*, 163.

35. See Rafael Falcón, "El tema del negro en el cuento puertorriqueño," *Cuadernos hispanoamericanos: Revista mensual de cultura hispánica* 451–52 (January–February 1988): 97–109. Falcón concludes his essay with a caveat regarding neo-Negrista literature for, as he judges, "todavía carecemos de obras que expresen una visión clara y definida de la lucha de clases que entraña el prejuicio racial en Puerto Rico, y que presenten las luchas y aportaciones del puertorriqueño negro como elemento vivo de nuestra colectividad nacional" [we still lack works that express a clear and definite vision of the class struggle, including the racial prejudice in Puerto Rico, and that present the struggles and contributions of the black Puerto Rican as dynamic element(s) of our national collectivity].

36. Rosario Ferré, "Amalia," in *Papeles de Pandora*, 65–80. Also in English in *The Youngest Doll*, 47–58.

37. Roland Barthes, *The Pleasure of the Text*, trans. Richard Miller (New York: Noonday Press, 1989), 41–42.

38. See Ferré's "La cocina de la escritura," in *La sartén por el mango: Encuentro de escritoras latinoamericanas*, ed. Patricia Elena González and Eliana Ortega (Rio Piedras, P.R.: Ediciones Huracán, 1985), 137–54.

39. Susan Andrade, "White Skin, Black Masks: Colonialism and Sexual Politics of Oroonoko," *Cultural Critique* 27 (spring 1994), 189–214.

40. Rosario Ferré, "Una conciencia musical," in *La escritora hispánica*, ed. Nora Erro-Orthman and Juan Cruz-Mendizábal (Miami, Fla.: Universal, 1990).

41. Ferré, "Una conciencia," 8–9.

42. Ngugi Wa Thiong'o, *Decolonising the Mind: The Politics of Language in African Literature* (Portsmouth, N.H.: Heinemann, 1986), 17.

43. Ferré, "Maquinolandera," in *Papeles de Pandora*, 204–23.

44. Ibid., 223.

45. Fernando Ortiz, *La música afro-cubana* (Madrid: Ediciones Júcar, 1975), 306–8.

46. Barthes, *Pleasure of the Text*, 61.

47. Kutzinski, *Sugar's Secrets*, 179, observes how formalist literary criticism has persistently "disguise[d] political choices as purely aesthetic ones"; an excellent case in point is the *jitanjáfora*, which has been traditionally defined as "mere playful onomatopoeia," thus dismissing its value "as a language with [its] own discrete history[ies]."

48. Andreas Huyssen, "Mass Culture as Woman: Modernism's Other," in *After*

the Great Divide: Modernism, Mass Culture, Postmodernism (Bloomington and Indianapolis: Indiana University Press, 1986), 62.

Part Two: The Plural Sites of Salsa
A Postmodern Preface

1. Juan Flores and María Milagros López, "Dossier Puerto Rico," *Social Text* 38 (spring 1994): 93–95, summarize the singular case of Puerto Rico in its contradictory position "that appears at once postnational and prenational" (94). The authors stress issues such as the "national question," economic dependence, consumption without production, social and ethnic inequality in the educational system, and "insertion into the global economy at points (like high finance and tourism) that are powerless to transform local life" (93).

2. Quoted in Leonardo Padura, "Willie Colón: Algo distinto," *La gaceta de Cuba*, January–February 1992, 12.

3. See Demetria Martínez's profile "The Salsa Padre," *Vista: Focus on Hispanic Americans*, 26 May 1990, 6–7, 12.

4. Lise Waxer, "Appropriation, Ethnicity, and the Negotiation of Insider-Outsider Roles in Latin Popular Music Performance." Paper presented at the 36th Annual Meeting of the Society for Ethnomusicology, Chicago, 10–13 October 1991.

5. Andrea Press and Elizabeth Cole, "Women like Us: Working-Class Women Respond to Television Representations of Abortion," in *Viewing, Reading, Listening: Audiences and Cultural Reception*, ed. Jon Cruz and Justin Lewis (Boulder, Colo.: Westview Press, 1994), 55–80.

Chapter Four: Situating Salsa

1. César Miguel Rondón, *El libro de la salsa: Crónica de la música del Caribe urbano* (Caracas, Venezuela: Editorial Arte, 1980), 210.

2. *Cocolo* also refers us to Cocolía, the artistic pseudonym of Domingo Cruz, a mulatto Puerto Rican bombardinista and dance orchestra director famous at the turn of the century. See Angel Quintero Rivera's *Patricios y plebeyos: Burgueses, hacendados, artesanos y obreros* (Rio Piedras, P.R.: Ediciones Huracán, 1988): 76–77.

3. In the *San Juan Star* of 14 June 1987, Carlos Galarza reported on the salsa concert under "Salseros Jam until Morning," and Jaime Pieras documented the rock concert under "Rockers Give Fans an Earful."

4. Produced and directed by Ana Maria García, *Cocolos y rockeros* documents the musical wars between salsa and rock music in Puerto Rico. Filmed in 1992, it received the Special Jury Award in San Juan's Cinemafest that year.

5. Elliott Castro Tirado's profile of Tony Vega, "Tony Vega: Un salsero," *Claridad* 12–18 (June 1992): 20–21, begins, significantly, with questions addressed to the reader that attempt to deessentialize the salsero archetype: "Si les digo Eladio Antonio Vega Ayala . . . ¿pensarían ustedes en un salsero? Si les digo que es blanco, de ojos claros y pelo lacio . . . ¿pensarían en un salsero?" [If I mention the name Eladio Antonio Vega Ayala . . . would you think of a salsero? If I say he is white, with green eyes and straight hair, . . . would you think of a salsero?]

6. Tony Vega, "Busca el ritmo," composed by Johnny Ortiz, in *Tony Vega con la Orquesta de Willie Rosario*, Rodven Records, TH-2972, 1992.

7. Castro Tirado, "Tony Vega," 20–21.

8. Wayka Pagán Agosto, "Esa humanidad no es casualidad: Andy Montañez," *Claridad*, 12–18 June 1992, 23.

9. Mark Slobin, "Micromusics of the West: A Comparative Approach," *Ethnomusicology*, 36 (winter 1992): 1–87.

10. Willie Colón explains salsa's popularity in Europe as a result of various factors, such as the presence of Latino groups that toured Latino communities dovetailed with the European following of jazz and its institutionalization through jazz festivals. Moreover, he ascribes this "easier" penetration of salsa in European countries to the open, tolerant attitudes of Europeans toward multicultural productions, in contrast to U.S. monocultural trends. See Leonardo Padura, "Willie Colón: Algo distinto," *La gaceta de Cuba*, January–February 1992, 11. See also Ramón Cintrón's summary of the first salsa festival in Paris, "Primer festival de Salsa en París (entre logros y tropiezos)," *Claridad*, 3–9 March 1995, 24, which he describes as very successful despite problems in publicity, organization, and production.

11. Orquesta de la Luz, *Somos diferentes*, Sony Discos and BMG Victor, CDZ-80851, 1992. The lyrics of the original song by Pablo Beltrán Ruiz appear in Carmencita Delgado de Rizo, ed., *Cancionero: Antología* (Bogotá, Colombia: Ediciones Gamma, 1991), 351.

12. See Guillermo Cabrera Infante, "El Son: El fantasma que recorre América," *El Nuevo Día*, 9 September 1984, 8. This newspaper piece is a brief version of Infante's earlier essay, titled "Salsa para una ensalada," in Rose S. Minc, ed., *Literatures in Transition: The Many Voices of the Caribbean Area* (Gaithersburg, Md.: Hispamérica and Montclair State College, 1982), 21–36.

13. Pierrette Hondagneu-Sotelo, "A Cultural History of Salsa, and Some Remarks on the Nature of Musical Creation and Meaning, Ethnic Identity, Hegemony and Resistance," master's thesis, University of California, Berkeley.

14. Rondón, *Libro de la salsa*, 182.

15. See John Fiske, "The Jeaning of America," in *Understanding Popular Culture* (Boston: Unwin Hyman, 1989), 1–23.

16. Richard Middleton, *Studying Popular Music* (Milton Keynes, U.K., and Philadelphia: Open University Press, 1990), 7–11, discusses *articulation*, already used by Stuart Hall and defined by Antonio Gramsci as "the most sophisticated method at present available of conceiving the relationship between musical forms and practices, on the one hand, and class interests and social structure, on the other."

17. Jeremy Marre and Hannah Charlton, *Beats of the Heart: Popular Music of the World* (London: Pluto Press, 1985), 73.

18. Leonardo Acosta, *Música y descolonización* (Havana: Editorial Arte y Literatura, 1982), 213.

19. Rondón's *El libro de la salsa* remains the most complete historical overview of the development of this music. See also Peter Manuel, *Popular Musics of the Non-Western World: An Introductory Survey* (New York and Oxford: Oxford University Press, 1988), 24–50; Jorge Duany, "Popular Music in Puerto Rico: Toward an Anthropology of Salsa," *Latin American Music Review* 5 (fall/winter 1984): 186–216; Hondagneu-Sotelo, "A Cultural History of Salsa"; and Sue Steward, "Cuba and the Roots of Salsa," in *Rhythms of the World*, ed. Francis Hanly and Tim May (London: BBC Books, 1989), 24–37.

20. Rondón, *El libro de la salsa*, 20.

21. Ibid.

22. Many of these diverse and conflicting definitions are culled by Sergio Santana in *¿Qué es la salsa? Buscando la melodía* (Medellín, Colombia: Ediciones Salsa y Cultura, 1992). My appreciation to Margarita de la Vega Hurtado for purchasing this book for me in Colombia. Peter Manuel, in "Puerto Rican Music and Cultural Identity: Creative Appropriation of Cuban Sources from Danza to Salsa," *Ethnomusicology* 38, no. 2 (spring–summer 1994), also argues for the recognition that *all*

Puerto Rican musics have originated in Cuban music. While he stresses how Puerto Ricans have "resignified" these forms to create their own cultural expressions, I disagree with the degree to which Cuban musical structures are favored over parallel Afro–Puerto Rican forms.

23. Santana, *¿Qué es la salsa?*, 76.

24. Félix M. Padilla, "Salsa: Puerto Rican and Latino Music," *Journal of Popular Culture* 24 (Summer 1990): 87–104.

25. Duany, "Popular Music in Puerto Rico," 187.

26. Steve Loza, in "The Origins of the Son," *Aztlán* 15, no. 1 (1984), 107, summarizes this correction. Manuel Pérez Beato, José Juan Arrom, and Alberto Muguercia have all refuted "the authenticity" of Ma Teodora as a historical figure, who was "most likely . . . fiction." See also Peter Manuel's summary of Cuban music in *Popular Musics*, 30.

27. See Cabrera Infante, "El Son: El fantasma que recorre América" and "Salsa para una ensalada." César Miguel Rondón honors Piñeiro's coining of the term *salsa* by using his song as an epigraph to his book.

28. Cabrera Infante, "Salsa para una ensalada," 35.

29. See Leonardo Padura, "Willie Colón," 12.

30. Rondón, *El libro de la salsa*, 25.

31. Peter Manuel, "Puerto Rican Music," 270.

32. Hondagneau-Sotelo, "Cultural History of Salsa," 1–10.

33. Duany, "Popular Music in Puerto Rico," 195–97.

34. Hondagneau-Sotelo, "Cultural History of Salsa," 14–25.

35. Angel Quintero Rivera, *Music, Social Classes, and the National Question in Puerto Rico* (Rio Piedras: University of Puerto Rico, Centro de Investigaciones Sociales, 1987), 12, 31.

Chapter Five: Ideological Negotiations

1. Angel Quintero Rivera, *Music, Social Classes, and the National Question in Puerto Rico* (Rio Piedras: University of Puerto Rico, Centro de Investigaciones Sociales, 1987), 6.

2. Ibid., 8.

3. Víctor Hernández Cruz, *Snaps* (New York: Vintage Books, 1969), 77.

4. Quintero Rivera, *Music*, 8–9.

5. Theodor Adorno, "On Popular Music," in *Studies in Philosophy and Social Science*, vol. 9 (New York: Institute for Social Research, 1941), 24–26.

6. Roberta L. Singer, "Tradition and Innovation in Contemporary Latin Popular Music in New York City," *Latin American Music Review* 4 (fall–winter 1983), 194.

7. In Ana Lydia Vega and Carmen Lugo Filippi, *Vírgenes y mártires* (Rio Piedras: Editorial Antillana, 1983), 81–88.

8. According to Jorge Duany, "Popular Music in Puerto Rico: Toward an Anthropology of Salsa," *Latin American Music Review* 5 (fall–winter 1984): 201, since its release in 1978 the song "Pedro Navaja"—and its character—have "become part of Puerto Rican folklore." Duany also describes the song as a reference to the "urban lower-class community in the United States" in its continuity with the literary and folkloric character of the *guapo* or *matón*. See also Manuel Cachán's analysis of this song as "a musical" version of the testimonio in Latin American literature, in "Bailando salsa con el super en Harlem: El testimonio caribeño del barrio," *Apuntes postmodernos/Postmodern Notes*, fall 1993, 59–64.

9. *La verdadera historia de Pedro Navaja*, produced by Teatro del Sesenta, is

now considered a legend; it probably was the most popular dramatic piece ever performed in Puerto Rico. See Lowell Fiet's historical assessment of its impact on Puerto Rican theatre in "La verdadera historia de Pedro Navaja: Leyenda y actualidad," *Claridad* 26 (August–1 September 1994), 16–17.

10. Vega, "Letra para salsa," in Vega and Lugo Filippi, *Vírgenes y mártires*, 88.

11. See Juan G. Gelpí, *Literatura y paternalismo en Puerto Rico* (San Juan: University of Puerto Rico Press, 1993), 188–91. Gelpí analyzes the open spaces of Vega's urban short stories as an oppositional gesture to the enclosed, domestic loci that prevailed in earlier patriarchal texts of Puerto Rican literature. He extends this oppositionality to include, metaphorically speaking, the aperture of elite modes of culture onto popular culture, as the presence of salsa references indicates in this short story.

12. I use these terms based on their definitions and deployment in "Discourse in the Novel," in *The Dialogic Imagination: Four Essays by M. M. Bakhtin*, ed. Michael Holquist, trans. Caryl Emerson and Michael Holquist (Austin: University of Texas Press, 1981), 259–422.

13. Taken from Charley Gerard and Marty Sheller, *SALSA! The Rhythm of Latin Music* (Crown Point, Ind.: White Cliffs Media, 1989), 15.

14. Adorno, "On Popular Music," 41. Richard Middleton, in *Studying Popular Music* (Milton Keynes, U.K., and Philadelphia: Open University Press, 1990), 34–63, devotes a chapter to a critique and reading of Adorno, reminding the reader of the "historical location" of Adorno's writings. While the latter's approach to popular music was formed during the 1930s, Middleton argues that during the 1940s "cultural totalitarianism becomes absolute," and it is also during this period that fascism and Stalinism emerge. Middleton also argues that Adorno's "ethnocentric and culture-centric perspective" (44) weakened his approach to musical production in the United States and in third world countries and that his view of the unitary subject, later questioned by poststructuralism, limited his analysis of audience and reception practices.

15. See Janos Marothy, *Music of the Bourgeois, Music of the Proletariat* (Budapest: Akademiai Kiado, 1974).

16. Adorno, "On Popular Music," 21–24.

17. George Lipsitz, *Time Passages: Collective Memory and American Popular Culture* (Minneapolis: University of Minnesota Press, 1990).

18. Middleton, *Studying Popular Music*, 268.

19. Ibid.

20. Ibid., 269. Middleton establishes two types of repetition in music. Musematic repetition is the "repetition of musemes," or short units that would include "riffs, call and response structures, and short, unchanging rhythmic patterns" (270). Discursive repetition, on the other hand, refers to the duplication of longer units such as the phrase, the sentence, or even complete sections. While these categories are usually related, respectively, with oral and written forms of musical composition, Middleton argues that "it would be better to see them not as crudely technologically determined but as actively summoned into development and strongly mediated by the needs of distinct socio-economic configurations."

21. Peter Manuel, in his introduction to *Popular Musics of the Non-Western World: An Introductory Survey* (New York and Oxford: Oxford University Press, 1988), 2–3, summarizes definitions of popular music that connect it with industrialized nations and with mass media. However, Manuel also shows that non-Western cultures have developed popular musical forms without such infrastructures.

22. See Duany, "Popular Music in Puerto Rico," 187.

23. César Miguel Rondón, *El libro de la salsa: crónica de la música del Caribe urbano* (Caracus, Venezuela: Editorial Arte, 1980), 102.

24. John Shepherd, "Value and Power in Music: An English Canadian Perspective," in *Relocating Cultural Studies: Developments in Theory and Research*, ed. Valda Blundell, John Shepherd, and Ian Taylor (London and New York: Routledge, 1993), 175.

25. Manuel Cachán, "Bailando salsa," 60, defines "commercial Salsa" as music produced for a consumer market, thus celebrating dancing and parties, what in Antillean culture has possessed strong religious values. "Politico-social Salsa" (my translation) integrates to music and dancing a political discourse that serves as a vehicle for appropriation and for the cultural struggle of the barrio. In my view, these definitions do not do justice to the simultaneous and plural meanings of any song, regardless of the initial intention.

26. Félix M. Padilla, "Salsa: Puerto Rican and Latino Music," *Journal of Popular Culture* 24 (summer 1990): 88.

27. Ibid., 91.

28. See Leonardo Padura, "Willie Colón: Algo distinto," *La gaceta de Cuba*, January–February 1992, 12. Leonardo Acosta, *Música y descolonización* (Havana, Cuba: Editorial Arte y Literatura, 1982), 74, identifies four major criteria established by Tin Pan Alley since 1914 in the realm of composition: (1) avoiding variations and emphasizing the musical theme, (2) limiting improvisation, (3) attaining novelty through a superficial element rather than creativity, (4) accelerated changes in musical evolution.

29. Peter Manuel, "Latin Music in the United States: Salsa and the Mass Media," *Journal of Communication* 41 (winter 1991): 110.

30. Ibid., 110.

31. Ibid., 111.

32. Ibid., 114.

33. Jeremy Marre and Hannah Charlton, *Beats of the Heart: Popular Music of the World* (London: Pluto Press, 1985), 81.

34. Iain Chambers, *Popular Culture: The Metropolitan Experience* (London and New York: Methuen, 1986), 135.

35. Edgardo Díaz Díaz, "El repertorio de salsa en dos perspectivas genéricas," paper presented at the first meeting of Iberoamerican ethnomusicologists, Lisbon, Portugal, March 1994. Given the dearth of ethnographic studies on dancing among Latinas/os, this study represents an important development for understanding Latina/o popular music as sociocultural practice. See also, by the same author, "La música bailable de los carnets: Forma y significado de su repertorio en Puerto Rico (1877–1930), *Revista musical puertorriqueña* 5 (January–June 1990): 3–21.

36. For an analysis of the role and authority of the band and its leader in deciding the musical repertoire, see Manuel Peña, "Ritual Structure in a Chicano Dance," *Latin American Music Review* 1, no. 47–73 (spring 1980); see also José Limón's discussion about dancing as "a site of contestation" within the very dance itself, "at the point of dance production," in *Dancing with the Devil: Society and Cultural Poetics in Mexican-American South Texas* (Madison: University of Wisconsin Press, 1994), 164.

37. Díaz Díaz, "Repertorio de salsa," 37.

38. Limón, *Dancing with the Devil*, 49. My emphasis on *they* needs further discussion. Most unique about Limón's ethnographic incursion is his own doubled subject position as anthropologist and as participant in this dance club scene. Although he is there as observer, he also participates as a Chicano male by dancing with Beatriz and by taking her out to dinner. The gender-inflected *they* is significant because Beatriz is also implicitly calling him to task for belonging to that class of men. As he mentions at the beginning of the chapter, he, as anthropologist, also wants something from her, not her body but definitely her experiences and her cultural knowledge of a

social event and world that he is, in many ways, trying to recover as a "working-class Mexican descent anthropologist" by learning how to dance again.

39. Ibid., 153–54. Edgardo Díaz Díaz, in "Repertorio de salsa," clearly documents through interviews with both men and women that men ascribe an exclusively physical and erotic meaning to dancing boleros (35), whereas women tend to be more wary of whom they choose to dance boleros with because they consider this intimate dance an expression of a serious emotional commitment (33–34).

40. Limón, *Dancing with the Devil*, 164.

41. Ibid., 163. Randy Martin, "Dance as a Social Movement" in *Social Text* 12:54–70.

42. Ibid., 166.

43. This and subsequent citations are part of the interviews held with working-class women in Detroit. Refer to Part Four of this book for more details.

44. Leslie Gotfrit, "Women Dancing Back: Disruption and the Politics of Pleasure," in *Postmodernism, Feminism, and Cultural Politics: Redrawing Educational Boundaries*, ed. Henry A. Giroux (Albany: State University of New York Press, 1991), 174–95.

45. Willie Colón, "The Rhythms," in *The Portable Lower East Side* (New York: The Portable Lower East Side, 1988), 9–12.

46. Adorno, "On Popular Music," 37–39.

47. Gotfrit, "Women Dancing Back," 176.

48. Limón, *Dancing with the Devil*, 165.

49. Gotfrit, "Women Dancing Back," 176.

50. Ibid.

51. Luis Rafael Sánchez, *La importancia de llamarse Daniel Santos* (Hanover, N.H.: Ediciones del Norte, 1988), 104.

52. *Danzón* was produced by Jorge Sánchez and directed by María Novaro. Mexico City: Macondo Cine Video, 1991.

53. See Frances R. Aparicio, "Salsa, maracas, and baile: Latin popular music in the poetry of Víctor Hernández Cruz," *MELUS* 16 (spring 1989–90): 43–58.

Chapter Six: Cultural (Mis)Translations and Crossover Nightmares

1. Leslie Gotfrit, "Women Dancing Back: Disruption and the Politics of Pleasure," in Henry A. Giroux, ed., *Postmodernism, Feminism, and Cultural Politics: Redrawing Educational Boundaries* (Albany: State University of New York Press, 1993), 84.

2. Tim Padgett, Peter Katel, and Niko Price, "Crossover Dreamers," in *Newsweek* 4 (November 1991), 75.

3. See Leonardo Acosta, *Música y descolonización* (Havana, Cuba: Editorial Arte y Literatura, 1982), 31. I want to thank Peter Manuel for pointing out this fact.

4. I want to thank Bridget M. Morgan for sharing this material with me. The musical score includes both English and Spanish lyrics and the music by Eliseo Grenet and arranged by Laurence Kempton (New York: Edward B. Marks Music Corporation, 1931).

5. See Cristóbal Díaz Ayala, *Música cubana del Areyto a la Nueva Trova*, 2nd ed. (San Juan, P.R.: Editorial Cubanacán, 1981), 127, 137.

6. Don Michael Randel, "Crossing Over with Rubén Blades," *Journal of the American Musicological Society* 44 (summer 1991): 301–23.

7. Ibid., 306.

8. Ibid., 307.

9. Ibid., 320.
10. Ibid.
11. Ibid., 320–21.
12. Ibid., 322.
13. Ibid.
14. Acosta, *Música y descolonización*, 45.
15. I employ these terms informed by Nathaniel Mackey's analysis of musical appropriations in "Other: From Noun to Verb," *Representations* 39 (summer 1992): 51–70.
16. Carlos Agudelo, "Latin Notas," *Billboard* (23 September 1989): 69.
17. Ibid.
18. See, for example, George Lipsitz, *Time Passages: Collective Memory and American Popular Culture* (Minneapolis: University of Minnesota Press, 1990); Jon Cruz, "Testimonies and Artifacts: Elite Appropriations of African American Music in the Nineteenth Century," in *Viewing, Reading, Listening: Audiences and Cultural Reception*, ed. Jon Cruz and Justin Lewis (Boulder: Westview Press, 1994): 125–41; Nathaniel Mackey, "Other"; and Acosta, *Música y descolonización*.
19. In *Dangerous Crossroads: Popular Music, Postmodernism and the Poetics of Place* (New York and London: Verso, 1994), George Lipsitz discusses this shift "as transnational corporations create integrated global markets and the nation state recedes as a source of identity and identification, popular culture becomes an ever more important public sphere" (7).
20. Middleton, *Studying Popular Music* (Milton Keynes, U.K., and Philadelphia: Open University Press, 1990), 8–11.
21. Willie Colón, quoted in Agudelo, "Latin Notas," 69.
22. Mackey, "Other," 64.

Part Three: Dissonant Melodies
Theoretical Pretexts

1. See Jonathan Culler, "Reading Woman," in *On Deconstruction: Theory and Criticism after Structuralism* (Ithaca, N.Y.: Cornell University Press, 1982), 43–64; Mary Jacobus, *Reading Woman: Essays in Feminist Criticism* (New York: Columbia University Press, 1986); Pamela L. Caughie, "Women Reading/Reading Women: A Review of Some Recent Books on Gender and Reading," *Papers in Language and Literature* 24 (summer 1988), 317–35; and Janice A. Radway, *Reading the Romance: Women, Patriarchy, and Popular Literature* (Chapel Hill: University of North Carolina Press, 1984, 1991).
2. Culler, "Reading Woman," 46.
3. See, for instance, Jane S. Jaquette, "Literary Archetypes and Female Role Alternatives: The Woman and the Novel in Latin America," in *Female and Male in Latin America*, ed. Ann Pescattello (Pittsburgh, Pa.: University of Pittsburgh Press, 1973), 3–27.
4. Neyssa Palmer, *Las mujeres en los cuentos de René Marqués* (Rio Piedras, P.R.: Editorial de la Universidad de Puerto Rico, 1988), 27.
5. Toril Moi, *Sexual/Textual Politics: Feminist Literary Theory* (1985; reprint London and New York: Routledge, 1990), 45.
6. Caughie, "Women Reading," 328.
7. Ibid., 318–19.
8. Cathy Schwichtenberg, "Reconceptualizing Gender: New Sites for Feminist Audience Research," in *Viewing, Reading, Listening: Audiences and Cultural Reception*, ed. Jon Cruz and Justin Lewis (Boulder, Colo.: Westview Press, 1994), 171.

Schwichtenberg's working definition of gender avoids the sorts of essentializing traps into which critics such as Jonathan Culler fall when approaching "reading woman" as a "differential definition": Culler states that "to read as a woman is to avoid reading as a man, to identify the specific defenses and distortions of male readings and provide correctives" ("Reading Woman," 54). While Culler potentially argues here for the oppositional value of women as readers, it ultimately makes women's identity contingent on man, that is, woman is what is not male nor masculine, a legacy of Freudian theories of penis envy and of woman as "lack."

9. Frances Aparicio, "'Así son': Salsa Music, Female Narratives, and Gender (De)Construction in Puerto Rico," *Poetics Today* 15 (December 1994): 659–84.

10. See Mary Ellison, *Lyrical Protest: Black Music's Struggle against Discrimination* (New York: Praeger, 1989), whose discussion of sexual politics in the blues and in black music in general is based on the assumption that the lyrics of the song are unmediated reflections of the singer's personal life. As for salsa music, José Arteaga Rodríguez's piece on violence as a recurring theme in this musical tradition, "Salsa y violencia: una aproximación sonoro-histórica," *Revista Musical Puertorriqueña* 4 (July–December 1988): 20–33, tends to criminalize salsa singers from New York as direct agents of the violence they sing about.

Chapter Seven: Woman as Absence

1. Peter Manuel points out that the habanera rhythm emerged in Cuba as early as 1803 and was a staple feature of the early- to mid-nineteenth century contradanza. I want to thank him for this historical clarification.

2. See Iris M. Zavala, "De héroes y heroínas en lo imaginario social: El discurso amoroso del bolero," *Casa de las Américas* 30 (March–April 1990):123–29. See also René A. Campos, "The Poetics of the Bolero in the Novels of Manuel Puig," in *World Literature Today* 65 (autumn 1991): 637–42.

3. Printed in *Un siglo de bolero* (Mexico City: EDUSA, n.d.), vol. 5. Also in *Cancionero: Antología*, ed. Carmencita Delgado de Rizo (Bogotá, Colombia: Ediciones Gamma, 1991), 245 (hereafter cited as *Cancionero*).

4. Zavala, "De héroes y heroínas," 124.

5. Ibid., 125.

6. This phrase is quoted from Luis Rafael Sánchez's *La importancia de llamarse Daniel Santos* (Hanover, N.H.: Ediciones del Norte, 1988), 104, in which he establishes a poetic contrast between the centrifugal movements of dancing to guarachas and the centripetal forces of the bolero. The association of the bolero with the eternal, its universality and timelessness, has also been discussed by Héctor Madera Ferrón in "El bolero es eterno," *Un siglo de bolero*, 3–5, in which he celebrates the popularity of this musical form throughout one hundred years.

7. Luis Rafael Sánchez, *La importancia*, 3. This phrase, which describes Latin America as bitter, barefoot, and speaking Spanish, becomes a leitmotif throughout the book. Its recurrence anchors the preeminence of the everyday life and culture of the working class and proletariat over the elite forms of culture in Latin America, a class dialectic that the bolero, according to Sánchez and others, truly bridges in its language of love.

8. Zavala, "De héroes y heroínas," 124.

9. Luis Miguel, *Romance*, Warner Music Netherlands CPXI-7150, 1991.

10. Zavala, "De héroes y heroínas," 125, and Madera Ferrón, "El bolero es eterno," 4.

11. Chuíto y La Calandria, *Siempre peleando*, Ansonia Records ACS 1520.

12. I have used Deborah Pacini Hernández's English version of "Aquí la mujer

se daña," which, not insignificantly, circulates as a bachata in the Dominican Republic. This suggests that these patriarchal perspectives and explicit articulations about the dangers of urbanizing women transcend national boundaries. Also, these songs act as cautionary tales among men, as Pacini Hernández reminds us in *Bachata: A Social History of a Dominican Popular Music* (Philadelphia: Temple University Press, 1995), 164.

13. Included in Daniel Santos y su conjunto, *El retrato*, Seeco Records SCLP-92870.

14. Sylvia Rexach, "Es tarde ya," in *Alma adentro: Poemario de las más bellas canciones románticas de Sylvia Rexach*, collected by Tutti Umpierre (San Juan, P.R.: Ramallo Brothers, 1987), 15.

15. Leonor García, in "Déjalo que se vaya," *Cancionero*, 101, also exhorts women to let the men in their lives leave.

16. Lolita de la Colina, "Ahora no," *Cancionero*, 18.

17. Sandra Lee Bartky, *Femininity and Domination: Studies in the Phenomenology of Oppression* (New York and London: Routledge, 1990), 67–68.

18. Don Fabián, "Infortunio," *Cancionero*, 178.

19. P. Galindo and E. Ramírez, "Malagueña," *Cancionero*, 247.

20. María Greever, "Maldición Gitana," *Cancionero*, 246.

21. "Un cigarrillo, la lluvia y tú," composed by Alberto Cortez and interpreted by Tito Rodríguez in *Los grandes éxitos de Tito Rodríguez*, West Side Latino, Th Rodven, CD-117, 1987.

22. Zavala, "De héroes y heroínas," 125.

23. Madera Ferrón, "El bolero," 3, celebrates the function of the bolero as the language of love deployed by men: " que en cien años y algo más, a ritmo de bolero le hemos dicho a la mujer amada, de mil formas distintas: ¡Te quiero!"

24. "Fichas negras," composed by Osvaldo Farrés, speaks about the love relationship as a game, an act of gambling, of taking a risk. Yet the male voice accuses the woman of perversity, whereas the male played his chips with trust and honesty. This song remains popular because of its diffusion by La Sonora Matancera. The text appears in *Cancionero*, 154.

25. See "Infortunio" by Don Fabián and "Ingrata" by Rafael Roncallo, *Cancionero*, 178 and 179, respectively. The figure of woman as traitor to man's love and feelings is commonplace in many traditions of popular music.

26. René Touzet, "Conversación en tiempo de bolero," *Cancionero*, 78.

27. José Alfredo Jiménez, "Amanecí en tus brazos," *Cancionero*, 4.

28. In this context, Gilberto Santa Rosa's revival of "Yo tengo una muñeca," composed by Juanito Tremble and interpreted by Orquesta Aragón, fails to represent woman as a thinking, feeling being despite the lyrics that overtly attempt to reconstruct women in a positive light. This song, indeed, articulates an ambivalence, or rather a contradiction, between the overt attempt to rescue women from negative textualizations and the masculine desire to objectify her, structured throughout the song in the signifier of the *muñeca* (the doll), which alludes to Woman as object, as possession, and as adornment. It is not arbitrary, then, that feminist writers such as Rosario Ferré have reappropriated and deployed the figure of the doll as a major structuring device in their stories. "Yo tengo una muñeca" is included in Orquesta Aragón's music, recently redigitalized by RCA: *That Cuban Cha-cha-chá: Orquesta Aragón*, BMG Music 2446–2–RL, 1956.

29. "Flores negras" by Sergio De Carlo, *Cancionero*, 157.

30. Agustín Lara, "Arráncame la vida," *Cancionero*, 10.

31. Campos, "Poetics of the Bolero," 638.

32. Bartky, *Femininity and Domination*, 26.

33. Campos, "Poetics of the Bolero," 638.

34. "Nuestro balance," composed by C. Novarro and interpreted by Tito Rodríguez in *Los grandes éxitos de Tito Rodríguez.*

35. Octavio Paz, *El laberinto de la soledad* (Mexico City: Fondo de Cultura Económica, 1959).

36. Daniel Santos, "El que canta," *Cancionero*, 136.

37. In "Is There a Fan in the House? The Affective Sensibility of Fandom," in *The Adoring Audience: Fan Culture and Popular Media*, ed. Lisa A. Lewis (London and New York: Routledge, 1992), 54, Lawrence Grossberg defines "sensibility" as "a particular form of engagement or mode of operation" that "defines the possible relationships between texts and audiences." He argues that single texts, genres or media can't fully account for the constructing of meanings or the "structures of pleasure" that audiences experience in a particular cultural context. Thus, he proposes "sensibility" as a concept that acknowledges the particular context in which "musical texts and practices, economic and race relations, images of performers and fans, social relations, aesthetic conventions, styles of language, movement, appearance and dance, media practices, ideological commitments" come together to constitute that specific semiotic moment of the productive.

38. When the interviewee states that "amor es el pan de la vida," he is quoting from Pedro Flores's "Obsesión," a well-known bolero that attempts to define love despite its ineffability and that reaffirms the "obsessive" nature of man for woman.

39. Hélène Cixous, "The Laugh of the Medusa," in *New French Feminisms*, ed. Elaine Marks and Isabel de Courtivron (New York: Schocken Books, 1981), 245–64.

40. Campos, "Poetics of the Bolero," 638.

41. It is not arbitrary that Luis Rafael Sánchez's textualization of Daniel Santos is informed and mediated by the figure of Don Juan. Julia Kristeva, in "Don Juan, or Loving to Be Able To," in *Tales of Love*, trans. Leon S. Roudiez (New York: Columbia University Press, 1987), 191–208, associates music, eroticism, and performance in Don Juan's constant deferral of love. It is the "pure jouissance of a conqueror," that infinite "eternal return" (193) that characterizes donjuanismo as musical: "Don Giovanni is musical precisely because he has no Ego. He has no internality, but, as his roamings, his flights, his many as well as unbearable residences show him to be, he is a multiplicity, a polyphony. Don Giovanni is the harmonization of the multiple" (193).

42. Luis Rafael Sánchez, *La importancia*, 205.

43. Zavala, "De héroes y heroínas," 125.

44. Jorge A. Morales, *Baladas de vellonera y otras consideraciones* (San Juan, P.R.: Editorial Easymoving Co., 1981), 1.

Chapter Eight: Patriarchal Synecdoches

1. Composed by Billo Frometa, a Dominican composer who resided in Venezuela and was director of the band Billo's Caracas Boy, "Las muchachas" was included in the Sonora Matancera's recording celebrating its sixtieth anniversary: *Sexagésimo Aniversario de la Sonora Matancera*, Discos Peerless, MC-TV 4003-9, 1984.

2. Edgardo Rodríguez Juliá, "El veranazo en que mangaron a Junior," in *El cruce de la Bahía de Guánica* (Rio Piedras, P.R.: Editorial Cultural, 1989), 99–130.

3. Ibid., 105.

4. See Edgardo Rodríguez Juliá, "Una noche con Iris Chacón," in *Una noche con Iris Chacón* (San Juan, P.R.: Editorial Antillana, 1986), 102–49. See also Juliá's historical novel, *La noche oscura del Niño Avilés* (Rio Piedras, P.R.: Ediciones Huracán, 1984).

5. Orquesta Aragón, "Tan Sabrosona," BMG Music, 2446-2-RL, 1956.

6. See Vera Kutzinski, *Sugar's Secrets: Race and the Erotics of Cuban Nationalism* (Charlottesville: University of Virginia Press, 1993), 172.

7. Fernando Ortiz, *La música afro-cubana* (Madrid: Biblioteca Júcar, 1975), 35.

8. Enrique Fernández, "Salsa × 2," in *Currents from the Dancing River: Contemporary Latino Fiction, Nonfiction, and Poetry*, ed. Ray González (New York: Harcourt Brace and Co., 1994), 1–10.

9. Antonio Benítez Rojo's *The Repeating Island*, trans. James E. Maraniss (Durham, N.C.: Duke University Press, 1992), a postmodern perspective on the geocultural entity of the Caribbean, allegorizes this culture as polyrhythm, chaos, and carnival, ideologemes that the author concludes are "feminine": "There is something strongly feminine in this extraordinary fiesta: its flux, its diffuse sensuality, its generative force, its capacity to nourish and conserve." (29).

10. Fernández, "Salsa × 2," 1.

11. Ibid., 2.

12. Ibid., 7.

13. Fernández's feminization of Latina/o culture may be read as a cultural allegory of the male/female power relations behind "emotional labor." That is, while Latin(o) America continuously feeds the ego of the masculine United States, providing indeed for "emotional caregiving," the United States does not recognize its parasitical or dependent relationship nor rewards it accordingly. See Sandra Lee Bartky's "Feeding Egos and Tending Wounds: Deference and Disaffection in Women's Emotional Labor," in *Femininity and Domination: Studies in the Phenomenology of Oppression* (New York and London: Routledge, 1990), 99–119.

14. While Fernández considers the term *merengue* (meringue) another instance of the convergence of food and sexual pleasure in Latina/o cultures, this is not exclusive to Latinas/os. As Rosalind Coward analyzes this convergence in *Female Desires: How They Are Sought, Bought and Packaged* (New York: Grove Weidenfeld, 1985), in Anglo cultures women are referred to as sweets, which to Coward signals the function of nourishment and possession that women embody in patriarchal societies as well as in the role of "inessential luxury," with which their "labor" is also associated (91). Thus, while the language of sweets constructs the feminine in the North, in Latina/o cultures a discourse about taste and spice "contaminate" the culture of the erotic. Structurally, however, the analogy is valid, for in both cultures patriarchal language positions women as objects of cannibalism.

15. Catherine Guzmán, "Pónmelo ahí que te lo voy a partir: Sex and Violence in the Merengue," in *Popular Culture and Literature in the Hispanic World: A Symposium*, ed. Rose Minc (Gaithersburg, Md.: Hispamérica, 1981), 173–83. I mention that this is an early article because nowadays the merengues of Juan Luis Guerra have surpassed in popularity those such as "Caña brava."

16. Among other songs, see Gerardo, "Rico Suave," *Mo'Ritmo*, Interscope Records 7-91619-4, 1991; El General, "Te ves buena," *Meren-Rap*, Prime Entertainment, 3229-4-RL, 1991; "Las mujeres de San Diego," lyrics by Lucho Bermúdez and Ramón de Zubiría, *Cancionero*, 225.

17. Deborah Pacini Hernández, *Bachata: A Social History of a Dominican Popular Music* (Philadelphia: Temple University Press, 1995), 173–78.

18. Rodríguez Juliá, "El veranazo," 108.

19. Robin Roberts, "Music Videos, Performance and Resistance: Feminist Rappers," *Journal of Popular Culture* 25 (fall 1991): 149.

20. Fransheska, *Menéalo*, New York, Prime Records, 3207-4-RL, 1991. The song "Menéalo" also is included in the anthology *Meren-Rap*.

21. Ortiz, *La música afro-cubana*, 36.

22. Lisa M, "Taste the Flavor of the Latin," *Flavor of the Latin*, Sony Discos DCC 80687, 1991.

23. Sylvia Walby, *Theorizing Patriarchy* (Oxford and Cambridge: Basil Blackwell, 1990), 107.

24. Bartky, *Femininity and Domination*, 74.

25. Judith Ortiz Cofer, "So Much for Mañana," in *Terms of Survival* (Houston: Arte Público Press, 1987), 37.

26. Santi y sus Duendes, "La gordita," *Meren-Rap.*

27. Toña La Negra, "La Negrita Concepción," *Toña la Negra: La sensación jarocha*, Discos Peerless MCP 2519-7, 1991.

Chapter Nine: Singing the Gender Wars

1. See Alba Nydia Rivera Ramos, ed., *La mujer puertorriqueña: Investigaciones psicosociales* (Rio Piedras, P.R.: Editorial Edil, 1991), particularly the chapter titled "Actitudes y autopercepción de un sector de mujeres puertorriqueñas," by Rivera Ramos and José Acevedo (3–18). Also relevant are *La mujer en Puerto Rico*, ed. Yamila Azize Vargas (Rio Piedras, P.R.: Ediciones Huracán, 1987); *La mujer en la sociedad puertorriqueña*, ed. Edna Acosta Belén (Rio Piedras: Ediciones Huracán, 1980); and Margarita Ostolaza Rey, *Política sexual en Puerto Rico* (Rio Piedras, P.R.: Ediciones Huracán, 1989).

2. Rivera Ramos and Acevedo, "Actitudes," 15.

3. This most popular of boleros, "Usted," authored by Gabriel Ruiz, has been interpreted by diverse singers throughout Latin America, including Rubén Blades. The lyrics appear in Carmencita Delgado de Rizo, ed., *Cancionero: Antología* (Bogotá, Colombia: Ediciones Gamma, 1991), 399 (hereafter cited as *Cancionero*).

4. See María Herrera-Sobek, *The Mexican Corrido: A Feminist Analysis* (Bloomington: Indiana University Press, 1990), for an analysis of images of women in this form of Mexican oral tradition. Anna M. Fernández Poncela, in "La constitución del género a través de la cultura popular: Cuentos y leyendas," paper presented at the third Coloquio del Programa Interdisciplinario de Estudios de la Mujer (PIEM), at the Colegio de México, Mexico City, November 1993, arrives at similar conclusions regarding the negative textualization of women who disobey and the concomitant idealization of the figures of the mother and the virgin.

5. Sander Gilman, *Difference and Pathology: Stereotypes of Sexuality, Race and Madness* (Ithaca, N.Y.: Cornell University Press, 1985), 17–18.

6. Ibid., 22.

7. Ibid., 25.

8. See César Miguel Rondón, *El libro de la salsa: Crónica de la música del Caribe urbano* (Caracas, Venezuela: Editorial Arte, 1980), 32.

9. Quoted in John Fiske, *Understanding Popular Culture* (Boston: Unwin Hyman, 1989), 168, in his analysis of the political potentiality of cultural texts.

10. Jessica Benjamin, "The Bonds of Love: Rational Violence and Erotic Domination" in *The Future of Difference*, ed. Hester Eisenstein and Alice Jardine (New Brunswick, N.J.: Rutgers University Press, 1990), 41–70, summarizes how the process of male individuation emphasizes maintaining boundaries and stressing difference between the Self and Other, a dynamic that discursively informs rationality in the Western world and the dualist, binary oppositions that emerge regarding gender.

11. José Arteaga Rodríguez's article, "Salsa y violencia: Una aproximación sonoro-histórica," *Revista Musical Puertorriqueña* 4 (July–December 1988): 20–33, does not even allude to violence against women in salsa. Peter Manuel's historical summary of salsa, "The Soul of the Barrio: 30 Years of Salsa," *NACLA: Report on the Americas* 28 (September/October 1994): 22–26, 28–29, does acknowl-

edge the invisibility of women in this musical industry, although he concludes that salsa lyrics are "mildly machista, though they display little of the crude and blatant sexism found in reggae, calypso, and hardcore rap." It should be noted that all of Manuel's incursion into gender issues in salsa was framed within a parenthetical statement. Elsa Fernández Mirallés, in a very short journalistic article titled "La salsa, ¿en contra de la mujer?" *El nuevo día*, 7 March 1979, pp. 21, 22, is perhaps one of the first female voices to bring to the foreground the problematic lyrics of salsa regarding gender roles and women in particular.

12. See, among others, Virginia W. Cooper, "Women in Popular Music: A Quantitative Analysis of Feminine Images over Time," *Sex Roles* 13, nos. 9–10 (1985): 499–506, and Timothy E. Scheurer, "Goddesses and Golddiggers: Images of Women in Popular Music of the 1930s," *Journal of Popular Culture* 24 (summer 1990): 23–38.

13. See Robin D. G. Kelley, "Kickin' Reality, Kickin' Ballistics: Gangsta Rap and Postindustrial Los Angeles," in *Race Rebels: Culture, Politics, and the Black Working Class* (New York: The Free Press, 1994), 183–227; and Tricia Rose, "Never Trust a Big Butt and a Smile," *Camera Obscura* 23 (1991): 109–31.

14. I take this quote from Robin D. G. Kelley's unpublished version of "Kickin' Reality," p. 4.

15. bell hooks, in "Feminist Movement to End Violence," *Feminist Theory: From Margin to Center* (Boston: South End Press, 1984), 121.

16. Ibid., 117.

17. Ostolaza Rey, "*Política sexual*," 43.

18. Septeto Nacional de Ignacio Piñeiro, *Sones cubanos*, Seeco SCCA-9278, 1992.

19. Sonia López y su combo, "Castígalo," *Sonia López* PDC-8701.

20. See Daniel Santos, "Yo la mato," guaracha included in *Daniel Santos y su conjunto de sociedad*, vol. 2, Ansonia ALP 1234, and Lisa M's "Ingrato," *Flavor of the Latin*, Sony Discos DCC 80687, 1991.

21. Las Chicas del Can, *Explosivo*, Rodven Records, 2970, 1992.

22. Delgado de Rizo, ed., *Cancionero*, 126.

23. Comisión para los Asuntos de la Mujer, *Ley para la prevención e intervención con la violencia doméstica* (No. 54, 15 August 1989, San Juan, Puerto Rico), 1.

24. In the first survey on domestic violence carried out by Doris Knudson and Yolanda Díaz, the women interviewed cited these three reasons for the abuse exerted by their male spouses. See Doris Knudson, "'Que nadie se entere': La esposa maltratada en Puerto Rico," in Yamila Azize Vargas, ed., *La mujer en Puerto Rico* (Rio Piedras, P.R.: Ediciones Huracán, 1987), 148.

25. Bienvenido Benes, "La cárcel de Sing-Sing," *Cancionero*, 189. Valeria Sarmiento's documentary about machismo in Latin America, *El hombre cuando es hombre* (A man when he is a man), also poignantly portrays two interviews with convicts who had killed their wives for jealousy and for disobedience.

26. Benjamin, "The Bonds of Love," 49.

27. This term is inflected by Gloria Anzaldúa's coinage of "linguistic terrorism" to refer to the ways in which Latina women are silenced not only by social institutions such as schools and government but also by the patriarchy in Mexican culture. See "How to Tame a Wild Tongue" in *Borderlands/La Frontera* (San Francisco: Spinsters/Aunt Lute, 1987): 53–64.

28. Rivera Ramos and Acevedo, "Actitudes," 13–16. The authors also explain this gap in perception as a result of men's and women's internalizing the insularist myth about Puerto Ricans.

29. El Gran Combo de Puerto Rico, "Oprobio," *Aquí no se sienta nadie*, Combo, Rico Record Productions RCSLP 2013, 1979.

30. Héctor Lavoe, "Bandolera," *Comedia*, Fania Records JM-00522, 1978.

31. According to Scheurer in "Goddesses and Golddiggers," 23–38, the image of the golddigger had not emerged before the 1930s: "the golddigger was something new, something slightly shocking, and something probably only the Depression could have created" (32).

32. Kelley, "Kickin' Reality," 217.

33. This summary is based on Javier Costa Clavell's documentation of Galician legends in *Bandolerismo, Romerías y jergas gallegas* (La Coruña, Spain: Editorial La Voz de Galicia, 1980). See particularly "Pepa A Loba, figura cumbre del bandolerismo gallego" (29–43).

34. "El bandido robado," a poem about a bandit who kills himself because of unrequited love, presents the figure of the male bandit in an ironic twist of fate in which he becomes the victim of an affective assault by the death of his wife. Thus, the woman becomes the bandit of his love: "La compañera amorosa / la del bandolero esposa, / la mujer de su ilusión, al ladrón de alma bravía / le había robado un día, / por lo visto, el corazón!" [The love companion / wife of the bandit / the woman of his illusion / had stolen one day from the courageous thief, even his heart!], in Constancio Bernaldo de Quiros y Pérez and Luis Ardila, *El bandolerismo andaluz* (Madrid: Ediciones Turner, 1973), 213–14.

35. Pedro Conga y su Orquesta Internacional, "Ladrona de amor," *No te quites la ropa*, Discos Musart CMPI 8008; Rubén Blades, "Ella se esconde," *Caminando*, Sony Records International DCC 80593, 1991. Also see "Ladrona de besos," a bolero composed by Ramón Inclán, in *Siglo de bolero* (Mexico City: EDUSA), 57.

36. Son de Azúcar, "Devoradora," *Más dulce!*, Sony Discos DIC-80681, 1991. Copyright © 1991 Sony/ATV Music Publishing LLC.

37. Milly y los vecinos, "Ese hombre," *14 Grandes Exitos Originales*, Capital Records H4F-42486, 1991.

38. La India, "Ese hombre," in *Dicen que soy*, Sony Records CDZ-81373, 1994. La India appeared performing this song as the closing cut in the television series *New York Undercover*.

39. Celia Cruz and Johnny Pacheco, "Las divorciadas," *De nuevo*, Música Latina Internacional, Vaya Records 4XT JMVS-106, 1985. See also Celia Cruz, "Que le den candela," in *Irrepetible*, Sony Discos CDZ-81452, 1994.

40. Lisa M and Santy y sus Duendes, "Tu Pum Pum," *Meren-Rap*, Prime Entertainment, 3229-4-RL, 1991.

41. El Gran Combo de Puerto Rico, "Psicología," *Treinta años de sabor: Gracias!*, Combo Records RCSA-2090, 1992.

42. Sandra Lee Bartky, "Foucault, Femininity, and the Modernization of Patriarchal Power," in *Femininity and Domination: Studies in the Phenomenology of Oppression* (New York and London: Routledge, 1990), 63–82.

43. Ibid., 78.

44. Ibid., 79.

45. Ibid., 80.

Chapter Ten: Singing Female Subjectivities

1. See Karen E. Petersen, "An Investigation into Women-Identified Music in the United States," in *Women and Music in Cross-Cultural Perspective*, ed. Ellen Koskoff (Urbana and Chicago: University of Illinois Press, 1989), 203–12. Also see Huyssen, *After the Great Divide: Modernism, Mass Culture, Postmodernism* (Bloomington and Indianapolis: Indiana University Press, 1986), 62.

2. See Cristóbal Díaz Ayala, *Música cubana, del Areyto a la Nueva Trova*, 2nd

ed. (San Juan, P.R.: Editorial Cubanacán, 1981); Pedro Malavet Vega, *La vellonera está directa: Felipe Rodríguez (La Voz) y los años 50*, 3rd ed. (Rio Piedras, P.R.: Ediciones Huracán, 1987), and *Del bolero a la Nueva Canción* (Ponce, P.R.: Editora Corripio, 1988); *Un siglo de bolero* [author unknown] (Mexico: EDUSA, n.d.).

3. See Díaz Ayala, *Música cubana*, 152–54, who dedicates a two-page section to "las compositoras cubanas." In addition to the Lecuona women (Ernestina, 1882–1951, and Margarita), the prominence of women composers in the development of the Cuban guajira and the *son* is evidenced by the compositions of Juana González, Coralia López, July Mendoza, Sara N. Rodríguez, and Cora Sánchez Agramonte. The role of women composers during the 1940s and 1950s was also central to the international popularity of Cuban music. For instance, Díaz Ayala mentions Cristina Saladriga's "Ojos malvados" and "Añorada Cuba," Trini Márquez's "Eres mi amor," Ela O'Farrill's "Ni llorar puedo llorar," and others. He closes this section with a reference to Concha Valdés Mirando, who, according to the author, "sorprende con sus atrevidas canciones" [surprises us with her daring compositions] and whose selected titles during the 1970s include "La mitad," "Las cosas buenas de la vida," "Tápame contigo," and "Orgasmo."

4. Umberto Valverde and Rafael Quintero, *Abran paso: Historia de las orquestas femeninas de Cali* (Cali, Colombia: Universidad del Valle, 1995), 37–49.

5. Rayda Cotto, "La mujer negra en la música folklórica y popular en Puerto Rico," *Claridad*, 25 September–1 October 1992, 25.

6. For instance, Olga Tañón received two major Lo Nuestro Awards for 1995, and La India appeared in Banco Popular's musical video for 1995, "Somos un solo pueblo." Albita, whose CD *No se parece a nada* (Sony Music Entertainment, EK66966, 1995) is fast outselling her previous recording, was invited to perform at the National Council of La Raza's annual fund-raising event. Because of her homo-erotic and androgynous lyrics and performance, she has been hailed by Madonna and others as a most promising figure in the Latin scene.

7. Taken from *Quince éxitos de Toña La Negra: Versiones originales*, RCA/Ariola Internacional, CSC-1270, 1986. The song, composed by Andrés Eloy Blanco, dates back to 1946.

8. Quoted from Coqui Santaliz, "Bolero de mujer," *Claridad*, 16–22 April 1993, 21. This article is a positive tribute to those women composers of the bolero in Puerto Rico who have remained truly invisible in our musical histories. Santaliz names these composers—Sylvia Rexach, Puchi Balseiro, Ketty Cabán, Karmen Mercado, Alyce Gracia, and María Alicea de Sharrón—as well as contemporary composers such as Sylvia Domenech, Rayda Cotto, Zoraida Santiago, Nilda Torres Feliciano, and Ivette Pacheco, among others, as an initial attempt to document their agency in the development of the bolero in Puerto Rico. She rightly asserts that "la cantera de mujeres que componen es interminable, mas no se conocen como se merecen" [the numerous women who compose is endless, yet they are not known as they should be]. While this article represents an effort in the right direction, its writing tends to essentialize women's compositions uniquely as a product of women's location within the affective, sentimental modes. Themes of solitude, passion, and pain consistently recur as markers of feminine modes of composition.

9. Historical information culled from Malavet Vega, *La vellonera está directa*, 196, and from Díaz Ayala, *Música cubana*, 228–57.

10. See Díaz Ayala, *Música cubana*, 274, and Jon Pareles, "La Lupe, a Singer, Is Dead at 53; Known as 'Queen of Latin Soul,'" *New York Times* Obituaries, 7 March 1992.

11. Pareles, "La Lupe," 11.

12. Díaz Ayala, *Música cubana*, 274.

13. Ibid., 275.

14. César Miguel Rondón, *El libro de la salsa: Crónica de la música del Caribe urbano* (Caracas, Venezula: Editorial Arte, 1980), 208.

15. Ibid., 209.

16. Ibid., 46.

17. Ibid., 45, 47.

18. Ibid., 47.

19. See Héctor Monclova Vázquez, "La Lupe más allá del mismo cuento," *Claridad*, 23–29 September 1994, 24, documenting the theatrical production of La Lupe's life and works. Titled *La Lupe vuelve*, it was produced, written, and scripted by Tite Curet Alonso and Zora Moreno. The script integrates La Lupe's songs in this "espectáculo biografía" that was shown on 23–24 September 1994. Zora Moreno, who performed as La Lupe, also interpreted the singer in Julio Axel Landrón's theatrical piece *Carnaval y pasión*.

20. "La Tirana," *La Lupe: The Best*, Sony Discos CDZ-81108, 1993. Also by La Lupe: *One of a Kind/Unica en su clase*, Tico Records TSLP-1416, 1977, and *La Lupe: En algo nuevo*, Música Latina Internacional JMTS-1438, 1980; with Tito Puente, *Tito Puente and La Lupe: La Pareja*, Tico Records JMTS-1430, 1978.

21. Catalino Curet Alonso, better known as El Tite Curet, is one of the most important composers of salsa music in Puerto Rico. His songs range from traditional love ballads to feminist rewritings of Puerto Rican history, as in "Anacaona," and to denouncements of U.S. colonialism, as in "Tiburón." For a summary of El Tite's importance in the development of salsa, see Rondón, *El libro de la salsa*, 211–13, 221–23.

22. In *La Lupe: The Best*.

23. "Canta bajo," composed by La Lupe and Pat Patric, with arrangements by Marty Sheller, in *La Lupe: One of a Kind*.

24. "Dueña del cantar," in *La Lupe: One of a Kind*.

Part Four: Así Somos, Así Son
Listening to the Listeners

1. El Gran Combo de Puerto Rico, *Aquí no se sienta nadie*, Combo Records RCLSP-2013, 1979.

2. Observation by a Puerto Rican man interviewed for this study.

3. Jean Franco, "What's Left of the Intelligentsia? The Uncertain Future of the Printed Word," *NACLA* 28 (September–October 1994): 21. See also José-Luis González, *El país de cuatro pisos y otros ensayos* (Rio Piedras: Ediciones Huracán, 1983), p.21, documenting the emerging centrality of popular culture, mass culture, and orality in the configuration of Puerto Rican cultural identity.

4. For John Fiske, "productive pleasure" is that "pleasure which results from [a] mix of productivity, relevance, and functionality, which is to say that the meanings I make from a text are pleasurable when I feel that they are my meanings and that they relate to my everyday life in a practical, direct way" (*Understanding Popular Culture* [Boston: Unwin Hyman, 1989]), 57.

5. Lawrence Grossberg, "Is There a Fan in the House? The Affective Sensibility of Fandom," in *The Adoring Audience: Fan Culture and Popular Media*, ed. Lisa A. Lewis (London and New York: Routledge, 1992), 50–65.

6. Jon Cruz and Justin Lewis, eds., *Viewing, Reading, Listening: Audiences and Cultural Reception* (Boulder, Colo.: Westview Press, 1994), 15. This anthology of essays is an important contribution to audience research not only for the theoretical proposals found throughout but also because these studies have integrated the voices of diverse audiences into their work.

7. Andreas Huyssen, "Mass Culture as Woman: Modernism's Other," in *After the Great Divide: Modernism, Mass Culture, Postmodernism* (Bloomington and Indianapolis: Indiana University Press, 1986), 62.

8. The constellation I refer to here is constituted by what Myriam Díaz-Diocarets describes as the intersection "of the extratextual with the textual: . . . there is a critical locus of an encounter among the I, the social being, the writing subject, and the subject of the utterance" (quoted by Iris M. Zavala, in "Las formas y funciones de una teoría crítica feminista: Feminismo dialógico," in *Breve historia feminista de la literatura española [en lengua castellana]* [Barcelona: Anthropos; San Juan: Editorial de la Universidad de Puerto Rico, 1993], 74).

9. Tania Modleski, "Femininity as Mas(s)querade," in *Feminism without Women: Culture and Criticism in a "Postfeminist" Age* (New York: Routledge, 1991), 32.

10. Fiske, *Understanding Popular Culture*, 121–22. See also Pierre Bourdieu's previous discussion of the "disgust at the facile" in *Distinction: A Social Critique of the Judgement of Taste* (Cambridge, Mass.: Harvard University Press, 1984), 486–88.

Chapter Eleven: Así Son: Constructing Woman

1. Pedro Malavet Vega, *La vellonera está directa: Felipe Rodríguez (La Voz) y los años 50*, 3rd ed. (Rio Piedras, P.R.: Ediciones Huracán, 1987), 393–409.

2. Ana Lydia Vega and Carmen Lugo Filippi, "Cuatro selecciones por una peseta," in *Vírgenes y mártires*, 127–37.

3. Mayra Muñoz Vázquez, "Matrimonio y divorcio en Puerto Rico," in *La mujer en la sociedad puertorriqueña*, ed. Edna Acosta-Belén (Rio Piedras, P.R.: Ediciones Huracán, 1980), 211–25. In a follow-up article, "La experiencia del divorcio desde la perspectiva de un grupo de mujeres puertorriqueñas," in *La mujer en Puerto Rico: Ensayos de investigación*, ed. Yamila Azize Vargas (Rio Piedras, P.R.: Ediciones Huracán, 1987), 155–70, Muñoz Vázquez argues that instead of defining divorce as the "fracaso de la pareja" [the failure of the couple], it needs to be analyzed as "una forma de resistencia o protesta usada principalmente por las mujeres para expresarse inconscientemente en contra de las condiciones nocivas u opresivas en su vida" [a form of resistance or protest principally used by women to express themselves, unconsciously, against the dangerous or oppressive conditions of their lives] (160). As the author predicted in her 1980 article, the rate of divorce did indeed rise, from about 40 percent to almost 50 percent by 1987.

4. Vega and Lugo Filippi, "Cuatro selecciones," 132, 134.

5. Ibid., 133, 135.

6. Adorno, "On Popular Music," in *Studies in Philosophy and Social Science*, vol. 9 (New York: Institute for Social Research, 1941), 42.

7. Vega and Lugo Filippi, "Cuatro selecciones," 137.

8. For a recent analysis of ideology, political status, and mass media in Puerto Rico, see Federico Subervi-Vélez and Nitza M. Hernández-López, "Mass Media in Puerto Rico" (with the assistance of Aline Frambes-Buxeda), *Centro de Estudios Puertorriqueños Bulletin* 3 (winter 1990–91): 17–31.

9. Vega and Lugo Filippi, "Cuatro selecciones," 129.

10. Cathy Schwichtenberg, "Reconceptualizing Gender: New Sites for Feminist Audience Research," in *Viewing, Reading, Listening: Audiences and Cultural Reception*, ed. Jon Cruz and Justin Lewis (Boulder, Colo.: Westview Press, 1994), 171.

11. Manthia Diawara et al., "A Symposium on Popular Culture and Political Correctness," *Social Text* 36 (fall 1993): 1–39.

12. John Fiske, *Understanding Popular Culture* (Boston: Unwin Hyman, 1989), 168.

13. I want to thank Lisa Quiroga and Wilson Valentín for serving as interviewers in this project. Lisa facilitated the interviews with UM Latinas, and Wilson served as the interviewer for all the Latino subjects. This was done to avoid as much as possible the influence of a Latina on the male responses as well as that of a professor on those of the female students. I did, however, lead all of the interviews with the Detroit women, none of whom knew about me nor about the gender focus of the project. All subjects were told that it was an interview about salsa music.

The interview format consisted of a series of initial short questions regarding age, place of birth, number of years in the United States, favorite salsa groups, and frequency of dancing. The rest of the interview consisted of questions about the two songs analyzed here, "Cuando fuiste mujer" and "Así son." The same general and open-ended questions regarding both songs were asked of each interviewee. Depending on the listener's degree of engagement with the song, some responses were very detailed and lengthy; others were brief and to the point.

14. Grossberg, in "Is There a Fan in the House? The Affective Sensibility of Fandom," in *The Audience: Fan Culture and Popular Media*, ed. Lisa A. Lewis (London and New York: Routledge, 1992), identifies this "ideology of authenticity" among rock and roll fans who distinguish between "authentic and co-opted rock" (62).

15. Janice Radway, "Interpretive Communities and Variable Literacies: The Function of Romance Reading," in *Rethinking Popular Culture: Contemporary Perspectives in Cultural Studies*, ed. Chandra Mukerji and Michael Schudson (Los Angeles and Berkeley: University of California Press, 1991), 465–86. Originally published in *Daedalus* 113 (summer 1974), 3.

16. Tania Modleski, "Some Functions of Feminist Criticism; Or, the Scandal of the Mute Body," in *Feminism without Women: Culture and Criticism in a "Postfeminist" Age* (New York: Routledge, 1991), 38.

17. Here I paraphrase Iris M. Zavala's definition of symbolic economy in "Las formas y funciones de una teoría crítica feminista. Feminismo dialógico," in *Breve historia feminista de la literatura española (en lengua castellana)* (Barcelona: Anthropos; San Juan: Editorial de la Universidad de Puerto Rico, 1993), 54.

18. Willie Colón, "Cuando fuiste mujer," in *Legal Alien/Top Secrets*, WAC Productions JM655, 1989.

19. Hélène Cixous, "The Laugh of the Medusa," in *New French Feminisms*, ed. Elaine Marks and Isabel de Courtivron (New York: Schocken Books, 1981) 249.

20. One Puerto Rican male student commented that "nuestra educación nos lleva a entender y prestar atención a los mensajes" [our education allows us to understand and to pay attention to the messages], and the Salvadoran interviewee asserted that "para mí estar en este país [United States] ha sido una escuela; he aprendido a compartir con mi esposa, mis hijos" [for me, being in this country has been a process of schooling; I have learned to share with my wife, my children].

21. In reference to "Cuando fuiste mujer," a Latino observed the following: "Aunque ella se enamorara de otro hombre, él está insinuando que se acuerde de él cuando la hizo mujer, dependiendo, ella puede tener un recuerdo grato o malo. Si él la hizo mujer con amor y cariño, el recuerdo es grato. Si él la hizo mujer en contra de su voluntad, lo recordará mal" [Even if she falls in love with another man, he insinuates that she should remember him when he made her a woman, depending on whether she has a pleasant or a negative memory. If he made her a woman with love and warmth, the memory is pleasant. If he made her a woman against her will, then she will remember him badly]. It is noticeable that the language of the lyrics, "fuiste mujer," contaminates these observations thoroughly.

22. Another respondent from Detroit similarly substituted the dominant male perspective with a female one: "es romántica porque está diciendo las cosas que una mujer piensa cuando está en desarrollo, está creciendo . . . está detallando las cosas que una mujer piensa al desarrollarse como mujer, en la experiencia, en el futuro de ella." [this is a romantic (song) because it is expressing what a woman thinks when she is developing, growing up . . . it is detailing what a woman thinks as she develops, in experiences, in her own future].

23. See Judith Ortiz Cofer, "Quinceañera," in *Silent Dancing* (Houston: Arte Público Press, 1990), 132–40. See also the poem of the same title both in *Silent Dancing*, 47, and in *Terms of Survival* (Houston: Arte Público Press, 1987), 9.

Chapter Twelve: Así Somos: Rewriting Patriarchy

1. Angela McRobbie and Jenny Garber, "Girls and Subcultures," in *Resistance through Rituals: Youth Subcultures in Post-War Britain*, ed. Stuart Hall and Tony Jefferson (London: Hutchinson, 1976), 216.

2. I have included the term *countervaluation*, proposed by José Limón and referred to by Janice Radway, *Reading the Romance: Women, Patriarchy, and Popular Literature* (Chapel Hill: University of North Carolina Press, 1984), 211–12, as "a process of inversion whereby the original socioeconomic limitations and devaluations of a subordinate group are first addressed by the folkloric performance and then transformed within or by it into something of value to the group. If the process is successful, Limón maintains, the performace contests by supplementation." Radway equates this with the function of romance reading for the women in her study, a fictional genre that "supplements the avenues traditionally open to women for emotional gratification by supplying them vicariously with the attention and nurturance they do not get enough of in the round of day-to-day existence."

3. Henry A. Giroux and Roger I. Simon, "Popular Culture as a Pedagogy of Pleasure and Meaning: Decolonizing the Body," in Henry A. Giroux, *Border Crossings: Cultural Workers and the Politics of Education* (New York: Routledge, 1993), 192, discuss the "persuasive" as "the ways in which hegemony functions on the terrain of popular culture through a variety of pedagogical processes that work not only to secure dominant interests but to offer as well the possibility of a politics of resistance and social transformation." In this context they develop the "related categories of consent, investment, ideology, and pleasure."

4. I follow Giroux and Simon's differentiation between two forms of consent: first, the orthodox version, which refers to the "ways in which the dominant logic is imposed on subordinated groups through the mechanizations of the culture industry." In the revisionist radical version, consent "is defined through more active forms of complicity in that subordinated groups are now viewed as partly negotiating their adaptation and place within the dominant culture" (193).

5. This observation was expressed by a Mexican-American woman, showing that although she does not identify with salsa as her own national tradition, she nonetheless is able to identify the analogous forms of Latin American patriarchy and their articulation in both Afro-Caribbean and Mexican songs.

6. It is essential to add that this song evoked visually the image of men at a bar listening to music and drinking their sorrows away. This was clear not only in the responses of the Puerto Rican man whose father owned a restaurant but also among three middle- and upper-class Latinas who associated these icons and cultural rituals with machismo. The class-based implications here are most poignant if indeed these Latinas associate machismo only with the social spaces of the working class or proletariat.

7. Giroux and Simon, "Popular Culture," 189.
8. Ibid., 190.
9. Ibid.

Afterword

1. For a discussion of this concept, see G. Tuchman, et al., eds. *Hearth and Home: Images of Women in the Mass Media* (New York: Oxford University Press), 1988. Also see Dominic Strinati, *An Introduction to Theories of Popular Culture* (London and New York: Routledge, 1995), 178–89.

2. Wild Mango, *Made in Mango,* Redwood Records RR9402CD, 1994.

3. Olga Tañón, *Siente el amor,* WEA Latina W2-97881-2, 1994. See also Celia Cruz, *Irrepetible,* RMM Records CDZ-81452, 1994.

4. Willie Colón, *Hecho en Puerto Rico,* Sony Discos CDZ-81040, 1993.

5. Wilson Valentín, "Memorializing Héctor Lavoe: Cultural Heroes and Popular Music in the Puerto Rican Community." Paper presented at the Second Puerto Rican Studies Association Conference, San Juan, September 26–29, 1996.

6. Néstor García Canclini, *Hybrid Cultures: Strategies for Entering and Leaving Modernity,* trans. Christopher L. Chiappari and Silvia L. López (Minneapolis: University of Minnesota Press, 1995), 229.

7. Ibid., 62.

8. Banco Popular de Puerto Rico, the major Puerto Rican–owned financial institution on the island, has been an important sponsor and mediator of Puerto Rican culture, particularly of musical performances. It has created a tradition of producing music videos for each Christmas season.

9. Sara del Valle, "Salsa Sinfónica: Un concierto balanceado," *Claridad,* 7–13 June 1996, 30.

10. Jeremy Marre and Hannah Charlton, *Beats of the Heart: Popular Music of the World* (London: Pluto Press, 1985), 80.

11. Néstor García Canclini, *Hybrid Cultures,* 93.

12. Jesús Martín Barbero, *Communication, Culture and Hegemony: From the Media to Mediations,* trans. Elizabeth Fox and Robert A. White (London: Sage Publications, 1993), 222–23.

Continued from page iv

"Caña Brava" by Toño Abreu. Copyright © 1960 by Peer International Corporation. Copyright Renewed. International Copyright Secured. Used by Permission.

"El Sancocho Prieto" by Luis Alberti. Copyright © 1955 by Peer International Corporation. Copyright Renewed. International Copyright Secured. Used by Permission.

"Usted" by Gabriel Ruiz & José Antonio Zorrilla. Copyright © 1951 by Promotora Hispano Americana de Música S.A. Administered by Peer International Corporation. Copyright Renewed. International Copyright Secured. Used by Permission.

"Oprobio" by Rafael Hernández. Copyright © 1931 by Peer International Corporation. Copyright Renewed. International Copyright Secured. Used by Permission.

"La Negrita Concepción" by Cuates Castilla. Copyright © 1943 by Promotora Hispano Americana de Música S.A. Administered by Peer International Corporation. Copyright Renewed. International Copyright Secured. Used by Permission.

"Angelitos Negros" by Andrés Eloy Blanco & Manuel Alvarez Maciste. Copyright © 1946 by Editorial Mexicana de Música Internacional S.A. Administered by Peer International Corporation. Copyright Renewed. International Copyright Secured. Used by Permission.

"Se Fue" by Pedro Flores. Copyright © 1941 by Peer International Corporation. Copyright Renewed. International Copyright Secured. Used by Permission.

"Malagueña Salerosa" by Galindo & Ramírez, also known as La Malagueña. Copyright © 1947 by Promotora Hispano Americana de Música S.A. Administered by Peer International Corporation. Copyright Renewed. International Copyright Secured. Used by Permission.

"Es Tarde Ya" by Sylvia Rexach. Copyright © 1959 by Southern Music Publishing Co. Inc. Copyright Renewed. International Copyright Secured. Used by Permission.

"Flores Negras" by Sergio de Karlo. Copyright © 1937 by Peer International Corporation. Copyright Renewed. International Copyright Secured. Used by Permission.

"Arráncame la Vida" by Agustín Lara. Copyright © 1934 by Peer International Corporation. Copyright Renewed. International Copyright Secured. Used by Permission.

"Las Muchachas" by Billo Frometa. Copyright © 1958 by Peer International Corporation. Copyright Renewed. International Copyright Secured. Used by Permission.

"Tan Sabrosona" by Rafael Lay & Richard Ergües. Copyright © 1956 by Peer International Corporation. Copyright Renewed. International Copyright Secured. Used by Permission.

"El Negrito del Batey" by Medardo Guzmán. Copyright © 1955 by Peer International Corporation. Copyright Renewed. International Copyright Secured. Used by Permission.

"Yo la Mato" by Pedro Flores. Copyright © 1967 by Peer International Corporation. Copyright Renewed. International Copyright Secured. Used by Permission.

"El Castigador" by Ignacio Pineiro. Copyright © 1933 by Peer International Corporation. Copyright Renewed. International Copyright Secured. Used by Permission.

"La Cárcel de Sing Sing" by Bienvenido Benes, also known as Historia de Sing Sing. Copyright © 1967 by Peer International Corporation. Copyright Renewed. International Copyright Secured. Used by Permission.

"Bandolera" by C. Víctor Cavalli. Copyright © 1950 by Promotora Hispano Americana de Música S.A. Copyright Renewed. Administered by Peer International Corporation. International Copyright Secured. Used by Permission.

"Cuando Fuiste Mujer" by Vilma Planas & Héctor Garrido. Copyright © 1981 by Peer International Corporation. International Copyright Secured. Used by Permission.

Victor Hernandez Cruz's poem "descarga en cueros," published in *Snaps* (Random House/Vintage Books, 1969), is reprinted by permission of the author.

Index of Songs and Recordings

✛

General Index

✠

Abreu, Toño, 148

Acosta, Leonardo, 34, 78, 114, 253n 7

Adorno, Theodor, 84, 90–91, 94, 103, 190, 196, 210, 261n 14

Afro-Puerto Rican music. *See* music

Aguirre Jr., Adalberto, xiv

AIDS: in salsa music, 88–89

Alejandro, Chico, 170

Alfonso X the Wise, 8

Almodóvar, Pedro, 181

Alonso, Manuel A., 9–10, 11, 17, 44, 45

Althusser, 111

Anzaldúa, Gloria, 270n 27

appropriation, by listeners, 219, 233; cross–cultural, xvii, 115; of plena, 33

Arnaz, Desi, 107, 172

Arteaga Rodríguez, José, 265n 10

articulation, 77, 241. *See also* appropriation, resemanticization

Astol, Félix, 14

audience research, 185–238; need for, xviii–xix, 187–90, 243–45

authenticity, 68, 71, 93, 114, 200

bachata, xvii, 104, 148

bandolera, 161, 163–65, 193, 229, 235

Barbero, Jesús Martín, 244

Bakhtin, 86, 99, 101

ballad, romantic, 95

Barretto, Ray, 80, 82

Barrio Obrero, 37, 139

Barthes, Roland, 60

Bartky, Sandra Lee, 135, 151, 169

bastonero, 11

Bauzá, Mario, 79

Beach Boys, The, 70, 142–43

Beatles, The, 70, 115

Bécquer, Gustavo Adolfo, 126

Beethoven, Ludwig van, 141

Bell, Monna, 133

Beltrán Ruiz, Pablo, 74

Benítez, Lucecita, 59, 60

Benítez Rojo, Antonio, xvi, 146

Billboard, 108

blacks: exclusion of, 9, 13–14, 28; in Puerto Rican literature, 56; on television, 35. *See also* music: Afro-Puerto Rican

Blades, Rubén, 32, 65, 68, 80, 81, 82, 83, 85, 93, 165, 223; as crossover, 108–116; listeners' preferences to, 199–201; lyrics by, 86–88

Blanco, Andrés Eloy, 175

Blanco, José, 42

Blanco, Tomás, 4, 6, 27, 45, 47, 50, 53, 147; writings by, 38–44

blues, 115

Bobbitt, Lorena, 168

bolero, xvi, 74, 76, 162, 180, 213, 227, 240; gendering in the, 138–41; in Puerto Rican fiction, 193–95; male responses to, 136–38; origins of, 126; patriarchal discourse in, 128–30, 154; rancheros, 133; reception of, 125; rewritings of, xviii, 138–41; and social classes, 139; and salsa erótica, 136–37; and transnationalism, 127; versus guarachas, 101–102, 177; women composers of, 130–32, 133. *See also* Santos, Daniel

bomba, 9, 27, 59, 81

bombardino, 13

Boone, Pat, 115

Boston Pops Orchestra, The, 242

Bourdieu, Pierre, 237

Brau, Salvador, 4, 23, 44, 45, 50; writings, 10–16

brujería, 51; in women-authored boleros, 132

Butler, Judith, 7
Byrne, David, 66, 115

Cabán Vale, Antonio. *See* Topo, El
Cabrera Infante, Guillermo, 79, 81, 92
Cachán, Manuel, 112
Calderón, Vitín, 24, 25
Callejo, Fernando, 13
calypso, 28
Campos, René, 133, 135, 137
capitalism: in Puerto Rico, 5, 29, 33, 158
carpe diem, 132
Carpentier, Alejo, 80
Carreta, La, 129
Carter, Jimmy, 25
Castilla, Cuates, 152
Castillo, Debra, 51, 56
Castro, Fidel, 79, 240
catholicism, 38
Caughie, Pamela, 122
Certeau, Michel de, 37
Chacón, Iris, 59, 60
Chambers, Iaian, 95, 99
Chantelle, 123
Chicago (musical group), 71
Chicano movement, 176
Chicas del Can, Las, 99, 123, 150, 160, 173
Chuíto el de Bayamón, 130
cimarrones, 82, 84, 141, 242
Cixous, Hélène, 137, 206
Claridad, 72
Clark, John, 28
class: conflict in Puerto Rico, 54; and gender, 42–44; and musical preferences, 199, 204, 230, 236. *See also* salsa: and class
clave, 89–90
Club Palladium, 79–80
Cocolía, 13, 258n 2
cocolo, 56, 85; versus rockero, 69–73
Colina, Lolita de la, 131
Colón, Willie, xviii, 65, 67, 68, 80, 82, 90, 94, 95, 99, 115, 116, 173, 193, 196, 200, 203, 204, 220; gender in, 205–209; listeners' responses to, 210–18; repertoire of, 240–41; song by, 88–89
colonial alienation, 58
colonialism: in Puerto Rico, 5–6, 18–20, 176, 196
combo, the, 90
Concepción, César, 33
Conga, Pedro, 165
consent, 222, 223, 228, 276n 4
convivencia, 5, 6

Cordero, Federico A., 15
Cortez, Alberto, 132
Cortijo, Rafael, 34, 36, 60, 92, 108; in Puerto Rican literature, 34–37; y su Combo, 35–37, 59, 111, 175
corridos, Mexican, 29, 82
countervaluation, 219, 233, 276n 2
country-dance, European, 11
courtly love, 130
creole: music, xvi; woman, 10
Crossover Dreams, 109
crossover music, xvii, 108–117; redefining, 116
Cruz, Celia, xii, 82, 95, 123, 142, 167, 175, 179, 242; feminism in, 173–74; repertoire of, 240–41
"Cuatro selecciones por una peseta," 188, 193–96
Cuba, 79–81, 105–108
Cubop, 79
cultural difference, 68, 76, 105–108
cultural hybridity, 68
cultural nationalism in Puerto Rico, 4
cultural studies, 78, 188–89, 227
Curet Alonso, Catalino "Tite," 77, 178, 179, 181, 182

dances: in Puerto Rico, 9
dancing: and gender roles, 96–99; social meanings of, 95–103, 104
danza, xvi, 18, 27, 241, 250n 1; feminization of, 16–20; historical development of, 8–26; as political music, 8, 20–24; representations of, 10; syncretism in, 14; transculturation of, 11–15
Danzón (film), 102–103
danzón, Cuban, 8, 126
Darío, Rubén, 126, 139
D'Castro, Alex, 72
décimas jíbaras, 240. *See also* jíbaro music
De León, Oscar, 80, 111
"Descarga en cueros," 83
descargas (jamming), 83
desclasamiento, 34
desire, 52, 127, 208; female, 208–209; intercultural, 67, 107–108, 116, 146; mimetic, 48; triangular, 50
dialogism: in salsa, 86–89
diaspora, Puerto Rican, 188
Díaz, Joe, 253n 13
Díaz Ayala, Cristóbal, 107, 178
Díaz Díaz, Edgardo, xviii, 11, 96–97
Díaz Quiñones, Arcadio, 5, 6, 38

Paz, Octavio, 136
Pedreira, Antonio, 4, 6, 38, 45, 50; writings of, 17–21
Pepa La Loba, 164–65
Peregrino, María Antonia, 175
Pérez Prado, Dámaso, 65, 67, 79, 175
Pérez-Rolón, Jorge, 33
performance: and gender, 173–74; by La Lupe, 178; and sexual politics, 181–82
Petrarch, 134
phallologocentrism, 137, 206
Piñeiro, Ignacio, 80, 92, 159, 161
Planas, Vilma, 206
plebeyismo, 52, 60
plena, xvi, 7, 27–44, 81, 82, 111; commercialization of, 33 (see also appropriation, resemanticization); contents, 29; and the danza, 27, 41; feminization of, 27, 41; instrumentation, 30; lyrics, 49–50; marginalization of, 27; origins of, 27, 29; in Puerto Rican literature, 34–38, 49; racialization of, 27, 41; and salsa music, 37; structure, 29; syncretism with mambo, 34; term, 27–28; and transnationalism, 30; versification, 29
Poison, 69
Ponce, xvi, 3, 6, 24, 28
popular culture: scholarship on, xviii, 188–89; in academia, xi, xv, xix; and pedagogy, xiv
Popular Democratic Party, 31
positivism, 10, 15–16
Postmodernism: in Puerto Rican literature, 5; and salsa music, 241–42
preciosismo, 126
prejudice, racial, 38–44
Presley, Elvis, 115
Pretto, Frank, 67
primitivism, 105, 157
productive moment, xviii, 231, 236
productive pleasure, 188, 195, 197, 226, 273n 4
Puente, Tito, 65, 79, 95, 113, 179
Puerto Rican Autonomist Party, 24
Puerto Rican literature, 3–7, 45–61; in U.S., 6. See also Hernández Cruz, Víctor; Ferré, Rosario; Filippi, Carmen Lugo; Sánchez, Luis Rafael; Vega, Ana Lydia
Puerto Rican Symphony Orchestra, 241
Puerto Rico, gendering of, 19

Queen, 69
Queen Latifah, 149
Quintero, Rafael, 172–73, 247n 3

Quintero Rivera, Angel, 13, 14, 16, 23, 54, 82, 242; works by, 83–91
Quiñones, Samuel R., 8

race: improving, 54; and interracial desire, 43; in Mexico, 153; in Puerto Rico, 38–44; "race" music, 32
racialization: of women, xvi, 45–61
racism: in Puerto Rico, 38–44, 53; treatment of in literature, 53; in Tomás Blanco's works, 38–40
radio, 94; in Puerto Rico, 33
Radway, Janice, 203, 233
Ramírez, Paco, 60
Ramos Otero, Manuel, 257n 30
ranchera, 76, 194, 195, 230
Randel, Don Michael, 108, 113, 116, 201
rap: African-American, 34, 157, 164; Latino, xvii, 148, 157
rappers, African-American women, 149
rape, 43
Ratt, 69
recording industry, U.S., 32
repetition, 59, 159–60; as eroticization, 59; types of, 91–92, 261n 20
resemanticization, 33. See also appropriation, articulation
Reynold, Franz, 247n 1
Rexach, Sylvia, 130–31
rhythm: and cultural identity, 99
Rivas, Olga Lucía, xii–xiii
Rivera, Danny, 24, 25
Rivera, Margot, 59, 172
Rivera, Ismael, 34, 36, 59, 60, 69, 72, 82, 108; in Puerto Rican literature, 59, 60
Rivera, Mon, 34, 81
Rivera Montalvo, Adela, 23
rock and roll, 70, 157, 172
rockero: versus cocolo, 27, 69–73, 200
Rodó, José Antonio, 19
Rodríguez, Albita, xii, xiii, 136, 174, 241, 242, 243
Rodríguez, Arsenio, 79
Rodríguez, Felipe, 177
Rodríguez, Tito, 79, 128, 132, 135, 138
Rodríguez de Tió, Lola, 21–24, 25
Rodríguez Juliá, Edgardo, xvi, 29, 32, 60, 143, 147, 149; on Rafael Cortijo, 34–37; treatment of women by, 46–48
Rohena, Roberto, 59
romance, Spanish, 29
romantic sensibility, 136. See also sensibility
romanticism, 16, 17

Romero, Deddie, xii, 242–43, 247n1
Rondón, César Miguel, 77, 81, 178, 179
Rondstadt, Linda, 115, 116
Rosa Nieves, Cesáreo, 8
Rose, Tricia, xiii, xiv, 34
Rubens, 40
Ruiz, Gabriel, 194
rumba, 81, 105, 107

Salazar, Max, 92
Saldívar-Hull, Sonia, xiv
salsa, 227; Anglo constructions of, xvii, 66–67, 99, 104–108; and class, 69–73, 87–88, 111–12, 199; contradictions in, xii; as Cuban music, 79–80; and cultural hybridity, 66; dancing to, 95–103; in English, 113–14; erótica, 93, 136–37, 205, 212; in Europe, 259n10; feminization of, 239–40; and gender politics, xiii, 117, 190, 195, 238; and globalization, 73–74, 116, 241; ideological plurality in, 61, 65–68, 77, 142; label, 67, 92; in literature, 193–96; machismo in, xiii; mainstreaming of, 66, 67, 73, 116–17 (see also appropriation, articulation); and maroon culture, 82, 83; and mass media, 92–95; and nationalism, xvii, 65–66, 68, 78–82; and postmodernism, xvi, 61, 65–68; and race, 69–73, 96, 111–12, 116, 241; reception of, 66, 67, 77, 99, 121, 124; repertoire, 240–41; representations of women in, xii–xiii, xvii, 121–24, 142–49, 155, 191–93, 205–210; and resistance, 66, 68, 77, 82, 124; and rock and roll, 69–72; romántica, xviii, 73, 78, 205, 240–41, 242–43; as sociomusical practice, 67; in Toronto, 67; and U.S. Latinos, 66, 81; in Venezuela, 69; violence in, 157
salsamigo, 67
salsódromo, 67
Salt'n Pepa, 149
San Juan Star, The, 70, 71
Sanabria, Izzy, 92
Sánchez, Luis Rafael, xvi, xviii, 35, 43, 124, 125, 127, 133; on Daniel Santos, 139–41; on music, 101–102
Santa Rosa, Gilberto, xiii, 72, 73, 136, 205, 241, 242
Santana, Carlos, 69, 71
Santi y sus duendes, 151–52, 168–69
Santiago, Eddie, 93, 99, 136, 143, 199
Santos, Daniel, 124, 125, 127, 128, 132, 134, 136, 142, 160, 161; in fiction, 139–41. *See*

also bolero
Sarlo, Beatriz, xviii, 248n10
Schwichtenberg, Cathy, 123, 197
Selena, xii
sensibility, 267n37. *See also* romantic sensibility
sexual politics, 124, 233
sexuality, female, 55; male, 48
Shakespeare, William, 139
Shepherd, John, 93
Showalter, Elaine, 4, 53
Sierra, Julia, 243
Silva, Mirta, 175–77
Silvestre, Sonia, 131
Simon, Paul, 115, 116
Singer, Roberta, 84
singers, female, 123–24
slavery, 147, 255n52
son, Cuban, 28, 76, 80–81, 82, 105, 107, 159
Son de Azúcar, 165–66
soneo, 84; in literature, 85–86
Sonora Matancera, La, 142
Sony, 243
Spanish language, eroticized, 147; in salsa music, 113–14
standardization, 90–91
strategy, 37
Strinati, Dominic, 249n8
subjectivity, female, 46, 47–48, 124, 154, 172–83; male, 129, 133, 135
subtext, 4, 5, 193
syncopation: in literature, 59
syncretism, musical, 14, 34
synecdoches: in the bolero, 134–35; patriarchal, 135, 142–49

Taberna India, La, 35
tango, 194, 195; tango-congo, 107
Tañón, Olga, xii, 174, 240, 242–43
Tavárez, Manuel G., 14, 23, 24, 25
teatro bufo: in Cuba, 105
terrorism, discursive, 161–62
Tex-Mex music, 97–98
Thiong'o, Ngugi wa, 58
timbales, 12
Tin Pan Alley, 94
Tjader, Cal, 92
Toña La Negra, 138, 152–53, 175–76
Tongolele, 177
Topo, El, 25
Touzet, René, 133
translation, cross-cultural, 105–108
tresillo elástico, 13, 14, 23

tropicalization, 105; of salsa music, 108
Tropicuba, Los, 177
Truman, Harry, 25

upa, 11. *See also* merengue

Valdelamar, Emma Elena, 133
Valdez, Miguelito, 172
Valentín, Wilson, 241
validation through visibility, 73
Valle, Joe, 33
Valle, Sara del, 241
vallenato, 82
Valverde, Mariana, 55
Valverde, Umberto, 172–73, 247n 3
Vargas, Wilfrido, 160
Vázquez, Consuelo, 133
Vega, Ana Lydia, xvi, xviii, 35, 102, 124, 167,
    181, 188, 197, 220, 230, 233; short stories,
    85–86, 193–96
Vega, Tony, 71–72
Venezuela: immigration to Puerto Rico, 11;
    salsa music in, 69
Ventura, Gilda, 58
Ventura, Johnny, 160
Veray, Amaury, 10, 11, 12, 13, 24
violence, sexual, 43; against women, 155–63

Wagner, Richard, 3
Walby, Sylvia, 150

Waxer, Lise, 243
Western culture, 104, 155
"When Women Love Men" (Ferré), 3–4,
    45–60
White, Hayden, 110
Wilde, Oscar, 140
witches. *See* brujería
Wild Mango, xii, 239–40
Wolfe, Gilbert L., 105–107
woman: as absence, 125–41, 232; as bando-
    lera, 229; construction of, 206–10, 229;
    idealized, 126–27; lost, 128–30, 138; objec-
    tification of, 135, 142–49, 266n 28; as
    prostitute, 229; as traitor, 235; woman's
    culture, 4, 53. *See also* feminism, gender,
    heterosexual conflict, salsa, women
women: bands, 172–73; black Puerto Rican,
    173; composers, 172, 272n 3, 272n 8; in-
    strumentalists, 172–73; rappers, 149;
    singers, 156, 165–69, 172–83, 242–43; sym-
    bolic annihilation of, 239
World War I, 29

Yoli, Lupe Victoria. *See* La Lupe

zarzuela, 107
Zavala, Iris, xviii, 125, 126, 130, 132, 133, 141;
    writings of, 138–39
Zona de carga y descarga, 3

FRANCES R. APARICIO is Associate Professor of Spanish and American Culture at the University of Michigan, where she has also directed the Latino Studies Program. Her books include *Versiones, Interpretaciones, Creaciones* (1991), which analyzes the poetics and practice of literary translation among modern Latin American writers; an anthology of Latino literatures for young readers (*Latino Voices*, 1994); and an English translation of Francisco Matos Paoli's *Canto de la locura/Song of Madness* (1989). She has also co-edited, with Suzanna Chávez-Silverman, a collection of essays titled *Tropicalizations: Transcultural Representations of* Latinidad, published by the University Press of New England. She is currently writing on the politics of bilingualism among U.S. Latinos.

UNIVERSITY PRESS OF NEW ENGLAND publishes books under its own imprint and is the publisher for Brandeis University Press, Dartmouth College, Middlebury College Press, University of New Hampshire, Tufts University, and Wesleyan University Press.

Library of Congress Cataloging-in-Publication Data
Aparicio, Frances R.
Listening to salsa : gender, Latin popular music, and Puerto Rican cultures / Frances R. Aparicio.
p.   cm. — (Music/culture)
Includes bibliographical references and index.
ISBN 0–8195–5306–9 (cl : alk. paper). — ISBN 0–8195–6308–0 (pa)
1. Salsa—Puerto Rico—History and criticism.   2. Feminism and music.   I. Series.
ML3535.5.A63   1997
781.64—dc21   97–9121